THE

CAMERA AND THE PENCIL;

OR THE

HELIOGRAPHIC ART,

ITS THEORY AND PRACTICE IN ALL ITS VARIOUS BRANCHES;
e. g.—DAGUERREOTYPY, PHOTOGRAPHY, &c.;

TOGETHER WITH ITS
HISTORY IN THE UNITED STATES AND IN EUROPE;

BEING AT ONCE A
THEORETICAL AND A PRACTICAL TREATISE,

AND DESIGNED ALIKE, AS A
TEXT-BOOK AND A HAND-BOOK.

Illustrated with Fine Engravings
ON STEEL AND ON WOOD.

BY M. A. ROOT,

PROFESSIONAL HELIOGRAPHIC ARTIST.—RECIPIENT OF EIGHTEEN FIRST PRIZES AWARDED BY INSTITUTIONS IN PHILADELPHIA, NEW YORK, BOSTON, WASHINGTON, HARRISBURG, ETC., FOR SUPERIOR ARTISTIC PRODUCTIONS IN THE ART.

Philadelphia:
M. A. ROOT, 808 CHESTNUT ST.
J. B. LIPPINCOTT & CO., 715 & 717 MARKET ST.
D. APPLETON & CO., 443 & 445 BROADWAY, N. Y.

1864.

MEARS & DUSENBERY, STEREOTYPERS, PHILADELPHIA.

C. A. ALVORD, PRINTER, NEW YORK.

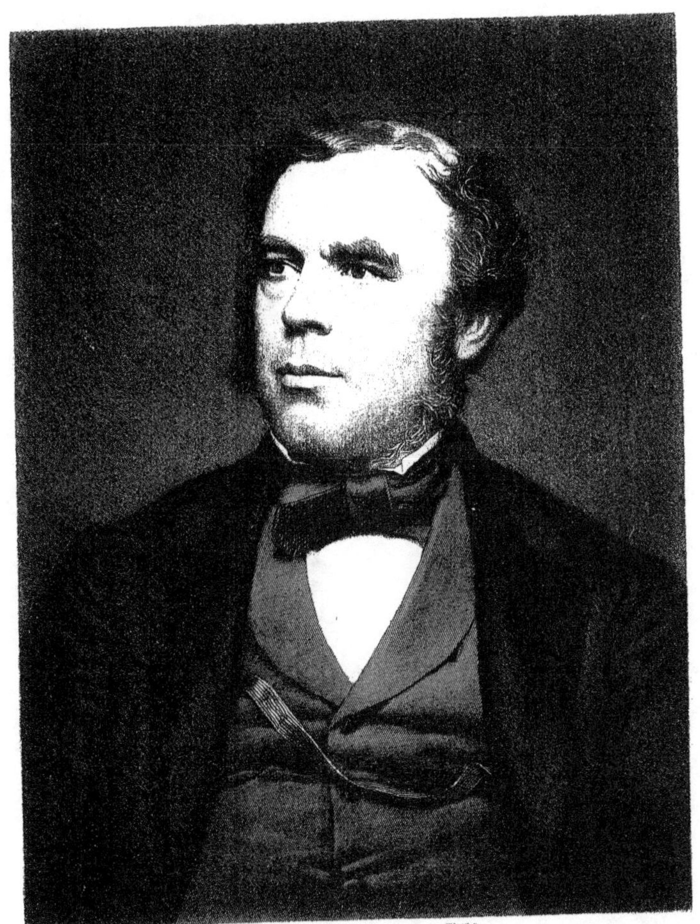

Engraved by John Sartain, Phil^a

Jno W Draper.

JOHN WILLIAM DRAPER, M.D. L.L.D.

PROFR OF CHEMISTRY AND PHYSIOLOGY IN THE UNIVERSITY OF NEW YORK

CONTENTS.

CHAPTER I.

THE FINE ARTS—HELIOGRAPHY, ETC.

CHAPTER II.

USES OF THE HELIOGRAPHIC ART.

CHAPTER III.

QUALIFICATIONS REQUISITE TO A FIRST-CLASS HELIOGRAPHER.

CHAPTER IV.

SUGGESTIONS AS TO THE FITTING UP OF HELIOGRAPHIC ROOMS.

CHAPTER V.

THE SUNBEAM.

CHAPTER VI.

HARMONY OF COLORS.

CHAPTER VII.

THE HUMAN FACE—MIRROR OF THE SOUL, AND CHIEF SUBJECT OF ART.

CHAPTER VIII.

THE HELIOGRAPHIC ARTIST AND HIS SITTERS.

CHAPTER IX.

SITTING ROOM—SKY-LIGHTS—OUT-DOOR VIEWS, ETC.

CHAPTER X.

HINTS UPON SITTING—EASE AND GRACE IN A PORTRAIT.

CHAPTER XI.

THE EYES—THEIR LANGUAGE, AND HOW TO DEAL WITH THEM.

CHAPTER XII.

SUGGESTIONS AS TO DEALING WITH DEFECTS AND BLEMISHES IN SITTER'S FACE.

CHAPTER XIII.

LIGHTS AND SHADOWS IN A PICTURE—THEIR USE AND VALUE.

CHAPTER XIV.

COSTUME IN PORTRAITURE—HOW DISPOSED.

CHAPTER XV.

THE ATMOSPHERE—WEATHER—LIGHT FLEECY CLOUDS.

CHAPTER XVI.

PERSONAL CONSIDERATIONS.

CHAPTER XVII.

HELIOGRAPHY AN IMPROVER OF ARTS AND ARTISTS.

CHAPTER XVIII.

EXPRESSION—THROUGH THE FACE.

CHAPTER XIX.

EXPRESSION—THROUGH THE FACE AND FIGURE.

CHAPTER XX.

EXPRESSION—THROUGH THE ANIMAL AND INANIMATE WORLDS.

CHAPTER XXI.

EXPRESSION—THROUGH ABNORMAL MOODS OF BODY AND MIND.

CHAPTER XXII.

MISCELLANEOUS FACTS.

CHAPTER XXIII.

OPINIONS OF ARTISTS AND ART-CRITICS UPON BEAUTY.

CHAPTER XXIV.

ART, WITH ITS INCIDENTS AND BELONGINGS.

CHAPTER XXV.

MISCELLANEOUS REMARKS FROM VARIOUS AUTHORS.

CHAPTER XXVI.

ON COLORING PHOTOGRAPHS.

CHAPTER XXVII.

PORTRAITS—SEVERAL VARIOUS MODES OF PRODUCING OR FINISHING PERMANENT SOLAR IMPRESSIONS.

CHAPTER XXVIII.

THE CAMERA AND THE MICROSCOPE—OR MICRO-PHOTOGRAPHY.

CHAPTER XXIX.

HISTORY OF THE HELIOGRAPHIC ART IN THE UNITED STATES.

CHAPTER XXX.

HISTORY OF THE HELIOGRAPHIC ART IN EUROPE.

CHAPTER XXXI.

THE HELIOGRAPHIC ART—ITS PRESENT STATE AND APPLIANCES, AND ITS FUTURE POSSIBILITIES.

CHAPTER XXXII.

HELIOGRAPHY—ITS ARTISTIC CHARACTER AND RELATIONS.

INTRODUCTION.

The appearance of this work may, naturally, suggest the inquiry, why the author should have assumed the care and labor, as well as the responsibility, of getting up and submitting to the public a Treatise on Heliography, when so many on the same subject are already in circulation,—some among which are of sterling value, and produced by writers of profound science and great practical accomplishment. It might fairly be exacted of one who would swell the number of these books, that he should either present something new, or should bring forward, in better shape, topics which had already been discussed. That in both these respects there was room for improvement, I have myself been long convinced, as, I trust, my reader will be by the examination of these volumes.

My reasons for undertaking this work were founded, in part, on what seemed to me *deficiencies* in the treatises now in vogue, and partly on other grounds to be presently noticed. The principal of these reasons are the following:—

1. It is a frequent complaint, among American Heliographers, that the books on their art are mostly written in a style too learned and technical, and therefore ill-suited to popular use. Their complaint appears to us not entirely groundless. Nearly all these books were penned by scientific men, who had cultivated the art simply as amateurs, and who, therefore, employed the same style as though dealing with ordinary themes of science. They wrote, as if addressing persons of their own class,—not reflecting, perhaps, that those by whom these books are chiefly required, rarely possess profound scientific attainments.

Professional Heliographers of that eminence, which alone would impart sterling value to a treatise from their hands, are, mostly, too busily occupied for thus using the pen, even if possessing sufficient skill in composition to qualify them for producing a book. So that we have not hitherto (to my knowledge) had a single heliographic treatise from a first-class *professionist.* I thought, therefore, that a book from a practical artist would be likely to meet the want thus generally expressed. Such a work I was especially impelled to undertake, as well as encouraged to carry forward to its completion, by the fact, that I was able to secure, through its whole progress, the most valuable assistance of a number of gentlemen of ability, of scholarship, and of long-practised aptitude in writing.

2. Several years' personal experience had impressed me with what I thought important deficiencies in every work on this subject within my knowledge. The mechanical and chemical appliances of the art were, indeed, not unfrequently treated with satisfactory fulness and skill; yet what may be termed its *artistic* requirements were scarcely touched upon: *e. g.* posture and costume, light and shadow, expression in its various modes, and numerous other minute yet important particulars, relating to the management of the sitting department, were by every writer almost totally ignored. And yet on a thorough acquaintance with these particulars, coupled with aptitude and tact in dealing with them, it mainly depends whether a picture shall be a veritable gem of art, or a baldly mechanical performance. The major part of my remarks on these points will be found in that portion of Volume I., commencing with the "Sitting Room," and extending through the four chapters on "Expression," including pages 96–179.

The reader might scarce credit me, were I to tell him of how much vigilant observation and laborious thought these few pages were the fruit. Day after day, and week after week, through several successive years, I kept careful watch, jotting down diurnally the results of my scrutiny, and testing them again and again, till, at last, I trust I have succeeded in presenting them in a shape so simple and lucid that to *read* will be to *understand.*

3. I have mentioned, elsewhere in this book, my early propensity for drawing and sketching, and my after employment, for several years, in a kindred profession. My assumption of heliography was a partial fulfilment of my juvenile prepossessions. In its adoption I carried with me my young aspirations for artistic distinction, together with the natural desire, that my vocation should stand, in general estimation, on the high platform I thought it deserved.

I soon learned that it did *not* so stand. Sun-painting, I was mortified to find, was considered a merely mechanical process, which might be learned in a few weeks, by a person of the most ordinary capacity and attainment.

Now, as might have been anticipated from my early biases, *I* put a very different estimate upon the art. I regarded it as decidedly one of the Fine Arts; nor this alone, but as standing high among these arts. My thoughts on this point will be found expressed in more than one place in this work. I felt, almost as if a personal affront to myself, the low repute in which the art and its practitioners were held. And this feeling was aggravated by the fact, not to be denied, that, owing to causes detailed otherwhere, there was, unhappily, too much ground for the common opinion respecting the profession. Its operants, with not very numerous exceptions, bore a reputation similar to that of those itinerant portrait-painters, who anticipate the death of their victims, by destroying every trait of *life-likeness* in the faces they *execute*.

As already remarked, my ambition forbade my *patiently* being ranked among *recognised* imbeciles and incapables. Why (I queried with myself) should not Heliography be placed beside Painting and Sculpture, and the Camera be held in like honor with the Pencil and the Chisel? Is that (methought) a low and vulgar art, which can bid defiance to time and space, and triumphantly look into the eye of the so-named "King of Terrors;" which grants me, at my own fireside, to behold the rocky heights once trodden by prophets and apostles, and, more inspiring still, by Him who was the "brightness of the Father's glory," "the chiefest among ten thousand and altogether lovely;" to gaze on the immemorial pyramids and catacombs of Egypt, and the mystic caverns of Ipsamboul and Ellora?—which, in a word, enables me, without crossing my threshold, to view the multitudinous populations of the total globe, past and present, with the monuments of beauty and grandeur, that immortalized their earth-existence? Finally, should that art be contemned, which is helping to train society, from its topmost to its nethermost stratum, to an appreciation of the beautiful? For, be it noted, the specimens, inferior as so many of them are, exhibited at the doors of the Heliographic Galleries, in numbers of our city streets, constitute a sort of artistic school for developing the idealistic capabilities of the masses that daily traverse those streets.

An art, then, which contributes so much, and in so many modes, towards elevating and refining all classes of the community, seemed to me to possess high claims to consideration. I trust, that the time and care and labor, unsparingly devoted to this book, have made it, in some fair degree, worthy of its subject.

It will be seen, that in several of the opening chapters (*e. g.* The Sunbeam and The Harmony of Colors, Chapters 5 and 6), I have dwelt at some length on the sciences that constitute the basis of heliography. The general object, as well as the propriety of so doing, must be patent to all, and needs no explaining. An incidental purpose was to intimate the high dignity of an art resting on foundations so august.

It will also be noted, that I have spoken in considerable detail (Chapter 5) of the high attributes, both intellectual and moral, essential to a first-class heliographer. To represent, in their just proportions, the beautiful and the sublime in natural scenery; to reproduce in like manner the creations of inspired human genius; and especially to delineate the human face and figure pervaded by an *expression*, that bids the soul shine glowingly out through the same; are to transcribe the matchless pencillings of the Divine Proto-Artist. To do this, how imperfectly soever, demands qualities, alike of head and of heart, in rapt accordance with the Infinite Creative Spirit.

In fine, the true heliographer, like the true artist in whatever sphere, should be an intermedium, through which the light of the Divine should pass unmodified and pure, producing imprints as distinctly and delicately limned, as are the images of natural objects on the surface of a crystal pool. How, then, we once again ask, can *that* art be ignoble and mean, which involves requisites and appliances so high, so important, and so numerous, as these?

The scientific foundations of the art and the qualifications of the artist having been stated, the book proceeds to discuss the particulars, that constitute or are incidentally related to the producing process. I must restrict myself to a mere enumeration of the remaining chapters, with their subjects annexed.

Chapter 7. The face, the chief subject of art, as being the soul's mirror; Chapter 8. On the proper bearing of the operant towards his sitters; Chapter 9. The sitting-room, its location, appurtenances, &c.; Chapter 10. On sitting, with its incidents; Chapter 11. The eyes, their language, &c.; Chapter 12. How to deal with defects and blemishes in the face; Chapter 13. Lights and shadows in the picture; Chapter 14. Costume, &c.; Chapter 15. The atmosphere, &c.; Chapter 16. Personal considerations; Chapter 17. Heliography an improver of the arts and sciences; Chapters 18, 19, 20, 21. Expression, through various mediums; Chapter 22. Miscellaneous facts;

Chapter 23. Opinions of artists and art-critics on beauty; Chapter 24. Art, its incidents and belongings; Chapter 25. Miscellaneous remarks; Chapter 26. Coloring photographs; Chapter 27. Portraits, &c.; Chapter 28. Camera and Microscope; Chapter 29. History of heliography in the United States; Chapter 30. History of same in Europe; Chapter 31. Present and future of heliography; Chapter 32. Character and relations of same.

In addition to the above subjects, the "Fine Arts in general;" the "Uses of Heliography;" and the "Fitting up of Heliographic Rooms," are discussed at length in the early portion of the book.

From the foregoing enumeration it will be seen, that in both the plan and the contents of this work, it differs largely from all other Heliographic Treatises in circulation. I think, that the matter constituting such difference will be found, to say the least, of not inferior interest to the residue of the work. I trust, moreover, that the general reader may draw from it not a little of both instruction and entertainment, while, to the professional heliographer, it may be a manual of sterling value.

My intention, on commencing the book, was to issue it in one volume, and a few circulars were given to the public expressing this intention. But, from the urgent advice of several scientific gentlemen and amateurs of distinction, having decided to enlarge and make it more complete, by inserting considerable new matter of interest and importance, my manuscript became so bulky, that it was deemed expedient to put it in two volumes instead of one,—the first embracing the theoretic basis of the art, and the second its practical processes, formulas, &c. Still, for all desiring it, the two volumes will be bound in one.

On some subjects the reader will find not a little repetition. One reason for this is, that I was specially anxious to impress these subjects on all within my reach; and another, that the book having been seven or eight years in hand, it was impossible to carry the whole in my mind, so as to avoid occasional reiteration. The first volume is illustrated by several fine steel engravings of distinguished men, some of whom have taken a deep interest in our art. The second is fully illustrated by engravings representing the instruments and appliances of the art.

In the cotemporary Heliographic Journals both of the United States and of Europe, several topics may be found often and earnestly discussed, which, eight years ago, were scarce ever alluded to. One of these is the claim of Heliography to be one of the Fine Arts, instead of a simply mechanical process; and, as such, requiring genius and accomplishment for achieving distinction therein, no less than Painting and Sculpture. A second is, that expression is a *sine qua non* in our art; and that extreme care and much skill in handling its accessories, *e. g.* arrangement, position, &c., are essential to excellence therein. In this work, these subjects are often and earnestly pressed on the attention,—and, in simplest justice to myself, I may remark, that the paragraphs treating of the same were written years before I had seen anything of the sort in print.

In the New York Photographic Journals, numerous articles on the same subjects have been furnished by me during the last ten successive years. These, with what appears in this book, constitute all I have seen of this character, till within a short time past, when they have begun to be discussed in both American and European Heliographic Journals and Books.

It may also be noted, that in speaking of our art in general, and of its agents and results, I commonly use the terms heliography, heliographer, and heliograph, in place of photography, &c. My reason is, that Heliography, "Sun-sketching," is a *correct general name* for the art in all its varieties; while Photography, "Light-sketching," with all its derivatives, is a *misnomer*, since it is not light, but *actinism*, which is the producer. "Heliochart," "Sun-paper," is the proper title of what is now called a photograph. It is not to be hoped (I presume) that this error will ever be amended in the popular speech, any more than that the right name "Breed's Hill," will ever be substituted for "Bunker Hill," in the account of the battle involved. The following are the words of the eminent heliographic author, T. F. Hardwich, page 83 of his sixth edition: "The actinic and luminous spectra are totally distinct from each other, and the word 'Photography,' which signifies 'taking pictures by *light*,' is in reality *inaccurate*."

Delamotte, in the introduction to his manual, remarks as follows: "As *light* is not the agent, through which the effects are produced, the word Heliography, 'Sun-drawing,' has been suggested as the more correct."

What remains to be said, of an introductory character, is reserved for the opening of the second volume. I would only observe, in closing, that by the profession, and by amateurs and others interested in the art, several of whom are *named* in the introduction to Volume II., I have been graciously assisted, in the way of information, as well as by all other means in their power, for which I would here express my sincerest acknowledgments.

HELIOGRAPHY

AND

OTHER FINE ARTS.

CHAPTER I.

THE FINE ARTS—HELIOGRAPHY, ETC.

Our country—High *materially*—Inferior *artistically*—Causes of this—Fine Arts, the development of innate tendencies—Amusement a necessity—Art supplies it—Elevates morally and spiritually—Refines intellectually and socially—Art among Greeks and Romans—America probable originator of new type of art—Heliography—How distinguished from other arts.

HOLDING, as I do, that Heliography is entitled to rank with the so-named Fine Arts, some remarks upon these arts, as a class, their basis in nature, and their various uses, may properly constitute the opening chapter of this volume.

That in material prosperity and mechanical utilities our country stands high, very high, in the scale of nations, there can be no doubt whatever. As little doubt can there be that in artistic culture many a cotemporary people are our superiors.

This, however, may be admitted without humiliation. Pioneers and tamers of a primitive world, as we have been hitherto, we have had neither leisure nor means for largely cultivating the mere embellishments of life. But with our present material attainments, it is quite time that the energy and inventive ability, which have accomplished so much here, should be turned towards the fine arts. And as vague, erroneous notions prevail as to the real nature of these arts, it may be well to state some reasons for their cultivation.

And, first, I would remark that, irrespective of all special uses of the arts, their cultivation may be urged on the simple ground that they answer to one of our natural wants, being the pre-ordained development of that law of beauty and harmony, whose germs are implanted in every soul. Thus, in even the most savage tribes yet discovered, some rude essays at embellishment are found. Not one of them is content with what are termed the indispensables of life; but among their most prized possessions are feathers and a thousand various trinkets, which they regard as making attractive themselves and their belongings.

It is similar with children, whether in the savage or civilized state. Trinkets and toys, and all things bright and showy, however rude, are among their earliest tastes. And I suspect that the fondness for tales in all kinds, common to both child and savage, is another manifestation of the same radical principle.

Such being the fact, we can press the cultivation of the fine arts on the ground that such is the will of God. Since most of his gifts are bestowed in the germ, the mere fact of his conferring certain *capacities* should be evidence enough of our obligation to labor for their development. But artistic culture has many specific uses.

Thus the arts open to their amateurs inexhaustible sources of enjoyment. It were superfluous arguing that men must needs have relaxation and amusement. Labor, the common lot, has not yet been made in itself pleasurable and attractive; generally wearisome, often positively repulsive, it would be insupportable but for seasons of relaxation.

If, then, mankind must and will have pleasure, what shall this be? Few questions are more momentous. For where there is no mental culture, sensuality is the main resource, and fatal excess its too frequent accompaniment. And even where excess is avoided, sensual indulgence, unchastened by the activity of the higher powers, is of debasing tendency.

But let the love of manifold beauty be developed, and how vast man's resources for enjoyment! Painting, sculpture, and architecture, music, poetry, and universal letters offer springs of pleasurable emotion, which, while ever new and fresh, are absolutely fathomless. Pure delights they are, too, harming neither him who tastes nor those connected with him.

And still better, these enjoyments are morally and spiritually elevating in tendency. Not that in point of fact all artists and amateurs reproduce, in their sentiments and life, the harmony and beauty of art. But this is not the fault of art itself. It does but show that the artistic element is not in them strong enough to hold in check other passions of a debasing kind and accomplish its own specific ends. In other phrase, though a veritable angel of blessing, it is not omnipotent.

How, indeed, can it do else than purify and exalt, since it brings the mind into sympathy with one of the most conspicuous of the divine attributes?

For, if wise design and benignant use be everywhere visible in creation, not less universal and perceptible are the forms and hues of beauty. How prodigally, indeed is that beauty poured out over earth and sky! And not alone, either, where man may take cognisance of it. In the very heart of sylvan wilds, where human foot never trod, countless flower-tribes, lovely and fragrant enough for a seraph's wreath, bloom and perish, it might seem, in vain. Why, too, was the interior of the muscle's shell painted with the rainbow's matchless hues, only to lie on the dark bed of Ocean, "a thousand fathoms down"? What numeration could reckon the kindred instances where, on birds, fishes, and insects, are lavished beauties of shape and tint beyond the reach of man's art, and yet with no discernible end to be subserved thereby?

Is it, then, presumption to suppose that such beauty exists because its Author delights in its creation? Why may we not believe that all this grace and loveliness are not

> "born to blush unseen,
> And waste their sweetness on the desert air,"

but that their Creator enjoys the contemplation of these exquisite works of his hands?

The artist, therefore, who by pencil or chisel, by pen or voice, brings before us shapes of beauty or grandeur; what does he but co-operate with the great Proto-Artist, and in his humble measure participate in His work of Creation? And he who, through culture, has become susceptible to the charms of multiform art, must, through the same susceptibility, love and enjoy also the divine manifestations of grandeur and loveliness. And the artist and amateur, who dwell thus delightedly on the derivative beauty incarnate in effects, are more likely than others to venerate and love the great Original Cause of beauty—the Being, who is himself the absolute, essential Beauty and Wisdom, Life and Love!

We plead, then, for the cultivation of art, both as a

means of recreation and refreshment to a toiling race, and not less for its genial and elevating influence on the character.

It is universally admitted, that the fine arts communicate to the mind that refinement, and to the life those accomplishments and graces, without which the one is incomplete and rude, and the other bald and bare. Of course men must first provide life's absolute essentials; nor will I object to their procuring, as a second step, its material conveniences and comforts. But I insist, that the very next stage, in a true development, is to secure that intellectual culture, of which the fine arts constitute a large share—embracing, perhaps, all not covered by the term science. Without this, we must be little higher or other than animals.

But through the portals of art we enter a vastly higher and nobler than the animal sphere: one in which the Divinity is our prototype and exemplar, and unseen angels our sympathizing and helpful associates. It is the domain of the beautiful; boundless, exhaustless, and infinitely various, like its Author and Supervisor. Thenceforward man, both the individual and social, has before him an illimitable work, fully worthy his most strenuous endeavors. This work is to shape and array his total life into harmony with the laws of beauty. Such work demands, that, commencing with what is most individual, we conform our feelings and thoughts, our speech and port, our movements and costume, to the standard prescribed by those laws; that, still further, we fashion, according to this standard, our domestic and public structures with their furniture and equipments; our implements to whatever use applied; and finally, whatever we touch and hear and look upon at home and abroad, so far as within our control. Life's ideal requires, that every human being, whether in his hours of labor or recreative leisure, should be encompassed by sights and sounds incarnating the most advanced existing conceptions of loveliness, grandeur, and nobleness, that so his nature's best elements may be kept alive and active, while enjoying the conditions of further expansion and growth.

To some extent this idea was actually embodied in life by the ancient Greeks and Romans. They made beauty and magnificence almost

> "As broad, as general, as the casing air,"

in many spheres, which in these modern days exhibit little save ugliness and meanness.

We cannot, however, doubt that we are destined to higher achievements even than theirs. It will assuredly be so, if that American energy, so prolific of prodigies in the domain of utility, shall fling its total self into the culture of art. And would we rid ourselves of that servile propensity to imitation, implanted in us by our constant intercourse with old Europe, and act fully out the originality springing from our novel conditions, in this respect, as we have done in so many others, I doubt not, that a new and magnificent type of universal art would be ushered into the world. The copyist—as the American has too generally been—can never equal his model, since he works not with the freshness and surging enthusiasm of a primal impulse. To be alike true and great, American art must be America's spirit and life, with all their individualities, idealized and encircled with the magic halo of beauty!

Our opening chapter has, thus far, been occupied with remarks upon art in general, and upon the principles that underlie and modify whichever of its specific forms it may assume. As the particular subject of this Treatise is Heliography, a few words respecting it will not be amiss in closing.

In the course of the present volume, I have repeatedly and earnestly advocated the proposition, that sun-painting is *not* (as but too commonly supposed) a mere *mechanical* process; but, contrariwise, is one of the fine arts, and in its *capabilities* is, at least, the *full equal* of the others bearing this name.

We may go still further. In the variety and extent of its *possible* applications, both useful and ornamental, Heliography promises to go even beyond its sister arts. From the extreme celerity with which these pictures may be taken, their numbers can be indefinitely multiplied; while their cheapness brings them within reach of all classes save absolute paupers. By consequence, in the humblest of cabins, not less than in the most sumptuous of palaces, they will be in future among the most frequent spectacles.

As the next chapter will be devoted to an enumeration of the *utilities* of heliography, I have contented myself *here* with briefly touching upon two or three points, wherein *this* differs greatly from the *other* fine arts—such difference being *decidedly in its favor.* To that expository chapter I would ask the reader's attention.

CHAPTER II.

USES OF THE HELIOGRAPHIC ART.

Cherishes domestic and social sentiments—Inspires to virtuous and noble deeds—Education largely the work of circumstances and conditions of men—Augments greatly men's knowledge and happiness—A substitute for travel—Cultivates artistic taste and love of beauty—Tends to improve other fine arts and their professors—Exemplifications of this.

THOUGH heliography is but a new-discovered art, and is, of course, far from having reached perfection, it has already conferred various and important benefits on society. These benefits must be augmented, as the art progresses. Let me specify some of these.

1st. In the order of nature, families are dispersed, by death or other causes; friends are severed; and the "old familiar faces" are no longer seen in our daily haunts. By heliography, our loved ones, dead or distant; our friends and acquaintances, however far removed, are retained within daily and hourly vision. To what extent domestic and social affections and sentiments are conserved and perpetuated by these "shadows" of the loved and valued originals, every one may judge. The cheapness of these pictures brings them within reach, substantially, of all.

In this competitious and selfish world of ours, whatever tends to vivify and strengthen the social feelings should be hailed as a benediction. With these literal transcripts of features and forms, once dear to us, ever at hand, we are scarcely more likely to forget, or grow cold to their originals, than we should be in their corporeal presence. How can we exaggerate the value of an art which produces effects like these?

2d. But not alone our near and dear are thus kept with us; the great and the good, the heroes, saints, and sages of all lands and all eras are, by these life-like "presentments," brought within the constant purview of the young, the middle-aged, and the old. The pure, the high, the noble traits beaming from these faces and forms,—who shall measure the greatness of their effect on the impressionable minds of those who catch sight of them at every turn? Who can behold the "mimic" Washington of Stuart or Peale, without recalling, for an instant at least, who and what was the original once enshrined in that majestic face and figure? And the representation of the "Divine Man of Nazareth,"—not, of course, a transcript from *actual life*, but the picture whereby an artist of supreme genius, in his most rapt devotional moods, made visible *his* conception of what must have been the aspect of One thus endowed and inspired,—could any individual look upon it daily, and not experience that a "virtue had gone out of it," and had done somewhat towards moulding his own dispositions and character?

Indeed, our education is accomplished far more by the circumstances amid which we live, than by all the direct, technical instruction we receive; and from infancy to old age we are continually acted upon for good and for evil by the sights and sounds with which we are familiar. And he who beholding, on every side within his dwelling, spectacles of the class above named, derives from them no elevating moral influence, must be made of almost hopelessly impenetrable stuff. But taking a still wider view, consider

3d. What this art is doing, and is still more largely to do hereafter for increasing, the knowledge and happiness of the masses. What, heretofore, the traveller alone could witness (and travelling was out of the reach of ninety-nine hundredths of mankind), even the humblest may now behold, substantially, without crossing his own threshold. The natural scenery, grand, beautiful, or picturesque, of every quarter of the globe; the noblest edifices, secular and religious, of the most highly civilized lands; together with the weird, fantastic piles, reared by semi-barbaric peoples to their "strange gods;" the multitudinous reliques still remaining of the skill and the power, the pomps and the glories of the most celebrated regions of the ancient world; the localities, on either continent, where conflicts have been waged, or events have occurred, which have acted powerfully on the destinies of nations, and perhaps have turned the currents of the world's history into new channels; the inhabitants of every zone, from the Arctic to the Antarctic Circle, with their costumes and their exterior ways of life; the finest existing specimens of art, ancient and modern, of foreign countries or our own; the most exciting, impressive, and awful acts or scenes which may occur anywhere at any moment—a thunder-storm, a tempest at sea, a great battle, in the very heat and fury of its crisis,—all these, and whatever else of interest the world may present to the sight, caught, as they may be, with absolute exactitude, by the infallible pencil of the sun, are now brought within reach of all, even the lowliest of the community.

But while the masses are thus supplied with abundant and infinitely various stores of knowledge and entertainment, they are, at the same time, receiving no small measure of artistic training. Of course, in the multitudes of heliographs sent abroad into the world, there are very many various degrees of excellence in execution and finish, and the observer of different specimens is naturally moved to compare one with another, and to form his own judgment of which are the superior and which the inferior. By this simple process, carried on, perhaps, for the most part, unconsciously or but semi-consciously, the community is being trained to a taste for art and a love of the beautiful. Thus sun-painting promises to do for the moderns, what art, in other forms, did for the ancient Greeks. And who can even imagine what would be the purifying and elevating effects of a relish and enjoyment of beauty, both in nature and art, universally diffused,—especially when combined, as it is among the moderns, with the influence flowing from the precepts and the life of the "Good Master"? But

4th. Heliography, we believe, is destined to do much for the improvement of the other fine arts and their professors. To the portraitist, for example, a good heliograph furnishes important aid in transferring a face and form to the canvass or ivory. By its means he is able to get a more exact outline of his sitter, besides being helped to catch his brightest and best expression. For obtaining such outline, as also the drapery and all other accessories, the sitter need not be subjected to the long, wearisome sessions formerly required, as these may be taken directly from the heliograph. And then a few brief sittings, devoted exclusively to studying the subject's type of mind and character, and thus settling the fittest mode of expressing the same in the countenance, will fully suffice,—especially if the heliographer has been fully successful in calling up and representing the sitter's best expression at the outset. In a word, this use of the heliograph is a mode of *economizing* both time and force, leaving to the painter more of both for producing the highest effects of his art.

The landscape-painter, the sculptor, and the architect, as well as all others, whose aim is visible representation, may in like manner derive essential help from copies of their originals.

But especially is heliography, with the late discovered devices for *instantaneous taking,* calculated to benefit other artists, by supplying them with most interesting "studies." For example, the clouds, seen occasionally to rise aloft like dark craggy mountains leaning against higher and lighter-tinted ones, above which appear still others, darker, grander, and more irregular in outline, and tipped with light,—the whole having a dark blue sky for a background,—all can be accurately and *instantly* pictured by the solar pencil.

So the high-rolling and high-capped billows of a storm-lashed sea, as they follow each other, dashing furiously against or curling triumphantly over the overtaken ship or the immovable rock, may be stamped upon the plate exactly as the eye beholds them, and almost as rapidly as the eye can take them in.

Again, waterfalls; choice bits of landscape; large moving masses of people assembled on occasions of festival or public celebration; and all kindred spectacles, may be reproduced in the same way.

And thus, taken on a small scale, they can, by methods recently devised, be enlarged to a magnitude of many feet square, without losing their original exactitude of truthfulness.

Such pieces, to an artist in colors, must be invaluable as "studies" of nature; while the imaginative artist, by idealizing them, may win an enviable reputation.

It will readily be seen how useful the art, with its

present facilities, must be for illustrating books, periodicals, &c.,—supplying them with reliable sketches of machinery, of architecture, of scenes of disaster or of jubilee, of portraits; and, in short, of whatever is suited to interest or instruct the public.

It seems, too, that the French savans are applying heliography to physical astronomy and the mathematical measurement of the heavenly bodies. Several valuable pictures of this class have already been taken, and the art promises to render important services in this direction.

I need pursue these remarks no further here, as the multiform utilities of the art will be found clearly and fully explained in the following chapters of this work.

CHAPTER III.

QUALIFICATIONS REQUISITE TO A FIRST-CLASS HELIOGRAPHER.

Heliographers mechanical or artistic—Former lack power of giving *expression* to portrait—Latter have it—Genius this power—Gift of nature, not fruit of effort—Camera requires not less genius than pencil—Heliographer, like painter, must rouse in sitter his best mood—How—Chemistry, natural philosophy, &c., essential to heliographers—Heliography in disrepute—Reasons—Motives which *should* inspire heliographer.

IN the heliographic, as in other arts, are found two classes of persons—the artists, and the mere mechanics. In all respects, save two or three, the latter may equal, if not even surpass, the former. For the solar pencil will transcribe, with rigorous exactness, the original submitted to it, alike in either case; while in the preparing of the impressible surfaces, and other processes chemical or manual, the dexterous-handed mechanic may transcend the artist. But when we come to the *expression*—that something which reveals the soul of the sitter, the individuality which differences him from all beings else—we find an antagonism between the two classes, as decided as between a living man and the wooden image of a man. As the mechanic can but put together dead materials, his work must needs be lifeless. The artist, on the contrary, creates, and into his work he "breathes the breath of life," and it "becomes a living soul." Mrs. Fanny Kemble, once contemplating a portrait by one of our famed artists, remarked, "Mr. —— paints a beauti ful picture, but it required Lawrence to put the soul in the eyes!" A complete verification of what is said above.

Whether the pencil or the camera be employed, this distinction equally holds. I believe the time is not distant, when the perfect handling of the latter will be acknowledged to be not less difficult than that of the former. And indifferent as the past repute of heliography has been, and dishonored as it has too often been by ignoramuses and charlatans, I believe it will, ere long, be regarded as a sphere wherein the most eminent of artistic geniuses, a Michael Angelo and a Raffaelle, a Titian, a Rubens, a Rembrandt, and a Stuart might find amplest scope for their powers.

But what are the special qualifications which go to make a first-class heliographer? Substantially the same (I think) with those required for an eminent painter. Not that the two operate in the same way. Both. however, aim at the same object, and unless they attain it, their attempts must be total failures. That object is the expression of the soul through the face, or the face and form.

Now even to discern what *is* that cast or character of the individual soul, which discriminates it from all other souls, requires genius—a quality known by its results, though perhaps impossible to define—and requires it as much in the heliographer as in the painter. Neither a mechanical painter nor a mechanical heliographer can perceive it. True, the former with his brush may represent, with precision, the face and form, and the latter can do the same, through the camera. But as neither has, by nature, the eye to *detect* the soul-expression, so neither can *represent* it. We repeat, then, that the first-class heliographer must possess the same art-genius, as the painter of kindred rank.

But after *seeing* the expression to be represented, the next step is to *represent* it by some means. The painter does this through color, light and shade, &c., put upon canvas. The heliographer uses the camera, in lieu of the pencil, and by various dispositions of light and shadow, must accomplish (if at all) the purpose effected by the painter with his pencil. Something, indeed, the heliographer, after using the camera, may do by means of colors, to *improve* and *heighten* the expression first obtained by the solar pencil. But unless this expression is, substantially, gotten at the outset, this subsequent employment of color will be of no avail.

But prior to the handling of either the pencil or the camera, a *preliminary* work must be done both by the painter and the heliographer; and to the execution of this work *genius* is indispensable. The sitter, before a transcript of him is taken, should be put into a *mood,* which shall make his face *diaphanous* with the expression of his highest and best, i. e. his *genuine, essential self.* He is not always *in* this mood at the commencement of his sitting to the painter or the heliographer; and his face may be of that rough, coarse mould, which, in the absence of emotional excitation, would give no adequate manifestation of the in-dwelling soul. So was it with Curran, who (as related in Chapter 24) sat to Lawrence *six times* before the painter could detect the *real* Curran by the *soul-irradiation* of his face. But how came this soul-irradiation there at last? It seems that Lawrence, as his usage was, had plied Curran with the various resources of his marvellous conversation, till, finally, he struck upon that chord of "Erin ma vourneen, Erin go bragh," to which the orator's highest nature responded

And *then* the expression required shone out from within, and touched up that gross, rugged mask with an empyreal grandeur and beauty.

In like manner the heliographer's subject often shows little of what he essentially is at the moment of sitting—the more especially as the very conditions of a heliographic sitting are apt to produce a dull, meaningless look, from the fact that the sitter must be *perfectly immovable* during the action of the camera. The operant, therefore, should tax all his intellectual resources, both before and during the session, to summon into activity in his sitter those elements which shall stamp on the face the distinguishing soul. Conversation is the principal form in which those resources are employed, though much is also done by the magnetism of his manners and presence. If successful in calling into the face the expression desired, it remains to tax all the powers of the camera in producing such a combination of lights and shadows as will secure an exact transfer of this expression to the plate. To use the camera, as it *may* be used, is possible only to genius, united with thorough knowledge and high accomplishment.

Indeed the public at large has little idea of what marvels of achievement this instrument is capable in the hands of genius; and the same might be said of the great majority of heliographers. Some suggestions on this topic may be found in the chapters of this volume relating to "Sitting, the Sitting-Room," and kindred matters. It will there be seen that this instrument, by a delicately skilful handling, may do for the face and figure, so far as concerns outline, light and shadow, &c., nearly every essential service which the pencil, with its manifold appliances, can do in the hand of a painter of genius.

Be it noted, moreover, that heliography is based upon chemistry and natural philosophy; and the heliographer who would master all departments of his profession must be versed to a considerable extent in both these branches of knowledge. But to deal familiarly with sciences as boundless as the world, or rather *all* worlds; to be able to pierce through the ofttimes thick mask of the material *outward* and discern the inner, spiritual *self;* and then to represent that self by such a delicate management of a *single* implement, as shall cast peculiarly-tempered lights and shadows upon the face and form, adapted by an almost inspired selection of attitude, with its accessories, to *receive* them aright;—are performances like these within the capacity of a dull, slow, ignorant operator? Or do they not rather (as already intimated), demand both genius and talent,—genius and talent, too, thoroughly instructed and disciplined by prolonged, careful study, observation, and experiment? For a first-class heliographer all these qualities and acquirements are, in my view, essential.

Thus far I have spoken of *intellectual* qualifications exclusively. But to a heliographer, who would be both eminent in fact and successful with the public, certain *moral* qualities are hardly, if at all, less requisite.

And first, speaking generally, no man can work to the best advantage, unless the mental and moral, the thinking and emotional elements of his being are in proximate accordance or equilibrium. To work with the head without the heart were itself ominous for his success; but to work with the heart in bitter opposition to the head were far worse. He who should attempt to run a race in fetters, or to breast a torrent with half the body paralyzed, were more likely to succeed than one at odds with himself.

As matter of history, I believe it will be found, with few exceptions, if any, that the great immortals in art have been characterized by moral properties mainly corresponding to, if not perfectly matching, their intellectual. Michael Angelo and Raffaelle, Correggio and Leonardo da Vinci, may be named as examples among the moderns across the water; while Washington Allston, Gilbert Stuart, Rembrandt Peale, and Henry Inman show alike favorably on this. If there are exceptions of any considerable moment to this rule, I cannot now recall them. Indeed how *could* a corrupt, debased creature detect in his subject the expression of goodness—not to say, how represent such goodness on canvas or in stone? It stands among the moral axioms, that no man can discern or understand in another a quality of which he has not in himself the germs,—and these germs, too, somewhat developed.

That the heliographer, like other artists, should possess a genial and measurably *harmonic* nature is essential, both because man, being dual-natured, cannot achieve his highest and best unless the two elements of his being work accordantly together; and because without goodness in himself, he cannot perceive and depict goodness in others; while it is a generally recognised principle that a picture devoid of this element cannot be a chef d'œuvre in art.

But coming down from this general view, there are certain specific moral qualities which may be seen at first glance to be exceedingly important to the heliographer.

1st. Amenity, cordiality, grace, and ease of manners—in one word, politeness—are well-deserving the most assiduous cultivation by him. In truth, politeness may, for its multiform good effects, almost be catalogued among the positive virtues. An exterior, prickly and touch-wounding, may despoil the rarest qualities of the major portion of their proper influence. Conversely, a gracious, winning demeanor has such potency that it often gives social currency to one whose delinquencies would otherwise "send him to Coventry." What stronger incentive than this for sterling worth to put on a *seemly* garb!

2d. Genial, habitual good-nature, so-named, is another important requisite to a heliographer. A bright, sunshiny face is a positive benefaction to all beholders. It enhances the sitter's cheerfulness, if already in good spirits, and dispels his gloom if in the opposite mood. Whereas a sour, sullen face in the operant may neutralize the rarest skill by freezing the very emotions that should impart to the sitter the expression wished. It were wiser for one of this saturnine, surly temper to

"*Affect* this virtue, if he have it not."

Best have it in very fact; for, though nature withheld it, assiduous, prolonged endeavor will attain a considerable measure of it.

3d. The would-be eminent heliographer must especially have patience, as few places more urgently require it than his operating room. For, from the nature of his art, a single day may bring under his hand a host of persons, comprising almost every type of organization; the ignorant and stolid, the flippant and conceited, the fastidious, the difficult, &c. To deal with all these, even so as to avoid giving mortal offence, often taxes his patience to an extent that might make him almost envy even the patriarch Job himself.

Let him, however, beware of yielding to impatience or irritation even with such as these; for they constitute perhaps the majority of those, by whom he must (if at all) win his bread, as well as his professional distinction. To the multiform annoyances from these sources let him oppose simply a genial, invincible patience, which will be to him like a water-proof overcoat in a sleety storm, keeping him substantially dry and warm.

Thus far in the present chapter I have spoken of the heliographer in his individual relation to his art, and to the public who furnish subjects for his art. Before closing it I would say something of the heliographic body at large, and of certain matters that vitally concern it.

I suppose it will not be denied, that in days past the estimation generally put upon our profession and its practitioners, has been a humiliating one; and that the art itself has shared in the humiliation of its professors. Why was this so?

Among many different reasons may be mentioned,

1st. The fact that, to a degree unparalleled among other professions and callings within my knowledge, the practitioners of this have been chargeable with bickerings and clashes; with covert attacks and contumelious insinuations of one against another; while they have rarely recognised each other's professional deserts and rightful standing.

2d. That, among several thousands of heliographic practitioners in our country, there are very few *genuine artists;* and the number of sun-paintings is scanty, which win approval from those competent to judge of their merits. And most heliographs being what they are, i. e. poor, even to paltriness, it is commercially right, that they should be vended at rates so ludicrously cheap, that the vender himself, if sane, can hardly feel other than contempt for his work.

3d. That, unlike other artists and even artisans, helio graphers have not formed associations for advancing their art and securing their own reciprocal benefit, but have maintained a selfish isolation, or, worse still, a semi-hostile attitude towards each other.

I might, perhaps, suggest still other reasons for the disrepute under which our art and its professors have lain, but the three specified are more than sufficient to account for it.

Now all who feel sincerely interested in our art—and the number is far greater than when the first draft of these lines was made—must desire to see this deplorable state of things rectified. Let us attempt to ascertain from what causes it sprang, as such knowledge must precede all endeavors to amend it.

A principal cause lies, I think, in the fact that, heretofore, the majority of heliographers have adopted this vocation from motives *purely mercenary*. That is, the desire and the hope of making money more rapidly, and of avoiding manual labor, which seemed less easy and less "genteel," than art-practice. Will any one deny that this is *fact*, however discreditable to those concerned? As any one, by a few days' attention, may learn to get, through the camera, some kind of copy of the object placed before it; and as the obtaining of such copy is the whole idea the unimaginative, unartistic, uncultured person has of a heliograph, the impression has gone abroad, that sun-painting is the easiest of all vocations both to acquire and to practise. Hence numbers, not merely of the illiterate and undisciplined, but of dullards without a spark of art-genius, or even of discernment of the nature and requirements of art, have rushed into this profession from the exclusively mercenary impulses above named.

Now, be it how it may with other vocations, mechanical, agricultural, and the like, I feel confident that no one ever became, I will not say one of the art-immortals, but even a tolerable artist, from mercenary instigations *solely*. Other motives of a far different quality are needed to urge him forward and sustain him in the toils and sacrifices and endurances, which the attainment of artistic eminence will certainly exact of him.

At the head of these motives, and an absolute *sine qua non*, is a love for the art elected, in and for itself. Without this, I do not believe a genuine artist to be a possible existence. And in this love solely some have found a stimulus adequate to carry them upward to the very summits of excellence and distinction.

Another motive, however, is allowable to humanity as a support and strengthener of the first, viz. the love of fame,

"That last infirmity of noble minds."

Milton, veritable religious hero as he was, acknowledges that one motive which inspired his immortal Epic was, "the hope of producing something which the world would not willingly let die." Ambition of this sort, however, never descends to unworthy means and modes for working out its ends. The love of art forbids the artist to seek repute otherwise than by superior excellence therein; and under these conditions, the love of fame may be a collateral excitant, help, and support in his work. Where one of these motives is dominant and controlling, or the two united, even the desire of drawing pecuniary advantage from art may be, not a hindrance, but rather a help.

Young speaks expressively of the love of fame in the following lines:—

"The love of praise, howe'er concealed by art,
Reigns more or less, and glows in every heart;
The proud, to gain it, toils on toils endure;
The modest shun it, but to make it sure."

On the joint authority, then, of years and of much and varied experience, I would advise every one who is not conscious of an intense and sustained love of heliography, on its own account, to take up *any other* vocation than the practice of this, be such other what it may.

And speaking of intellectual and moral elements together, we should specify genius and love of the art, as two elements without which the striving to become a first-class heliographer would be a perfectly desperate undertaking.

When individuals possessing these two elements adopt the profession, and all beside abandon, or are driven from a field wherein they were not made to shine, then will heliography and its practitioners assume the honorable rank which both ought to hold.

Two other means by which the profession might be benefited, both in reality and in general repute, are, 1st, Heliographic Associations, akin to the Art-Associations which have long subsisted, and with such excellent effects; and 2d, Heliographic Journals, ably conducted and liberally patronized. The nature and possible advantages of both these are well enough understood, and beginnings in both have already been made among us.

The main thing, however, is that all heliographers should love their art; should appreciate its wondrous capabilities and possibilities; and should strive to place it in the high rank to which it is entitled. So these elements exist and act, all else desirable will follow in course.

CHAPTER IV.

SOME SUGGESTIONS AS TO THE FITTING UP OF HELIOGRAHIC ROOMS.

Expression essential to picture—Infants and children physiognomists—Average and intensified expression of face—Proper aims of artist—Difficulties of heliographer and painter as to getting expression—Both must act on sitter—How—Heliographer by fitting up of rooms—Enumeration of particulars in fitting up—All influenced by surroundings.

No artist needs be told that expression constitutes the chief beauty and power of the human face, both in the living original and in its "counterfeit presentment" by art. In our familiar associates the degree of this facial expression is often unnoticed and unknown; while in a stranger, casually encountered, we may, at the outset, be strongly impressed by it. The child, and even the infant, are very sensitive to this trait. From some persons they instinctively shrink—not unfrequently with tears and seeming fright—while to others they fondly cling, with a ready permission of handlings and caresses.*

In this fact lies a valuable security for social order,

---

* We have heard (says the editor of the *N. Y. Photographic Journal*) an anecdote of the late Daniel Webster, illustrative of this fact. Mr. Webster was visiting a friend, and while waiting in the parlor, his thoughts became abstracted, and perhaps were not of the most pleasant kind, for a little girl, running into the room, shrieked violently on catching sight of him, and it was with the utmost difficulty her nervous excitement could be calmed. By this time, the expression of Mr. W.'s face had changed, and the moment the child looked at him again she rushed into his arms and caressed him, as if he had been her father.

insuring, as it does, that men shall ultimately be known for what they really are. In vain do the profligate, the base, the wicked, and the selfish mimic those outward indications which pertain naturally to the pure, the good, and the generous. The inward unworthiness, despite all effort, *will* glare through the fleshly mask.

The face has an *average* expression, stamped thereon by the soul's *habitual* workings; but the momentary passions and emotions of joy, grief, anger, love, or hate, may, especially if intense, obliterate, or partially shadow, its wonted characteristics.

So, too, the average expression may be intensified by an extraordinary excitation of its habitual feelings.

These remarks bear directly on the purpose of this chapter. For what should the artist, heliographic or other, aim at, while exercising his art? Not *merely* to get an exact outline of his sitter's face. Nor *solely* to so fill up and color his sketch, that in shape, features, and tints, it shall be true to the original. These items are, indeed, important,—nay, essential to a *perfect* portrait. All these, however, are insufficient, in the absence of that expression which reveals the soul within,—that *individuality* which distinguishes *this* from all human beings beside. If the artist cannot detect and seize *this*, he makes no portrait.

Both the painter and the heliographer encounter difficulties in the matter of expression. From the stillness of the place; the moveless, and maybe constrained attitude of the sitter, producing weariness and ennui; his facial expression is often unnaturally dull and inanimate; and rarely of the bright, genial cast which it may, and in other conditions does, exhibit. To both artists, therefore, it is of vital moment that some means should, if possible, be devised to counteract these untoward influences, and summon into the face, at the time of sitting, the finest expression of which it is susceptible.

Now as the stamping of the image, by the heliographer, is the work of but a few seconds, he has not the same facilities for getting the desired expression as the painter, who may have many and prolonged sittings. On the other hand, if he can call it into the face but for an instant, his camera can infallibly seize and transcribe it; and here he has the advantage of the former. It is, then, a question of incalculable import, by what methods (if any) can the heliographer call up, in readiness for the *instant* of taking, the precise expression he would transfer to his plate?

His aim, of course, must be to act upon the *mind*, that is, upon both the *intellect* and *feelings* of his sitter. But *how?*

By the *circumstances* (for one item) surrounding the individual, both prior to and at the precise instant of sitting. It is peculiar to the heliographer's vocation, that his customers,—especially in busy seasons,—come in numbers, and remain awaiting each his turn for being taken. A portion, of course, must be subjected to a considerable delay before being reached; and this often proves wearisome, and sometimes positively irritating,—either of which moods is but a sorry preparative for a successful session. To *preclude these* moods on the one hand, and to *awaken* the *right* mood on the other, were a great desideratum.

Much, I think, might be done toward both these ends by a proper adjustment and fitting up of the heliographic rooms. Without attempting to furnish a complete plan for such fitting up, I will venture a few suggestions, which each artist may modify according to his own taste and judgment. And

1st. I would supply the *waiting-room* with books sufficiently various to interest the majority, at least, of all comers. Not bulky, grave, or abstract works, but such as may fitly occupy the fragments of time in question. Such works, abundant in our day, might do much, both for staving off *ennui*, and for awaking the better moods.

2d. I would have lying on the tables, and in portfolios, an ample variety of the finest engravings, prints, &c., to be procured; together with curiosities of different kinds, more especially such as have classic, romantic, and historic associations connected with them—*e. g.*, medals, coins, vases, urns, &c., whether originals or copies.

3d. But, over and above these specialties, I would make all things in and about the rooms converge to the single point of producing in the sitter a genial, elevated tone of sentiment and emotion. To myself our rectangular, formal apartments seem the very reverse of fitted to inspire either artist or sitter. The curve is recognised as the authentic "line of beauty." I will not, however, venture to dictate whether the curve, as appearing in the circle, or in some other of the conic sections, should determine the shape of the rooms. I will merely give it as my opinion that the highest artistic taste demands some one of these as the shaping principle of the construction.

4th. Having achieved the greatest attainable beauty in the *general outline*, I would apply the same formative principle to every even the smallest item in the equipment of the rooms.

Thus, for the customary rectangle in the windows, I would substitute some mode of the curve. In some, if not all of them, too, I would set that exquisite *stained glass* to which the mediæval cathedrals owed so much of their impressiveness. I would also drape them with ample and splendid curtains, taking special heed, however, that a pure artistic taste be not sacrificed to mere richness.

The garnishing of the walls, either with paper-hangings or paint, furnishes scope for a diversity of tastes, either or any of which may be artistically beautiful. On these walls I would suspend finely-executed and appropriate pictures in various styles, heliographic and other; while marble or other busts and statues should occupy the most suitable locations. In regard to these pictures and busts, I would have them so various, as to correspond to the leading types of character which might be expected among the sitters, and to be calculated to call into vivid action the feelings pertaining to these characters.

These pictures and heliographs should be all of the choicest quality; as walls crowded with specimens good, bad, and indifferent, suitable and unsuitable, would do more harm than service. Individuals of both sexes, who have been renowned for high traits and noble deeds, might well be introduced largely. It were best to affix the name to each, as this would enhance the interest. It were well, too, to have a considerable number of heliographs made in the establishment here suspended—taking care that they were of the very finest execution and finish. So far as possible, let all the heliographs exhibited be those produced in the establishment.

Especially would I have suspended from the walls several cages of singing-birds. The notes of these charming little creatures, their beautiful forms and plumage, and their graceful movements and pretty ways are to nearly all persons exceedingly agreeable; and, diverting the mind from a consciousness of self, they tend to awaken emotions and call up recollections and associations which impart to the face an amiable, genial ex pression.

Finally, in selecting the (technically named) furniture of the rooms, *e. g.*, carpets, tables, chairs, sofas, &c., I would adhere to the same principle. That is, I would have every article shaped and finished in accordance with our best conceptions of beauty and grace.

At the close of each day, every room should be thoroughly swept, and every utensil and article of furniture cleansed and arranged in their proper places. Before opening, on the following morning, the apartments and all their contents should be dusted, and fresh boquets of flowers disposed in appropriate locations. The general appearance of neatness and order in the rooms, together with the beauty and fragrance of these floral embellishments, will act agreeably on the feelings of the visitants; and being naturally observed by them, and spoken of to others, will enhance the reputation of the establishment, and thus advance both the fame and the pecuniary interests of its proprietor.

In sum, I would have the heliographic rooms a temple of beauty and grandeur, so that those entering therein may inhale a spirit which shall illumine their faces with the expression which the true artist would desire to perpetuate.

CHAPTER V.

THE SUNBEAM.

The sun the heliographer's instrument—Deified by Pagans—Newton's theory of light—Young's theory—Field's theory—Light, heat, actinism—Light a compound of seven colors, according to Newton—According to Brewster, &c., three—Effect of light on health, development, &c.—Heat and its incidents, *e. g.* absorption by the atmosphere, latency, influence on climate—Franklin's experiment—Actinism the heliographic element—This a proximate cause of germination—Decomposes and alters the arrangement of bodies—Electricity in sunbeam—Sunbeam weighed.

As the sunbeam is the chief instrumentality of the heliographic artist, it would seem not only proper, but indispensable, that such artist should master whatever is known concerning it. And his attention is more especially called to this subject *now*, from the fact, that recent discoveries have added largely to all our previous knowledge.

It cannot be wondered at that so many heathen nations should have numbered the sun among their divinities. For certainly there is no other *created* object, which images so variously and vividly the *uncreated* Creator. In truth, not merely the brightness and beauty, but the very *vitality* of the vegetable, the animal, and the human races, depend absolutely on the solar ray. And the fact is demonstrable, that the withdrawal of this ray would speedily be followed by the universal extinction of all material existence.

But, though *we* are better instructed, than to copy antiquity in yielding to the *creature* the homage due to the Creator alone, it is none the less true, that in the solar orb we behold one of the most expressive and glorious of all existing types of that great, inscrutable Being, from whose fiat the universe sprang. And so infinitely diverse and important are the agencies of the sunbeam in all the spheres of both nature and human art, that some account of its composition and properties may be interesting and perhaps useful to all.

Without going into detail, it may be well to note the principal theories, which have obtained concerning the abstract nature of light.

As by Newton himself, so by his followers, light is regarded as an emission of material particles from luminous bodies, corresponding to the aromas issuing from all odorous substances; the former causing the sensation of seeing, as the latter do that of smelling. On the other hand, Young, Frenel, Harris, &c., constitute a school, which maintains, that light is a mere undulation of a subtile ether, precisely as sound is an undulation of atmospheric air; the one causing vision by impinging against the visual nerves, as the other does hearing by contact with the auditory nerves.

A theory differing from both these and (so far as I know) peculiar to himself, is advanced by George Field, author of some of the profoundest and most ingenious works yet published on the subject. He considers light the product of two concurrent forces; 1st, oxygen, or the "whitening power," originating in the sun; and 2d, hydrogen, or the "blackening power," existing either in our atmosphere, or in planetary space. This oxygen darted from the solar orb, impinges against and combines with the aërial hydrogen; thus producing *combustion* with its wonted two-fold result, light and heat. Light, therefore, as a *total*, and the several colors, into which it is divided by the various refracting, reflecting, and absorbent properties of bodies, are regarded by him as oxydes of hydrogen. He holds, moreover, that magnetism, electricity, galvanism, and all other elementary existences, are the result of the same two principles, that constitute light. Now it is familiarly known, that the three elements above named are products of chemical action. Field's theory of light differs from others in maintaining the same to be true of *this* also.

But the *practical* philosophy of to-day ignores this whole class of topics, and inquires merely whether the sunbeam be simple or composite, and what are its effects upon vegetable and animal life. To treat cursorily these two questions will be all I shall here essay.

It has long been known, that the solar beam was not *simple*, but a compound of at least three elements; light, heat, and a third, of which, though some of its effects had been noted, comparatively little was understood. With whatever knowledge existed on this subject were commingled, till recently, a swarm of fables which progressive science has exploded. It is now demonstrated, that in the sunbeam, in its primary state, are combined and equably interdiffused light, heat, and a third principle, to which has been given the name of "actinism." This name comes from the Greek word, Ακτις—"Sunbeam,"—and denotes simply "ray-power," or "power of the ray." It is not a very felicitous name, since it entirely fails to *discriminate* its subject. For certainly light and heat are "ray-powers" equally with itself. We must, however, make the best of this title for the present.

The precise composition of the sunbeam was discovered by the artificial prism, though nature's own prism, the rainbow, had, for thousands of years foregone, intimated the same knowledge. A beam of *white* light, that is, of light coming *unmodified* from the sun, being made to pass through a peculiarly-shaped glass, sustains several interesting changes. First, the solar ray is thus discovered to be not light *simply*, but light in union with the two other principles of heat and actinism.

Secondly, it is found, that light itself is soluble into *seven* distinct colors, according to the doctrine of Newton and of most natural philosophers long after him, viz., red, orange, yellow, green, blue, indigo, and violet; these colors being of various degrees of refrangibility—the red appearing at the one extremity of the spectrum, as *least* refrangible, and the violet at the other, as *most* refrangible. By certain delicate experimentations, Sir John Herschell discovered two colors *additional* to the original seven; one beyond the violet, named by him, "lavender;" the second beyond the red, and named by him "crimson;" or "extreme red."

Sir David Brewster, however, ascertained, by careful experiment, that the "seven colors" of Newton, as also the "nine colors" of Herschell, were demonstrably reducible to three, viz., red, yellow, and blue; which *alone* he pronounces undecomposable or primary colors; all the others being readily produced by combinations of these radical three.

But the prism, *besides* thus affecting the *luminous* portion of the solar beam, affects no less its two other components, heat and actinism. At the red extremity of the spectrum it concentrates the main body of the calorific rays, while it gathers the actinic rays at the blue extreme. Thus the bulb of a delicately sensitive thermometer, being held in the blue ray, will stand at 56° F.; in the yellow it will rise to 62° F.; while in the red, or just beyond it, it will rise to 79° F.—making 23° difference between the temperature of the blue and the red. It is, moreover, ascertained that the heat-rays are intensest of all *outside* of the red ray, and that the actinic rays act most powerfully *beyond* the blue ray.

These three constituents of the solar beam have each its own special office in carrying forward the innumerable processes of both the inanimate and the living worlds. By reiterated experiments a few of the most important functions of each have been discovered and noted down.

These I will now attempt briefly to describe.

I. Of Light. This, by unanimous recognition, is the sole colorist, and thus the grand beautifier of the visible universe. The azure of the firmamental vault; the green of the meadow, forest, and ocean; the gorgeous splendors of the painted clouds; the variously exquisite tints of the flowers, of the plumed and insect tribes, and of the precious gems; and finally, those matchless pencillings which often make the infantile or female face a lovelier spectacle than any and every other the world can display; these, one and all, point to and borrow their chief beauty from the sun's *luminous* rays. This fact is shown by experimentation so simple, that all may put it to the test.

Thus the potato and other vegetables, sprouting in a dark cellar, are seen to shoot up *pallid* stalks. But, on a few days' exposure to the sunshine, the *white* stalk takes on a *deep green.*

On the same principle, tropic vegetation wears a tint of green as much more richly dark than that of the extra-tropic zone, as the degree of sunlight enjoyed by the torrid transcends that which visits the temperate parallels of our globe.

But while thus imparting color and beauty to the

vegetable world, light works out another result on which the very life of the animal races depends. It has been discovered that the *green* of all vegetable growths is owing to a substance elaborated in their cellular tissues by the action of light. This substance has been denominated chlorophyll. That light, and neither of the two other constituents of the sunbeam, produces this substance, has been determined by numerous facts, of which the following is a specimen. In the warm, moist weather of spring, the sun's *light* is, for successive days, occasionally obscured wholly by clouds, while its calorific and actinic forces are in free, energetic operation. During such intervals, a forest has been known to germinate and put forth its leaves to nigh their full compass, notwithstanding the obscuration of the *luminous* rays. But in such conditions it has been noted that the leaves, in lieu of exhibiting their *wonted* hue, wear a *pale, bluish-white* tinge. A single day, however, of *unobstructed* sunlight has been known to elaborate this coloring chlorophyll so rapidly that, ere its close, the foliage has put on its customary depth of green. This may sound improbable, but it is avouched by the most reliable authorities.

Now, by analysis, chlorophyll has been discovered to be a composite of oxygen gas and carbon. In intimate connection with its production commences a second most curious and interesting process. This is the generation of the *woody tissue* of the plant, which is found to be effected by the same agency of light. This woody tissue is mostly carbon, and of this carbon the principal portion is derived from the atmosphere. It is quite familiarly known that carbonic acid—a compound of carbon with oxygen gas—is one among the constituents of atmospheric air. On this fact is based a beautiful and marvellous arrangement, whereby the animal and the vegetable worlds are interlinked and made vitally dependent, the one on the other. Thus all animals, including man, inhale air, which is a composite mainly of nitrogen and oxygen gases, as a prime indispensable of existence. The lungs decompose this inbreathed air, and its oxygen, uniting with a portion of the superabundant carbon of the blood, generates a species of *combustion* which supplies the requisite animal heat, while at the same time clarifying the blood. The result of *this* combustion, like that of our fires, burning lamps, &c., is carbonic acid, which passes by respiration from the lungs into the atmosphere.

The amount of oxygen thus consumed by the countless varieties of animal existence, as well as in other modes, would, but for some replenishing arrangement, in no long time exhaust the atmosphere of this vital element. But, by a beautiful *compensatory* appointment, carbonic acid has been ordained to be as literally the "breath of life" to all *vegetable* beings, as oxygen is to animal. Through their leaves, which are their lungs, it is absorbed from the atmosphere decomposed into its two constituents. The carbon goes to form the plant's woody fibre, while the disengaged oxygen is dismissed into the atmosphere to replace what had been consumed by animal respiration and otherwise.

The first who called general attention to the fact (if not absolutely its discoverer) that plants, under the action of light, *exhale* oxygen and *inhale* carbonic acid gas, was Dr. Joseph Priestly, who may almost be pronounced the father of modern chemistry.

M. Labillardière discovered that light is necessary to the development of *pores* in plants; while Michellotti of

Turin found light to be injurious to young plants and animals.

Thus it is, that the animal and the vegetable worlds are so inseparably connected and interdependent, that were either annihilated, a swift dissolution would no less befall the other.

What a beautiful anomaly, too, seems the fact, that the *solid tissues* of all vegetable growths, whether the granite compactness of the oak and hickory, or the impenetrable hardness of the lignum vitæ, are a product of the noiseless agency of light; that soft, delicate substance (if *substance* we may name it) which, launched in floods from its parent orb, and hurrying earthward with thought's own speed, impinges against that most exquisitely sensitive of organs, the eye, without causing any other sensations than those of refreshment and delight.*

I have already stated one proof, that these results are wrought by light and not by heat or actinism. I will just allude to one or two more.

Thus a plant, sequestered from light while exposed to the other two elements, will indeed grow at its ordinary rate; but *besides* being *white* instead of *green*, as mentioned, it will grow up soft and brittle, and will never elaborate its proper *woody fibre*.

* Says a modern writer: "Not only does light fly from the sun with a velocity a million and a half times greater than that of a cannon-ball, but it darts from every reflecting surface with like velocity, and reaches the tender structure of the eye so gently, that, as it falls upon the little web of nerves there spread to receive it, it imparts the most pleasing sensations. Philosophers once tried to *weigh* the sunbeam. They constructed a most delicate balance, and suddenly let in upon it a beam of light—the lever of the balance being so delicately hung that the fluttering of a fly would have disturbed it. Everything being prepared, they took their places and keenly watched the result. The sunbeam that was to decide the experiment had flown through 95,000,000 of miles in eight minutes, and shot upon the balance with unabated velocity. But the balance moved not, and the philosophers were mute."

Again, it has been ascertained, that with the going down of the sun the plant nearly ceases to decompose the carbonic acid that constitutes its chief nutriment. Thus it would seem, that night is appointed as a season of repose, not less for the vegetable than the animal world, as the day is ordained as a period of labor for both.

But how shall it be explained, that the plant does not *entirely* suspend the decompounding of carbonic acid by night, if light be essential to this process? May not the *diminished* action still remaining be caused by a portion of light, which continues unabsorbed by the darkness? Heat, as we know, has the property of becoming *latent*, under certain conditions. It is by many believed, that light possesses a quality akin to this; that, during the day, a portion of it is absorbed by bodies on the earth's surface, and, remaining invisible while the sun is above the horizon, is disengaged during the night-hours. Thus the pale, diffused light, which enables us to see partially by night, even when the moon and stars are muffled in dense clouds, is supposed to come from this source, as is also the light emitted by certain gems in the dark. It may be, then, that the partial decomposition of carbonic acid performed by vegetables at night is caused by the light thus liberated from its latent state.

Among the numerous other agencies of light I shall here speak of but one; I mean its power and influence on the health and well-being of animals. I believe it is almost uniformly the case, that sick persons suffer most from their maladies during the dark hours, and enjoy more or less alleviation of their pains while the sun is above the horizon. It is quite common, that those suffering from violent irritation of the lungs and throat, commence coughing at sunset, and perforce continue this tormenting process without intermission until sunrise, when it ceases, to be renewed only at the coming on of another evening.

But there are facts far more striking, which illustrate the genial influences of this element. Savage tribes of both the tropics and the temperate zones,—of the former more especially,—live almost wholly in the open air, and therefore in the sunshine, wearing the while but scanty clothing. Now, malformation, sickness, and debility of constitution are well nigh unknown to these races, while, on the other hand, they are very common with the dwellers in the dark lanes and cellars of our large cities. It is said, that numbers of the poor in the French city of Lille had been used to live in certain dark recesses under the fortifications, until the magistrates, finding that the majority of those born there were somehow deformed or diseased, passed an edict compelling the removal of these people elsewhere. It is believed, too, that cretinism and the goitre, repulsive maladies prevailing among the Alps and Pyrenees, are owing to the absence of sunlight, as their victims dwell in deep, shady glens, which the solar ray but partially penetrates.

But a still more curious proof of the potent agency of light was discovered by a French naturalist. He found that tadpoles could not undergo their wonted transformation into frogs, if kept sequestered from sunlight, although they continued increasing in size and weight as *tadpoles!* It would seem, then, that those corporeal transmutations, through which such multitudes of the insect and reptile tribes pass, are vitally dependent on the influence of the sun's *luminous* rays.

But I must pass to the remaining branches of my subject.

II. Of Heat. It is estimated, that when the heat-rays,

in their passage from the sun to the earth, enter the atmosphere enveloping the latter, they are so much affected by this aërial fluid, that one-third of them becomes absorbed and two-thirds only reach the surface of our globe. It would seem, then, that one office of our atmosphere is to protect animal and vegetable life from that unmodified power of the sun's heat, which would be its destruction. Few, perhaps, are aware of the quantity of heat received from that orb. If you imagine our globe entirely incased with a coating of solid ice forty feet thick, the heat derived from the sun in a single year would, it is calculated, suffice to melt the whole immense mass.

I have already mentioned the remarkable property possessed by heat of becoming *latent*. Thus a volume of ice, which is water *solidified* at 32° F., when subjected to 172° F. of heat, becomes liquid, and yet the resulting water remains precisely at the temperature of the ice, or 32° F. Consequently 140° F. of heat have become latent, so as to be inappreciable by any known test. Again, when water passes into steam, or is evaporated, 1000° F. of heat become latent, since steam is of exactly the same *sensible* temperature with boiling water, which stands at 212° F. For this singular property of caloric we discover a most wise and beneficent use. Thus, as the sun reaches the limit of his northern journey on the 21st of June, his rays *then* reach us most directly and of course in greater abundance, and it would seem, therefore, that our hottest weather should date here. As a general rule, however, our intensest summer heats fall a month or more later; and if, in fact, we should pass from the biting airs of winter and the boisterous, penetrating breezes of spring to a May and June of such melting heats, as characterize our July and August, not only severe suffering, but debility and disease would be the almost unavoidable result. But from this evil we are secured by this provision of latent caloric. By the *gradual* liquefaction of the ices and snows of winter and spring, large quantities of the solar heat become progressively latent, and therefore do not inflict discomfort on sensitive beings. The same result flows from the immense evaporations incessantly going on in every volume of water, great or small, on the globe under the solar rays in their greatest intensity. Nor are even these the only methods ordained for attempering, on our behalf, the fierce heats of opening summer while we are by degrees growing inured to them. In fact, every object on the earth's surface, animate and inanimate, organic or inorganic, as also the soil itself, has the property of absorbing considerable proportions of caloric, and reserving it until the various exigencies of the animal and vegetable kingdoms require its disengagement.

While, then, in these and kindred ways living creatures are prepared for the transition from cold to heat, on the approach of winter there occurs a process exactly the reverse and for a reverse purpose. On the 20th of December we should expect our intensest cold, as then receiving the minimum quantity of the sun's heat, on account of his position in relation to us. Yet the last half of January and the main part of February constitute usually our severest season. And the reason is, that, by the transmutation of immense bodies of water into ice with the consequent disengagement of the latent caloric that kept them liquid, and the condensation of aërial vapors into snow, with the liberation of the semi-latent heat, which had previously been absorbed by the earth and the objects on its surface, the severity of the cold is so far mitigated that our systems become fitted for what they must encounter. What human parent, even the tenderest and most affectionate, *so* cares for the well-being of his children?

Most persons, I presume, have read of an experiment performed by Dr. Franklin to ascertain whether the *color* of a substance had any connection with its capacity of absorbing and radiating heat. Laying several differently colored pieces of cloth on the snow where they were exposed to the sun, he found considerable difference in the rapidity with which the snow melted under them. His experiment has been repeated by Sir Humphrey Davy and others, and the result reached by them all is, that black possesses most absorbent power, to which succeed in order brown, green, red, yellow, and white. It is ascertained, moreover, that the power of a substance to *radiate* caloric corresponds exactly to its power of *absorbing* it. In selecting the color of our garments for summer's heat or winter's cold, this knowledge may, perhaps, be of some service.

The same principle, as regards color, pervades the whole vegetable world. The damask rose which bears its beautiful ruddy tint because it reflects merely the *red* ray of the solar beam, while absorbing the rest, imbibes also a larger share of the *heat-rays* than the *white* rose of the same bulk, which reflects the sun's entire light and absorbs none, and of consequence absorbs fewer of the heat-rays. The bulb of a delicate thermometer, placed successively within the corollas of these two flowers, exhibits the mercury as rising considerably higher in the red than in the white one.

It appears, then, that those exquisite flower-tribes, which look like beautiful characters in which God has written His immeasurable love all over the green page of earth, subserve ends of *utility* not less than embellishment to man's abode. First, imbibing the solar heat, and thus aiding to shield living creatures from its too intense summer fervors; next absorbing from the atmosphere that carbonic acid which, *unmodified*, is hostile to all animal life; they then exhale into the air their own fragrant breath freighted with that oxygen which is a prime necessity of universal animate existence. And all the while their delicate loveliness is a perpetual charm and blessing to the eye, while their wondrous organism speaks more potently, than sermon or homily of man, of the wisdom and goodness of their Creator.

"'Neath cloistered boughs each floral bell, that swingeth
And tolls its perfume on the passing air,
Makes Sabbath in the fields, and ever ringeth
A call to prayer."

That heat is the principal agent in the generation of winds, from the irresistible tornado to the gentlest zephyr; that it also enacts an important part in the development of electricity and magnetism, elements so essential as to be almost identical with the very currents of universal life, is too well known to require notice here. Omitting also much else that is interesting on this subject, I proceed to the third principle in the Sunbeam.

III. Actinism. As this is the principle with which the heliographer is chiefly concerned in the exercise of his art, it is highly desirable he should be acquainted with whatever, as yet, is known of its relations and effects. And since less is known of actinism than of either light or heat, he, as well as the student of science, has before him a large field for experiment and investigation. In consequence of Daguerre's discovery, it has been studied mainly in reference to its influence on the mineral and inorganic world. Something, however, is known of its action on vegetable and animal structures, and of this I will briefly speak.

With the depositing of the seed beneath the soil, we detect the first operation of this principle. By experiments, which I need not detail, it has been ascertained that actinism, with little if any aid from light and heat, is the proximate cause of *germination*. You may exclude the two last, and yet, under the radiation of the former in connection with moisture, a seed will sprout in twenty-four hours. Conversely, exclude actinism and expose the seed to light and heat, and it will remain for days without signs of germination. In fact, until germination has occurred, and the plant has risen above the surface, light—strange to say—is a *positive hindrance* to the commencement of growth. So also is heat,—at least in that unmodified state in which it comes from the sun. One actual reason, then,—though we may not be aware of it—for burying seeds in the earth is, that the soil may serve as a screen from the full power of the solar light and heat. Actinism, a chemical force, of which one of the principal functions is to decompound and alter the arrangement of the particles in whatever it touches, is enabled to pierce through the earthy covering to the seed. It then transmutes the starch of the seed into gum and sugar, which are the proper nutriment of the vegetable embryon. The tiny root penetrates the husk and shoots downward, while the baby stem pushes its way upward into the air. *Then* light and heat join forces with actinism, and continue operating with it in all after stages of the plant's life. Probably very few of the whole number of offices executed by each in vegetive growth are as yet known; though we do know that neither of the three *singly*, nor either two of them united, will suffice to perfect the plant, but that *all* must coöperate in the process. That actinism, however, performs an important part in the work is obvious from its being the emphatically decomposing power, while decomposition is incessantly required in vegetable nutrition; doing for the plant very much what the gastric juice does for the animal.

Little has been hitherto ascertained in regard to the effect of this principle on animal life. Analogy, however, would intimate that it must be considerable. It is, indeed, most likely that a part at least of the influence ascribed to light on animal health and development belongs properly to actinism.

Many interesting discoveries have been made touching the relation of actinism to inorganic substances, such having been the direction given to it by its connection with the heliographic art. Thus, the chlorine and hydrogen gases will not effect a chemical union in darkness. But, on their exposure to sunshine, an immediate combination is produced by actinic influence.

So, again, peroxalate of iron in solution remains unchanged in a dark place. But, brought into sunshine in a glass vessel, it commences a vehement fermentation, which terminates by precipitating small crystals of protoxalate of iron of a brilliant yellow color.

Actinism, as we have seen to be the case with light and heat, is to some extent *absorbed* by certain bodies; for, if you first expose chlorine to the solar ray, it will *then* combine with hydrogen even in darkness.

As a decompounding force, actinism effects some change in the atomic arrangement of every body whereon it falls, be it the firmest rock or the softest wood or leaf. Were it not, then, for *counteracting* and *reparative* agencies in the economy of creation, this delicate-seeming power, though the tender nurse of the vegetable infant, would eventually crumble into ruins the total frame-work of the universe! But no sooner

> "Comes still evening on,
> And in her sober livery all things garbs,"

than the action of this disturbing force is suspended. That *rest,* which is indispensable to man and beast, is not less so to vegetable beings. This rest is a *restorative* to the latter, as to the former, and stays the advance of decomposition beyond the degree in which it subserves the ends of life and well-being.

In a succeeding chapter, I shall briefly describe the heliographic process, with the agency of actinism therein and the chemical substances contributing to the result. Before closing this chapter, however, I will mention that, by an ingenious apparatus, heliographic pictures have been produced in absolute darkness; arrangements having been made to exclude light *entirely,* and heat *mostly,* while the actinic rays were allowed free course. This establishes the point beyond question, that the actinic, and neither of the other two constituents of the sunbeam, is the *working* instrument of the heliographic artist. In accordance with this is the fact that cloudy weather is *equally* favorable, to say the least, to the production of pictures with days of brightest sunshine; and that the prodigal radiance of tropic climes is less propitious to the successful practice of this art than the paler sunshine of our chilly north.

It was long a matter of debate whether or not electricity made a fourth constituent of the solar ray. But the recent experiments of the German Baron Reichenbach have completely settled this question in the affirmative. I will, therefore, now close this imperfect account of a matter in itself highly interesting as well as important, with the hope that my professional brethren may be induced to cultivate a field which, though as yet but partially explored, is known to be incalculably rich, in such a manner as may largely augment our existing knowledge.

I may here casually mention that, in a subsequent chapter detailing my method of practice in the production of heliographs, I naturally must touch again on the subject of the present chapter.

CHAPTER VI.

HARMONY OF COLORS.

The love of ornament innate and universal—Constituents of visual beauty, form and color—Harmony of colors—Its meaning—Knowledge of this practically useful, *e. g.* in dress, embellishment, &c.—Our guides in using colors for costume, *e. g.* climate, size, form, complexion, &c., of person; also, age, social position, &c.; and still further, time, place, and occasion—The best portraits are those which, retaining *likeness,* conceal defects and blemishes, and *heighten* charms and beauties—Exposition of the effects of various colors on the appearance—Definition of harmony of analogy and harmony of contrast in colors—Also of primary, and secondary or complementary colors—Colors emblematic of dispositions and character—Illustrative quotations from the poets.

A TASTE for ornament and embellishment, or, to speak most comprehensively, a love of beauty, is undeniably an innate, ineradicable property of our nature. And that the Creator designed this taste or love to be satisfied, and has, therefore, provided means for this satisfaction, as expressly and abundantly as for that of any among our appetites, even those most essential to life, our own eyes assure us, whether we direct them to the firmament above us, or over the globe we inhabit.

Of *visual* beauty, the two *material* constituents are form and color. That each of these is based on mathematical principles of its own, which determine the quantity and arrangement necessary to the production of the result named beauty, there can be no question whatever. For the Deity operates not by *casual* agencies, nor has *accident* any part in the evolution of His designs. The floating of a dust-grain in the air depends upon laws no less exact and indefeasible than the journey of Neptune through his immeasurable circuit. But whether, for various causes, more attention has been devoted to the study of *form* than that of *color*, or whether the latter subject has greater *intrinsic* difficulties than the former, I believe it is unquestionable, that the principles and regulating laws of the former are far better understood than those of the latter. This is the more to be regretted in relation to matters of every day concern, because while defects of form may be measurably disguised and redeemed by extraordinary beauty of coloring, the most exquisite symmetry of form may be marred, if not utterly spoiled, by a tasteless ugliness of coloring.

Such, however, being the state of the case, it should not be expected by the reader, as I certainly do not myself expect, that *full* justice will be done, in this chapter, to the subject of color. All I hope is, that some suggestions may be offered, which may prove valuable to such as may have occasion to employ colors either for professional or personal uses.

In this, as in all other cases, nature is our great object of study; our main source of information; our paramount and infallible guide wheresoever and so far as we can apprehend her directions. The Deity is the great proto-artist, the one perfect harmonist of colors, and the material creation is the measureless sphere of His workings. Would we learn what is meant by the "harmony of colors," we have only to examine the products of that divine pencil. In the mineral, the vegetable, the animal, and the aromal worlds, may be witnessed an infinity of specimens, either and all illustrating the principle in perfection. You may select the many-tinted gems that irradiate the mountain's dark caverns; the delicately pencilled shells that beautify the green depths of the sea; the myriad-hued flowers that decorate spring, summer, and autumn in succession, or those wingéd flowers, the birds and insects, that traverse the airy realms; the gorgeous assemblage of clouds that wait on the departing sun, or the glad splendors that play over the face of young morning; or, finally, that most exquisite of all combinations of colors, which constitutes the magic of a beautiful human countenance. Of all these specimens, select which you will, and you have the very thing of which we speak. And if you can but detect the *philosophy* of the thing; that is, the *order* in which these colors are arranged, the *proportion* each bears in the combination, and the *grounds* of both, you will then possess the law to guide you in your own use of colors.

Such knowledge is important to the public on various accounts; such as the purposes of the toilet, the fitting up of our dwellings, and for many other similar objects. I do not consider it necessary to argue the point, that dress is a subject deserving careful consideration. If there are those, who charge such consideration to the score of a reprehensible vanity and criminal folly, I shall attempt no argument with them, but feel safe in the example of Him who garnished "the rose of Sharon and the lily of the valley" with that exquisite beauty which mocks all human skill, and dims the "array of Solomon in all his glory."

One of the leading principles in regard to coloring, is that it should bear a strict relation to climate. In nature such is invariably the case. In the dazzling light and beneath the intense fervors of the tropic sun, the flowers, birds, and insects wear a corresponding gorgeousness of tint, and the grass and foliage a kindred vividness of green. Of course, then, the dress and other equipments of the inhabitants should bear relation to this fact. And they actually do so, whatever the cause may be, whether a knowledge of principles or mere intuition. Thus the various reds and yellows, which go by the name of "warm" or "gay" colors, are employed profusely, in the way of ornament, by the denizens of hot climates; nor do we deem it in *them* an affront to correct taste. So, also, whether from knowledge or intuition, we find the chief materials of their dress to be of a white color, this being the least absorptive and most reflective of colors, and therefore most conducive to coolness.

Again, in temperate climates, where the sun's light and heat are less vivid and intense, we see a corresponding difference in the aspect of both vegetable and animal worlds; universally there is less prodigality of life itself. The forest and the meadow are robed in a paler green; the flowers, exquisite as they are, exhibit a less gorgeous coloring, and the feathered tribes charm rather by the sweetness of their minstrelsy than by the splendor of their plumage. Perfect taste, then, requires that in the colors of our dress and other appointments, we should have a general regard to the aspect of nature, as modified by our geographic position.

Bearing in mind these general considerations which respect a people as a whole, let us now touch on some of the specialties which concern each individual. And as, if we can ascertain the true principles of harmonic coloring belonging to a single class of subjects, we can easily transmute these into universal laws, so for the sake of clearness and simplicity we select for our subject the female dress in its relation to colors, this being certainly as important as any other, and as little under the guardianship of a cultivated taste.

At the outset, then, it is manifest that in choosing the

predominant color of a lady's dress, as well as the *subordinate* colors employed as ornament, strict regard should be had to her size, her configuration, and especially her complexion and style of expression. The point to be aimed at in all this is, that so far as depends on her garb, she should *look as well as nature aided by art will permit;* and that, therefore, defects should be supplied, redundancies thrown into the shade, and actual beauties be brought conspicuously into view. The philosophy of which may be stated thus: nature aims ever at the highest beauty, the utmost perfection; but in moulding the human body her creative force is intercepted by several causes which belong to our present stage of being; such as the stubborn, unpliable quality of the material composing the body, the defects inherited from ancestors, the casualties to which the individual is exposed during corporeal development, &c. In consequence of all these obstructions, *faultless, complete* beauty is rarely, if ever seen. In striving, then, by art to rectify deformities or imperfections, we do not *contravene* and impeach, but rather *coöperate* with and *justify* nature. That is, by help of powers furnished by herself, we do somewhat towards bringing to view that ideal of beauty which nature aimed at and would have attained, had she been dealing with that more ductile and tractable material of which the *spiritual body* is compounded.

On the same principle, the *true artist*, when limning a human face, does not represent it *exactly as it is*, with every casual wart, pimple, and freckle that now disfigure it, but just as it would be if her moulding idea, instead of being partially thwarted by the intractability of the material she wrought with, had been brought out and expressed. Therefore, you say of a portrait by the pencil of an artist-genius, that "it is an excellent likeness, but much handsomer than the original." Acting according to the same law, by cultivation, grafting, &c., we elevate the puny, sour, worthless native apple into that large, beautiful, delicious fruit which delights three senses, instead of affronting all. Shakspeare, the high priest and interpreter of nature, has said the whole thing in a few lines:

"You see, we marry
A gentler scion to the wildest stock;
And make conceive a *bark of baser kind*
By *bud of nobler race.* This is an art
Which does *mend nature—change it* rather; but
The *art itself is nature.*"

This principle is of universal application, and we are fully authorized by nature herself to apply it equally to a lady's toilet as to aught beside. Therefore, we say that dress should do its utmost towards producing the ideal of the species of beauty it adorns.

For example, a lady, inclined to stoutness and of extra height, should select a color for the principal robe which disguises these deviations from the "juste milieu." Black, which *absorbs* all luminous rays, has the effect to *diminish* the apparent bulk, and black, therefore, is her appropriate color.

White, which *reflects* all light-rays, operates to *magnify* the apparent size, and thus garments of this color would give her too much of the Glumdalclitch aspect. Contrariwise, a small-sized woman should eschew black, unless she chooses to resemble the Lilliputian ladies seen by the immortal Gulliver, and adopt *white,* which to the beholder's eye will retrieve the short-comings of nature.

Suppose, again, a lady has a complexion of *extra ruddiness.* In choosing a bonnet, she should, if possible.

adopt a tint which will *mitigate* this excess. A head-dress of a *deeper red* than her complexion will, by comparison, produce this effect, while one of pink or any still lighter red will exaggerate the original ruddiness.

On the same principle, a *sallow* complexion should eschew a *light-blue* bonnet, which *aggravates* its defect, and adopt one of transparent white, which conceals it.

A *pale* complexion is improved, by a *pale-green* head-dress into a delicate pink hue, through the operation of the principle of *harmonious contrast in colors* which I shall presently explain; while one of *lemon-yellow* would heighten this paleness to very ghastliness.

Once more, the delicate red and white complexion, nature's master-piece of coloring, should avoid head-gear of crimson or any deep red, as by contrast giving it a pale appearance, and adopt a *light blue,* or *light green,* or *transparent white,* either of which will at least leave to it its original beauty, if it does not enhance it.

The grounds of the foregoing suggestions may be better understood from a brief description of certain peculiarities in the nature of the sun's luminous rays. Of the several kinds of harmony of colors, the two principal are the "harmony of analogy," and the "harmony of contrast."

By the harmony of analogy is meant that order in which the colors occur, as they are displayed in the prismatic spectrum. That is, from one of the primitive colors you pass, by scarce distinguishable gradations, through numerous intermediate shades of color to the next primitive, and so onward through the whole. Complete specimens of this species of harmony may often be witnessed in the sunrise and sunset clouds and skies. Somewhat of the same is seen frequently in extensive prospects, embracing sky, land, and water, though in general variety is given to this spectacle by the occasional introduction of the harmony of contrast.

What is meant by this latter phrase may, perhaps, be apprehended most clearly from the following diagrams, which help to illustrate certain peculiarities of color.

FIGURE 1.

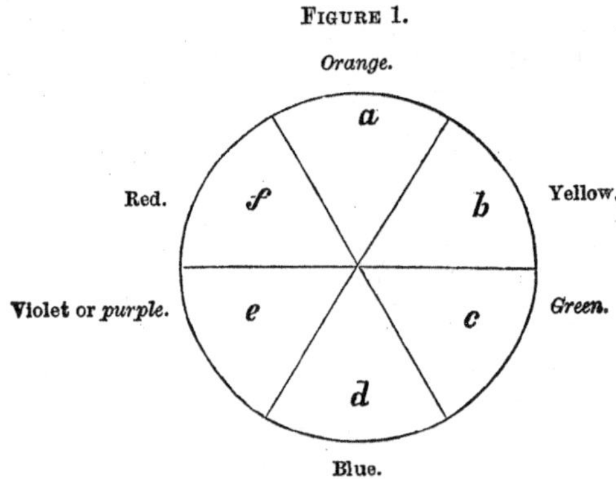

There are several points here requiring notice. In figure 1st, it will be observed that the primary color, blue, occupies full double the space in the spectrum of the other two primaries, red and yellow. Thus representing the proportions by figures, 2 will stand for red; 3 for yellow; and 5 for blue.

The intermediate colors noted down in this diagram are called secondaries; and a peculiarity belonging to them is, that the secondary standing *opposite* to a particular primary is formed by combining the two other primaries. Thus green, standing over against red, is a compound of blue and yellow; orange, opposed to blue, of red and yellow; and violet, opposite yellow, of blue and red. These secondaries are commonly called the *complements* of the opposing primaries, because, being a composite of two primaries, they constitute, when added to the third primary, white light, or the whole of the solar luminous ray. If you lay a *red* substance on a white surface, and gaze at it steadily a few moments, you will perceive around it a halo of *green*. So a blue object exhibits an orange ring, and a yellow a violet one.

FIGURE 2.

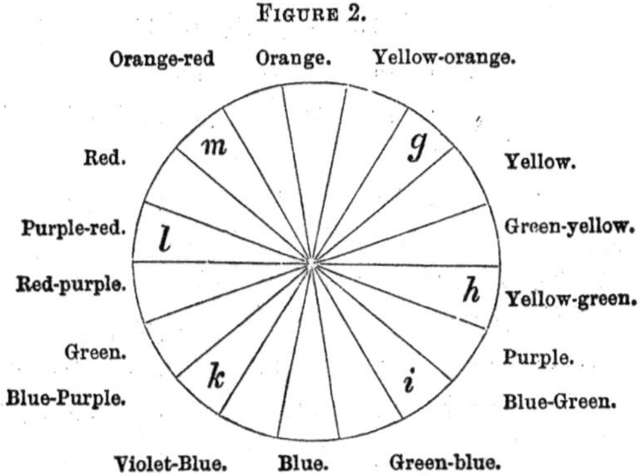

Modifications of these secondary or composite colors, as is seen in figure 2d, may be multiplied indefinitely by combining the secondaries, and thus forming *tertiaries;* by combining the tertiaries into another shade; and so so on for hundreds of times or more. But the same principle continues to hold, that each of these shades or tints has a complement, as we saw in figure 1st, which complement is a union of the tints, that do *not* enter into its own combination.

These complemental colors are also named "contrasts," and as they harmonize with the colors over against them, we thus arrive at the phrase, "harmony of contrasts."

Let one, then, study carefully the harmony of analogy, as illustrated by the solar spectrum, or on a still more splendid scale in the rainbow and the tinted clouds; let him also master the harmony of contrast through the requisite methods; and I am confident we should no longer be shocked by those practical barbarisms of taste now prevalent in so many spheres.

As I have already said, my object in this chapter is not to specify minutely the requirements of a pure taste in the costume of one or another person. It is rather to present a few general principles, which may aid the reader in deciding what is most appropriate to him or herself. I will, therefore, subjoin a few suggestions to those already advanced.

It would seem obvious enough, that in selecting alike the colors and the fashion of a garb, special regard should be paid to the age, the general characteristics, and the social position, not less than to the complexion, the shape, and the size of the individual concerned. For a middle-aged lady to array herself like a girl of eighteen, or for an old lady to wear the garb of one or the other, or for either of the three to make an exchange with either of the other two, would be an absurdity too glaring to require one word of exposition. Again, for a lady of grave dispositions and reserved deportment, whether middle-aged or young, to put on the gay or semi-gay costume, which seems not only appropriate, but almost essential to one of vivacious, lively temperament, and frank, cordial manners, is a self-demonstrated incongruity, even though her own feelings (as, I believe, would commonly occur) should not interdict it. And then, the intuitions of society, which are not apt to be far astray in such matters, intimate that the position of the head of a family should have some bearing on the costume of its members. For example, the lady of a clergyman, or of a man exercising any other function of kindred gravity, would be likely to offend the susceptibilities of the judicious and refined by appearing in that rainbow-tinted garb, which would be appropriate enough to the messenger of Olympus,* or one holding a similar office.

But there are yet other qualifying circumstances to be kept in view, such as time, place, occasion, and the like. No sane person, for example, would dress for attending a funeral, as for attending a theatre or ball; or for supervising her domestic affairs, as for receiving morning or afternoon calls. An instinctive feeling prevails well nigh universally, that the affairs with which one is occupied, and the mood belonging to the time, should exert a controlling influence on the quality of the garb. Thus red and yellow, which for obvious reasons are named "warm colors," harmonize well in their several shades with *festive* and *joyous* scenes. So also does white, which is counted an emblem of cheerfulness, dignity, and peace, as well as of innocence, purity and delicacy, all of which traits must characterize such scenes to give them favor with persons of refinement.

Green, the complemental of red, harmonizes with it to make a festive garb of that *medium* liveliness, which pleases many tastes of the more chastened quality.

Blue is called the coldest of the colors, but is interesting for its symbolic associations. Thus it is reckoned an emblem of constancy and generosity, as appears in the sailor's phrase, "true-blue." Being also the color of heaven and of the human eye, it is taken for a symbol of intelligence and of divinity, and the ancients pronounced the mantle of Minerva, or Wisdom, to be blue, as also the robes of the Muses. These intimations point out many occasions of the comparatively graver description for which this color would be appropriate.

Moreover, orange, which is deemed the warmest of

---

* Iris.

colors, as combining red and yellow, being the complemental of blue, orange and blue for persons of certain complexions, would constitute a very striking harmony of contrast even in a festival costume.

So, for a lady of good height and proportions, and with that exquisitely white skin sometimes witnessed, jet black is a charming color for almost every occasion.

I venture to call black a color, as also white, though the ordinary writers on color deny the name to both. *Why* they do so, I know not, since both produce in us the *sensation* of color, and both are composites in varying proportions of the three primitive colors; in black, blue predominating, red coming next, and yellow last; while in white, yellow predominates, red comes next, and blue is subordinate to both. What are termed negative or neutral colors, are those compounded either of the three primaries, or secondaries, or tertiaries, in such proportions that neither is predominant. Black and white are the extremes, and grays the intermediates of these.

The neutral grays and the semi-neutral drabs, &c., are admirably fitted for a lady's *service*-dress while attending to household concerns, or while walking abroad or journeying, and thus exposed to dust and soil of various kinds.

Supposing the above-mentioned conditions observed, the complexion and the color of the hair are the two things which mainly determine the colors to be employed in the dress. Of the Caucasian race, the two principal complexions are named the blonde and the brunette. The blonde is said to be a subdued orange color, or a union of red and yellow; while the brunette is a brown, —that is, a black in which yellow, or red and yellow, or green and orange predominate according to its shades. Of course both the blonde and the brunette are more or less mingled on the face with carnation or roseate tints.

The light hair which commonly accompanies the blonde complexion, is also a subdued orange, and takes different names according as one or another color predominates in it. Thus, if yellow predominates, it is called flaxen or golden; if red, chestnut or auburn; if brown, simply light, or light-brown. The hair of the brunette is usually black or dark-brown, though there are not a few exceptions to this rule.

The prevalent blue eye of the blonde presents the harmony of contrast with the orange of the hair and complexion,—orange being the complemental of blue,—while the ordinary black or dark eye of the brunette exhibits the harmony of analogy with the dark hair.

Having thus stated briefly the circumstances of various kinds to be regarded in selecting the colors of the costume, I have, perhaps, done all that should be expected in a chapter which aims rather to state and illustrate *principles* than to furnish practical formulas. Before closing, however, I will offer a few applications of these principles to particular cases.

For example, sky blue in the dress harmonizes, by agreeable contrast, with the blonde complexion and hair, since the orange tint of this complexion is the complemental of blue, besides that the latter color is pleasing for its emblematic quality.

On the other hand, yellow and red bordering on the orange combination, contrast brilliantly with black or dark hair, since blue, the complemental of orange, is predominant in these hues.

Light-green is becoming to colorless complexions or those faintly colored, because, having red for its complemental, it casts a delicate rosy tint upon the face.

On the other hand, dark-green best suits an *over-ruddy* complexion, since, having light-red for its complemental, it softens this excess of red by a reflection of the latter hue.

Violet or purple in direct contiguity with blonde complexions is not becoming, since its complemental being yellow, a greenish-yellow hue is cast upon the face. If used at all, it should be of so very dark a shade, as to make the skin look white by contrast.

I have already intimated that black or dark draperies make persons appear smaller, and white or light draperies larger, than they actually are. Consequently, stout persons look best in the former, and diminutive persons in the latter. Black shoes, for the same reason, are best suited to not very small feet, while a delicate-sized foot is charming in a white satin slipper. So a dress vertically striped increases the apparent height, while a dress with horizontal stripes is apt to produce a squat, dumpy appearance.

Without going into further details of this kind, let me refer the reader who would see this subject handled with sufficient minuteness, as well as eminent ability, to Field's Chromatography, in connection with numerous articles in the London Art Journal.

I trust it may enhance the interest, if not the intrinsic value, of this chapter, if, in closing, I cite from the poets a few passages which exhibit their accurate perceptions of the harmonies both of analogy and contrast in color, as well as their use of colors, as symbolical of human passions and affections. It is almost superfluous to say that here, as everywhere else, we find Shakspeare speaking with a knowledge that seems like inspiration.

HARMONY OF ANALOGY.

"There was a pretty *redness in her lip*,
A little *riper* and more *lusty red*,

Than that *mixed* in her *cheek;* 'twas just the difference
Betwixt the *constant red* and *mingled damask.*"

SHAKSPEARE.

"A *pudency* so *rosy*, that I thought her
As chaste as *unsunned snow.*"

SHAKSPEARE.

CONTRAST.

"My *bloody* hand will rather
The multitudinous seas *incarnadine*,
Making their *greenness red.*"

SHAKSPEARE.

"My mistaking eyes,
That have been so *bedazzled* with *the sun*,
That everything I look on seemeth *green.*"

SHAKSPEARE.

ANALOGY.

"*Beauty's ensign* yet
Is *crimson* in thy *lips* and in thy *cheeks*,
And Death's *pale flag* is not advancèd there."

SHAKSPEARE.

"*White* and *azure* laced
With *blue* of Heaven's own tinct."

SHAKSPEARE.

"Through whose *white skin*
With *damask* eyes the *ruby blood* doth peep."

MARLOWE.

CONTRAST.

"Here Love his *golden* shafts employs; here lights
His constant *lamp*, and waves his *purple* wings."

MILTON.

"Aurora now, in *radiant purple* drest,
Shone from the portals of the *golden* east."

TASSO.

I subjoin from the poets, a few examples of the use of colors in symbolizing sentiments, passions, and affections:

"I have marked
A thousand *blushing apparitions* start
Into her face; a thousand *innocent shames*
In angel whiteness bear away those blushes."

SHAKSPEARE.

"And thus the *native hue* of *resolution*
Is sicklied o'er with the *pale cast* of thought."

SHAKSPEARE.

"Go, *prick* thy *face*, and *over-red* thy fear,
Thou *lily-livered* boy; those *linen cheeks*
Are counsellors to *fear*."

SHAKSPEARE.

"'Tis not alone my *inky cloak*, good mother,
Nor customary suit of *solemn black*,
That can denote me truly."

SHAKSPEARE.

"Glittering in *golden coats*, like images,
And gorgeous as the sun at midsummer."

SHAKSPEARE.

"Long, pity, let the nations view
Thy *sky-worn* robes of *tenderest blue*;
And eyes of dewy light."

COLLINS.

"The *blushes* of the *opening rose*
Thy *tender modesty* disclose;
The *snow-white lilies* of the vale
Diffusing fragrance to the gale,
Careless, and sweet, and mild, we see
In *them* a *lovely type* of *thee*."

RUSSIAN ANECDOTES.

"O welcome *pure-eyed* Faith, *white-handed* Hope,
Thou hovering angel girt with *golden wings*,
And thou, *unblemished* form of Chastity."

MILTON.

"Celestial, *rosy-red*, Love's *proper hue*."

MILTON.

"O'erlaid with *black*, staid Wisdom's hue."

MILTON.

"Hence, loathèd Melancholy,
Of Cerberus and blackest *midnight born*."

MILTON.

"*Rosy-fingered* Aurora."

HOMER.

"*Blooming youth* and *gay delight*
Sit on thy *rosy cheeks* confest."

PRIOR.

There are numerous other points of interest pertaining to our subject, which would amply repay discussion; such as the physical nature of light and colors, the correspondence between colors and sounds, and the singular analogy between the harmonies of the two, &c. My limits, however, forbid my touching on these, even were they not, perhaps, too purely scientific for a work like this. But to the reader, who may desire to penetrate more deeply into the topics here discussed, I would recommend the examination of the following works, constituting my principal helps in the preparation of this article, viz.: Field's Chromatics and Chromatography; the London Art Journal from its commencement; Lectures on Painting by Sir Joshua Reynolds; do. by James Barry; do. by John Opie; do. by Henry Fuseli; do. by B. R. Haydon; and Modern Painters, by an Oxford Student. Either and all of these will be found instructive and entertaining both by the artist and amateur.

CHAPTER VII.

THE HUMAN FACE—THE MIRROR OF THE SOUL AND THE CHIEF SUBJECT OF ART.

The face the most perfect medium of expression—"Mosaics," by Saunders—The face an index of the soul—Views of Lavater, Bacon, Haller, Browne, and Southey—Language of the face changeless and universal—The forehead, nose, and chin indicative of *original* character; eyes and mouth of *changeable* character—The eye extraordinarily expressive—Reasons—The lips very expressive—Varieties of lips—Human faces the most interesting of sights—Applications of the term face to inanimate things—National types of face and head, *e. g.* Greek and Italian features marking certain races—Examples—The eyes, what qualities expressed by various colors, &c., of—Noses—What is indicated by different forms—Anecdote of Napoleon—Cerebrum and cerebellum—Mental properties intimated by different shapes of these.

I HAVE taken the ground in this treatise that expression is a "sine qua non in art;" and have vindicated my position by showing that man, the animal, and inanimate nature, each and all derive from this their whole significance and their chief interest. As the human face, then, is the most perfect of all mediums of expression; the medium, too, for expressing that intelligence and affection whereon rests man's claim to be "made in the image of God;" it seems essential to the completeness of my work that I should speak with somewhat of minuteness of itself and its characteristics.

For the chief materials of this chapter I am indebted to the "Mosaics" of the accomplished author of "Salad for the Solitary," &c. His charming essay on the

"Human Face Divine," with its wealth of apt citations from many rare works, has saved for me the necessity of looking beyond itself. With this general acknowledgment of obligation, I take from his pages what serves my purpose, without distinguishing it from matter gotten elsewhere.

The face is to a man what the dial is to a clock, or a table of contents to a book, viz., the index of the soul. And that the animate and inanimate worlds have physiognomies not less expressive of interior meanings than is man's, we have elsewhere shown.

Lavater says, "Faces are as legible as books; the main difference being that they are sooner read and far less deceptive." Bacon, Haller, Sir Thomas Browne, and Southey have all recorded their faith in the face being a reflector of the soul.

Measurably every one talks by means of his own countenance, and believes in the indications of the countenances of others. What oratory can be more vital with meaning than the telegraphic glances of the eye?

The significance of sounds is uncertain and limited to special places and times; while the language of the face is immutable and universal. It is the mind's short-hand, crowding much matter into a small compass.

For the original character scrutinize the unchanging features—the forehead, the nose, and the chin—for the secondary or acquired character, the changeable features, *i. e.*, the eyes and the mouth. The eye has extraordinary expressiveness, since, in addition to its own intrinsic expression, it serves as a mirror wherein meet and are reflected the various expressions of the other parts of the face.

The lips are exceedingly expressive; being capable of manifesting every cast of character, from the most delicate sensibility to the lowest brutality. The most flexible of the features, they change oftener and to a greater degree than any other, and thus mark the nicest shades of character and even of passing emotion.

How plainly, in the close-shut month, with its encircling muscles rising into a sort of ridge, do we read firm, resolute will; while in loose flabby lips we seem to behold not less plainly a vacillating, irresolute disposition!

In unusually thin lips we discern sharpness and asceticism of temper; while in extra thick lips we find sensual proclivities accompanied mostly by good nature and generous tendencies.

Saunders holds the face to be not alone the *vehicle* of *feeling*, but the *instrument* of wisdom as well; affirming that no one can be utterly stupid who has much commerce with human faces. In confirmation of his doctrine he instances artists and barbers as being, from their familiarity with faces, more intelligent on the average than musicians and shoemakers, whose vocations do not necessitate this familiarity.

Of all sights, the most generally and permanently interesting is that of human faces. The face, shadowed by grief or furrowed deeply by prolonged adversity, who can view without tenderness or pity? The innocent, gleeful face of the infant; the bright, wide-awake face of the finely-moulded boy; the diaphanous face of the beautiful and amiable woman, a very world of sweet meanings; and the face of the high-souled, august man, surcharged alike with wisdom, nobleness, and power; who can contemplate these, or either of them, without a more than ordinary interest and sympathy?

How universal, as well as high, is our estimate of the face, is evinced by our habitual use of the word to denote the expression of inanimate equally with animate objects. Thus, face of the earth, of the waters of the sky; face of affairs, &c., are phrases constantly and everywhere in vogue.

It is a curious philosophic fact that general and prolonged addiction to a special pursuit, or class of pursuits, will produce a distinctive cast of physiognomy and conformation of head. Thus, the Greeks and the Italians, long devoted to the arts, and growing up, generation after generation, within view of the finest artistic creations, have the most ideal faces and heads in the world, even in these distant days. In fact, the keen-eyed physiognomist may find in every nation a cast of countenance peculiar to itself; and, still further, may discover in particular districts and even families faces or single features distinctively marking them. Thus, the race of Hapsburgh have a peculiar under lip, and that of Bourbon a pear-shaped face; while in one section of Tuscany is seen the Boccaccio face, and in another the Dante face, and finally in Genoa the Bonaparte face.

It is curious to note in Caracalla and others of the brutalized Roman emperors, the same bull neck and broad hind-head, which are so plainly visible in the performers of the prize ring. Like propensities and habits can mould to one or another pattern the muscle and even the solid bone. And the physiognomies of the depraved women of Rome's corrupter days reappear in those of the times of Charles Second of England, and of France's Louis Fifteenth.

In the color, as well as other marks of the eye, experience has found intimations of peculiar casts of mind and character. Thus, dark-blue eyes are held to be commonest in persons of delicate, refined natures, and light-blue in the active and hardy. Gray and greenish eyes are nearly identical in their significances with the light-blue. Hazel eyes usually intimate a vigorous, profound, masculine mind. Shakspeare's eyes were hazel; Swift's blue; Milton's, Scott's, and Byron's gray, which is the special color of genius. Black eyes are thought to be mostly indicative of strong passions, combined with quick, penetrating intellects.

The traditional and historic beauties, from the Grecian Helen and the Oriental Shirene to Madame de Maintenon and Mary of Scotland, were distinguished by the large, lustrous eye,—the same, probably, attributed by Homer to Juno in the epithet "Ox-eye."

The fact that nearly all the bodily tissues meet and are blended in the eye, may indicate its importance and its representative character.

The nose is by no means an insignificant feature of the face; as is most unpleasantly shown by any casualty that destroys or mars it.

Physiognomists reckon four classes of noses, viz., Grecian, denoting imagination, equanimity, and patience,—Roman, courage, energy, magnanimity,—Cat or Tiger, cunning, vindictiveness, obstinacy, selfishness,—Pug, imbecility and indecision. You find the Grecian among scientific, literary, artistic men,—the Roman among active, efficient men and warriors,—the Pug among the flippant, contemptuous, and sneering.

These four classes are distributed into numerous varieties, *e. g.*, aquiline, snub, thin, flat, &c.,—each and all indicating characteristics more or less decided and distinctive. Napoleon says he selected for performing any important head-work long-nosed men, if properly educated,—holding that "the brain, lungs, and heart of such must be cool and clear, as the respiration was bold and free."

Phrenologists assign to the cerebellum, or hinder portion of the cranium, the organs of sense, common to man and the inferior animals; and to the cerebrum, or front cranium, the organs of the mind or soul. According to the greater or less development of one class or the other, do the mental or animal qualities hold the ascendant.

Thus, a small, triangular forehead, however large the entire head, denotes paucity of intellect. A forehead high and broad, prominent and gently arched, bespeaks great genius or talent; while one with irregular protuberances intimates a choleric, fitful temper. Deep, vertical lines between the eye-brows commonly denote mental vigor coupled with concentrativeness.

But we must close. That, in a considerable degree, the face is an index to both the intellectual and moral character, is beyond dispute. Indeed we are all physiognomists in practice, if not in theory. And who better than young children, and even veritable infants in arms? Everybody knows by experience that certain persons strongly *attract*, while others not less strongly *repel* these little ones; and that these antagonist influences come mostly, at least, from an *unreasoning*, instinctive perception of physiognomic expression is, I suppose, unanimously recognised.

As the face is altogether the most important subject for representation by the portraitist whether with the camera or the pencil,—since *its* true expression, when transcribed, is the revelation of the real man,—so it seemed to me especially important that a summary should here be given of what observation has taught about the face and its indications.

And thanks to the fascinating author of "Mosaics," the contents of his rich pages have greatly lightened our task.

CHAPTER VIII.

THE HELIOGRAPHIC ARTIST AND HIS SITTERS.

The operant must try to please all—The selfish and impatient must be conciliated—Proper conduct of the operant here—Heliographic sittings should be brief—Difficulties specified—Anecdote of Reynolds.

THE present chapter will be devoted to sitting, and sundry incidents connected therewith. The heliographer will concede to my age and experience the privilege of speaking in a homely, advisory strain. And

1st. Let us never lose sight of the fact that we must, if practicable, *please all* who seek our services. Nor let us lose sight or recollection of the myriad difficulties which must needs be encountered and completely mastered, if we would achieve high excellence and a durable reputation in our art.

Often—perhaps most commonly—the heliographer's business comes upon him in "lumps," and his sitters in crowds. This point is dependent upon the season of the year, the particular weather of the moment, and the general circumstances of the "times." In auspicious, genial weather our galleries may be thronged by numbers, consisting partly of family-groups, and partly of individual women and men; all strangers alike to each other and to the operant. Usually, *all* are somewhat in haste for a sitting, while many of them are constitutionally selfish, and not overstocked with either patience or politeness. The last-named are very apt to demand being waited upon at once, and to threaten going otherwhere if denied, or if requested to delay for a few minutes only, even though such denial and request be of absolute necessity.

Now we all, of course, desire to secure the patronage of *every visitant,* and, in the hope of detaining them long enough, we are extremely prone to promise compliance with their wishes. In this mood of excited, anxious feeling we commence our task with whatever judgment, skill, and expedition we can command,—goaded the while by our subject's point-blank demand of *perfection,* as a *sine qua non!*

While the artist is disposing his sitter for taking, he should keep up a cheerful, genial, appropriate conversation, either with his sitter or with some other person or persons present in order to summon, if possible, a *genuinely characteristic expression* into the face.

If the sitter's features are very mobile and variable, and the desired expression, therefore, is liable to flit too soon away, then a large mirror, or "cheval-glass," upon castors, may be stationed before him, wherein he may behold his own image. He may then, with some effort, discern in that reflected face the expression wished for, and may endeavor to retain it unaltered for the few seconds required for its being arrested and fixed by the solar pencil.

2d. I apprehend that there are few heliographers who, while taking the portraits of their sitters, are accustomed to instruct them in the general matter of sitting, including the items of posture, expression, &c., or to engage them in rousing and genial conversation immediately before the commencement of the process, or the exposure of the plate to the object.

When all is prepared for letting on the sunbeam to

secure the impression, some operants will exclaim, "A good expression, sir"—"Please keep still, miss, and *look pleasantly*,—'tis going on," &c., &c.,—and even these few useless and perhaps worse than useless phrases are uttered in a low, chilling, abrupt tone, and mostly, too, *after* the admission of the light and the commencement of the process! And yet, at this precise moment there are imperatively required that affable, gracious, prompt, social quality,—that instantly discriminating, truthful, artistic eye, that ripe judgment, and that skilled, dexterous hand,—and superadded to all the rest that excitant, exhilarating, *magnetic* influence which the felicitously-tempered artist brings instinctively to bear upon his sitter, when the *soul* of the latter is to be roused to give *expression* to the face!

3d. If groups, either of adults or of children, are to be taken, an instant or two alone are granted wherein to *compose* our picture,—to arrange the most effective lights and shadows,—to select the best aspect of each face,—to place the instrument in position,—to summon by conversation and whatever else into each countenance, and strive to *keep* there, the most intelligent and genial expression until the momentary exposure of the plate has been effected and the impression secured. After all this, the image, of course, must be developed, fixed, finished, and exhibited to the sitter. If the attempt be satisfactory, we must proceed, in like manner, to wait on other impatient expectants, handling all the numerous parts of the delicate process with the utmost practicable expedition.

No one, therefore, can *appreciate*, or in the slightest degree *apprehend*, the difficulties encountered daily and hourly by the heliographer, save a capable, sensitive practitioner himself. He must deal with and overcome, too, on the *instant*, a multitude of vexations, perplexities, and obstacles in mere manipulation, of which *outsiders* neither know nor can know anything at all.

The heliographer, then, who would win friends and customers, and achieve a reputable name, must be good-tempered, just, patient, and forbearing; prompt, gracious, and courteous towards all callers without exception. The artist (be it remembered) of highest capacity, and the most efficient manager of the camera, must ofttimes encounter persons who are excessively hard to please; some for lack of native judgment, coupled with ignorance of art; some through a foolish pride or vanity, and a thirst for praise; others because it is their nature to differ from others and indulge in indiscriminate fault-finding.

Others, again, will find fault with the face exclusively, and will call another day for another trial,—desiring, *in fact,* a new sitting, in order to view themselves in a different article of apparel, such as a collar, a cape, another style of head-dress, or of arranging the hair, or, it may be, in an entirely new dress, though they will, all the while, speak of the face *exclusively*.

Thus I have often heard persons, on first seeing, and before examining, a truly exquisite heliograph of *themselves,* exclaim, with both hands uplifted, "O frightful,—it is not at all like,—it is perfectly horrible!"

The artist, in response, appeals to the nature of his art, and the necessary truthfulness of his camera, and refers the objecting sitter to the mirror; but is told, "I never *did* like the daguerreotype, nor can I abide the photograph," &c., &c. "I must have a picture painted by Mr ———; *his* likenesses are beautiful!" And yet this very artist depends upon and idealizes the best daguerreotype or photograph he can get taken,—merely, as he will say, to save trouble to the sitter and time for himself!

All portraitive artists are liable to meet with eccentric persons like the above, and should deal with them good-humoredly and philosophically.

If the artist has shrewdness and tact, he will be careful to exhibit a new portrait of one who may be disposed to fault-finding *first* to a friend, or to some third person, who will be likely to speak favorably of it, at first sight, and influence the judgment of the pettish, eccentric individual.

B. R. Haydon, the great English historic painter, remarks that "Amiability, courtesy, and tact were prominent traits in the character of Sir Joshua Reynolds,"—a statement illustrated by the following incident:—

"My portrait is not at all *like*, Sir Joshua," said a beautiful woman of fashion whom he had been painting. Reynolds, bowing low, replied, with his hand to his deaf ear, "I am delighted that your grace is pleased with it." "Pleased!—I am really not at all pleased," said she. "I am quite delighted," bowed Reynolds. In despair she entreated an artist, just then entering, whom she knew, to get Reynolds out of his error. This artist roared in Sir Joshua's ear, "Her grace—does not—think—her—portrait—like!" "Not think it like?" replied Reynolds. "Not like?" Then, bowing, he said in the mildest voice, as if he had now just heard, "Then, we'll *make* it like!—we'll make it like!" This is an epitome of his whole life.

4th. But let me not be misapprehended. I do not assume to instruct my brother heliographers, or my unprofessional readers, *how* to express the various passions. I can teach no man how to *invent.* I will say, however, that he, whose eye and hand are obedient to his conceptions, may easily wear a smile upon his face, exchange a lively word with both old and young, and yet not be rude; and occasionally exchange little graceful acts of politeness which may arrest and charm the eyes of the recipient, and still not be intrusive. If he knows his own place and keeps it, *such* familiarity will breed *not* contempt, but confidence.

A genuine, soul-originated smile on the face of the artist is more than likely to summon a *corresponding* smile into the face of the sitter, and the power of a smile to give *attractiveness* to a portrait is more easily perceived than described.

A modern writer says, "Smiles and speech are characteristic of man, and are bestowed upon him to express thought and affection."

"A beautiful smile is to the female countenance what the sunbeam is to the landscape. It embellishes an inferior face, and redeems an ugly one. A smile, however, should not become habitual; insipidity is the result; nor should the mouth break into a smile on one side, the other remaining passive and unmoved; for this imparts an air of deceit and grotesqueness to the face. A disagreeable smile distorts the line of beauty, and is more repulsive than a frown. There are many kinds of smiles, each having a distinctive character; some announce goodness and sweetness, others betray sarcasm, bitterness, and pride; some soften the countenance by their languishing tenderness, others brighten by their brilliant and spiritual vivacity. Gazing and peering before a mirror cannot aid in acquiring beautiful smiles half so well as to turn the gaze inward, to watch that the heart keeps unsullied from the reflection of evil, illumined and beautified by sweet thoughts."

CHAPTER IX.

SITTING-ROOM—SKY-LIGHT—OUT-DOOR VIEWS, ETC., ETC.

Diffused light essential—Angle for falling rays—Upper story best—Side and sky-light—Size and arrangement of the latter—Preparations for cloudy weather—Curtains, and their disposition—Out-door views, and their conditions—Heliographers should study the best paintings, &c.—Examples—Miscellaneous directions.

As our pictures are produced by means of the sunbeam, the sitting-room should be so constructed as to furnish a *diffused* light, whereby the object, animate or inanimate, may be illumined *completely*, *i. e.* lighted up on all sides; while the principal mass of the rays should fall in such manner and with such degree of power, as to give clearly defined shadows at an angle of about 45°, or more or less, as circumstances may require. By this disposal of the light, and this arrangement of the room, the highest artistic effect is attained, and the utmost possible excellence may be imparted to the picture.

My personal observation and experimentation have assured me as to the expediency of the following plan for the light of a heliographic sitting room.

Thus, the topmost apartment of a building should be secured, having an unobstructed northern or north-western exposure, together with perfect facilities for communicating with the street. A second-floor room for heliographic uses is preferable to one on the ground-floor, because free from damp, and less affected by changes of weather.

Its easier accessibility, too, makes it preferable to a fourth or fifth story room.

SIDE-LIGHT AND SKY-LIGHT COMBINED.

If an attic is to be used as a sitting-room, I would advise the construction of a side or a front light equally wide with the sky-light, and facing, if practicable, the north or the north-west.

When the room is spacious enough to allow the using of long-focussed lenses, a sky-light placed above its centre, at the north end, 12 or 14 or 15 feet wide, by 14 or 16 or 18 feet long, with the front or side light uniting with the top-light, and reaching to within 3 or 4 feet of the floor, will permit the artist (if large groups are to be taken) to give his subjects any position he may desire in the room, and to secure any required effect of shadow; since he is able to station the camera on either the right or the left of the subjects, and to work all around the room by changing the shades under the sky-light, or with the backs of the subjects towards the sun, *i. e.* with a northern exposure,—this attitude being most favorable alike for the subjects themselves and for fine effects of light and shadow.

If the side or front light be divided into three windows, or sash running up and down, and each window be double-sashed (so that with its shades, it can, if needful, be lowered from the top), with very narrow casings; such windows will be very convenient for taking children, as well as for general uses in cloudy weather, since the transparent curtain (and each window should have its separate shade) can be so raised as to admit side-light somewhat in the rear and on the background, or on one side of the subject, when stationed in the centre of the room,—not, of course, to deaden the power of the light from above, but to mellow or soften down and to render translucent those abrupt, coarse, inky shadows beneath the brows, nose, and chin, which are so objectionable in many pictures taken by means of the sky-light exclusively.

The height of the sky-light above the floor should be proportioned to its size. If large-sized, it may be 10, 12, or 14 feet high; if small, 9 or 10 feet will be preferable; especially when heliographic negatives are to be produced, which require stronger light and more protracted sittings than do positives.

Every sky-light, if over six feet wide, should have two transparent curtains suspended over head under the glass, on wires and rings, so that one or both of them can (if desired) be pushed towards the front or side light, in order to obtain good artistic shadows from above, by permitting the light to fall upon the subject in a concentrated mass,—an arrangement which supplies shadow sufficiently strong at an angle of about 45°.

In taking an out-door view, *e. g.* a building, a landscape, or street-scene for the stereoscope, or some kindred purpose, we should be careful to select the most appropriate hour of the day, and should place the camera so as to get the finest artistic effects from the lights and shadows. A skilful management of the lights and shadows is also essential to the portraitist who would produce a well rounded, distinctly "relieved," and lifelike face. How many *such* faces do we see at the doors and in the galleries of the contemporary heliographers of this country? Scarcely one in the thousand! But, instead, we behold flat, meaningless *maps* of the face, with little or no shadow, but with half of the face white, and the other in a shadow, *flattened* through a side or reflected light from a side screen.

These, of course, are made by dull ignoramuses, by mere *mechanism*, and sold by thousands to the unenlightened portion of the community. Hence the present low repute of our wonder-working art.

The heliographer, whether professional or amateur, may learn much about the magic effects of light and shadow, as also derive other benefits, from carefully studying the paintings, engravings, &c., of eminent artists, as, for example, "The Women of Shakspeare," "The Beauties of Moore," the productions of Finden, Heath, &c. It would be profitable especially to study the engraving of Da Vinci's "Lord's Supper;" to note how much is expressed by the arrangement and posture of each figure; and most of all, by each face, in which one may almost read the thoughts agitated within, and the words about to break forth.

What, by these artists, is done by other means, the heliographer should aim to effect by the camera, and if he have genius and skill sufficient to call into use all the powers of this instrument, he may produce pictures not less true to nature than those above specified.

Good small single portraits; or those with the head and bust; or those in the crayon or vignette style, may be taken at a tolerably sized high side-light window, if the lights and shadows are skilfully managed, with the aid of transparent curtains to soften the light below, and with side reflections, if used at all, kept at proper distance.

If only a side-light window can be had, or a side and top light combined, it should be 6 or 8 feet wide, and 10 or 12 or 15 feet high. Such a light can be advantageously used in taking single portraits, or groups of two or three.

If the whole light *must* come through a flat roof above

the middle of the room, the window should be at least 10 or 12 feet wide, and 16 or 20 feet long, and built according to the directions in "side-light and sky-light combined," not flat, but roof-like—*i. e.* in three sashes, one pitching east, one west, and one north. This will bring the light nearer to the floor and stronger at the sides, and will also light up a group of several, clearly at both extremes or sides of the room, as well as in the middle of the picture; and will enable the artist to place the back of the sitter towards the south-east in the morning, and the south-west in the afternoon—such being the best arrangement of the light for the eyes and face.

The panes of glass should be 16 by 20 inches in size, and ground on the under side, if not protected from the sun; having their lower ends lapping at least one inch over the upper ends of those below them, and being set in thin putty and paint. The lower end of each pane should be kept separated from the pane below it, by resting upon trammel-hook wires, hooked over the ends of each pane,—an arrangement which will keep each in its place, and allow the air to circulate between the panes, —thus preventing capillary attraction, which causes tight-set glass roofs to leak.

The ceiling should be "flared" away 5 or 6 feet back into the room east, south, and west (if the room faces north and south), so that the rays may fall on the floor, or the sitter, 7 or 8 feet back of the opening above. By this means, a well-defined, mild light is thrown upon the sitter, or group of sitters, if placed a little away from beneath the opening above, clearly illuminating alike the head, the figure, and the dress. Care should be used that the light be not brilliant or dazzling, but mild and soft, as well as clear, and so falling as to make well-defined, transparent shadows, especially under the brows, nose, and chin.

The "high lights" should be distinctly located on the forehead, nose, cheeks, and chin; and broad, flat lights and shadows avoided. The high lights, the shadows, and the middle tints should be, especially on the face, in perfect harmony.

The walls of the heliographic sitting-room should be painted or papered with a warm light-blue, or straw, or cinnamon color, while the floor should be covered with a light carpet. This arrangement will tend to diffuse a mild, agreeable, uniform light throughout the apartment.

For an artist's painting-room, a dark-slate, or dark-cinnamon, or brown is more suitable, as these colors absorb, instead of reflecting, the light.

Finally, special care should be taken that the sitting-room be appropriately and neatly fitted up, and supplied with every convenience for the business, as well as comfort for sitters and visitors; and be kept during the day in perfect order. The instruments, headrests, chairs, screens, backgrounds, &c., should be fixed in their proper places after each party has left the room, that all things may be pleasant to the eye of the next sitter, and calculated to awaken agreeable feelings.

The same good order should prevail throughout the chemical room, which should be so arranged, as to prevent all fumes of chemicals from reaching and annoying visitors to the apartments.

PORTRAITS OF CHILDREN.

In cloudy weather, or while taking children, both top-shades may be pushed up to the front, while the side-light shades are raised, or (what is better) lowered from the top. Impressions may thus be caught in a few seconds.

This process, however, involves a considerable sacrifice, through the necessity of broad light, as well as of seizing the impression almost instantly.

Such pictures, though not very creditable to the heliographer, regarded solely as specimens of art, are, nevertheless, if perfectly truthful, highly acceptable to parents; and, when the loved originals are deceased, are deemed invaluable.

It is, then, the *interest* of the artist, if not his *duty*, to secure the *most faithful* impressions possible of these little ones, even though such may be lacking in mere artistic merit.

However difficult of management children may be, no effort should be spared for producing a *pleasing* picture of them. Nor should any time devoted to this object be regarded as lost. Therefore, I would advise the operant to indulge and play with them, and strive thus to win their confidence and good-will. These, with a little tact, he will rarely fail to gain, and in this way will both please the fond parents and enhance his own reputation. But if, taking the opposite course, he manifests a morose or irritable temper, he will assuredly forfeit his "good name," even though he may occasionally produce a creditable picture.

It may not be irrelevant to this topic to recite an incident of my own experience.

I once permitted my temper, which is generally under command, to be ruffled by the slight of a "sitting" child. He was the only son of an authoress as intelligent and amiable as she is widely popular.* Losing patience, after several unsuccessful trials, and scarcely aware of what I

* The late Mrs. Alice B. Haven, formerly Mrs. J. C. Neal.

did, I hastily tapped the boy's hand with my fingers' ends, while fixing upon him a stern look.

He gazed an instant in my face; the tears started; his heart seemed broken.

The mother calmly remarked, "This is the first time he was ever chastised or spoken to severely."

Her mild, gentle tones in addressing first myself, and then her boy, administered a rebuke to me which, I think, will never be forgotten, or cease to have a practical influence. I trust, too, that the record of this simple incident may be of service to all who read it and manage the camera in taking the portraits of young children.

Impartial justice to myself, however, requires that I should state *why* I acted as I did in this case. Both before commencing operations and while engaged therein, I was assured by the lady that, unless the picture was faultless, unless it was felicitous in arrangement and perfect in expression, she must decline accepting it. Acting under these instructions, I was, of course, unusually anxious to succeed; for, over and above pecuniary considerations, my repute as an artist was at stake.

Repeated trials had been defeated by the refractoriness of the boy. For, in defiance of his mother's injunctions, he kept incessantly changing his position, nor were my own entreaties of any more avail. Moreover, he was monopolizing my time; and several other persons were impatiently waiting, and threatening to leave. As a final resort, I adopted the authoritative mode, as I had, with others, been accustomed to do successfully.

But ever after my failure here, I made it a point (as in fact I always had done previously), to go directly to the child, and talk and play familiarly with him, and, if possible, to put some amusing or pleasant object in his hands; assuring him, by these various means, that I was friendly, and that my purpose was to give him pleasure, and not in any way to harm him. By this method of proceeding, I almost invariably obtained a good picture of a child.

CHAPTER X.

HINTS UPON SITTING—EASE AND GRACE IN A PORTRAIT.

The attitude should be chosen by the operant—What it should be—Management of lights and shadows—Legs of gentlemen and hands of ladies, how placed—How to take certain faces—Directions about colors—Useless accessories to be avoided—Mode of ameliorating blemishes—Groups, &c.

As frequently intimated elsewhere in this treatise, the proper attitude of a person sitting for a portrait should be left, mainly at least, to the judgment and taste of the heliographic operant. At the same time it may be policy, as well as courtesy, to ask intelligent sitters whether they have a preference for any special view of the face, posture, arrangement, &c.; and, if so, to inform them what artistic experience has shown to be intrinsically best, subjoining the reasons why.

The sitter's position should be unconstrained and perfectly easy, the hands and feet neither projecting too much, nor drawn too far back, but placed in the focus of the instrument, or nearly so.

The sitter's age should also be considered. For example, the appearance of the elderly should be calm and sedate, instead of spirited; while the young, of either sex, should express, by the position of the head and face, energy of thought, feeling, and action, rather than a grave, meditative cast of mind, unless where they are specially moved and interested.

The head should be easily and gracefully turned to

the right or the left,—not too high or too low, but so as to express intellect or meaning in lieu of constraint. Especially should be avoided that appearance of a spasmodic twist of the head, or jerk of the neck-muscles, which are found in the portraits of some operators, whose conceit is quite as manifest as their artistic knowledge and skill!

The eyes should be directed a little farther to the left or right, than the face, and if a front view be taken, to some object above or near the camera, in a nearly front direction from the face, if the color or shape of the eyes will admit; but rarely toward the lens or tube, as the face would thus take on a *stare* or a dissatisfied or dolorous look.

The lights and shadows on the face, or other parts of the picture, must be managed with the greatest care, in order to produce rotundity, relief, harmony, and life-like effect. When the broad or short side of the face is mostly in shadow, the shaded cheek should, if possible, be tipped with light, to give it a pleasing fulness and natural-seeming roundness.

If portraying a gentleman cross-legged, avoid all long, straight lines or right angles, and do not throw the limb nearest the camera over the other, but *vice versa.*

The hands of a lady may rest easily upon the lap, and should be presented edgewise, neither too high nor too low, which will give them a small, delicate appearance. Or one hand or arm may be laid upon a table, while the other hand may hold a book or some other object, if the sitter so choose. For myself, however, I think a pretty hand is much the prettiest when empty. [*See plate.*]

A thick hand should show the thumb in the foreground, with the fingers bent a little inward; while a long hand had best exhibit its back. A handsomely shaped hand, neither too long nor too short, should display full two-thirds of itself, with the fingers hanging easily and gracefully down.

A slight bending of the body forward and to one side will, by its graceful appearance, produce a good artistic effect.

If a shawl, or boa, or like article of dress, be thrown lightly over the shoulders, and tastefully disposed, so as to hide some defect, and distribute light and shadow properly, it will generally serve to balance other parts. and thereby make the entire impression agreeable.

The portrait of a full, round face, with small eyes and nose and large mouth, should be taken in nearly half-profile, so as to show one side of the face in full, with very little of the other side.

A face of moderate fulness, with aquiline nose and handsome eyes and mouth, should be taken in three-fourths profile; while one having strongly pronounced features, should be presented nearly full in front view.

If in the same picture two persons are to be portrayed, both sitting, the one should be represented as leaning lightly on the other's chair, and the face of each should be turned partly towards the other, as if a conversation was going on. Or they may be placed opposite to each other at a table, the one with the right and the other with the left arm resting thereon, and the persons of both gently bending towards each other, as though they were conversing; or one may be seated, while the other stands nigh him, leaning familiarly on the latter's shoulder or chair-back.

Again, the arrangement of family groups should, save in exceptional cases, be surrendered wholly to the judgment of the intelligent and skilful artist. Care, however, should always be taken to station the several persons of the group all at the same focal distance.

As regards dress, vivid colors and intensely illumined objects should uniformly be avoided. This monition applies more especially to white, yellow, light-blue, and scarlet. Plain-colored dresses, neither too light nor too dark, are most appropriate, and always furnish the most pleasing heliographs.

The sitter should be so placed in the room as to project short shadows; the light being sufficiently subdued to preserve the half-tints, while the time of exposure is long enough simply to develope the image completely, without, meanwhile, "overdoing," (*i. e.* solarizing) or flattening the pictures.

So, too, all strong cross-lights and reflections should be carefully avoided, and special pains taken to impart the utmost rotundity, boldness, and force to all portions of the figure.

USELESS AND OFFENSIVE ACCESSORIES IN A PORTRAIT.

Hands, hats, and numerous other accompaniments, *e. g.* landscape or fancy back-grounds, curtains, &c., should (in my opinion) be rigorously banished from the picture, as tending to impair the likeness. So a high chair-back behind the head both interferes (I think) with the effect of the face, and offends correct taste. Whereas, a low chair-back, with one side in view and in focus, is not only far more appropriate, but proves, not unfrequently, a valuable accessory.

VIGNETTE OR CRAYON STYLE.

A vignette portrait, *i. e.* the head and shoulders in the crayon style, I generally find more pleasing to the true artist and connoisseur, than either full-length or half

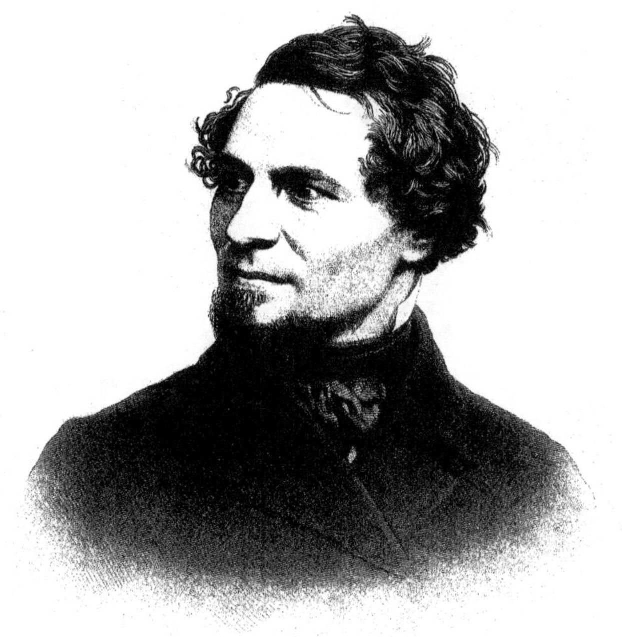

Dag^e by M.A.Root.

John Sartain

figures. The apparent size of the head can be augmented by placing it somewhat above the middle of the plate; and as the image is produced by the centre of the lenses, there is less liability to distortion in it. So that if proper heed be given to the subject's posture, and a suitable arrangement of light and shadow be made, a vignette portrait may be rendered more truthful, life-like, and artistically effective, than one wherein the head surmounts a half or a full-length figure.

Although, then, there are many subjects who, when left to their own selection, are apt to insist upon having a half or whole length, with both hands introduced, yet the true artist, for the credit of both himself and his art, will recommend the vignette, which (as above stated) comprises the head alone, or head and shoulders merely.

POSTURE, ETC., ETC.

Stuart, the eminent portraitist, like Reynolds, Lawrence, and other distinguished artists of recent date, usually gave to his pictures a wide margin; making the head, the figure, and the entire portrait proportionate in size to the bulk of the individual and the superficies of the canvas.

In representing a head and bust merely, the chin should be placed slightly above the centre of the picture, while the eye nearest the spectator in a three-quarters face is generally midway in the breadth of the picture.

The heliographer who possesses correct judgment and taste, combined with proper feeling, while earnestly striving to secure the most truthful expression of his subject's face, as seen in repose, will meanwhile also note critically all the important points, which may serve to communicate to his picture genuine artistic effect.

A profile, or a two-thirds or three-quarters face, should

have at least as broad a margin before the face, as behind the head, and not unfrequently a broader one.

As a faithful likeness is the chief desideratum in portraiture, the mere head and bust are preferable to a larger proportion of the figure, or one including either or both of the hands.

In sum, the picture should embrace not much over half the length of the body; though it should, if practicable, when more than the head is taken, indicate the breadth across the shoulders, with the relative size of the body, when the portrait is set in an oval "mat," or "spangel."

Artists generally prefer painting short shadows on the narrow side of the face in a two-thirds or three-fourths view. This arrangement succeeds, for the most part, in producing an agreeable picture.

Occasionally we encounter an admirer of Rembrandt's or Van Dyck's manner, wherein the shadows are so broad and strong, as to shade deeply nearly half the face. Unfortunately, however, for the heliographer, most of his patrons, like England's "Queen Bess," prefer "pictures without any shadow at all!"

If you would give to a spare, thin face, with high cheek-bones and deep wrinkles, a fuller, younger, and more attractive appearance, you must reverse the general rule.

Thus, to impart to the face and head the utmost possible boldness, energy, rotundity, &c., place the subject so that in a two-thirds or three-fourths view of the face, the face may, from the point of sight, or eye, or the part focussed upon, be almost totally in shadow; or so that the shadow may fall from the cheek-bone backwards towards the ear. By this means, with a clear, distinct shadow on the side of the nose and face, and a soft, mellow light along the cheek, a picture is obtained upon a flat surface which, wondrously "relieved" from its background, exhibits all the roundness and solidity of nature. Provided, however, that the material and color of the background be favorable, and the subject so placed, that a suitable tint or shadow of the background may be had, *i. e.*, one which is neither too dark nor too light to contrast happily with the complexion or the color of the hair and the dress.

For heliographs of a lady in a white or light-colored dress, the ground should be dark, and removed far behind the sitter, or beyond the focus, so as to give an ethereal or faintly visible appearance to the ground, and relief to the figure. A lady's white dress, or collar, or cape may be beautifully represented by covering the part exposed in strongest light with a black veil, or piece of dark muslin, and cautiously withdrawing it at the expiration of one-third or one-half the time of exposure required for bringing the figure fully out; and this, without disturbing the sitter or stirring the dress.

A lady or gentleman in dark dress should sit before a ground somewhat lighter than the dress. Not *too* light, however, as in this case the outline would be hard or sharp.

The color of the background may be of dark drab or dark blue for a short distance, and light blue for a longer; or of a warm, cinnamon-colored cloth, with short nap. Cloth is better than painted muslin for a background. All these should be carefully kept at a proper distance from the sitter, and are most effective if kept in motion during the session, as then seams or spots are not copied.

The artist, who is fully alive to all the requirements of his profession, will find that nearly every successive subject needs a different arrangement of light and shadow, with a different location in the room, view of the face, &c. Accordingly his genius (for nothing else can) will suggest such a change in the position of the camera, in the background, and in all other conditions, as is required for the object aimed at.

And as the reputation alike of himself and his establishment must rest on the artistic merits of his productions, so every successive picture is a proof, patent to all capable judges, either for or against his pretension to the title of artist.

CHAPTER XI.

THE EYES—THEIR LANGUAGE, AND HOW TO DEAL WITH THEM.

The eyes specially important in a portrait—How to direct and depict them—Same determined by color and surroundings—Catch-lights, what, and for what purpose.

THE eyes, which are most emphatically the index of the face, require of the artist the most scrupulous attention. Says a modern writer, "An eye can threaten like the loaded gun, or can insult like hissing or kicking; or by beams of kindness can make the heart dance with joy. There is an honesty in the eye in which the mouth does not participate. 'The artist,' said Michael Angelo, 'must have his measure in his eye.' Eyes are bold as lions—bold, running, leaping. They speak all languages; they need no encyclopedia to aid in the interpretation of their language; they respect neither rank nor fortune, virtue nor sex, but they go through and through you in a moment of time.

"Vain and forgotten are all the fine offers of hospitality, if there is no holiday in the eye. How many inclinations are avowed by the eye, though the lips dissemble! As soon as men are off their centres, the eyes show it."

In order that they may wear the most favorable expression in a picture, the proper direction should be given to them. What such direction is to be, must depend on their size, form, color, &c.

Thus, if they are blue, or light, or weak, they should either be directed towards a point somewhat low; or be turned away from the light towards a dim corner of the room; or be bent upon a screen covered with dark green velvet, or with some other cloth non-reflective of light.

If the eyes are full, round, or prominent, and thus are liable to catch too much light, let them rest upon or nigh some object on the distant floor, without strain or the least effort, so as to give them a somewhat languid expression. Let the sitter, meanwhile, be instructed to wink his eyes as often as inclined, that he may avoid a constrained or wild look therein. And to give the eyes an agreeable expression, the "catch-lights," or white spots in them, should be thrown close to the upper lid, while made as small as possible.

These so-named "catch-lights" are small spots of reflected light seen on all sound eyes, except when these are in shadow. They serve to impart to the eyes a life-like, bright expression. Yet, I have known intelligent persons to reject portraits which, by their admission, were well-nigh faultless, on the very account of the beautiful, round "catch-lights" on the eyes. And it required no slight explanatory labor on my part to remove this their error, and to convince them of the importance of these supposed blemishes in giving expression to the eyes.

A small screen, fixed upon a stand-rod with thumb-screw, movable and elevatable, green or dark in color, on which some object is placed for the subject to look at, will be found more agreeable to the eyes than a screen of any other reflective color, or a pin or spot upon the wall or other object.

If the subject has light eyes, and desires a two-thirds or a three-quarters face, it is best to take a nearly front view of the person, with the head turned more or less aside, and the eyes directed towards an object somewhat on the right or left of the straight-forward line. The eye, however, should not be turned furtively back towards an object fronting the person, as if watching a pickpocket's movements. I have seen pictures that suggested this idea so vividly, as to be absolutely ludicrous,—*e. g.*, pictures having the body turned one way and the face another, while the eyes were pointed backwards in a direction with the person,—and all this, strangely enough, in so-styled first-class galleries!

Contrariwise, by making the position of the head *intermediate* between the direction of the eyes and that in which the person fronts, that spiral line is obtained which is so prized in art, and is to many familiar under the title of "Hogarth's line of beauty." The Greek sculptors invariably observed this line in attitudes of repose, by turning the head towards the right, when the left foot was withdrawn behind the other, and *vice versa*. They took special pains to procure the twining spiral; and this may be had even in a bust-portrait, by turning the eyes somewhat more in the direction whither the head points.

If the eyes are dark, and a nearly front view of the face is desired, it is generally best to take a two-thirds or three-fourths view of the person, with the eyes turned aside somewhat further than the face towards the camera. Thus, one eye is brought to look rather across the nose, while both eyes look towards the artist, or the camera, or some object nigh it. In this way the subject will probably obtain the view of his face most familiar to himself, as being that so often looked upon in his mirror. [*See plate.*]

If the subject has very light blue eyes, or light eyes of whatever shade, the face should be turned partially away from the light, provided the features will allow it. If the rays come through a sky-light, let him be placed more directly beneath them, so that all the shadows may fall more vertically, and the shadows of the eyebrows partially protect the vision. Light or blue eyes may thus be made to look dark and clear, and even to resemble black eyes. Extremes, however, or shadows too much elongated, should be specially avoided.

In that condition of the face which produces in it the appearance of intent, concentrated thought, the eyes do not converge to a focal point, as when looking on a near object; on the contrary, they turn outward, being involuntarily thrown into that position by the spontaneous action of the muscles,—thus presenting to the brain two different fields of vision, which, by producing indistinctness, leave the mind free to its own conceptions or meditations.

If the subject has light, flaxen hair, and a fair complexion, he should be stationed further from the light; or the intenseness of the light should be mitigated by the elevation or the lowering of the window-shades. Or a thin tissue-paper screen may be extended above the head to break the strong light, and to protect the hair and eyes, and light portions of the dress, such as caps, collars, capes, &c.*

* This protecting screen may be made of thin tissue-paper, or fine, thin mull muslin, or other transparent material, stretched upon a light wire ring or frame, or on an umbrella frame—and suspended some distance above the head of the sitter, to soften the light and protect the hair, eyes, &c.

CHAPTER XII.

SUGGESTIONS AS TO DEALING WITH DEFECTS AND BLEMISHES IN SITTER'S FACE.

How to deal with personal defects, *e.g.* cross-eyes, irregular features, loss of teeth, &c.; extra shortness or tallness, thinness or corpulence, imperfection of nose, forehead, skin, &c.—Few faces of perfect model.

CROSS-EYED persons may be much "flattered," and their defects greatly meliorated by directing the eye which turns most towards the nose, towards an object in the opposite quarter, or else turning both eyes towards an opposite object. Thus, without the least impairment of likeness, the particular blemish is much disguised, while the appearance of both eyes is essentially bettered.

In taking persons irregularly featured (and few are otherwise), extra care should be used to lessen existing defects; to avoid presenting them just as they are; and, above all, to take heed they be not exaggerated.

The keen observant will notice that many persons, when laughing, smiling, or even speaking, use the muscles of one side of the face more than those of the other. Persons, however, who, in their various expressions, use the muscles of one side of the face more than those of the other, have no real ground of dissatisfaction, when they see this reality portrayed in a picture; since it is a fact that most persons, with faces perfectly symmetrical, are devoid of any *marked* mental character. A silly, meaningless smile is one in which both corners of the mouth are equally elevated, as if drawn up by a cord attached to the ears.

Again, from the loss of teeth, or some casualty, one side of the face may be longer than the other. To disguise this defect in the portrait, let the longer side be placed nighest the camera, whereby the parts beyond the point or objects focussed upon are naturally somewhat magnified; since the lines issuing from the point focussed upon (unlike those in perspective, which converge to a point), *diverge* in directions corresponding to the curves of the lenses. By this means the aspect of the features on the shorter side of the face may be perceptibly magnified, and thus improved in appearance, without injury to the likeness. Whereas by the opposite course the defect will be exaggerated. [*See engravings.*]

A perfect face is extremely rare. Yet in every face there is some single view which is preferable to any other. The eye of an accomplished artist will, almost instantly, select that view which produces the most attractive portrait.

Thus, if the nose be very full or crooked on one side; or if the mouth be awry, or otherwise out of symmetry; or if one eye be weak or contracted, or more prominent than the other: these blemishes may be partially neutralized by selecting the most favorable aspect of the face, while the likeness is thus improved, instead of impaired.

If the subject be blind in one eye, the defect may be partially concealed, and yet an exact likeness secured, by taking a two-thirds or three-fourths view of the face, or perhaps even a profile view. Of course the most intelligent view should be gotten which is compatible with securing the truthfulness of each feature.

Half-length figures, with one or both of the hands displayed, are appropriate for gentlemen *sometimes*, and for

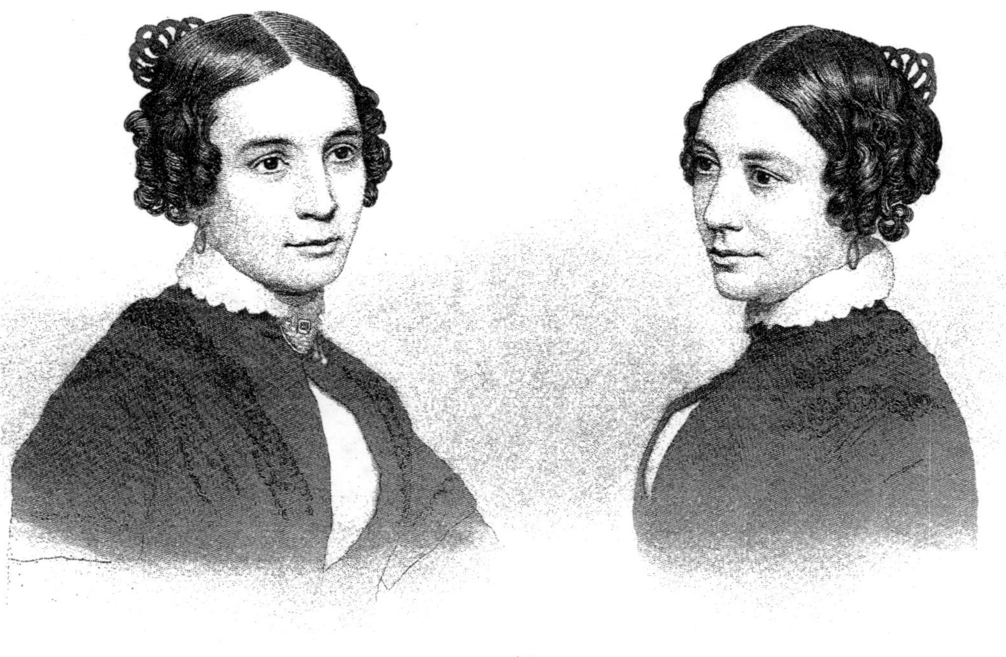

Nature corrected. Nature distorted.

ladies *almost always*. And, for a large-sized lady, a three-fourths or full length, by diminishing the apparent volume of the figure, is frequently more acceptable to her than a mere half-length.

A little "flattery," so named, is relished by most men, and even by *some* women. If, then, without impairing either the likeness, or the artistic excellence of the picture, or compromising our professional repute, we can please our subjects by "flattering" them somewhat in respect to these *minor points*, which do, after all, essentially aid in "making up" the picture, our efforts to please will, most probably, secure a twofold remuneration, in extended popularity and augmented custom.

The obese person seldom, if ever, objects to being represented as something less in bulk; or the small-sized one to appearing a trifle larger than the reality.

So the individual of *extra* height and thinness *would* be depicted, as somewhat shorter and ampler; the short-necked, dumpy one, as a little taller; and the aged, care-worn, visage-furrowed sire, or grandsire, as a few years younger. While, therefore, ever adhering to *fidelity* in representation, a moderate heed to the "art of pleasing" may foster our pecuniary interests without detriment to any interest beside.

If the subject be decidedly corpulent, the posture should be more erect, or somewhat forward-leaning, or else inclining slightly to the right or the left; so that the face, when in the focus of the lenses, may be nearly as far towards the front, as is the dress. Thus may be avoided the undue magnifying of the chest or of the general figure. Generally a two-thirds view of the figure and a nearly front view of the face of a bulky subject, with the eyes directed towards the camera, and with short shadows, will be likelier than any other to prove acceptable. [*See plate.*]

A tall, slender person may secure an aspect of ease and grace by inclining somewhat towards the left or right, or by bending a little backward, or by sitting low in his seat. The favorable appearance of a picture depends much on an attention to these minutiæ.

In representing the head and bust of a large person, the camera should be nearly, if not quite, level with the chin.

Portrait painters commonly place the subject on a platform or seat, a few inches higher than their own. The heliographer should either raise or depress his camera to attain the same results, and avoid foreshortening the face.

When the subject has a short nose, or one having, like Clay's, a short ridge but a long base, and thus exhibiting the nostrils to an unusual extent, special care should be taken to avoid magnifying this blemish, or foreshortening the nose or face. On the contrary, the camera should be elevated as high as the middle of the face, while the chin is dropped a little down towards the chest, though not so far as to compress the muscles of the cheeks or neck. Meanwhile, let the artist strive to secure the utmost freedom and ease by loosening the sitter's cravat, by giving to his head the most unconstrained position possible, &c.

If the subject has a long or a Roman nose, a two-thirds or a three-quarters face, with the head somewhat raised and the camera somewhat lowered, in order to show best the nasal cartilage, will generally give the most truthful likeness, while not distorting but rather flattering the picture. By this management the too prominent is diminished in appearance without either impairing the resemblance, or exaggerating the irregular features.

If the subject's head is broad, high, and intellectual, while the lower part of the face is thin, the camera may be placed slightly lower than the chin, and the head thrown a little upward. But if the head be small, while the inferior portion of the face is full and heavy, and the person generally corpulent, the camera should be elevated, while the head is brought, and the whole person inclined, slightly forward. It is likely that the portrait may thus be somewhat "flattered," through a partial sacrifice of literal truth. Better, however, to "flatter" innocently in a picture than to exaggerate unavoidable blemishes.

Persons having a rough and coarse or a freckled skin (both of which blemishes are more distinctly visible in the heliograph than in the original, since in such picture yellow shows stronger and darker than black), may so prepare the skin before sitting, that these defects will be but slightly, if at all, discernible in the picture. This is effected by smartly rubbing the whole face immediately before the sitting, with a soft scarlet flannel cloth, or a handkerchief, or even the bare hand; the result of which is a glowing flush upon the surface. By employing this simple expedient; by letting the light fall *directly* upon the cheek; and by having taken a view of the face, which gives the shadows on its broad side; the skin may be made to appear quite delicate and smooth, as well as nearly free from freckles; and all this without overdoing or solarizing the picture.

In estimating the merits of a picture, one consideration is more essential than all others; *i. e.*, it should be like the original. Verity of likeness is the first point of excellence. Some portraitists, in the past, have often given the preference to a *fancied* former likeness over the actual present one, and have assumed certain traits of resemblance which probably never existed.

Again, in many instances, they persist in looking forward to a period when the likeness, now partial, shall be perfect. "O, sir," said a disappointed mother, when the artist had finished a portrait of her child, "you have indeed done it beautifully, but it isn't in the least like my little boy!" "My dear madam," replied the far-seeing artist, "he will *grow* like it—astonishingly so!"

The time was when portraitists were frequently well paid, and with thanks also, for an indifferent painting, resembling the original but slightly. Thanks, however, to heliography, *its* productions have taught the public to see and judge for themselves.

As I have often intimated already, every manager of a camera should be an artist in feeling and judgment, if not in the full sense of the term. He should not only be able to see at a glance the best view of each face and feature, but to rouse the intellectual faculties of his sitter by impinging mind against mind, and to sketch the moral as well as the physical lineaments,—in a word, to secure the most natural and the best expression of which such sitter is capable after summoning the same into his face by conversation, and whatever other influences he may deem appropriate.

CHAPTER XIII.

LIGHTS AND SHADOWS IN A PICTURE—THEIR USE AND VALUE.

Importance of proper management of lights and shadows—Description of how Nature uses these in landscapes—Artists should follow her method as closely as possible—Not the painter and heliographer alone, but the architect—Remarks of Sir Charles Bell.

ALTHOUGH persons ignorant of artistic effect may find fault with the most effectively disposed lights and shadows, I would yet counsel every heliographer to give his productions the highest possible artistic value. This he should do not alone for his own-reputation, but for the honor of his art and its professors.

If insensible to these motives, he may well doubt his possession of the qualities indispensable to his profession. At all events, a skilful, delicate use of lights and shadows is essential to the production of those heads truthfully modelled and well "rounded up," which can win for their author the proud title of artist.

"Do architects," queries Sir Charles Bell, "while arranging the masses of their buildings for effect, study enough how the shadows will fall?"

It seems, then, that even in a structure of wood or stone care should be used that the shadows shall be cast so as to secure an aspect of appropriateness and beauty;

and that without such care all labors else are comparatively futile.

How noble an expression may be stamped upon an edifice by managing this department skilfully is shown in the Parisian palace of the Louvre, and in Oxford, Cambridge, and other colleges and buildings in England, of which excellent photographs are frequently to be met with. There are also many other heliographs of noble specimens of architecture, effectively taken by experienced and genuine artists.

If, then, light and shadow be essential to the artistic excellence of a building, how much more so to the perfect image of the human face and figure!

Wherever there is bright light, shadows are of extraordinary prominence and importance,—and this alike in nature and in art, the transcript of nature. Commonly, indeed, shadows are more conspicuous than the objects that produce them. For, while equally large with these objects, they are darker than their darkest parts, since the aspect of the objects is modified both by direct and by reflected lights. Their broad, equable spaces, therefore, strongly impress the eye; especially as their outlines are defined by lines sharper than nature ever uses in defining objects themselves.

Hold some small object above a piece of white paper in bright sunshine, and you may note two things,—first, that the object shows a soft outline, while the shadow exhibits a sharp, decisive edge,—and second, that the shadow is of a very much darker hue than the object. An eminent art-critic affirms that such a shadow will be threefold darker than a piece of black cloth laid in the light.

In a landscape, then, on a clear, sunshiny day, the shadows are actually the most conspicuous things next to the strongest lights. In fact, it is chiefly by them that what forms, and especially the peculiarities of forms, *are*, is perceived. For instance, the roughness of the bark of a tree can be seen neither in light nor in shade, but is defined by the shadows of its ridges. To represent vivid light, therefore, we must first get sharp, visible shadows.

Again, in nature, the intensest lights and darkest shadows are always sparingly employed; and this invariably in points, and never in masses. If the light be in a large mass, it is *subdued;* and the shadow, if broad, is feeble. The interval between such contrasted light and shadow is occupied by middle tints and pale grays. Into this scene nature introduces here and there a spot of high light, and here and there one of intense gloom; the effect of which is to vivify the whole. Her invariable rule, then, would seem to be to furnish the same amount of deepest shadow as of intensest light, and neither more nor less,—points of each answering to those of the other, and both showing vividly out from the rest of the landscape.

Such is nature's method of managing light and shadow; and herein the artist has a model which he should strive, to the extent of his ability, to copy. Masses of diffused, soft light, balanced by masses of expanded, mild shadow; the space betwixt the two filled by carefully graduated middle tints; while here and there, a keen, bright spot of light is set off by equivalent spots of deep shadow,—*here* is the programme which the wielders of the pencil and the camera should alike endeavor to conform to; and the nigher they approach it, the more do they exhibit the genius and executive skill of the artist.

It is impossible, on paper, to tell the heliographer *how* he can make his one simple instrument execute a work so complex and delicate. But if he have the eye of genius, there need but industry and perseverance in observing and experimenting to discover the *modus operandi*,—besides that, he may be essentially aided by an accomplished artist handling the camera before his eyes.

What we call "relief,"—*i. e.* the apparent *standing out* of the object from its ground,—is effected by the *contrasting* of light and shadow. So, would you produce breadth and splendor of effect, join together masses of light objects and corresponding masses of dark objects. Again, to get harmony and softness, sink some objects wholly or partially in shadow, and let their outlines be insensibly lost in the ground. Finally, to create vivacity and spirit, make, in some parts of the picture, abrupt breaks and sharp transitions.

CHAPTER XIV.

COSTUME IN PORTRAITURE—HOW DISPOSED.

The costume in a portrait of great importance—Directions about its arrangement—The disposition of the hair also of consequence—Instructions on this point with regard to women and to men—Facts, in relation to this subject, derived from noting the insane—How to station groups for taking, &c.—"Small things" of great moment—Stories may be told by pictures—How, and examples given.

As the attractiveness of a picture depends very much upon the artistic disposition of its drapery, whether it be that of a lady or a gentleman, this matter should receive special attention.

To give to the dress an easy and graceful or an elegantly careless appearance, is more difficult than may at first be thought. Indeed it requires a rare judgment and taste, coupled with a vigilant eye, and an unrelaxing attention, and these are not qualities of universal prevalence.

And yet not a few subjects pettishly object to the slightest handling or interference by the artist with their drapery or their hair. The operant should, of course, explain the *meaning* of such interference, and ask permission to employ it. If the party consents, the operant should loosen the cravat and spring away the collar, so as to give the utmost freedom to the neck and head. He should, moreover, adjust the coat, and draw the vest together, or else so raise it that it may partially cover the shirt-bosom, since the whiteness of this bosom, when exposed to intense light, not only solarizes, but impairs the aspect of the face by counteracting or subduing the beautiful middle tints thereon, and by partially destroying the lights and shadows which give roundness and force to the picture.

A lady's costume should receive special attention, in order to give it an appearance of amplitude and of falling from the figure in many graceful folds.

The most intellectual expression of a gentleman's face and head is generally gotten from the side showing the parting of the hair, as the intellectual organs are thus brought into view.

Fine hair, when curling naturally, or adjusted loosely, contributes much towards giving a noble expression to the head and an attractive cast to the features. The hair of a gentleman, when sitting for a heliograph, should never be carefully oiled and brushed down according to the fashion of the hair-dressers. Contrariwise it should be laid loosely up, and tossed lock above lock, so as to impart thereto a careless-seeming aspect.

If the hair, either of a lady or a gentleman, be very black, it should be so ruffled on the rounding of the head as to absorb instead of reflecting the light, and thus to neutralize the glossy lustre occasioned by the reflection of the light falling upon it. Else the hair will appear too light or gray, and the effect will be unpleasing.

In fact, hair, whether light or dark, looks in a picture by far the best if sufficiently ruffled up to let the light fall into and be absorbed by it, in lieu of being reflected from the crown or the sides of the head; since in the latter case it will wear a dry, unnatural appearance.

We are told that "those who have the care of the insane, testify that, by allowing to female patients combs and mirrors, their minds are soothed; that when the mind is brought to take some pride in personal appearance, it is always quieted; and that, when shaved, patients are invariably horrified at themselves. There is no evidence of folly or weakness in this. The hair is the glory of woman, and a well-regulated mind cultivates the exterior. Of all personal points the hair is the most characteristic and conclusive. We have seen a strikingly recognisable portrait of a well-known character, in which only hair, eye-brows, and mustaches were given! By a proper arrangement of the hair (says Walker), great defects in personal beauty are most effectually remedied. Possibly these items may suggest to those who have charge of female prisoners and of the insane, some useful ideas as regards restoring them to healthy minds."

In arranging groups, whether of adults or of children, some should be made to occupy lower seats than the rest; some should stand, while others should sit on stools or an ottoman, leaning lightly and with a lounging grace upon their companions; all, meanwhile, having some special object in view, to concentrate attention, so that the picture may bear an obvious meaning and relate an intelligible story.

Be it understood, however, that these subjects should *not* stand with the stiff precision of soldiers in a platoon. Contrariwise, they should be disposed in one or more pyramids; some being represented with nearly full face, others in profile, and still others with two-thirds face.

Meanwhile special care should be taken to arrange the group in correspondence with the curves of the lenses, at the same time, that each individual should be exactly in the focus of the instrument.

With all the misnamed "small things," above enumerated, the heliographer should be perfectly familiar, since they contribute greatly towards producing a fine picture; nor can he obtain the most life-like, artistic, agreeable portrait possible, without giving heed to each and all of them.

ILLUSTRATIONS BY HELIOGRAPHY.

Heliography, in its several branches, may, by skilled operants guided by sound judgment and good taste, be employed to illustrate many interesting events, very expressively and beautifully. And numerous simple incidents and subjects can be truthfully and vividly represented by a single figure or by a felicitous pose of a single person.

Two or more individuals, by a little effort, may be made to express, with clearness and force, the subject of a whole paragraph,—with *such* clearness and force indeed, that the picture shall all but *speak* the thoughts of the author and the artist.

Let me mention a few simple examples.

1st. The young artist,—drawing upon a slate.

2d. The young arithmetician,—puzzled with a sum on a slate.

3d. Schoolboy's first lessons in writing, &c.

4th. Separation of two fondly loving hearts,—a young man going to sea, as a sailor, or going abroad,—and a young lady with her face buried in a handkerchief, weeping, and resting her face on her lover's shoulder, while both are overwhelmed with sadness.

5th. His return,—their joyous meeting, &c.

Thus, many little domestic scenes might be effectively illustrated, as also scenes, both joyous and grave, in the writings of numerous authors. Shakspeare is full of interesting topics for representation. His "Seven Ages," for instance, would furnish admirable scope for the genius of a young enthusiast.

Collins's Ode to the Passions, if pictured skilfully, and

with suitable accessories, might be well illustrated by a few talented women who were capable of varied action and expression.

The five senses might be beautifully represented by grouping several little children in a series of pictures, each supplied with proper accessories,—for example, a sea-shell held by one child to the ear of another, might symbolize hearing,—an opera-glass or microscope, seeing,—fruit, &c., tasting,—flowers, smelling, &c.

The old arm-chair, with a female sitting in or standing by it, might be happily illustrated and made to tell its sad story in a few skilfully composed pictures,—in some of which it might be well to represent her as weeping. These few simple examples may intimate some of the utilities and beauties of which, in competent hands, heliography is susceptible.

CHAPTER XV.

THE ATMOSPHERE,—THE WEATHER,—LIGHT, FLEECY CLOUDS, ETC.

Effect of changes of weather upon chemical coatings—Various exemplifications of this—Perplexity of a noted artist—Suggestions of how the operant should deal with his critics and advisers.

CHANGES of weather affect the action of the sunbeam upon the chemical coating which receives the impression, and accelerate or retard the development of such impression.

Thus, in our climate, after a severe storm, or several rainy or damp days in succession, it often clears up, and for some days scarce a single cloud is visible. The sky is blue; the air seems clear and pure; and the heliographer's visitants, even if distinguished for scientific attainments, remark, "what a favorable day for your art; with *such* a light your pictures must be exquisite, as well as rapidly taken!"

These persons, however, are here in error; for the "clear sky" they allude to *absorbs* the needful light; whereas thin, fleecy clouds, by reflecting the light, quicken the chemical action of the camera, as well as the development of the image.

Observing operants have, I presume, frequently noted these phenomena, without ever having seen a *cause* assigned for the effect produced in operating, or for the *peculiar* action of the sunbeam on the chemically prepared surface, while exposed to the image in the camera.

After a heavy rain or several consecutive wet days, or more especially a thunder-storm, the heliographer, if taking daguerreotypes, should use *extra* care to preserve his whole apparatus and materials dry and in perfect order. Otherwise he will encounter a host of difficulties and vexations. He will certainly be baffled in his endeavors to produce well-developed, bright, and rich-toned pictures at short sessions. And his failure will be the more signal if the atmosphere be clear, or not charged with electricity, or devoid of white, fleecy clouds and of haziness. Such clouds, as remarked above, serve as reflectors, while electricity operates to intensify and quicken the action of the actinic rays.

On a certain occasion, after several successive days like those above described, followed by a thunder-gust accompanied with lightning, the sun rose clear and the firmament showed a cloudless azure. At about noon of such a day, I called upon one of the most popular daguerreotypists of New York city, who told me that an eminent theologian had submitted already to nine or ten trials for his daguerreotype portrait. During my stay, five additional trials were made. Not one, however, of the whole fourteen or fifteen, proved satisfactory. Our popular friend was (technically speaking) "lost in the fog;" and, manlike, owned frankly, that "he knew not what to do." He ventured, indeed, the hypothetical remark, that "the atmosphere was damp," &c.

At the first glance I discovered that his laboratory was damp, his iodine and buffs saturated with moisture; and his plates covered with the polishing material, rouge, &c. I found, moreover, that the atmosphere was but slightly charged with electricity, while free alike from fleecy clouds and vaporous haze; and that the sky wore that intense blue which swallows up the light. Here were superabundant causes to account for his repeated failures, since *either* of them would frequently suffice. In photographing, however, such difficulties are less numerous.

A FEW FRIENDLY HINTS TO THE ARTIST.

A few suggestions to my professional brethren respecting certain items of demeanor will, I trust, be graciously listened to, both in view of my lengthened experience in the premises, and of the kindly spirit that prompts them.

For example, you are overborne by a crowd of customers, each clamoring for the first sitting, since the time of each is limited to the minute,—one being obliged to leave the city in the next train, and a second in the next steamer for California or Europe; and each, of course, wishing to obtain not merely a life-like portrait, but *also* a transcendent specimen of cis-Atlantic art to exhibit and talk about abroad.

Such an experience may be yours any and every day of the six; *how* are you to deport yourself?

My advice, based on much observation, is substantially this. Curb your temper strictly,—ignore the very name of "nervousness,"—be courteous to all without exception and at all times,—pay a prompt, affable attention to all in their turn, whatever their vocation or social standing,—move heedfully, as well as quickly, in the performance of your duties, while exerting your utmost dexterity in handling the implements of your art;—speak to each but briefly, and then exclusively to the purpose,—and manifest to all, as they successively take their places before the camera, your solicitude to give them the utmost possible satisfaction.

If you will *thus* act, my own experience makes me quite confident that nineteen out of twenty of your sitters would appreciate your efforts and give you their approval; would patiently await your convenience; would accord you their personal influence; and, finally, would at least pronounce you a gentleman, even if nature had forbidden your being an artist.

Another not unimportant question is, how shall the artist demean himself towards his critics?

If sensitive, he may be both offended and grieved by the comments of the conceited and pretentious upon his performances. In such case he had best consider that, though fault-finders are not invariably the most intelligent and judicious critics, yet their remarks, if carefully weighed, may prove valuable helps to his after efforts. I would, therefore, as a friend, advise that *volunteer* strictures, be they what they may, should be accepted with good-humored patience.

Still further. I am confident that every high-minded devotee to his art will not merely receive with patience, but will eagerly court, the frank critiques of eminent artists and accomplished connoisseurs. If he does *not*, he deprives himself of a valuable means of improvement, and very unwisely "stands in his own light."

CHAPTER XVI.

PERSONAL CONSIDERATIONS.

Various personal matters stated—Account of the Author's early training—Of his pursuits for some years of his mature life—And the preparation thus made by him for his subsequent success in Heliography—Importance of drawing and sketching to all artists, and to persons in all pursuits of life—Measures which *must* soon be adopted to secure patronage in the sun-painting profession.

As my name has, for several years, been somewhat conspicuously associated with the art of which I am treating, I hope the reader may not think me presumptuously deviating from my subject if I here speak briefly of myself, of the aims pursued by me, and the course adopted in their pursuit.

Much of the generally conceded superiority of my heliographic pictures, in their several kinds, must, I think, be ascribed to my strong partiality for drawing and sketching, and to my study and practice of the same, as a vocation, during my early years. Having, for three of those years, pursued "drawing from nature," or making crayon portraits from life, I crossed the Alleghenies in 1832, nearly thirty years ago, to seek the instructions of Sully of Philadelphia, or of some eminent New York artist, as preparatory to a visit to Italy.

Circumstances preventing the execution of this purpose, I followed a somewhat kindred profession for several years, at the close of which I adopted the then newly promulged art of Daguerre,—a step I was, in part, moved to take with the view of gratifying, so far I might, my love for art.

Having thus exercised, to no small degree, the faculties involved in art-practice; having acquainted myself with numerous treatises on art, and meditated much upon the topics thereby suggested; I naturally found heliography a most fascinating pursuit. As an art based on the most important sciences, as well as for various other reasons, it struck me, at the outset, as well suited to furnish scope to the most comprehensive genius and the highest and most various culture.

And I hope to see it ere long in the hands exclusively of the ablest and most eminent practical artists. Then, and not earlier, will it be rightly appreciated, secure its merited rank, and receive the encouragement needed to redeem it from the contaminating grasp of operants whose incompetence is matched only by their disrepute.

The present state of heliography on both sides the Atlantic,—low certainly, in comparison with its possibilities,—indicates, that important improvements therein are urgently needed. And my own opinion is, that the day is not distant, when every heliographic establishment, that would secure patronage, must, as a *sine qua non*, have an able and accomplished artist, as the sole superintendent and manager of the sitting department.

The daguerreotype picture undoubtedly has given, and must give place, in some degree, to the paper and collodion pictures, since these can be indefinitely multiplied from each negative, and by help of the colorists can furnish likenesses more truthful in drawing and life-like in color, whether of miniature or life-size, than have heretofore been obtained. By consequence, even distinguished painters will soon be constrained to acknowledge the utility of heliography, and to give it some of their attention both theoretically and practically.

The aim of the true heliographer should ever be to produce such a picture, as will secure the approval of the best judges, whether his sitter can appreciate it, or not. And to effect this, he must be qualified to understand and bring into use all the various powers of the camera, as also to apprehend and sympathize in mood and feeling with every successive sitter. It is to be lamented, that drawing is so neglected in this country, since it is highly useful to mechanics of all classes, and to farmers and professional men generally.

Still more requisite, however, is drawing to the architect and to the artist of whatever kind. To the heliographer, above all others, is a familiarity with light and shade, perspective, and kindred matters, essential to achieving eminent success; outweighing even the most transcendent skill in coloration.

And, as already hinted, I believe the time is near, when every establishment, that would win the patronage of the most intelligent, must have one, by both nature and cultivation an artist, to arrange properly the sitting-room; to place the subject in the best position; to determine the most favorable view of the face and the most fitting disposition of light and shadow; to secure the finest middle tints; and, most essential of all, to obtain the highest and most genial expression of the sitter.

It then remains so to adjust the camera, that the impression gotten may be as truthful and agreeable, as possible, both as a likeness and a work of art.

CHAPTER XVII.

HELIOGRAPHY AN IMPROVER OF ARTS AND ARTISTS.

Predictions that heliography would ruin the business of other pictorial artists—Proved false by event—All art-genius more encouraged now than ever before—Heliography cultivating popular taste and judgment—Portrait and miniature painters improved by this art—70,000 heliographs produced by the Author —Means for advancing the art—Clearness, rather than graces of composition, aimed at in this work.

THE heliographic art hau no sooner reached such a development that a tolerably faithful representation of the human face and form might be produced by it, than pictorial artists of every class predicted that *their* vocation would be ruined, and universal art be degraded by its fatal instrumentality.

That the reverse has been the event, is now generally conceded. For it is obvious that artistic genius, in its every kind, is better appreciated and more amply encouraged at this moment, than it ever was before heliography had attained its present degree of excellence and of popular favor.

I have repeatedly suggested that the numerous pictures, exhibited at the doors of heliographers, operated powerfully for developing and training an artistic taste in the public. That important effects have already been thus wrought, is evidenced by many and various tokens.

Thus, all classes of the community, alike the poor and the rich, the high and the humble of state, manifest a constantly growing desire to procure portraits of themselves, or of their kindred and friends. Nor this alone. They show a taste also for the products of all the other fine arts, *e. g.* paintings, sculptures, engravings, &c. These signs indicate that the entire people are becoming, to some extent, artistically educated, and thus competent to appreciate the works of artists of every description, both in respect of their fidelity to nature and their artistic finish.

That heliography and its achievements have acted auspiciously upon portrait and miniature painters, is beyond all doubt. It is seen in the greater truthfulness of their representations,—a result flowing from a more diligent and profound study of nature. Meanwhile, instead of receiving *injury,* they have derived essential *benefit* from the newly-discovered art. For they have been constrained to present not merely the exact lineaments, facial and figural, of their subjects, but also what is vastly more important, that *expression* which reveals the mind—the heart—the *individualizing* soul of the same. Otherwise, their pictures are pronounced undeserving the name of portraits.

To those (if such exist) who may contemn the heliographic art; who may sneer at suggestions offered by one of its humble professors concerning the requisites of a good portrait, such as correctness, ease, and grace in arrangement, position, light and shade, expression, &c.; I shall make no apology for having ventured to express my views. They are, in fact, not addressed to such, but to persons of good sense, sound judgment, and correct feeling; and especially to those who are co-workers with myself in heliography. To the latter I submit my remarks, with the hope that they may amend or improve upon them, wherever there is *need* of the one, or room for the other.

It is worth noting, that while the portraitist or the miniature painter has devoted his study and labor to painting, say, 500 or 1000 faces, I have taken nearly 70,000. He, indeed, has enjoyed the advantage of giving from 3 to 7 or 10 hours, or even double or treble the time, to each picture. I, on the contrary, could spare but a few moments for each specimen. And during this brief period, I must, perforce, decide upon the most favorable disposition of light and shade; upon the most easy and becoming posture; upon the best facial expression, &c. All this, together with the taking, the developing, the fixing, and the incasing of the impression, must (if a daguerreotype) be accomplished within 10 or 15 or 20 minutes. And then this hurriedly-executed specimen must be handed to the applicant, who may, perhaps, convey it to Europe, or some other trans-oceanic region, and there exhibit it as a *sample* of American heliography.

If ladies and gentlemen would grant to a first-class heliographer an opportunity to produce a truly artistic specimen of his workmanship, as propitious, in all respects, as that allowed to the painter for getting up his portrait,—in which concession are implied time and facilities for correction, for elaborating all details, &c.,—if this, I say, should be done, while the entire control of the sitting-department was also assigned to an operant of highest ability and accomplishment,—then, I am perfectly confident, heliography would speedily assume a very high rank among the fine arts.

The suggestions comprised in several preceding chapters, were mostly noted down by me while busily engaged in the sitting-department, and were prompted by what I discovered to be the exigencies of the time and the occasion. I doubt not that others, inspired with a passion for art in general, and enthusiastic for their special vocation, have felt the impulses of the same or of kindred thoughts, and have carefully followed their lead. If so, I doubt not they are as fully persuaded as myself, of the importance of these hints.

Not having encountered such in any work designed for the use of heliographers, I have supposed I might be rendering a service to the profession by putting them within their reach.

In executing this task, I have striven incessantly for the utmost attainable clearness and minuteness of statement and exposition; and to compass this end, I have not shrunk from considerable repetition. However desirable may be the graces of composition, they are of far less value in a treatise like this, than *perfect intelligibility.* If the reader finds that, pressed by the exactions of the subject, I have occasionally sacrificed *the former,* I trust he will also find that I have rarely, if ever, missed of the latter.

In short, I hope my *meaning* will always and at once be discovered. Whether, *when* discovered, that meaning is of any value, my reader must determine.

CHAPTER XVIII.

EXPRESSION—THROUGH THE FACE.

Expression essential in a portrait—The artist an imitator of the Creative Power—Genius alone can detect and depict expression—Simon Magus—Genius *improved,* not *acquired,* by study—The painter has the advantage of the heliographer in detecting expression, from having many sittings—Lawrence, his supposed mode of doing this—Prometheus—The heliographer must act at once, with perhaps numbers awaiting their "turn"—None should attempt heliography but those conscious of genius—Otherwise, they should seek different vocations—Phaëton and his fate, what it may symbolize—Historic and ideal portraits—Their nature and modes of proceeding—Ideal representations of Christ, the Virgin Mother—Of Washington, Napoleon, &c.

In the course of this work I have repeatedly and most emphatically urged that expression is *essential* to a portrait, whether taken with a camel's hair pencil, or with the pencil of the sun. Nor can this point be pressed too often or too forcibly. For a portrait, so styled, however splendidly colored, and however skilfully finished its manifold accessories, is worse than worthless if the pictured face does not show the *soul* of the original,—that *individuality* or *selfhood,* which differences *him* from all beings, past, present, or future. The creative power never repeats itself; but in every successive performance presents somewhat varying from all existences that have been or are.

Now the true artist, of whatever class, is substantially an imitator of the Supreme Proto-Artist. His leading aim is to reproduce, as exactly as possible, the creations of the Divine Original. Therefore he must detect and "fix" the expression marking the *personality* of his subject, or he shows himself, virtually, an incapable and a sham.

But in what manner and by what means shall he pierce the "iron mask" of the human face (the chief medium of expression); enter those mysterious realms where abide the soul's motive powers; awake these powers to such activity, that the soul must show perforce, in the facial mirror, its *essential quality;* and, finally, transfer to his tablet a life-like "presentment" of the soul thus moved?

To do all this is the prerogative of *genius* exclusively; mere *talent* cannot effect it, neither can industry, nor the highest mechanical aptitude. And such genius is an original endowment; it can never be acquired by education, labor, money, or even prayers.

Simon, the Magian, offered a large sum for the purchase of the "Holy Ghost," on beholding the far greater than *magic* wonders wrought thereby. "Thy money perish with thee," replied Peter,—adding that this marvel-working power was simply "the gift of God."

Such a gift is genius as well. Of course genius, like other *native* qualities, can be improved and refined. But no culture will give it where its germs were not implanted. He, then, who is not clearly conscious of being thus endowed, had best adopt, without delay, some other vocation, wherein such powers as he possesses may be usefully and reputably employed. Art is certainly not his sphere.

Now, as I have repeatedly said, the heliographer, not less than the painter and sculptor, can never, without this genius, be more than a mere mechanic, or, far worse, a charlatan. Perfection itself, in the manipulative and other accessory departments, cannot even *begin* to fulfil the requisites of a true heliographic portrait, if it exhibits not that shadow of the soul which genius intuitively discerns, summons forth, and "fixes."

But *how* can the heliographer detect and call up this expression within the brief period of his process? Unquestionably the painter has *here* a certain advantage over the heliographer; as will appear from a simple illustration.

Suppose Lawrence, eminent for portraitive expression, were called upon to paint one of the celebrities of the land. Being an adept in form, coloring, composition, &c., he feels unquestionably no solicitude about these. His sole anxiety (I suppose) might be thus voiced,— "Shall I succeed in giving to the public, who have often *seen* my sitter, such a life-like representation of him, that all beholders shall exclaim, '*this* is the very individual himself!—his eyes follow us everywhere, and compel us to turn our own away!'

"This result" (he continues) "I *must* produce, or I compromise, perhaps fatally, the high repute I have heretofore won."

Such we may fancy to be his premeditations.

Let us now suppose the sitter placed in the position deemed most effective, and the painter, brush in hand, before his easel.

Of course much mere mechanical work must be done, occupying, perhaps, several sittings, ere the moment arrives for essaying the most essential part of the process, *i. e.*, the stamping upon the face an expression of the soul's individuality.

When, according to the Greek myth, Prometheus fashioned a form of clay, it was the last act of the creative process to interpenetrate that form with the *life giving* fire from heaven.

So, in creating Adam, "God, having formed man of the dust of the ground, breathed into his nostrils the breath of life, and man became a living soul."

The artist, a *quasi-creator*, must copy, throughout, the process of his Divine Exemplar.

I presume, that the painter is, from the outset, busily searching for the individualizing expression which will represent his sitter's soul. To this end he exerts his best conversational powers, while bringing to bear on his subject that fine *magnetism* which is the circumambient atmosphere of genius.

I suppose several sittings must be needful for attaining this end, as he may wish to study his subject while in different moods, and acted on by various influences. For this "thousand-stringed harp" sends not back the same tones to the touch of every wind. While, in response to the "sweet south" or the balmy west, it may "discourse excellent music," the rude, boisterous north or the sour, cutting east may wring from it what might seem shrieks of agony or howls of defiant wrath. Wind and weather, and myriad other conditions of man's embroiled lot may, for the time, forbid an exhibition of one's *higher*, or even *average* self. However excruciating your thirst, you cannot draw water from a spring, ordinarily the purest and sweetest, when stricken solid by a freezing blast, or roiled into mud by some passing hoof.

The artist-painter, therefore, by the several sittings accorded him, may scrutinize his subject in many of his various moods, mental and corporeal. And thus he eventually ascertains, by the mysterious intuition of genius, what his sitter's *individuality* is, when acting under the most genial conditions. This individuality he then bids shine out from the canvas.

From the foregoing premises several inferences logically follow.

As already intimated, the painter, while authorized to demand from his sitter numerous visits, may also fix upon the most auspicious seasons; and, above all, is secure from perturbing interruptions the while. If, then, with so many valuable helps, superadded to artistic genius, he fails of achieving the one indispensable object, his failure must be a veritable enigma.

Contrariwise, the heliographer may have his anteroom thronged with visitants, of numerous diversities of intelligence, character, and social state, all awaiting their turn, often impatiently, and not always silently. To each he can give but a few hurried moments. Within these he must (if at all) detect and represent the *selfhood* of each; besides performing all the other items, which the painter executes at, maybe, half a dozen sessions, sufficiently far apart.

If, then, despite these embarrassments and hindrances, the heliographer can, for the most part, produce pictures exhibiting this life-like expression,—may we not say of his genius, that it is more flashingly intuitive than even that of the painter of the same grade?

My conclusion from the foregoing remarks is this.

If an individual is *assured* by that ultimate intuition, which no words can define, that he is endowed with a genius for art, *then* let him, modestly yet firmly, enter the heliographic room, and plant himself by the camera.

If, contrariwise, he is pretty sure, or even strongly suspicious, that by the primordial decree he belongs to that vast majority who are destined to deal with the actualities of common life, *then* let him avoid such locality. Else he is a "trespasser on the close."

Apollo, the sun-god, once permitted his son, Phaëton,

to take the "ribbons" of the solar chariot for a twenty-four hours' drive round our globe. The youth got so bewildered that he could neither guide nor hold in his horses; thereby setting sky and earth on fire, and getting pitched headlong down upon the ground; while the too yielding sire was left to repair damages!

Now all who would become copartners with the sun,—as every heliographer *must* do,—had best ponder this wise old Greek myth. Its meaning, anglo-saxonized, is "mind your own business,"—"let the cordwainer stick to his last," &c.

If I have spoken with seeming severity, be it noted I am battling for a noble art which has been desecrated by a host of incompetents and charlatans; invaders of its fair precincts for the ignoble purpose of escaping *manual labor.* As if what occupied the hands of both the "first and the second Adam," were a thing so disreputable as to be shunned at whatever cost!

That all *intelligent* readers will appreciate and endorse my suggestions, I feel quite sure. Upon the dull and the malignant I have no words to waste.

Let me subjoin a few qualifying remarks to remove the appearance of having contradicted myself and familiar fact.

Thus, I said that the artist, being a secondary creator, should tread, as nearly as practicable, in the footprints of the Divine Proto-Artist.

But, if such be truth, what shall be said of *historic* and *ideal* pictures? For Raffaelle, Correggio, and many other of the world's most eminent artists, have produced portraits of the "Man of Sorrows;" of the Virgin Mother; of the Apostolic Twelve; of angels, &c., &c. *Here,* of course, they *could* not copy the *seen* workmanship of the Divine Artist.

Let me attempt to solve this seeming enigma.

The Creator gives us many, if not most things, not in a finished state, but in "the rough," as we call it. By our own efforts we may vastly improve them, or may reshape them, and thus fit them for our uses. By these self-same efforts, the while, we develop and discipline our own faculties.

To apply these suggestions to the case in hand, let me remark, that I have, all along, been considering *how* it is that the painter or the heliographer reproduces, in the pictured face, the *soul* or *individuality* of his sitter—the latter being *present* and *living*. All the foregoing pages were devoted to this point,—the historic or ideal in portraiture having no share therein.

A few hints, however, on this species of portraits may not be amiss.

What, then, are the historic and the ideal in portraiture? Whether they are different species, or one species under different titles, needs not here be settled.

I alluded above to the representations of the Christ, of the Virgin, &c., by the great Italian and other masters. *Why* did they assume to paint pictures so named, when they, of course, never saw the originals?

I suppose their intent was simply and solely to present, in visible shape, an image of the *qualities* belonging to the individuals delineated. The degree of their success in this venturous endeavor must be measured by the closeness of *coincidence* between this image and the impression made upon the intelligence and feeling of accomplished connoisseurs by the chronicles narrating the words and deeds of such individuals.

"Hence," says an intelligent critic, "the necessity of the artist's possessing genius competent to appreciate the distinguishing qualities of the character to be represented. Raffaelle and Albert Durer, both men of eminent genius, were yet of different mental conformation. Hence, Durer's representations of Christ realize, perhaps, more truly than Raffaelle's, or those of any other painter on record, the 'Man of Sorrows,' while Raffaelle, with not less truth and genius, has rather delighted to picture him as 'fairer than the sons of men, the chief among ten thousand, the One altogether lovely.'"

If we are malcontent with even the noblest existing representations of the Divine Nazarene, let us not be so unjust as to blame the Artist. For how can the finite grasp the indefinable?

I have never yet seen a picture of "the Virgin," which did not disappoint me. Indeed, how *could* the pictured conception of a single mind make visible to us our indefinite idea of a being, occupying a position so exalted and momentous in the history of humanity on earth and even beyond it?

So much for what I have entitled Ideal portraiture. Historic portraiture, I suspect, is but Ideal portraiture, differently named.

In limning a historic scene, I suppose the artist, if possessing any authentic materials, endeavors to obtain from them the ground-plan of his hero's face and form, and then to fill out this plan so as to image the *qualities* of the individual,—paying, the while, but scant regard to any special features, which might seem not to accord with, or positively to negative the fact of his heroism.

"Compare," says the critic just quoted, "the very different (pen and ink) portraits given of the same persons by Clarendon, Hume, Scott, Macaulay, &c.; owing doubtless not less to the differing mental conformation of these authors, than to their educational prejudices and their political biases."

Once surveying our Rothermel's fine picture of Patrick

Henry addressing the Virginia House of Delegates, I asked him, "if that was an authentic portrait of the great orator?"

"It is a *historic* portrait," was the artist's response,—a confirmation, the reader will perceive, of the suggestions presented above.

In portraying "Macedonia's madman," or Hannibal, or Julius Cæsar, &c.—supposing no reliable portraits of them to have come down to us—the historic becomes, of necessity, the purely ideal painter; since, in striving to represent the faces and forms of his subjects, he is, and *must* be, guided solely by his conception of their attributes.

Where, however, as in the case of Washington, or Franklin, or Napoleon, authentic portraits are extant, the question may arise, whether the historic painter is bound to adhere rigorously to these representations.

I think not. I hold that he may exalt and idealize these literal transcripts, if this be required for representing more perfectly their qualities and achievements.

Note, for example, the familiar picture of Napoleon crossing the Alps. You here behold a superb-looking man bestriding a magnificent, high-rearing battle-charger. Whereas, in literal verity, the Napoleon of that date and that scene was a hatchet-faced, tangle-haired, yellow-skinned youngster, who, occasionally walking, for most of the time bestrode a little donkey instead of a genuine Bucephalus!

Nevertheless that picture makes perceptible an essential, undeniable truth, *i e.*, the existence in its subject of those wondrous qualities which, while he was at large, kept a quarter part of our globe in vehement commotion; and even when he was islanded 1200 miles from the nearest mainland, and there girt by hostile bayonets, compelled the whole of armed Europe "to sleep with one eye open!"

Were an artist about attempting to idealize a portrait of Washington, might he not borrow some inspiration for his work from the following remarks of Lord Brougham?

"In Washington we may contemplate every excellence, military and civil, applied to the service of his country and of mankind; a triumphant warrior, unshaken in confidence when the most sanguine had a right to despair; a successful ruler in all the difficulties of a course wholly untried; directing the formation of a new government for a great people, the first time so rash an experiment had ever been tried by man; voluntarily and unostentatiously retiring from supreme power with the veneration of all parties, of all nations, of all mankind, that the rights of man might be conserved, and that his example might never be appealed to by vulgar tyrants. It will be the duty of the historian and the sage, in all ages, to omit no occasion of commemorating this illustrious man; and, until time shall be no more, will a test of the progress made by our race in wisdom and virtue be derived from the veneration paid to the immortal name of Washington."*

Having thus spoken of expression through the medium of the *face*, I shall proceed in the next chapter to speak of expression through the *form* and its belongings.

---

* Long after penning the above sentences, I met with the following remarks of Quatremère de Quincy, which strikingly confirm the doctrine there advanced.

"Though Alexander is described by his historians as of a diminutive height, the *kind of truth required in the historical style* would by no means render it necessary that he should be represented in the midst of his companions in arms under inferior proportions. That painter would evince a false respect for truth, who should represent Hannibal with but one eye, and Marshal Vendome hump-backed."

CHAPTER XIX.

EXPRESSION—THROUGH THE FACE AND FIGURE.

Not the face only, but the whole body, its attitudes, movements, &c., are vehicles of expression—M. Angelo, Raffaelle, Hogarth, Lawrence, and Gilbert Stuart, famed as expressionists—Skilled in calling up in sitter best expression—Mode of doing this—Anecdote of Mr. Clay, and the taking of his daguerreotype in 1848—Poor portraits of Clay, Webster, &c., especially of the last-named—Sydney Smith's remark—Webster's speeches on Boston Common and Bunker Hill—Lafayette—Surviving veterans of Bunker Hill Battle—Sir Charles Bell on anatomy of expression—Sonnet of Judge Conrad—Modes of rousing expression in sitters—An actor—A lady as nun—Anecdote of Washington, when being painted by Stuart—Interesting facts of the taking of Washington's portraits by Stuart and Peale—Bishop White—Posture in representing statesmen and other public speakers—In representing literary persons—Irving, Bryant, Longfellow, Dickens—Costume and accessories—Swedenborg's theory of *"spheres"*—Effect of the presence of various classes of persons on others—Remarks of a venerable artist.

In the preceding chapter, I spoke exclusively of the face as a vehicle of expression. The face, however, is but one among several mediums whereby the soul manifests itself to the beholder. The whole body, with its various attitudes and movements, subserves the same purpose.

I design, in this chapter, to treat at some length of corporeal expression, and to present some suggestions applicable to all branches of the general subject.

Michael Angelo and Raffaelle, Hogarth and Lawrence,—to whom we may justly add our own Gilbert

Stuart,—were preëminently gifted with the power to call up in the original the expression desired, as also to seize and transfer it to the canvas. In short, they were veritable men of genius, qualified to confer, on equal terms, with the largest and loftiest intellects, and to catch and fix the flashes of the divine fire sparkling in the eyes and radiating from the faces of their subjects, when these were in their most elevated and genial moods. Undeniably it was with them a leading object, during every session, to awaken these moods in their sitters; and this object they strove to secure by their own conversational powers, and, when possible, by those of others, who might be present.

What a pity that such artists could not have been employed to perpetuate the faces and forms of several eminent countrymen of ours, who have recently passed from this mortal stage! Is it not deplorable that, of existing portraits of men of this order,—especially those transferred from heliographs,—so very few display that intelligent, spirited, noble cast of countenance which we instinctively ascribe to the originals, and which properly signalizes true greatness? Who can doubt that these countenances *would* have displayed such a cast, had the minds of the originals been suitably aroused at the time of the pictures being taken, by those manifold expedients, conversational and other, which the veritable artist, and he alone, can employ?

As an illustration of what may be effected by these expedients, let me introduce the following anecdote.

In 1848, an appointment being made for my taking the daguerreotype of Henry Clay, I requested the mayor of our city and the sheriff of the county, together with several other of Mr. Clay's friends, who were present, to keep the statesman in brisk conversation till I was ready to expose the plates to the image; as I wished to catch the intellectual, lively look natural to him under such conditions.

The mayor, turning to Mr. Clay, said, "Mr. Root desires us to continue talking, as he wishes to daguerreotype your *thoughts;* to catch, if possible, your very smiles."

"Smiles!" exclaimed Mr. Clay,—"I can give him *frowns,* if he wants *them;*" upon which he smiled, while his face was radiant with intelligence as well. And in twenty seconds three good portraits were taken at once; the plates were removed from the instruments and four fresh ones got ready. In a few seconds more, Mr. Clay the while conversing pleasantly with his friends, all else was prepared, and then his likeness again was daguerreotyped by four cameras at once; all representing him, as we *then* saw him engaged in conversation, mentally aroused, and wearing a cheerful, intellectual, and noble expression of countenance. Thus seven portraits were taken in but thirteen minutes,—with such success, too, that Mr. Clay remarked, after inspecting them:—

"Mr. Root, I consider these as decidedly the best and most satisfactory likenesses that I have ever had taken, and I have had many." These words he left in my register with his autograph.

One of these portraits has since been engraved, as the finest likeness of him extant; and may be seen in the "Portrait Gallery of American Statesmen," published by Messrs. Rice & Hart, successors to J. B. Longacre, Esq.

To recur, for a moment, to the subject I was considering prior to the introduction of this anecdote, numbers of the heliographs of our eminent men, members of Congress, and others, taken by unthinking, machine-like operators, actually look as if the originals *contemned* the art, and had no faith in the ability of the individual to whom they had consented to give their time, and were sorely afflicted by the process of sitting.

As specimens of portraitive abortions, I may instance several which purport to represent Webster, Clay, Jackson, Taylor, Everett, &c. Represent! Possibly they *may* represent,—though even *that* very inadequately,—the perishable material organism. But for all else than this, like the poet,

"We start, for *soul* is wanting there!"

I think none of these abortive pretensions affect me so painfully as a (so-named) portrait of Webster which is often to be met with. That magnificent frame seems languid, relaxed, drooping, and as if ready to sink down into a *boneless heap;* while the august face, so fitted to ray out the highest and largest intelligence, conjoined with overmastering power, exhibits, in the dull, vacant gaze and the corners of the mouth drawn down, an aspect of feebleness and listlessness, both physical and mental, a malcontent gloom, and a lack of interest in all existing things.

Now that, in certain abnormal moods, Webster might have looked somewhat as here depicted, is not wholly improbable.

But suppose he did. Was *such* the look which artists like those above enumerated, would have sent into the world, to pass with cotemporaries who were strangers to the grand originals, as also with far posterity, as a true "presentment" of one of fame's immortals?

What would that prince of wits, Sydney Smith, have said of this (so-called) *authentic* portrait of the statesman?—he who, on seeing Webster in England, ex-

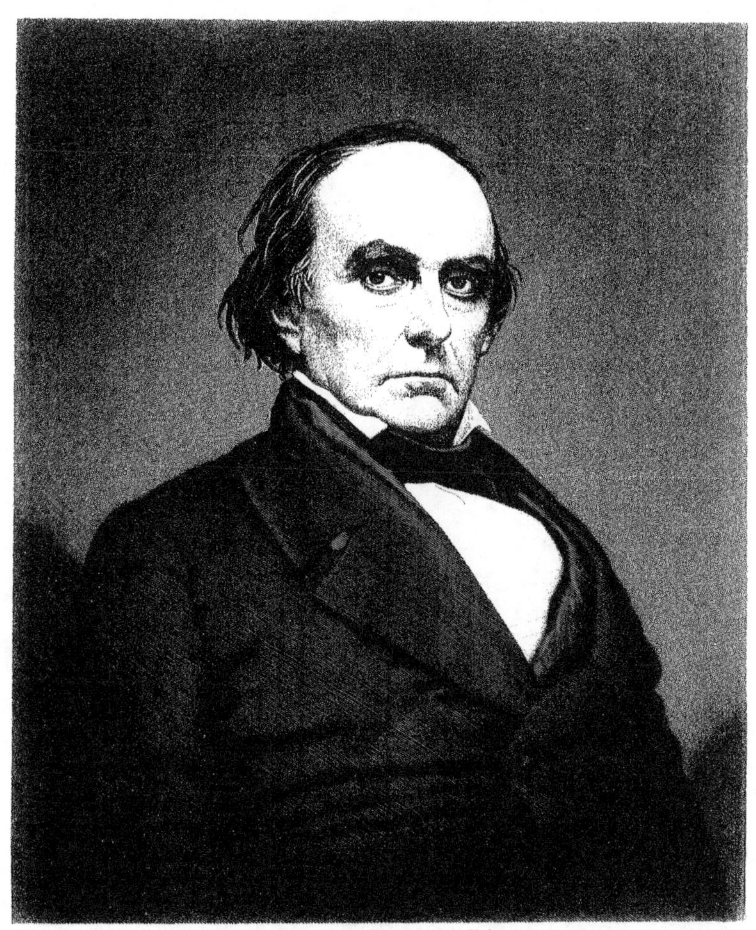

Engraved by John Sartain, Phil.

Danl Webster

After Dag. by J.A.Whipple

claimed, "What a magnificent head!—what a noble figure!—what dignity of demeanor and movement are his! He reminds me of a small cathedral!"

In truth, that impotent-looking, dismal shadow bears but a faint resemblance to the original I was privileged to see and hear, on two or three public occasions, some years ago.

One of these was when, from an elevated platform on Boston Common, he addressed a vast and sympathizing auditory on sundry themes of national interest. One of the subjects, on which he dilated largely, was the patriotic career of Henry Clay, with the many important services that marked that career.

Many causes conspired to rouse into energetic action his whole faculties of mind and body.

Thus, the importance of his topics, urgently appealing, as they did, to those patriotic sentiments which were among the strongest in his nature; the aspect of the multitudinous throng drinking eagerly in every syllable from his lips, and sending up frequent thunder-bursts of approving acclamation, which were reëchoed from those hills, so memorable both in history and tradition, as encircling the nursery-field of the revolution; and finally the simple fact that he was under full sail, with a smart breeze, on his proper element, which was to harangue popular bodies on great and absorbing subjects,—all these circumstances, combined with the operation upon him of what may be termed the concentrated magnetism of the enthusiastically sympathizing crowd, had the effect so coveted by every public speaker, *i. e.*, to rouse his entire nature into the intensest activity.

By consequence, you *then* and *there* beheld the veritable Webster, "one and indivisible." No *words* of mine could image his appearance on the occasion. It were the appropriate work for a first-class painter or sculptor.

Suffice it for me to say, that not alone the eyes, face, and head of the orator, but the form, with every individual limb and muscle, were intensely alive with expression. The spectacle verified Shakspeare's saying about the Grecian coquette,

"Her *foot* speaks."

A second occasion, whereon thousands saw and heard the orator, was more striking still. It was at the laying of the corner-stone of the Bunker Hill Monument; when, standing on that immortal battle-ground, he addressed an immense multitude, among whom were most of the few surviving veterans of that conflict, and the "nation's guest," Lafayette.

The associations of the spot were of a quality that could hardly be paralleled, or even approached, otherwhere. I shall merely glance at these, and then leave to my reader to *imagine* what must have been their influence upon him who was, that day, the cynosure of all eyes.

He stood upon that spot where the revolution, with all its stupendous and beneficent issues, was transmuted from a doubt, a trembling hope, into a certainty, a solid, inexpugnable fact; and where young Independence was baptized in a tide of the noblest blood of pilgrim-planted Massachusetts, and of the New Continent. It was a spot where the mind was moved to expatiate over the whole varied fortunes of that terrible eight-years' contest, wherein, virtually, "one chased a thousand, and two put ten thousand to flight;" upon its desperate straits and intervals of midnight darkness; and upon its occasional gleams of success, brightening and broadening more and more, till uprose at last, the full, unclouded day-star of triumph, whereby "the little one became a thousand, and the small one a strong nation."

Before him were the battered human reliques of that sanguinary fight, appealing to all the higher feelings of the American bosom. Before him, too, was the revered hero of almost fabulous experiences; once the boy-friend of Washington, and summoning before imagination's eye that august, majestic presence; a brave warrior and leading actor in the revolutions of two continents; and now come over the ocean as the enthusiastically honored guest of a people who thus, "in their day of greatness, and with the outstretching of *manly* arms, welcomed him who had supported their tottering infancy."

And for this picture, so crowded with all kindling memories and thoughts, what an appropriate setting was supplied by that unmatched panoramic landscape which spread around the sacred hill, whose every rood was memorable for those incidents of high-souled performance and endurance which glorify our common nature!

Let the reader imagine, as well as he may, what the *effect* must have been of these excitants upon the orator's high-toned mind and heart, and how vividly this effect must have showed itself through his rarely moulded organs of expression.

And while his imagination is thus occupied, let him also call up other instances of Webster's standing forward as the mouthpiece of grand occasions; such as the bi-centennial anniversary of the Pilgrims' landing at Plymouth, the nullification conflict in the national Senate, the completion of the Bunker Hill Monument, &c., &c. And I dare affirm, without qualification, that the reader's conclusion will be, that the picture above mentioned, so far from being a faithful representation of its pretended original, is a gross libel thereon, and richly deserving of indictment.

I have employed the instance of Webster to illustrate the principle I am discussing, simply because I have been more familiar with his public appearances than with those of his distinguished compeers. My remarks, however, equally apply to Clay and Calhoun, to Preston and Everett, and to numbers beside. Whoever has heard *these*, when aroused by momentous occasions and themes; and has noted how every corporeal movement, as well as flash of the eye and shadow upon the face, has helped to intensify the power of their utterances, will concede the truth of my suggestions about expression and its various modes.

But what is the fault or deficiency of the Webster portrait above spoken of?

Simply and solely the want of expression, *i. e.* of *livingness;* of that *individuality* which differences one human being from each and every other.

In Sir Charles Bell's Treatise, entitled "The Anatomy of Expression," we have what may be styled the *material* rationale of expression, both facial and corporeal. He has discovered a vast network of nerves which, by their varied action upon the muscles, serve to image forth all the diverse passions and emotions originating in the mind,—each having a movement or posture corresponding to and representing it. These nerves do not spread over the face exclusively; but also over the entire neck and chest, and thence through the total frame. So that vehement feeling, or, in fact, any feeling that rises much above the average, is not revealed by the face alone, but by all parts of the body as well.

The *wherefore* of this anatomy shows. "It is curious," remarks Sir Charles, "that expression appears to precede the intellectual operations. The smile, that dimples an infant's cheek, and which, in after years, corresponds with pleasurable and complex emotions, cannot *originate* from such emotions, for it is not first seen when the infant is awake, but often while asleep. This expression is, in fact, the spontaneous operation and classification of the muscles which await the development of the faculties to accompany them closely, when they do arise, and in some measure to control them during life." [*See* pp. 198–9.]

From what has been said, the conclusion is urged irresistibly upon us, that expression is a *sine qua non* towards displaying what a man really is, whether in an original or a portrait.*

I have suggested certain means of arousing, in the individual to be portrayed, the expression desired at the

* As apropos to the subject I am discussing, I trust I may be pardoned for introducing here the opinion of a connoisseur and a poet, (the late Judge Conrad) upon the *expressiveness* of a heliograph. It is entitled

SONNET

ON ROOT'S DAGUERREOTYPE OF MR. FORREST.

"Light-born and limned by Heaven! It is no cheat,
No image; but himself, his living shade!
With hurried pulse the heart leaps forth to greet
The man, who merits more than Tully said
Of his own Roscius,—that the histrion's power
Was but a leaf amid his garland wreath;
His swaying spirit ruled the magic hour,
But his vast virtues knew no day, no death.
He *seems* not now, but *is*. And I do know,
Or think I do, what meaning from those lips
Would break; and on that bold and manly brow
There hangs a light, that knows not an eclipse,
The light of a true soul. If art can give
The bodied soul *this* life, who doubts the soul will live?'

moment of portrayal. There are other means, which may be of service to the same end.

Thus; learn, if possible, what pursuits, or class of thoughts most interest the sitter. These may be what occupy his time chiefly, or upon occasion merely. Having learned this, endeavor, so far as may be, to awaken in him the thoughts referred to, as *then* the corresponding expression, be it of face or form, or of both, will appear spontaneously.

An experiment or two, made by myself, will illustrate my meaning.

I was required to portray a distinguished actor, as representing Othello, in a scene of the drama so named. At first, the actor, being wholly unexcited, bore not the slightest resemblance to the "jealous Moor." Observing this, I requested him to throw himself, by a strenuous act of imagination, into the *personality* of Othello, just as he was wont to do on the stage. In making the trial, he walked to and fro, for some time, mentally rehearsing the part, till he had succeeded in calling up the expression desired, which I transferred perfectly to the plate. The picture told the story distinctly and fully.

So, on being requested to represent a lady, as a nun in the act of prayer, I proposed, that she should assume a kneeling posture and put up a fervent mental petition. She complied; and her face soon exhibited an expression of devout thought and emotion, which I succeeded in impressing upon the plate.

As a further illustration, I subjoin an anecdote which Bishop White used to relate, and which he had from our eminent portraitist, Gilbert Stuart.

The latter, being engaged in taking a portrait of Washington, endeavored, according to his custom, to summon into the hero's countenance its most interested and noblest expression. In so doing, he alluded to Braddock's defeat, to the crossing of the Delaware, to Valley Forge, &c., &c. It was all in vain. Washington's face remained listless, and finally became even depressed. Well nigh discouraged, the artist at last bethought himself of referring to "Old Virginia," its rural life and sports, its peculiar customs, &c., &c.

Instantly the sitter's face lighted up, and he struck into a conversation upon these topics with keenest zest and animated interest. And thus Stuart was enabled to catch that fugitive *somewhat* which threatened to elude him, and to produce the portrait which has ever since been esteemed a model.

This anecdote was related to Bishop White by Stuart, while the latter was painting the former's portrait,—related, too, for the very purpose of *enkindling* the mind of the excellent prelate; an effect, we may be assured, it produced.

Possibly it may not be generally known that Washington and Bishop White were warm friends, and that the latter was the first chaplain in Washington's army.

It may also be worth recording that Rembrandt Peale painted Washington's portrait at the same time with Stuart; the two being thus engaged on alternate days.

Each had three sittings of three hours. Peale worked in the building called the Philosophical Hall, now owned and occupied by the American Philosophical Society, on Fifth street, below Chestnut, and standing nearly opposite Stuart's room, which was on the south-east corner of Fifth and Chestnut, and owned by William Smith. This was in 1795. Occupied from 1846 to 1856 by M. A. R., where this work was commenced.

Stuart's first portrait was a failure, which was thus accounted for:—Jay's Treaty was yet unsigned, and

Washington felt great anxiety on the subject. This anxiety was heightened by the appearance of certain anonymous letters which were charged to the authorship of Washington,—it being reported that they were found in a portfolio, taken from a runaway servant of his. At the final sitting, Peale's father asked Washington if he wrote those letters. His reply was, "No servant of mine ever left me,—no portfolio or letters of mine have ever been taken from me." At the close of the sitting, the elder Peale at once reported Washington's disclaimer all over the city; and no more was said about the anonymous letters by Washington's enemies.

Gouverneur Morris stood to Stuart for his *full length* portrait of Washington; while the outstretched hand of the figure was painted from a wax-cast of Stuart's own hand. These facts I received from the lips of the venerable Rembrandt Peale, Esq., the only survivor of the many artists who painted Washington.

To take a good full-length standing figure of a public speaker, or even of a private gentleman, so that the picture shall express the true character of the individual, and that the *pose* shall be natural, easy, and graceful, will tax the highest artistic powers of an experienced operant.

Small full-lengths, showing the feet naturally and happily placed, may be made pretty and graceful pictures.

Larger sizes, in which a faithful likeness is the principal desideratum, may be taken, while standing, nearly as low as the knees; or even below, if necessary to represent faithfully the height and size of person.

Ladies, when portrayed standing, should be taken at full length; and if a front view of the person be sketched, the face should be turned away; and vice versa. Special care should be used to secure a graceful disposition of their hands in all standing figures.

These instances suggest the propriety of representing statesmen, lawyers, clergymen, and public speakers generally, in a *standing posture;* since in that posture they usually put forth those efforts which stir into activity their highest and best faculties both of mind and heart. It is, moreover, in that posture *only* that the *whole body* coöperates with the face in manifesting outwardly the soul within.

I may further remark that, in the standing position, the falling of the shoulders imparts to the head most of freedom, grace, and dignity of movement.

But suppose you were required to represent a historian or a poet, a romancer or an editor; in short, any person whose chief excitations of intellect are experienced, and his favorite labors performed, while wielding the pen at the desk. To place such a one in a standing position would well nigh certainly defeat the end desired; since he would be more likely to feel embarrassed and awkward than inspired with enthusiasm, in consequence of the novelty and strangeness of his attitude.

Contrariwise, you should place your subject in conditions which may remind him strongly of the locality, with its accompaniments, whence thoughts have emanated, which have not alone exalted and thrilled his own soul in solitude, but which may have illumined and warmed the souls of myriads who never saw him; whence, too, have issued forth images of beauty and grandeur which, while delighting himself, may also have called out the acclaims of admiring and raptured multitudes.

Thus, in representing Washington Irving, who would not, if possible, call up in him the precise mental mood, from which sprang the inimitable "History of New Amsterdam;" the marvellous tale of Rip Van Winkle; the unmatched adventures of Ichabod Crane; the chivalrous "Tales of the Alhambra;" and the countless other creations, merry or pathetic, which have unsealed the fountains alike of smiles and of tears in the bosoms of the dwellers of two continents?

Would you not also have Bryant, at the instant of taking, think and feel just as when the august panorama of "Thanatopsis" unrolled itself before his inward sight; Longfellow as when those exquisite melodies of his "set themselves to music" for his inward hearing; and Dickens as when he accompanied the illustrious "Pickwick" in his desperately adventurous travels; or attended the child-angel, "Little Nell," in her weary earth-wanderings toward that *not* untimely grave, which unclosed the portal of her proper home in the highest heaven? And Morris you would fain behold as when the "Lines to my Mother's Bible," or of "Woodman, spare that Tree," swam in the tears called forth by grateful memory, as he traced them upon paper; and Willis, in various moods, either in the person of David bewailing Absalom, or in his own person annihilating some envious, impudent assailant.

Such, assuredly, are the mental states which you would fain produce in the individuals named, for the sufficient reason that they stamp the noblest attainable expression on the face and the form.

Be it noted, moreover, that among the subsidiary means for producing such states are the posture, the costume, and the surroundings generally.

After all, however, the most essential of all requisites for the artist; that, without which all qualities else, backed by all appliances, are of little avail; is original genius. And, as previously hinted, one of the leading traits of such genius is a power of acting potently on other minds, not exclusively by thought and word, but also by a noiseless influence which, for lack of a better term, we may entitle magnetism.

According to the greatest of modern Mystics,—the Christian Pythagoras,—every human is encompassed by a so-named "sphere;" a somewhat corresponding to the fragrant effluence surrounding the rose-bush, the cinnamon tree, and the magnolia. "These spheres" (he says) "encompass all spirits, flowing forth from the life of the affections, and of the thoughts derived thence." "*Sympathy* between different persons results from a *similitude* between their spheres, and *antipathy* from *dissimilitude*."

Now whether this philosopher be right or wrong in the *precise items* of his theory, all experience evinces that there is a *somewhat* exhaling from every person, which, apart from both his acts and his words, exerts a certain influence and makes a certain impression upon others, despite his own volition or wish, and without volition or wish on their part.

Thus, the *mere presence* of some individuals is repressive, depressive, and even stupefying to those in their company.

Of others the same simple presence is enlivening, animating, rousing, kindling.

Others again there are, in whose society our worst feelings are stirred into tormenting activity.

And there exist still others, in whose companionship our whole better nature is wakened and exalted into active predominance.

All this, I repeat, is matter of our daily experience.

Now it is a known property of genius to act powerfully on men's minds either for good or for evil. Suppose, then, an artistic genius to be united with those *moral* attributes which elsewhere I have spoken of as essential to eminence in art, it is obvious that the influence of an individual thus dowered must be very potent upon those with whom he comes in contact. It is on this account that I have insisted so strongly upon the necessity of genius to all such as venture to imitate the Divinity in His work of creation.

If, however, it be concluded that the portraitist, in whatever kind, should possess alike genius and culture, it is not my humble self who exact these high attributes, but the very nature of the pictorial and plastic arts.

How severely these requisitions must press upon the heliographer, whose process is, of necessity, restricted to a few brief moments, is obvious enough. And the more severely still, since to these high powers must be added that electric celerity of thought and performance which is among the rarest of human endowments.

Among the many difficulties he must cope with, by no means the slightest consists in the temperaments of his subjects. Pithily remarks Sir Charles Bell, "one man is so constituted that he *will* have his joke, though it may hurt his dearest friend; and another has so little imagination that even in the delirium of fever he is dull."

In a recent conversation with a venerable artist of much distinction, he made, substantially, the following suggestions:—

"The heliographic artist may justly plead some excuse for his short-comings in portraying alike distinguished persons and others, as he is usually limited, by his sitters, to a few moments for accomplishing a marvellous and very difficult work. As his art acquires importance, and rises in public estimation, he will be indulged with more patience by his sitters, who will also place a higher value upon his efforts."

I need not say that I was happy to find my own frequent remarks in various portions of this volume thus corroborated by an authority so respectable.

CHAPTER XX.

EXPRESSION—THROUGH THE ANIMAL AND INANIMATE WORLDS.

Expression pertains to the animal, vegetable, and mineral worlds, *e. g.* the lion, what ideas he expresses, what sort of man he typifies; the tiger, do. do.; the fox, bull-dog, snake, do. do.;—The inanimate world has expression—Macbeth, witches, blasted heath, &c., accordance between persons and scene—The crucifixion of Christ, and the accompanying darkness, earthquake, and other prodigies—Milton's description of earth's perturbations, on the eating of the fatal apple—Mountains expressive—Three different ones described, typifying three classes of men—Frigid zones and Sahara Desert, what sorts of human beings and conditions symbolized by them—Swamps and fens, what they represent—The face of earth, as a whole, symbolical of the character and state of the race.

HITHERTO I have spoken solely of the human face and figure, as vehicles of expression. But the subject is far from being *thus* exhausted. For the animal, the vegetable, and the mineral worlds, in their own manner, are not less charged with expression. In illustration of this fact, let us glance first at the animal kingdom.

If philosophy and poetry are not wholly astray, expression should be discernible in the faces and figures of all animals, domesticated or wild. For both teach, that the animal, of whatever species, is a fragment, or partial manifestation of man; and, conversely, that man is an aggregate of all the several properties existing in the spheres below himself, animal, vegetable, and mineral.

Hence, if, through man's material organism, spiritual

meaning be expressed, so must it be through the kingdoms beneath him.

Thus, has the lion's face no expression? What was the epithet, "lion-hearted," attached to the first English Richard, meant to express?

Probably *this*,—tremendous physical force; a disposition which, from its energy and excitancy, *may* rush into *cruelty* when fully roused; but which in ordinary moods, blends magnanimity with power; and finally the capacity to overwhelm and destroy all opposers, coupled with the habitual inclination to spare the dead and the unresistant. Such would seem the significance of the broad square face, combined with the formidable muscles and harrow-like claws of the desert-king.

Does he not vividly typify the Hercules, or the Samson, the heroes of rough, violent times; themselves hardly less rough and violent, than the foes they triumphantly encounter; but, unlike these, possessing a grandeur of soul, which bids to spare such, as can resist and ravage no longer?

Has not the tiger, too, *his* expression? An exaggeration of the household cat; with hardly less physical might than the lion, though with none of his reputed magnanimity; cruel and sanguinary to the core; sly, treacherous, and persistent in his endeavors to get as many victims, as possible, within the gripe of his ruthless fangs; do you not read this character in that face of his, so luridly lighted up with those green, blazing eyes? And certainly history, if not your own experience, furnishes numbers of both men and women embodying the tiger-element.

Again, from Æsop's time, at least, the fox has been regarded as the type of the cunning man, who pursues his ends by covert, tortuous methods; working in darkness, and not in sunshine; scudding away from whoever fronts him boldly, but creeping back to effect his destructive purposes, if he can surprise his victim asleep or unprepared. Are not these traits visible in his face, figure, and movements?

As antitype of Reynard, note the luckless hare; luckless in many ways, and especially in *this*, that the so-named "great" everywhere make a favorite amusement of hunting poor "Puss" to death, with the accompaniments of yelling hound and clamorous horn.

Who has not seen among human beings numerous archetypes of the fox and the hare?

Of the bull-dog I need say but a word. His head and neck bear a most extraordinary resemblance to those of the prize-ring heroes, and the characteristics of the two are identical.

But the snake, with his ugly coil while at rest; his stealthy, twisting movements when advancing; his forked, quick-darting, fiery tongue, and his whole aspect, when roused to anger; does he not image to you a human being who is cunning and treacherous in his methods of proceeding, while dangerous and deadly in his intents?

I have not room for further sketches of this kind. But the hints already given may by the reader be carried as far as he will through the several species of the animal kingdom.

Expression, however, does not stop with the animals; it appears hardly less distinctly in the inanimate than in the animal world. Mother earth has many a different expression, wherein we may witness striking correspondences to the states of her human children.

Where, for instance, did Macbeth encounter the weird, frightful beings who predicted the fate which should carry him to a throne along the dark, tortuous, blood-slippery ways of betrayed hospitality, treason, and midnight murder?

On a "blasted heath," but partially visible by the few shimmering stars of a clouded sky! A rough, bleak region, with dank mosses and noisome weeds, and sombre-hued, withered shrubs in place of the fresh green growths so gladdening to eye and soul; here and there the fragment of a dead tree, which had been robbed of vitality by the thunder-stroke, or the slow-sapping consumption of arboreal disease; and, topping this dread aggregate, a black-hued pool, bordered with tangled, foulest vegetation, dotted with green, slimy patches, all alive with hideous reptiles; and so looking like an eye darting forth basest, obscenest thoughts and feelings,—did not this scene express vividly the career that lay before Macbeth? Do we not, by instinct, recognise a natural affinity between this locality and the crimes here brought in vision before the future criminal in whose bosom the pandemonian fires are already smouldering?

And how was it with Mother Earth when the tragedy of tragedies was enacted,—the infliction of a felon death on "the Lord of life and glory"? Did her face wear its wonted smiling aspect, and did nature move on in her wonted courses?

It could not be so. But, instead, the sun hid his face in shame; the earth heaved with earthquake-sobs and groans; the long-dumb graves sprang up into life; and the inanimate world everywhere showed a shuddering sensitiveness to the horribly unnatural deed then in process of perpetration.

Milton has attributed similar perturbations to earth at the eating of the "fatal apple" by Eve.

> "Earth felt the wound, and Nature from her seat.
> Sighing through all her works, gave signs of woe,
> That all was lost."

And when Adam followed her example,

> "Earth trembled from her entrails, as again
> In pangs; and Nature gave a second groan.
> Sky lowered, and muttering thunder, some sad drops
> Wept at completing of the *mortal* sin
> *Original.*"

We may, however, find the same principle illustrated by the ordinary, perennial aspects of nature.

Mountains, for example, have an expression of their own. Speaking generally, I should say they expressed the preëminence of the individual man; that grandeur and power of soul, whereby he towers above his fellows and attracts their regards to himself. And the *varieties* of mountains we may suppose to symbolize the *diversities* of human greatness.

For example, one mountain, while rising to a vast height, is of symmetrical configuration, and brightly verdant to its very summit.

What more striking emblem of a character, at once eminently great and completely balanced; the intellectual and moral qualities all exalted to a high pitch, yet in such equilibrium, that no one or more stands above the rest? Such a character was Washington.

A second mountain, equally lofty as the first, is strikingly irregular in conformation. Here is an expanse of vivid green; there a a patch of dun-hued, bristly shrubs, and gnarled tangled vines; here again is a huge rocky ledge, encircled with thickly scattered boulders; and there, finally, a group of tall, superb trees, the graceful beech, or the majestic maple, whose very veins run sweetness for whosoever chooses to receive it. How better than by this symbolize a man *irregularly* great and good; a composite of virtues and faults, of beauties and blemishes, of fertilities and barrennesses,—a sun marked with many a *spot*, yet still a sun.

But yonder looms up a third mountain. Differing greatly from the two former, it appears, on a superficial glance, little other than a huge mound of rough, verdureless crags and stones. Hardness, barrenness, deformity, and desolation would seem there more aptly imaged in a single emblem. But a closer inspection shows a copious fountain of clear, cold water gushing from the heart of that rocky mass. The tired, heated wayfarer blesses the liquid benignity, and many an animal, too, is refreshed by the bounty of this pitiless-seeming giver. And far on through the plain below the rock-born streamlet carries greenness, fertility, and beauty, blessing multitudes who know not its origin; and so it will continue to do, till its existence becomes absorbed by the all-central ocean. Still further—Within the bosom of that forbidding mound are exhaustless stores of coal and iron, from which numbers draw the needful means of life and enjoyment.

Have we not here the type of a third great and good man,—one who, beneath a rough, hard exterior, shelters numerous sterling virtues of rarest quality, and is prodigal of benefits to multitudes of human kind? Do you not here discover many, at least, of the features of Ethan Allen and "Old Put?" But, passing from particulars to generals, does not the surface of our globe, as a total, reflect vividly the various conditions, mental and moral, of the human race that occupies it?

As thus: How many millions of our kind pass through life with their intellectual capacities frozen up in a cold, drear ignorance!

If now you glance over earth's frigid zones, you behold in their vast expanses of eternal ice and snow this mental barrenness most vividly symbolized; and this in a thousand minutest particulars.

Note one particular. From these immense ice-fields a huge mass gets sometimes detached, and, floating into mid-ocean, dashes destruction against many a ship, full-freighted alike with wealth and with human life.

So from the frozen sea of ignorance a great mass gets occasionally severed, which, floating blindly off, dashes ruinously against the social weal, and, with no definite malign intent, works mischief beyond the estimate of statistics or of imagination's self. For examples, recall the Jacquerie insurrection, or the first French revolution.

Again, traverse in imagination the great African Sahara, and what see you and hear you there? The formidable shapes and voices of lions, who "roar after their prey and seek their meat from God," together with the sharp barks and dismal moans of their attendant jackals; the sanguinary atrocities and hideous growls of tigers, panthers, and others of their kind; innumerable serpents, from the dragon that arrested the march of a Roman army to the "fiery, flying serpent" which wrought havoc upon the Hebrews under Moses,—what does this desert express in human society?

Traverse the cellars of New York "Five Points," or of London "St. Giles's," or of Paris "Cité," as presented at the bar of supernal justice by Dickens and Sue, the prosecuting attorneys of civilization, and tell me if you do not here witness a counterpart of that African desert, with its monstrous and loathsome containings?

I might further point your attention to earth's numerous swamps and fens, brimming with hideous reptiles, and dank, poisonous, sense-offending vegetal growths; eternally exhaling miasms, on whose viewless pinions a thousand mortal pestilences float; to volcanic mountains which, even when quietest, spout forth noxious gases and redden luridly the face of earth and sky, but which, in their roused moods, eject ashy clouds, and stormy showers, and lava-torrents which bury whole cities with their inhabitants; and then I might bid you note those corrupted *human* masses which at all times spread a fatal contagion about them, but in exasperated conditions become veritable Ætnas and Vesuviuses, the terror and the menaced destruction of the society that embosoms them! Do not the former plainly emblem the latter?

Not, however, to multiply these parallelisms further, we remark generally that in this our earth, scarred and blotched, volcano-spouting, fen-reeking, and reptile-swarming, desert-flaming, and frost-bound, the intelligent observer may see reflected, or expressed, the multiform defects, vices, crimes, and woes of the race that occupies its surface.

If, then, we can trace expression through all the departments of creation; if we find in this the one characteristic that imparts a living interest to the human, the animal, and the inanimate worlds alike; should it not, beyond all particulars else, secure the attention of all who would be artists in very deed and truth?

CHAPTER XXI.

EXPRESSION OF ABNORMAL MOODS OF BODY AND MIND.

Disease, like health, subject to laws—Various diseases exhibit various expressions—Sundry examples of these—Abnormal passions have each their own expressions—Instances given—Wisdom of this ordination—The actor must study these expressions—Important for all to do this.

SAYS a modern writer, "The laws of disease are as beautiful as the laws of health." And with equal truth we might say that the process of decomposition is as curious and full of interest as that of growth.

In the three preceding chapters I have spoken of the expression of persons and things in their healthy and normal condition. Equally curious and hardly less worthy of notice is the expression of the same, when in a diseased or abnormal state.

An observant, acute physician learns at once to detect, by the external appearances of his patient, what disease he is attacked with, and in what part of the organism this disease is seated. Our friend, Dr. S. S. Brooks of this city, has given us a few notes on this subject which we here transcribe, not so much as affording full indications, as suggesting in what direction to look for such.

Thus he remarks that in a disease of the brain or nervous system, the forehead, brows, and eyes give the explanation of the ailment.

Morbid conditions of the chest write their signatures on the middle of the face,—especially the nose.

The mouth and the lips, by their change from the customary aspect, show the presence of abdominal affections.

In acute disease of the head, the eyes are fixed and staring, or wild and vacant-looking, while the brows are knit. At one time the pupil may be contracted, and the sick one start as if frightened, and scream aloud on being touched,—or the pupil may be dilated and insensitive to light, while the patient is motionless or unconscious.

When the chest is acutely diseased, the wings of the nose are dilated or in rapid motion.

Again, in acute abdominal disease, the lips are drawn back, so as to show the teeth or gums, while the countenance is pale or sunken.

And doubtless a sufficient amount of observation would detect distinctly marked signs indicative of *every* malady from which man suffers, so that a glance at the face and figure might determine the character and intensity of such malady.

But the self-same law applies not alone to physical diseases, but to what may be called diseases of the mind; that is, excesses of the passions and appetites, whatever their kind. Anger, malice, revenge, and the whole dark brood of the malign elements of the soul, imprint their marks upon the face and form. So plainly, indeed, that the very infant understands and is alarmed and repelled by them. Nor less can the same infant read the kindly affections upon the exterior, and is thus often attracted to the arms of a total stranger. And so winning is the expression of these affections that they often impart what we entitle beauty to a face whose features are irregular almost to deformity. So, too, the malignant passions will cast upon a face which, in its normal state, is supremely beautiful, a shadow that produces on the beholder the effect of veritable ugliness.

It is a wise and beneficent ordination of Providence that the internal dispositions thus stamp themselves on the exterior. For by this means we are warned on the one hand to beware of the base and malicious of heart, and on the other are taught in whom we may securely place our trust.

All the various expressions of which the face and the figure are susceptible are carefully studied by the actor, and his professional skill is measured and his reputation in a great degree determined by the closeness with which he can copy and represent them. It were well that we all were accustomed to observe far more carefully than we do the expressions indicating the propensities and characters of those among whom we live. We might thus be taught whom to avoid and whose acquaintance to cultivate, with much greater certainty than any words could give.

Our purpose in this supplementary chapter has been not so much to impart definite instruction to the reader, as to point out the direction in which such reader may seek it for himself. That the heliographer, as well as all other artists, should make himself familiar with the numerous varieties of expression here indicated, is too obvious to require more than the mere mention.

CHAPTER XXII.

MISCELLANEOUS FACTS.

Peculiarities in the eyes of various individuals; *e. g.* 1st. Incapacity of distinguishing certain colors; 2d. Beholding the same objects of different sizes—Instances in relation to sun and moon—Causes of these anomalies unknown—The subject worth investigation—Expression through names—Various examples among savage tribes—Origin and use of names of whatever kind—Illustrations among both ancients and moderns, *e. g.* Cicero, Cæsar, Scipio, Smith, Brown, White, &c.—Heraldry, with its emblems, due to the same origin.

A FEW items more or less related to subjects discussed in various parts of this volume, I have thought might be interesting enough to deserve recording. They are, therefore, introduced here under the above caption. The first two of them I entitle

OCULAR ANOMALIES.

1. Many of my readers may, perhaps, be aware that some persons are, organically, incapable of distinguishing certain colors. That is, some colors, as, for example, the red, or the green, or the blue, *do not exist for them,*—and, so far as they are concerned, are absolutely blotted out of the prismatic spectrum of the sunbeam. I have even known persons engaged in heliography who had this imperfection of vision. What can be the *cause* of this fact so strangely *exceptional?* The discovery of its *rationale* would be well worthy the attention and the endeavors of experimentists of leisure.

2. Size, proportion, and relation are principles which, in some eyes, would seem to be all ajar.

Thus, the *apparent* bulk of the sun and the moon, so far as we can learn, is, to the average of beholders, pretty nearly the same.

One of my acquaintances, however, a shrewd observer, whose senses have been actively and habitually exercised, as being the avenues whereby the quite extensive knowledge possessed by him has entered his mind, tells me, gravely, that the *sun's disc looks to him as large as a coach-wheel!* That he speaks in perfect sincerity, I have no doubt.

A second acquaintance, not less intelligent and keenly observant than the first—of the same class of mind and mode of education, and belonging to the same sphere in life—assures me that these heavenly bodies wear, to his vision, about the compass of his hat-crown,—their size being, if anything, rather less than greater.

Here are two instances wherein visual organs, to all appearance equally healthful and perfect, utter reports completely clashing,—the defect in the one and the variance in the other flowing from causes entirely unknown.

Is it not both possible and probable that useful results might be attained, were persons possessing the requisite capacity and leisure to take up these subjects and probe them thoroughly?

For one, I have no doubt of the fact.

A third of these items I entitle

EXPRESSION AS INTIMATED BY NAMES.

In one of the chapters of this volume, I speak of the animal races and of the inanimate world as wearing an expression of their own, and this expression a partially *human* one, *i. e.* suggestive of human qualities. I alluded to the customs of savage tribes in the assumption of names or designative titles. Alike from the animate and the inanimate worlds they borrow such appellatives as are fancied by them to symbolize their characters, or some special element or elements of the same.

Thus, in "The Last of the Mohicans" we find, among its personages, "Chingachgook," or "the Serpent," and "Le Cerf Agile," "the Active Stag,"—names significant of certain qualities supposed to characterize those to whom they belonged.

So in Bowen's History of the Indian Tribes, we find "Meomouni," "the Cloud out of which the Rain comes"—"Wakawn," "the Snake"—"Chittee Toholo," "the Snake that makes a Noise"—"Monkaushka," "the Trembling Earth"—"Tooan Tuh," "the Spring Frog," &c., &c.

These are but instances of a principle which, at the outset, was, doubtless, universal and without exceptions. Names being, originally, as matter not only of convenience, but of almost absolute necessity, bestowed in order that individuals might be discriminated one from another while present, or so spoken of in their absence, that it might be known who was meant; it mattered little by *what particular thing* they were signalized, so that all recognised it at the instant of hearing. Again, it was sometimes a feature of face, or a peculiarity of shape or of aspect; sometimes a prominent trait of mind or of heart; sometimes a striking incident in the life; and sometimes the ordinary vocation or pursuit; from which sprang a family name that has endured thousands of years.

Illustrations of this principle might be quoted in abundance from the records of antiquity. I will alude merely to the titles, Cicero, Cæsar, and Scipio. Thus, the immortal orator, Marcus Tullius, is said to have received the cognomen, Cicero, from "cicer," "a bean"—he having been marked on the face with a *bean-shaped wart.*

So, Caius Julius derived the cognomen "Cæsar," from "cæsus," "cut"—in consequence of his having been taken from the womb of his deceased mother by a surgical operation.

Finally, the cognomen "Scipio," subjoined to the family name of an illustrious Roman race, signifies "a staff,"—intimating the important part enacted by this family in upholding the fabric of the state.

Coming down to times comparatively recent, we find the far and wide spread patronymic of Smith. Originally it was one of the most honorable of titles, indicating, in its possessor, one of the most useful of citizens, as well as of the main harbingers of civilization. For it was *the smith* who forged alike the weapons of war for men's defence against their foes; and the implements of the chase, from which they drew, in part, their subsistence; and of agriculture, which constitutes the basis of our present advanced condition.

A host of kindred examples will occur to my reader on a moment's reflection.

Again, in the class of names, of which White, Brown, Green, Black, &c., are specimens, we find a reference to the complexion, or color of the dress, or some one or more particular of the individual's belongings.

In Scott's Rob Roy we have, in the hero's title, Robert the Red,—Roy signifying red,—an allusion to the color of his hair.

So, in Highland Annals, you find "the Black Comyn," "the Red Comyn," &c.,—the prefixes being drawn from the tint of the hair or the complexion.

Once more. In French Chronicles we find "Philip the Fair"—"Louis the Fat"—"Philip Augustus," &c.—

the appellatives having been borrowed from some property either corporeal or mental.

In sum, the total science of heraldry is based on the same principle, *i. e.* the adoption of some *distinctive* emblem which represents or intimates some property of body or mind, or some event in the life of those assuming it, or signalized by it.

How wide-reaching and profound, then, is this subject of expression, may be conjectured from the foregoing hints superadded to the much that is suggested in other parts of this treatise.

Somewhere, however, I must abruptly *make* an end, for the subject itself is all but illimitable.

CHAPTER XXIII.

OPINIONS OF ARTISTS AND ART-CRITICS UPON BEAUTY.

Opinions of artists and art-critics upon beauty, physical, intellectual, moral, and ideal; *e.g.* Phidias, Plato, Cicero, &c., among the ancients; and M. Angelo, Raffaelle, Reynolds, Barry, Opie, Lawrence, Haydon, Cousin, Ruskin, Jeffrey, Alison, Burke, Michelet, &c., among the moderns—Sundry original comments on the same.

In the course of the present volume, it has fallen into the logical sequence of my design to touch, more or less extensively, on art and artists; on beauty, genius, taste; and on expression, light and shadow, composition, and kindred topics, which come naturally under these general heads. In discussing these various points, I have hitherto drawn upon my own observation and experience more largely than upon any resources beside. I have been accustomed, however, in the few leisure hours accorded me, to glance over such volumes of distinguished artists and connoisseurs, as came in my way and dealt with the same subjects as myself, and to transcribe or pencil-mark the passages, which especially struck me as worthy of consideration. These passages have so accumulated on my hands that I have concluded they might add to the value of my book, if arranged in some tolerable order and published with the rest of its contents.

On some of the topics, here referred to, there will be found more or less antagonism of opinions; but instruction and inspiration may be gathered from the clashes of view, and even the errors of men of genius and ability.

So that, with some partial attempts at ranging *like* things under the captions that cover them, I shall present the remarks, as they stand in my commonplace book. And

1st. Beauty,—what is said of it by various individuals, to whom it had been a theme of much contemplation?

Cousin, the eminent French eclectic, has given one of the most thorough and satisfactory analyses of beauty (in my judgment), of any writer I have examined. I will presently note down some of his utterances, after citing from certain others, who came earlier under my eye.

James Barry (the painter) remarks, "It is evident, that beauty and perfection are but different names for the same thing; and consequently the most beautiful form of body must be that, which in all its qualities most perfectly corresponds with the idea we have of its species, of whatever kind, sex, or age.

"But grace is more eminently observable in the female, because her sensibility and tenderness are greater than the male's, and the superior softness and delicacy of her bodily frame is more in unison with those tender sensations."

Says Ruskin, "*Repose* is the most unfailing test of beauty. No work of art can be great without it,—nothing can be ignoble that possesses it, and nothing right that has it not. By this light we shall see three colossal images standing side by side, looming in their great rest of spirituality above the whole world-horizon —Phidias, Michael Angelo, and Dante; and then, separated from their great religious thrones only by less fulness and earnestness of faith, Homer and Shakspeare.

"In all perfectly beautiful objects there is found the opposition of one part to another, and a reciprocal balance obtained.

"The most lovely objects in nature are only partially transparent. The utmost possible sense of beauty is conveyed by a smooth, feebly translucent, but not lustrous, surface of white and pale, warm red, subdued by the purest and most delicate grays, as in the finer portions of the human frame.

"The beauty of the animal form is in exact proportion to the moral and intellectual virtue expressed by it.

"The sources of beauty are not presented by any great work of art in a form of pure transcript or copy. They invariably receive the reflection of the mind under whose shadow they have passed, and are modified or colored by its image.

"Any material object which can give us pleasure in the simple contemplation of its outward qualities, without any direct and definite exertion of the intellect, is, in some way and in some degree, beautiful.

"The artist who would attain beauty, must not at all avoid or slight nature, but must study it profoundly as his most important source of improvement. He must not contemplate merely those beauties which may be presented to his view at the moment, but should also consider wherein they differ from others inferior to them. For example, how beautiful that smile! How eloquent those lips! Let him ask himself what is meant by these qualifying terms."

Asks B. R. Haydon, "What is beauty, without which all our previous principles, exemplified by practice, would fail to enchant the world? No modern artists, not excepting Raffaelle, Correggio, or Michael Angelo, ever equalled the ancients in this quality of face and figure. The ancients seem to have hit exactly what degree of fitness, proportion, unity, curve, and color in nature and art was adapted to excite the emotion of beauty in the human mind, and never to have failed once, down even to the form of a milk-jug.

"It is quite clear that every artist must, by form, by color, by expression—whatever may be the theory—excite the emotion of beauty in his spectators. Sometimes the form and face, which contain virtue, are ugly, like those of Socrates; and sometimes, however detestable sin may be, the most noble, the most heroic, the most beautiful form and face express it, like those of Satan.

"Though beauty may always be applied, morally, to virtue, and ugliness always to vice, yet sometimes the medium between extremes is the cause; and sometimes proportion, fitness, undulation of line, perhaps association from form, color, and expression may as often be the cause,—yet, I maintain, there is something in the form and the color that rouses the emotion of beauty before any association can take place from intellectual expression; and that association is *subsequent* to the first impression on the brain, and not *prior* to it; or co-instantaneous with it, if the impression be the first made on the individual."

Says Lord Jeffrey, "Beauty is that property in objects which is recommended to the power of taste,—the reverse of ugliness,—the primary and most general object of love and admiration."

Haydon remarks, "The more one dwells on the emotions of Beauty, strictly so meant, the more is he inclined to believe that, morally, mentally, and physically, it has its origin altogether in woman. Consider the face and form of woman in its perfection and its associations, as the standard of all beauty, morally or by form;—and, according as every object in nature approaches to or departs from such standard by color, form, or association, the emotion produced by this object is or is not entitled to be considered the emotion of the beautiful, and has ever done so from her first appearance in the world.

"Lord Jeffrey says, 'Men, whose organization is perfect, do not agree about beauty. The question here arises, whether the organization alluded to be that of the eye or the brain? To settle *this* were to settle the whole matter.'

"Thus some men have perfect sight, and yet do not see color or take any delight in it,—others (like myself) have imperfect sight, and yet have the most exquisite sensations from the perception of colors. So a man may have the dullest vision and yet see beauty; and possess the most perfect sight, and yet not see beauty in anything.

"The form of a tree is beautiful; and the form of a fine woman, of a column, and of a vase. 'But' (remarks Jeffrey) 'how can it be said that the form of a woman has anything in common with the form of a tree?'

"Simply because the vase, the column, and the tree, and the woman can be proved to merit the name of beautiful only as they each partake more or less of the womanly form. They are each beautiful through possessing principles in common which excite the emotion by form.

"All love worth anything has been, since the world began, love at first sight.

> 'They have changed eyes, delicate Ariel;
> I'll set thee free for this.'
>
> TEMPEST.

"Surely love at first sight is emotion from beauty *antecedent* to *experience,* or the slightest knowledge of each other's virtues; for the most celebrated lovers have been distinguished for mutual beauty of face and figure, and for instant infatuation.

"Jeffrey denies any organization of brain for the impressions of color, as for those of beauty; and suspects the enthusiasm of great artists for color to be what he terms *jargon.*

"So the intense sensibility to the beauty of color in nature, felt and expressed by Titian, or Rubens, or Paul Veronese, or Tintoretto, or Correggio, or our own Reynolds, was *jargon!*

"The beauty of emotion, independent of expression or association, based on form, is the beauty with which the great artist has to do, and which the Greeks attained in a more perfect degree than any other nation that ever existed.

"Alison denies the existence of any innate beauty in certain constructions and proportions of the human face or figure, and holds that the beauty depends on the expressions they convey.

"I maintain" (says Haydon) "that there is a decided emotion of beauty excited by certain proportions and constructions of the human figure, as well as in brute forms, or forms without life."

"Many countenances" (says Alison) "however beautiful, are not *permanently* so. Domestic harassings destroy them."

"Never" (replies Haydon)—"a face constructively beautiful in form no expression can destroy. Malignity, revenge, anger, hypocrisy, anxiety may vary its expressions, but never destroy its beauty; for you will always find them the bad passions of a beautiful countenance.

"Character, color, expression can never excite the emotion of beauty, if form, the basis, be defective.

"Alison (speaking of Mrs. Siddons) says, 'Every expression, however various, was equally beautiful; and had there been permanent beauty in any *form*, that could not have been the case.'

"But had not the permanent construction of Mrs. Siddons's face been beautiful as it was, none of her various expressions could have been so; for let expression vary a face as it will, again remember they are but the variations of a form perfect in its original formation.

"Beauty consists in something more than the raven locks, the oval, rosy cheeks, the lustrous eye with silken lashes, and the strawberry lip of a lovely woman. Let these be added to a well proportioned or perfectly shaped face, like that of Venus, and we have beauty in reality.

"We do not bestow the term beauty on the Hercules, but on the Apollo,—not on the gladiator, but the Bacchus,—not on the Juno or the Minerva, but the Venus,—because the manly form is never termed beautiful, save as it approaches, without losing its own special characteristics, the tenderness and delicacy of woman's form. In fact, the manly form has nothing essentially beautiful, physically or by association, unless it approaches the form of woman.

"Form alone, independent of mind or intention as expressed by the countenance, has the power to excite this divine emotion of beauty. Else how could the limbs alone of the Elgin marbles, without head or face, have made the hearts of the world vibrate at first sight? Yet proportion, fitness, relation, unity, and perfect construction in any face, form, limb, or vase will *not* excite the emotion of beauty, if the curves of that face, or form, or limb, or vase extend to excess or approach to deficiency. The *elliptic* is the regulating curve in the form and features of a perfect woman.

"When Adam first saw Eve, what *experience* could he

have had of the emotion of beauty from *form?* None And yet such an impression was made by this creature so lovely fair,

> 'That what seemed fair in all the world, seemed now
> Mean, or in her summed up; in her contained;
> And in her looks, which from that time infused
> Sweetness into my heart, unfelt before;
> And into all things from her air inspired
> The spirit of love.'
> 'On she came;
> Grace was in all her steps, Heaven in her eye,
> In every gesture dignity and love.'

"Afterwards Adam might analyze the emotion; but we affirm the object made the impression *first*,—continued to make, and will continue to make the impression on all future generations; and the impression so made is the emotion of beauty.

"Though convinced that the basis of beauty is the form of woman, yet the emotion, as explained, may be illustrated by two divisions:—

"1st. Beauty purely intellectual, which is not excited through the organ of sight at the instant, but by association and memory of previous impressions.

"2d. Beauty purely physical, where the impression is made by form and color at once on the brain by the nerve and through the eye, independent of all association.

"Finally, everything in the world which causes the emotion of beauty, and can be positively defined by form and color, we would call the beauty physical, which by its construction first makes the impression on the brain; and subsequently excites the association and belongs to the art of design,—while all beauty which excites the emotion by the association and relation presented to the imagination, and is not at the moment present to the sight, we would call the beauty intellectual.

"In both cases nothing is beautiful, physically or intellectually, in thought or in form, but what has a feminine tendency, and can be traced to the perfection in form and sympathies of woman; while all emotions of sublimity are based on the attributes and associations of God.

"A great part of the beauty of the celebrated description of Eve, in Paradise Lost, consists in using only general, indistinct expressions, every reader making out the detail according to his own particular imagination; his own idea of beauty, grace, expression, dignity, or loveliness. But a painter, when representing Eve on canvas, is obliged to give a determinate form, and his own idea of beauty distinctly expressed."

Michelet remarks, "Titian preferred to paint beautiful women at thirty. Rubens goes readily up to forty, and even beyond.

"Van Dyck does not recognise age at all; with him art is free. He held a sovereign contempt for time.

"That powerful magician, Rembrandt, does more; by a gesture, a word, a look, a smile, he banishes all age. The life, the goodness, and the intelligence suffice to charm us. What was the model? Beautiful and adorable? I do not remember,—I have entirely forgotten.

"By the ignorant Medieval art youth and beauty were held as synonymous. For the Mother of Christ it gives us stiff, insipid little girls.

"The conception of beauty always involves a mental impression or action. Exclude feeling and thought, and no place will be found for beauty. An able writer says, 'It will be a convenient and natural arrangement of the subject to consider beauty in relation, 1st, to sensation,—2d to thought or reflection,—3d, to moral sentiments,—

and 4th, to associated emotions. Conclude with a few remarks on the uses of beauty.'

"In its simplest essence beauty is best defined by the Bible phrase, 'pleasant to the eye.' Visual pleasure is the germinal form of beauty. 'Truly the light is sweet, and a pleasant thing it is for the eyes to behold the sun.'

"But the word receives far more extensive and complex applications. By the transitions of language it often expresses that of which visual pleasure is no component, or a very small one. An infant's delight in a brilliant object, or some vivid color, illustrates the simplest form of beauty.

"The mother, looking fondly at the infant's smiling face, and hearing its crow of joy, has a more compact feeling of the beautiful.

"A philosopher, watching the two, exclaims, 'What *beautiful* illustrations of my theory!'—using the epithet partly in its metaphorical sense, but *also* in expression of a kind of beauty, viz., that of *fitness*.

The *symmetrical* beauty of the human face and head is mainly dependent on the bony structures. The beauty of *expression*, or the beauty belonging to variety, results from the action of the muscles in the play of the features.

"The importance of the human figure, as a type of beauty, has in all times been recognised. Vitruvius says, 'No building can possess the attributes of composition, in which symmetry and proportion are disregarded; nor unless there exists that perfect conformation of parts which may be observed in a well-formed human being. So the members of architecture may be said to depend, in a certain sense, on those of the human body.' The chief characteristic of the typical female form being pure and simple beauty, while that of the typical male form is beauty modified by massive strength, the basis on which each of the figures is constructed, might be presumed to have reference to the sensations it would awaken, the one of loveliness, the other of strength; yet the relative proportions of the parts in each case ought to develope the same æsthetic laws, though in different modes. Such are the properties of *fitness* which characterize the beauty of the Venus as compared with that of the Hercules of the ancients, and render these statues the perfect types of the sexes.

"How are we to account for the fact, that if a face, though defective in symmetry and contour, is expressive of certain mental states of emotion, it is universally preferred to one, which is faultlessly *regular*, but wanting in *expressiveness?*

"The answer is, that in a human being we require more than a fine configuration of feature; we desire certain qualities of heart and mind, indicated in what we term a *pleasing* as distinguished from a *beautiful* face. In saying that *this* is the more *beautiful, that* the more *pleasing* face, we imply that we prefer the beauty of *emotion,* or mind, to that of *sense,*—yet still we unconsciously refer to a standard of beauty involving the idea of symmetry or harmonious color. The face which is *pleasing* in expression is (we say) *beautiful* in expression. We have pleasure in both; though a greater pleasure in the expressive one. But that which we characterize as beautiful *par excellence,* is that which is of a certain mould or color. The pleasure, however, which is derived from mere physical beauty of face, can never compete with that which is an indication of beauty of character."

Cousin remarks, "Is it not an incontestable fact, that before certain objects, under very different circumstances, we pronounce the following judgment?—This object is beautiful. This affirmation is not always explicit. Sometimes it manifests itself only by a cry of admiration; sometimes it silently rises in the mind that scarcely has a consciousness of it. The forms of this phenomenon vary, but the phenomenon itself is attested by the most common and most certain observation, and all languages bear witness to it.

"But, although sensible objects, with most men, oftenest provoke the judgment of the beautiful, they do not *alone* possess this advantage; the domain of beauty is more extensive than the domain of the physical world exposed to our view; it has no bounds but those of entire nature and of the soul and genius of man.

"Among *sensible* objects, colors, sounds, figures, movements, are capable of producing the idea and the sentiment of the beautiful. All these beauties are arranged under that species of beauty which (right or wrong) is called *physical beauty.*

"If from the world of sense we elevate ourselves to that of mind, truth, and science, we shall there find beauties more severe, but not less real. The universal laws that govern bodies; those that govern intelligences; the great principles that contain and produce long deductions; the genius that creates, in the artist, poet, or philosopher,—all these are beautiful, as well as nature herself; this is what is called *intellectual beauty.*

"Finally, if we consider the moral world and its laws,—the idea of liberty, virtue, and devotedness; here the austere justice of an Aristides, there the heroism of a Leonidas, the prodigies of charity or patriotism, we shall certainly find a third order of beauty that still surpasses the other two,—to wit, *moral beauty.*

"Physical beauty, however, is the sign of an *internal* beauty, which is spiritual and moral beauty;—and this is the foundation, the principle, the unity of the beautiful.

"As often as you give birth within me to the idea of the beautiful, you give me an internal and exquisite joy, always followed by a sentiment of *love* for the object that caused it. The more beautiful an object is, the more lively is the joy it gives the soul, and the more profound is the love, without being passionate.

"The beauty of woman has settled and unsettled the affairs of empires and the fate of republics, when diplomacy and the sword have proved futile.

"Certainly" (observes Lucian) "more women have obtained honor for their beauty, than for all other virtues besides."

"And Tasso has said, that 'beauty and grace are the power and arms of a woman;' while Ariosto declares, that 'after every other gift of arms had been exhausted on man, there remained for woman only beauty, the most victorious of the whole.' There is a great and terrible testimony to the power of female beauty in the history which Homer gives us of Helen."

Says the poet,

> "Fair tresses man's imperial race ensnare,
> And Beauty draws us by a single hair."

"But where are we to detect this especial source of power in beauty? Often, forsooth, in a dimple,—sometimes beneath the shade of an eyelid,—or perhaps among the tresses of a little fantastic curl!

"How often have we wept with affection over a lock of hair, or some such dear memento of a departed friend!

"With what loving devotion the heart cleaves to the

slightest thing, that brings back to us a name hallowed in our affections!"

Fuseli says, "A genuine perception of beauty is the highest degree of education, the ultimate polish of man, the master-key of the mind; it makes us better than we were before. Elevated or charmed by the contemplation of superior works of art, our mind passes from the images themselves to their authors; and from them to the race which reared the powers that furnish us with models for imitation or multiply our pleasures."

Thus far we have transcribed the utterances of sundry eminent men upon various classes of beauty, which may be brought under the single head of *real beauty.* It remains, that we cite a few passages upon what goes by the title of

IDEAL BEAUTY.

And here let Cousin first speak. "All the beauties hitherto enumerated, compose what is called the *really* beautiful. But above real beauty is a beauty of another order—ideal beauty. The ideal resides neither in an individual, nor in a collection of individuals. Nature or experience furnishes us the *occasion* of conceiving it, but it is essentially distinct. Let it once be conceived, and then all natural figures, though never so beautiful, are only *images* of a superior beauty, which they do not *realize.* For the Ideal constantly recedes, as we approach it. Its last termination is in the Infinite, that is to say, in God,—or, to speak more correctly, the true and absolute Ideal is nothing else than God Himself."

Plato's remarks upon this species of beauty may wear somewhat of a mystical aspect, but will, I think, reward the reader's careful consideration. They are as follows:

"Eternal beauty, unbegotten and imperishable; exempt from decay as well as increase; which is not beautiful in such a part and ugly in such another; not beautiful only at such a time, in such a place, in such a relation; not beautiful for some and ugly for others; beauty that has no sensible form, no visage, no hands, nothing corporeal; which is not such a thought, or such a particular science; which resides not in any being different from itself, as an animal, the earth, or the heavens, or any other thing; which is absolutely identical and invariable by itself; in which all other beauties participate, though in such a way that their birth or their destruction neither diminishes nor increases, nor at all changes it.

"In order to arrive at this perfect beauty it is necessary to *commence* with the beauties of this lower world; and, the eyes being fixed upon the supreme beauty, to elevate ourselves unceasingly towards it by passing (so to speak) through all the degrees of the scale, from a single beautiful body to two, from two to all others; from beautiful bodies to beautiful sentiments; from beautiful sentiments to beautiful thoughts; until from thought to thought we arrive at the highest thought, which has no other object than the beautiful itself, until we end by knowing it as it is in itself. O, that which can give value to this life is the spectacle of the eternal beauty. What would be the destiny of a mortal to whom it should be granted to contemplate the beautiful without alloy in its purity and simplicity; no longer clothed with the flesh and hues of humanity, and with all those vain charms that are doomed to perish; to whom it should be given to see face to face, under its sole form, the *Divine Beauty?*"

To this passage from Plato's "Banquet" I subjoin the following from his Timæus:—

"The artist who, with eye fixed upon the Immutable Being, and using such a model, reproduces its idea and its excellence, cannot fail to produce a whole whose beauty is complete; while he, who fixes his eye upon what is transitory, will, with this perishable model, make nothing beautiful."

Cicero, in his De Oratore, referring to the same subject, says, "Phidias, that great artist, when he made the form of Jupiter or Minerva, did not contemplate a model, whose resemblance he would express; but in the depth of his soul resided a perfect type of beauty upon which he fixed his look, and which guided his hand and his art."

Ruskin remarks, "An ideal form, in the common use of the term, is one containing all or most of the fully developed types or characters of its species.

"Strictly speaking, ideal works of art represent the results of acts of imagination.

"A perfect ideal may be wrought out of every face around us by the earnest study and penetration of the written history thereon, and the banishing of the blots and stains, wherein we still see, in all that is human, the visible and instant operation of unconquered sin."

"Every natural object," (says Cousin) "however beautiful, is defective on some side. Everything that is real is imperfect. *Here* the horrible and the hideous are united to the sublime,—*there* elegance and grace are separated from grandeur and force. The traits of beauty are scattered and diverse. To re-unite them arbitrarily; to borrow from such a face a mouth, eyes from such another, without any rule that shall govern this choice and direct these borrowings, is to compose monsters; to admit a rule is already to admit an ideal different from all individuals. It is this ideal that the true artist forms to himself in studying nature. Without nature he would never have conceived this ideal,—but with this ideal he judges nature herself; rectifies her; and dares undertake to measure himself with her.

"It is difficult to sketch an infallible standard of a beautiful woman. Canova was obliged to have sixty different women sit for his Venus; and how shall we dare point to any one woman, and say that she is perfectly beautiful?

"When Zeuxis drew his famous picture of Helen, he modelled his portrait from the separate charms of five different virgins.

"The process, which Raphael says he pursued in painting his Galatea was this,—'I am destitute of beautiful *models*,—I use a certain ideal, which I form for myself.'"

Says Proclus, "He who takes for his models such forms merely as nature produces, will never attain perfection; for the works of nature are full of dissonances and disproportion, and fall very short of the true standard of beauty. On this account Demetrius was blamed for being too natural, and Dionysius was ironically called the man-painter. Lysippus, on the contrary, adhering to the precept of Aristotle, given to painters and poets, boasted that he made men, not as they were, but as they ought to be; and Phidias astonished all those who beheld the forms he gave to his gods and heroes, not, according to Cicero, by copying any object ever presented to his sight, but by contemplating the more perfect idea of beauty in his mind, to the imitation of which all his skill and labor were directed.

"From this care to advance their art even beyond nature itself in its individual productions, arises that admiration, that almost adoration, which is paid by all competent judges to those divine remains of antiquity which have come down to us. Hence Phidias, Lysippus and other great sculptors are still held in veneration; and Apelles, Zeuxis, and other excellent painters, though their works have perished, are and for ever will be admired."

COMMENTS ON THE FOREGOING.

I trust it may not seem presumptuous, if I present a few remarks of my own upon the foregoing citations, and the interesting subject to which they relate.

They indicate, it will be perceived, that somewhat different theories exist among artists and art-critics, as to what beauty *is*, and how the impression of beauty is stamped upon our minds. Some hold that in certain objects, of both the physical and the spiritual worlds, there is a property which produces this impression *directly* and antecedently to all analysis or association. That these are right in their views,—at least in a great degree,—I have no doubt.

Others maintain that beauty is altogether a matter of association; or that one object is beautiful and another ugly solely in consequence of certain ideas or feelings which have become connected with them,—as pleasure or pain, or whatever else. That these persons are in error,—partially, at all events,—I feel confident. Equally confident, however, do I feel that, in regard to what are entitled intellectual and moral beauty, their views are mainly if not entirely correct. For, from the very nature of the case, the capacity of discerning and enjoying these two species of the beautiful implies somewhat of cultivation and mental development; and the unavoidable result of cultivation is to environ our *primary* ideas and feelings with a multiplicity of *secondary* or *associate* ideas and feelings.

Still more determinately is the capability to perceive and delight in ideal beauty the fruit of high culture,—a culture, too, which has produced, to a more than average degree, a *harmonious* development of the several elements of our complex nature.

It has occurred to me, that by passing, in *reverse* order, through the process whereby (according to Plato) the perception of ideal beauty is attained; that is, by *descending* from God into material nature, instead of *ascending* from material nature to God,—we might reach a theory, or at least a conception, of the beautiful, which would conciliate present antagonisms and divergencies of opinion on the subject, and exhibit the whole matter in a simpler, compacter form, than is anywhere found in the books. Let me, albeit with much diffidence, try the experiment.

What, then, is the *ultimate* source of beauty? Undeniably for beauty, as for all things conceivable else, that source is to be found in God. Beauty, therefore, is one of the Divine manifestations. Thus contemplated, it stands on the same footing with the Power manifested in the primal creation and the continuous upholding and regulation of the universe,—with the wisdom that adapts infallible methods and means to the accomplishment of the fittest ends,—with the benevolence, goodness, or love that has devised such multitudinous provisions for the welfare and enjoyment of all living creatures,—and with numerous other of the Divine attributes which, without specifying, will at once occur to all. All these alike exhibit,—and may we not reverently suppose it to be one at least of their main *purposes* to exhibit to ourselves, in such modes and degrees as our finite, imperfect natures can comprehend,—the character and will of the unseen, yet omnipresent, Author of universal life?

Were it worth the while to go into minute analysis, we might query whether beauty be not one of the modifications or forms assumed by the Divine benevolence or love, since its specific effect is to delight, elevate, better its percipients,—and how could we more exactly describe the intent of the Divine Benignity, than in these self-same terms?

The whole boundless universe, material and spiritual, —what is it but an aggregate of means whereby the Deity is revealed to His creatures,—a mirror that reflects with greater or less distinctness and completeness His image? For the life that is in the material creation; in the animal kingdom; and in human kind, is alike a perpetual influx from Him, and traces of his character are plainly discernible throughout each and all. In that quality of physical things which gives us that delightful impression which we call beauty,—what do we behold but one aspect of His nature?

Again, in those entities of the spiritual universe which inspire the still more delightful and august sentiments, which we name intellectual and moral beauty,—what do we perceive other than the self-same aspect or element of the Divine Nature disclosed more fully and by modes differing from the former?

And, finally, what is ideal beauty, but the same characteristic of the Universal Father, shown us through a *specific operation* of those human minds which He spake into being, fashioned to be *what they* are, and continually inspires to "go up higher and still higher?"

It is not presumed that in this view there is anything wholly new,—far less, anything at all brilliant. To myself, however, it seems to have at least the single advantage of placing the whole matter in an easily comprehensible shape. I cannot but look upon the majority of the discussions we meet with about the origin and nature of the Beautiful, as fruitless and even idle. For if it be, as I think it is, a fact that all or nearly all persons of well-tempered native faculties, whether educated or uneducated, *agree* in calling a rose, or pine tree, or a certain type of animal form, or of human face, beautiful, —and thus agree *because* these objects make substantially the same impression upon them all,—what *practical* difference does it make whether that impression is derived from the objects *directly* and "at first hand," or whether it comes from certain *collateral* ideas, unconsciously associated with the objects in the minds of the beholders? In either case, the great fact remains undeniable, that the *cause* of the impression, whatever it be, is *from* and *in* the ultimate Cause of all existences, and that beauty is one of His manifestations.

The question whether *physical* beauty be not the envelope or reflection of a higher or spiritual beauty, appears to me no question at all. For what are, what can be, all physical entities, but embodiments and representations of entities spiritual? The former could no more subsist without an ever indwelling, universally perfused spiritual life, than the human body could subsist without its in-living soul.

So, by certain causes, certain impressions are made upon us, which we variously denominate intellectual, moral, and ideal beauty. What matters it whether these causes be *simple* or *complex*,—made up of *primary* elements, or of primary combined with secondary or associate elements? It still remains a truth that these causes, be they what they may, are from the Infinite of causes, and are representations or manifestations of the same.

To sum up, with somewhat of reiteration. The total universe, with its infinitely diverse existences, is, of necessity, an aggregation of methods and means, whereby the character and will of the Creator are expressed to us. Beauty is the name we have agreed to affix to *one* of these expressions; and as the universe comprises the three elements of physical, intellectual, and moral, this expression must needs appear in all the three.

A thousand questions, indeed, may be, as they have been, raised by perverted metaphysics upon this subject, and argued without hope of solution. But for their contestants, as for all beside, the great verity stands untouched, that beauty *is*,—that it appears in each of the several kingdoms composing the universe,—and that as these kingdoms come from God, beauty must necessarily be one among the multitudinous modes of Divine manifestation.

The question about the best means and appliances for *expressing* beauty in art is a totally different one. How to use lines, colors, lights and shades, &c., may properly occupy the attention of artists and art-critics, for investigation and reiterated experiment can alone solve the problem.

But the question here considered is wholly as to the origin and quality of beauty; and this, I think, may best be answered by going directly to the Author of existence, and beholding, in all that *is*, an aggregate of expressions of Himself. Power, wisdom, goodness, mercy,—these attributes of Divinity may be clearly traced through the moral, intellectual, and physical kingdoms. Not less clearly through the same kingdoms may beauty be traced. And for myself, at least, this account of beauty, its origin and nature, abundantly suffices.

CHAPTER XXIV.

ART, WITH ITS INCIDENTS AND BELONGINGS.

Opinions of ancient and modern writers on the same—Sublimity and Beauty, for art-purposes, comprised by the latter term: Ruskin, Grace Darling, Florence Nightingale, Cousin, Symonds—Remarks on Genius: Reynolds, Fuseli, Haydon—Imagination, Invention, Passion, Taste: Ruskin, Burke—Drawing or Design: Fuseli, Barry—Grace: Allston—Repose: Ruskin, Michelet—Composition: Ruskin, Haydon—Color: Opie, Fuseli—Symmetry: Symonds—Light and Shadow: Quintilian, Reynolds, &c., Ovid—Expression: Reynolds, Du Piles, Lawrence, Curran, Stuart, Trumbull, Inman, Bell, Aristides, Timanthes, Stothard, &c.—Portrait: Howard, Northcote, &c.—Sculpture: Agesander, Barry, Haydon, Allston, &c.

In attempting to bring the miscellaneous remarks of various distinguished persons, collected in my leisure moments, into such partial order, at least, as might make them more useful to the reflective reader, it seemed to me most logical to put the paragraphs on beauty at the head of the series. For, rigorously speaking, beauty furnishes alike the field *in* which, and the materials *with* which, art works. To describe, then, what beauty *is*, naturally precedes the description of what art *is*, and what it *does* or *aims* to do.

And here let me offer a suggestion for which I cannot cite chapter and verse, and therefore must merely ask that it pass for what it may seem *intrinsically* worth. It is this, that the terms sublime and beautiful, though, in popular use, they may denote different things, should, in the highest generalization, and in the view of high art, be held to denote only different branches or degrees of the one great total of beauty. For, as a general rule, the perception of beauty gives pleasure or delight of some species. So, also and equally, does the perception of sublimity. Therefore it is, that men *enjoy* whatever embraces either of these elements. But the pleasure derived from the sublime differs from that caused by the beautiful, certainly in *degree*, and, perhaps, in kind. It is commonly more absorbing and overmastering, tinged with awe, and not seldom with terror. Still, both are alike characterized as being sources of enjoyment, and therefore both are subjects of art.

Note, too, how in poetic, and even in ordinary speech, the epithets denoting the one are, interchangeably, often applied to the other. Thus, we speak of the "*awful beauty*" of a thunder-storm or a tempest-vexed ocean,—two scenes familiarly cited as examples of the sublime. Again,

> "And if the *freshening sea*
> Made them a *terror*, 'twas a *pleasing fear*;
> For I was, as it were, a child of thee,
> And sported with thy billows, far and near;"

says Byron, in his celebrated Address to the Ocean.

"Pleasing fear" is a phrase *combining* the two several emotions produced by beauty and sublimity, as these terms are popularly understood. They fully substantiate my suggestion above made.

A passage just lighted upon in Ruskin, goes far to confirm my view. "Sublimity is not a *specific* term,—not a term descriptive of the effect of a *particular class* of ideas. Anything which *elevates* the mind is sublime, and elevation of mind is produced by the contemplation of *greatness* of any kind; but chiefly, of course, by the greatness of the *noblest* things. Sublimity is, therefore, only another word for the *effect* of *greatness* upon the *feelings.* Greatness of matter, space, power, virtue, or beauty, are thus *all sublime;* and there is, perhaps, no desirable quality of a work of art, which, in its perfection, is not, in some way or degree, sublime."

Sublimity, then, according to this ablest of present art-critics, is beauty in a high, or the highest, *degree.* The devotion of Leonidas and his three hundred, at Thermopylæ, was heroic, *i. e.* great, noble in the highest degree, and, *therefore,* sublime. But can any one deny that the devotion of those heroes was not *also* beautiful? Beautiful? Why, it was beauty in its very essence; a consecration to *principle,* to what was believed right, which, at the distance of 3000 years, inspires a *pleasure* glistening through tears, that, instead of *enervating,* kindles an *emulative* desire to follow, under such conditions as are furnished, so glorious a leading!

Grace Darling,—Florence Nightingale,—their deeds, under the circumstances, were sublime—but were they not beautiful? Yes, they were sublimely beautful—*i. e.* beautiful in an exalted degree.

I might illustrate by examples numberless; but these (I think) will suffice to show that, for purposes of art at least, what are commonly termed the sublime and the beautiful, both fall under the single designation of beauty,—and that, therefore, we may philosophically say that beauty is the domain of art.

Cousin remarks, "The sole object of art is the beautiful. Art abandons itself as soon as it shuns this.

"The arts are called the fine arts, because their sole object is to produce the disinterested emotion of beauty, without regard to the utility either of the spectator or the artist.

"The problem of art is to reach the soul through the body. Art offers to the senses, forms, colors, sounds, words, so arranged, that they excite in the soul concealed behind the senses, the inexpressible emotion of beauty.

"Art is the free reproduction of the beautiful; not of a *single* natural beauty, but of ideal beauty, as the human imagination conceives it by the aid of data, which nature furnishes it. The ideal beauty envelops the infinite;—the end of art, then, is to produce works that, like those of nature, or even in a still higher degree, may have the charm of the Infinite.

"Every work of art, whatever may be its form, small or great, figured, sung, or uttered,—every work of art, truly beautiful or sublime, throws the soul into a gentle or severe revery, that elevates it towards the Infinite."

Symonds says, "Art is inclusive of nature. It is nature, and something more. Nature is substance existing in certain forms and modes and conditions of being, full of forces, which are latent or actively at work,—and man is in the midst of them. If he is content with nature *as he finds it,* he is a dwarfed, undeveloped being. But it is not so; for it is obvious, that there ever arises in his mind a dissatisfaction with the world about him. He has capacities of enjoyment, which this rude, uninformed nature will not satisfy; his thoughts grow, and nature is compelled to grow in co-ordination with his thoughts. Hence arises art."

Cousin says, "Let us be thoroughly penetrated by the thought, that art is to itself a kind of religion. God manifests Himself to us by the idea of the True, by the idea of the Good, by the idea of the Beautiful. Each one of these leads to God, because it comes from him. True beauty is ideal beauty, and ideal beauty is a reflection of the Infinite. So, independently of all official alliance with religion and morals, art is by itself essentially religious and moral; for, far from wanting its own law.

its own genius, it everywhere expresses in its works eternal beauty."

(I may here remark, that most of the passages in this collection, though applicable, to a certain extent, to the whole five of what are usually reckoned the fine arts, viz. painting, sculpture, architecture, poetry, and music, yet have a more particular reference to the first two of these.)

Cousin says, "The arts have a common end, and entirely different means. Hence there are general rules common to all, and particular rules to each."

The foregoing paragraphs must suffice for the present as brief, specific definitions or descriptions by standard writers of the nature, origin, and objects of art. These points will be found more fully dealt with further on in the accounts of and remarks upon various artists which are there cited.

It remains here to cite sundry passages upon what I have entitled the incidents or belongings of art,—in other phrase, the powers, means, and appliances employed therein. And

1. GENIUS.

Reynolds (Sir Joshua) remarks, "Genius is supposed to be the power of producing excellencies which are beyond the reach of the rules of art,—a power which no precepts can teach and no industry acquire. When the arts were in their infancy, the power of merely drawing the likeness of any object was considered one of its greatest efforts. The common people, ignorant of the principles of art, employ a similar language to this day.

"When, however, it is found that most men may be taught to do this, it should be remembered that it is the man of genius only who excels in invention, expression dignity, and grace,—in short, those qualities or excellencies, the power of producing which cannot be taught by any promulgated or known rules.

"What is now entitled genius begins not where rules, abstractly considered, end, but where the trite and vulgar rules heretofore in vogue have no longer any place.

"When an artist is sure that he is upon firm ground, supported by the authority and practice of his predecessors, of the greatest reputation, he may then assume the boldness and intrepidity of genius."

Says Beechey, "The painter of genius first masters the subject he is to represent by reading or other means, and then works his imagination up into a species of enthusiasm, till in a degree he perceives the whole event before his eyes; when, as with the quickness of lightning, he puts his rough sketch on paper or canvas. By consequence his work has the air of genius stamped upon it; while the contrary method of proceeding will inevitably result in tameness, and produce pictures wearing the semblance of mere copies.

"Genius is mainly exerted upon historical subjects, and the art of the portrait-painter is often lost in the obscurity of his subject."

Says Reynolds, "A readiness in taking such hints as escape the dull and ignorant makes, in my opinion, no inconsiderable part of that mental faculty which is called genius."

Fuseli says, "It is the lot of genius to be opposed, and to be invigorated by opposition. All extremes touch each other; frigid praise and frigid censure wait on easily attainable or common powers; but the successful adventurer in the realms of discovery, in spite of the shrugs, checks, and sneers of the timid, the malign, and the envious, leaps on an unknown or long-lost shore, ennobles it with his name, and grasps immortality.

"Genius is the pupil of nature; perceives, is dazzled, and imperfectly transmits one of her features; thus saw Michael Angelo, Raffaelle, Titian, Correggio. We find Michael Angelo more sublime, but we sympathize more with Raffaelle. When Reynolds said that M. Angelo had more imagination, and Raffaelle more fancy, he meant to say that the one had more sublimity, more elementary fire; the other was richer in social imagery, in genial conceits, and artificial variety. Simplicity is the stamen of M. Angelo; varied propriety that of Raffaelle."

Says Henry Howard, "The principles of the fine arts exist originally in the deep recesses of our nature, waiting for genius to discover and apply them."

Haydon remarks, "The theory of Reynolds was that of the Johnsonian period, though Burke was a living thunderbolt of refutation. Johnson said, 'Genius was nothing but a mind of large *general* powers, accidentally determined to some particular object,'—and Madame de Stael, in Corinne, said that 'genius was only the ordinary faculties of us all carried to a greater pitch of refinement than most men possess them;—but neither theory goes far enough; genius is a natural and not an acquired power which accident develops but cannot create."

Says Cousin, "Genius alone has the power to convert conceptions into creations. Genius creates,—it does not imitate. But genius, it may be said, is then superior to nature, since it does not imitate it, and nature is the work of God. No—genius is not the rival of God, but it is the interpreter of Him. Doubtless in one sense art is an imitation, for *absolute* creation belongs to God alone.

"Art being the free reproduction of beauty, the power

in us capable of reproducing it is called genius. Genius is essentially the power of doing, of inventing, of creating."

Says Fuseli, "By genius I mean that power, which enlarges the circle of human knowledge; which discovers new materials of nature, or combines the known with novelty; while *talent* arranges, cultivates, polishes the discoveries of genius."

Says Cousin, "Genius is nothing else than taste in action; that is to say, the three powers of taste carried to their culmination, and armed with a new and mysterious power,—the power of execution.

"The habit of contemplating and brooding over the ideas of great geniuses, till you find yourself warmed by the contact, is the true method of forming an artist-like mind. It is impossible, in the presence of those great men, to think or invent in a *mean* manner. A state of mind is acquired, that accepts those ideas only, which relish of grandeur and simplicity."

We will next present a few paragraphs upon another of the intellectual faculties employed in art, viz.

2. IMAGINATION.

Ruskin remarks, "The imagination has three totally distinct functions:—

"1st. It combines, and by combination creates new forms.

"2d. It treats or regards both the simple images and its own combinations in peculiar ways.

"3d. It penetrates, analyzes, and reaches truths discoverable by no other faculty.

"Whatever portions of a picture are taken honestly and without alteration from nature have, so far as they go, the *look* of imagination, because all that nature does is *imaginative,—i. e.,* perfect as a whole, and made up of imperfect features.

"Claude was almost wholly unimaginative, and depended on a painful but untaught study of nature. He had much feeling for abstract beauty of form, though none for harmony of expression.

"Gaspar Poussin had the same want of imagination, disguised by more masculine qualities of mind and grander reachings after sympathy.

"In Salvator Rosa the imagination is vigorous, and the composition dexterous and clever,—all, however, rendered valueless by coarseness of feeling and habitual non-reference to nature.

"Nicolo Poussin is always imaginative in landscape; but Tintoret and Titian are unapproachable in this power.

"A sure test of an imaginative work is, that it always looks as if it had been gathered straight from nature.

"Imagination never deigns to touch anything but truth; and of this we may be assured, that where there is an appearance of falsehood, the imagination has had no hand.

"The virtue of the imagination is its reaching, by intuition and intensity of gaze, a more essential truth than is seen at the surface of things.

"The first and noblest use of imagination is to enable us to bring sensibly to our sight the things which are recorded as belonging to our future state, or as invisibly surrounding us in this.

"Its second and ordinary use is to empower us to traverse the scenes of all other history, and force the facts to become again visible, so as to make upon us the same impression which they would have made if we had witnessed them; and in the minor necessities of life, to enable us, out of any present good, to gather the utmost measure of enjoyment, by investing it with happy associations, and in any present evil, to lighten it by summoning back the images of other hours; and also to give to all mental truths some visible type in allegory, simile, or personification which shall more deeply enforce them; and, finally, when the mind is utterly outwearied, to refresh it with such innocent play as shall be most in harmony with the suggestive voices of natural things, permitting it to possess living companionship instead of silent beauty, and create for itself fairies in the grass and naiads in the wave."

Says Reynolds, "Those who depend on a native vigor of imagination, generally burst forth at once in fulness of beauty. Of this Homer, probably, and Shakspeare more assuredly, are signal examples. M. Angelo possessed the poetic part of our art in a most eminent degree. We will not say that M. Angelo was eminently poetic *only* because he was greatly mechanical; but we are sure that mechanic excellence invigorated and emboldened his mind to carry painting into the regions of poetry, and to emulate that art in its most adventurous flights. M. Angelo possessed both qualifications equally."

Says Ruskin, "The play and power of imagination depend altogether on our being able to forget ourselves, and enter, like possessing spirits, into the bodies of things about us.

"The most imaginative men always study the hardest, and are the most thirsty for new knowledge."

Says Haydon, "If you have genius, the whole will flash upon that 'inward eye which is the bliss of solitude,' with the object you have in view in selecting it; the principal figure to express it; the line it makes;

the color to convey the story delightfully; and the light and shadow to develop the masses clearly."

Says Ruskin, "The imagination sees the heart and inner nature, and makes them felt; but is often obscure, mysterious, and interrupted in its giving of outer detail."

3. INVENTION.

Under this head we shall give but a few brief citations, and these contain little more than definitions of the term. Our space will allow no more.

Fuseli says, "To *invent* is to *find;* to find something presupposes its existence somewhere, implicitly or explicitly, scattered or in a mass.

"The element and realm of invention are form, in its widest meaning,—the visible universe enveloping our senses,—and the invisible one that agitates our minds with visions begotten by fancy on sense."

Ruskin says, "One characteristic of *great* art is, that it must be *inventive,*—that is, produced by the imagination. It must not only present grounds for noble emotion, but furnish these grounds by *imaginative power.*"

Reynolds says, "Invention is one of the great tokens of genius; but, if we consult experience, we shall find that we learn to invent by being conversant with the inventions of others, as, by reading the thoughts of others, we learn to think."

Says Haydon, "If an expression must be seen before it can be done, there is an end of invention. There is an end, too, of all the petty and thoughtless presumption of portrait-painters' placing their art for a moment on a level with high art.

"The greatest art in practice is the art of using nature for poetical invention. This is intuitive, and cannot be communicated by words or deduction. It is visible in the very first productions of a youth. It must not be too individual. It must be like nature, and not too much like nature. It must be nature restored to her essential properties, and nothing more or less."

Says Opie, "The study of excellent works of every class is a certain way, to improve if not to create an *inventive* faculty; and I have no doubt that a person comparatively poor in natural gifts, who steadily pursues his purpose; examines engravings and paintings; reads works on art; and uses all the means open to him; would soon eclipse the strongest in native ability, who neglects the same and trusts to himself alone,—for whether we will it or no, nine hundred and ninety-nine out of a thousand of our thoughts are necessarily suggested by the works of others."

4. PASSION.

Ruskin remarks, "The use and value of passion are not as a subject of contemplation in itself, but as it breaks up the fountains of the 'great deep' of the human mind, or displays its mightiness and ribbed majesty; as mountains are best seen in their stability among the coil of clouds.

"In a picture, all grief that convulses the features is ignoble, because it is commonly shallow, and certainly temporary, as in children; though in the shock and shiver of a strong man's features, under sudden and violent grief, there may be something of sublime."

5. TASTE.

Ruskin says, "Perfect taste is the faculty of receiving the greatest possible pleasure from those material sources which are attractive to our moral nature in its purity and perfection. He who receives little pleasure from these sources wants taste; he who receives pleasure from any other sources has false or bad taste."

Barry remarks, "The term taste, as applied to objects of vision, is a metaphor taken from our corporeal sense of tasting; and thus used, means that quick-discerning faculty or power of mind by which we accurately distinguish the good, bad, and indifferent; the beauty or deformity either in nature or in the arts which imitate nature. It is a necessary ingredient not only in the design of the great artist, but also in the judgment of an intelligent observer."

Burke says, "Taste is that faculty or faculties of the mind which are affected by or form a judgment of the works of imagination or the elegant arts."

Reynolds says, "The natural appetite of the human mind is for truth. It is the same taste which relishes a demonstration in geometry; which is pleased with the resemblance of a picture to the original, and with the harmony of music."

Upon this passage Haydon remarks, "It is *not* the same taste which relishes a demonstration in geometry; the harmony of music; or the beauty of a picture; but a very different taste. It may be the same love of truth, but not the same taste; because if taste be, as assuredly it is, the power of selecting the beautiful from the ugly in nature, poetry, painting, or music, the taste which relishes a mathematical demonstration is *not* the faculty of selecting the beautiful from the ugly, but the true from the false,—a very different power producing a very different emotion, and referable at once to an organization of the brain altogether different."

Cousin remarks, "Three faculties enter into that complex faculty called taste,—imagination, sentiment, reason.

Taste feels, judges, discusses, analyzes, but does not invent. Genius is before all, inventive and creative."

6. DRAWING OR DESIGN.

Opie remarks, "Of the several branches of painting, separately considered, design or drawing is, undoubtedly, the most important; for on drawing not only form, but action, expression, character, beauty, grace, and greatness chiefly depend. Color represents nothing, and lights and shadows have no meaning till they are circumscribed by form. Drawing, therefore, is evidently the foundation and first element of the art, without which all the others, ideal or practical, are not merely useless, but nonentities."

Fuseli says, "By the word design I mean not what the word denotes in a *general* sense—the plan of a *whole*, but what it means in its narrowest and most specific sense—the drawing of the figures and component parts of the subject. The arts of design have been so named from their nearly exclusive power of representing *form*."

Barry says, "Titian's style of drawing is not remarkable for any excellence. His forms, therefore, though well enough rendered, are generally imperfect. He was scientific and ideal only in his coloring.

"Correggio's taste in drawing was very ideal; but as his ideas were not always well and solidly founded, his truth of drawing is often incorrect and affected from overmuch delicacy, grace, and sentiment. The Madonna and Magdalen are both exceedingly beautiful; are both remarkable for delicacy and elegance; and the beauty, grace, and interesting sensibility of these and other female figures of Correggio strongly show how short Raffaelle was of perfection in this class of figures.

"When we speak of the superior intelligence of design

in the antique statues, we mean a few only. The torso of the Belvidere is, as to perfection, really unique. There is nothing that can be put into the same class with it. The Laocoön, the Apollo, the Venus, the Fighting Gladiator, the Farnese Hercules, and a few others come next, and can hardly be overrated."

Annibale Caracci says, "First make a good *outline*, and then, whatever you do in the *middle*, it must be a good picture.

"In all the various schools and academies that have been instituted in every country where painting has obtained a local habitation, what has invariably been their object? Has it not been design alone? If you ask them what the first requisite in a painter is, will they not answer, Drawing? What the second? Drawing? What the third? Drawing? They tell you, indeed, to acquire coloring, chiaroscuro, composition, &c.; but they *insist* on your becoming draughtsmen.

"Both Raffaelle and M. Angelo, great as they were in design, fell extremely short of the ancients,—the former in elevation, refinement, and precision; the latter in variety, delicacy, and discrimination. M. Angelo undoubtedly stands highest, but Raffaelle is probably the safer and more eligible model for imitation. He, therefore, who wishes to be a painter or a poet, must, like Imlac, enlarge his sphere of attention, keep his fancy ever on the wing, and overlook no kind of knowledge."

Says Fuseli, "Rembrandt was, I think, a genius of the first order in whatever relates to *form*. In spite of the most portentous deformity, and without considering the spell of the chiaroscuro, such were his powers of nature; such the grandeur, pathos, and simplicity of his composition, from the most elevated or extensive arrangement to the homeliest and meanest, that the best cultivated eye, the purest sensibility, and the most refined taste dwell upon them equally enthralled. Shakspeare alone excepted, no one combined with so much transcendent, so many (in all other men) unpardonable faults, and reconciled us to them. He possessed the full empire of light and shade, and of all the tints floating between them; he tinged his pencil, with equal success, in the cool of dawn, in the noontide ray, in the livid flash, in evanescent twilight, and rendered darkness visible."

Howard says, "Beauty, character, grace and grandeur, expression, motion and energy, the noblest and most intellectual qualities of the art, all depend on drawing; which deserves, therefore, to be the determined aim of the student's systematic and persevering application. He must strenuously labor to render his eye mathematically true, and his hand firm, prompt, and obedient, that he may transcribe with facility and fidelity all the appearances of his model.

"No painter proves the value of style, by its *absence*, more than Rubens. To express, in the outward form, the internal workings of the mind of man, is the legitimate and principal effort of the painter; a knowledge of the effects of each on the other should be his constant and especial aim.

"Pamphilus recommended to his scholars the study of arithmetic, and may thereby have meant to inculcate the science of proportion. At any rate, the Greeks must have been thoroughly aware of the importance of the latter, as their works abundantly show. The relative proportions of the human figure, as adopted by the ancients, have been partly preserved by Vitruvius, and seem to be founded on geometrical principles."

Says Haydon, "Poets are not endured if their grammar is bad, or their language obscure, or their versification defective; and why should drawing, form, construction, color, light and shadow, and surface, the grammar of our art, on the same principle, be excused more than in the poet?

"It is to the Greeks we owe, as we owe everything in art, the geometrical principles of arranging figures, or parts taken as lines in the way most agreeable to the eye, and most effective in telling a story to the understanding, without confusion, distraction, or pain."

Beechey says, "The basis of all superior art is ability in *drawing* the human figure,—in other words, the knowledge of its anatomy. The valuable days of Reynolds's youth passed away without his attaining this most essential result of youthful study. But when the power of design was most essential to his object, he acquired it in an admirable degree; and no painter ever drew the head with more taste and decision than he."

Haydon says, "Lawrence *drew* better than Reynolds; but Reynolds was never guilty of many ignorances of composition and design, of which the former was guilty every day. In invention there is no comparison. Reynolds was a genius, and so a genius in color; whereas, Lawrence had no eye, and I remember but one head by him of exquisite color, that compares with Reynolds's—a head of Lord Bathurst. Gonsalvi, and perhaps the emperor of Austria, may be added."

7. GRACE.

Fuseli says, "By grace I mean that artless balance of motion and repose sprung from character, founded on propriety, which neither falls short of the demands nor overleaps the modesty of nature. Applied to execution it means that dexterous power which hides the means by which it was attained, the difficulties it has conquered."

Washington Allston remarks, "It is needless to say how I was affected by Raffaelle, the greatest master of the affections in our art. In beauty he has often been surpassed, but in *grace,* the native grace of character; in the expression of intellect; and, above all, of *sanctity,* he has no equal. What particularly struck me in his works was the genuine life that seemed, without impairing the distinctive character, to pervade them all; for even his humblest figures have a something either in look, air, or gesture, akin to the *venustas* (*grace*) of his own nature. This power of infusing one's own life, as it were, into that which is feigned, appears to me to be the prerogative of genius solely."

Ruskin says, "On the gentleness and decision of just feeling there follows a *grace* of action, and through continuance of this a *grace* of form which by no discipline may be taught or attained."

8. REPOSE.

Ruskin says, "There is probably no necessity more imperatively felt by the artist; no test more unfailing of the greatness of artistical treatment, than that of the appearance of *repose;* and yet there is no quality whose semblance in mere matter is more difficult to define or illustrate.

"As opposed to passion, changefulness, or laborious exertion, *repose* is the especial and separating characteristic of the eternal mind and power; it is the '*I am*' of the Creator opposed to the '*I become*' of all creatures; it is the sign alike of the supreme knowledge which is incapable of surprise, the supreme power which is incapable of labor, the supreme volition which is incapable of change.

"No work of art can be great without repose, and all art is great in proportion to the appearance of it. It is the most unfailing test of beauty, whether of matter or of motion; nothing can be ignoble that possesses it, nothing right that has it not."

Michelet says, "It must ever be borne in mind that, however great may be the charm of variety, expression, and change of movement, there is still a deep desire in the eye and in the mind for repose. A face always changing in expression would induce a feeling in the spectator far less agreeable than even the monotony and lifelessness of unbroken repose."

9. COMPOSITION.

Fuseli says, "Composition has physical and moral elements,—the former are perspective and light with shade,—the latter unity, propriety, and perspicuity."

Ruskin says, "The essential characters of composition, properly so called, are these. The mind, which desires the new feature, summons up before it those images which it supposes to be of the kind wanted; of these it takes the one it supposes to be fittest and tries it; if it will not answer, it tries another, until it has obtained such an association as pleases it."

Haydon says, "There are several modes of arranging figures and parts,—that is, of composing; as, for instance,

"1st. The circle, or the ellipsis, as in Ananias.

"2d. The pyramid with two wings, as in Elymas.

"3d. The large group with one figure, as in Christ.

"4th. The three distant groups, as in the 'Beautiful Gate.'

"5th. The serpentine line, like that of Rubens, and of many others, who may occur to artists.

"It is agreeable to have your lights diagonally at acute or obtuse angles; but never at right angles, unless for a specific purpose. Thus, beauty of form, truth of expression, harmony of color, shape of light and shadow, distinction but not separation of groups, inclinations of lines, whether of figure or drapery, make up the quantities of the various parts which define the whole of that quantity called composition.

"The *greatest* poets, musicians, painters, and sculptors have been the greatest composers. However brilliant their imaginations; however intense their capacities; however mellifluous their language or harmonious their color; it was the power of arranging their materials which rendered their genius useful to their fellow-creatures.

"There is one great principle of composition, if not the greatest, and this, I am quite sure, it will require very little eloquence to enforce. Let your color be exquisite; let your light and shadow be perfect; let your expression be touching; let your forms be heroic; let your lines be the very thing, and your subject be full of action.

"You will miss the sympathy of the world; you will interest little the hearts of mankind; if you do not lay it down, as irrefutable law, that no composition can be complete, or will even be interesting, or deserving of praise, that has not a beautiful woman, except as a series.

"This was the secret of Raffaelle's and Correggio's magic over our hearts; and, be assured, it is the truest, the deepest, and the most delightful, and one in which I defy refutation. For it appeals to our convictions at once, that a picture without a beautiful woman is, and must be, in opposition to all the sympathies of mankind

—especially in an art, the object of which is to instruct by beauty.

"Another cunning and touching secret of Raffaelle's and Correggio's power over us was, that, in every face of a beautiful woman painted by them, they gave a tender air of sympathy and love; so that, in most of their women, if you clear away all the figures, *but* those of the women, you may, without the least alteration of look, put a lover declaring his passion on his knee, and you will find the expression in the woman's face do exactly.

"Reynolds's portraits are all historical pictures in composition; all his smaller parts support and carry off his larger qualities. He appears to have hit the exact point, composed of neither too many parts, nor too few; and, as models of the degree of composition to be admitted into portrait, are (in my opinion) finer examples, than either the portraits of Titian, Rubens, Raffaelle, Sebastion del Piombo, or Vandyke.

"The first object in composition is to please the eye. Composition is the means of conveying the story to the mind. All objects, however exquisite individually, must be sacrificed to this. Raffaelle's great excellence was in expression.

"In composition Lawrence was a child, and Reynolds a great master. Reynolds, from his knowledge of perspective, always planted his men upon their feet, while Lawrence's nobility stood upon their tiptoes, and will do so while canvas lasts. Reynolds was the philosopher of art,—Lawrence the gentleman, with a tendency to dandyism."

Reynolds says, "When a young artist is first told that his composition and his attitudes must be contrasted; that he must turn the head adversely to the position of the body, in order to produce grace and animation; that his outline must be undulating and swelling, to give grandeur; that the eye must be gratified with a variety of colors, and with light and shadow; when he hears this, along with such animating words as spirit, dignity, energy, grace, greatness of style, and brilliancy of tints; —he is liable to push these directions too far. He should, therefore, be on his guard, reflect, and be governed by calm judgment and correct taste.

"The Apollo, the Venus, the Laocoön, the Gladiator, have some recommendation beside simplicity. They have a certain composition of action,—have contrasts sufficient to give grace and energy in a high degree."

Burnet says, "An artist ought always to recollect that he paints for the higher, not for the lower classes of men; and as his business is to convey pleasure, not pain, a little intercourse with society will convince him that men in all ranks have often enough to vex them, or to produce a variance with their fellow-creatures, without hanging up on their walls representations tending to increase either the one or the other feeling. In the early ages representations of vice were necessary, as strong lessons of morality; but as mankind grew more enlightened, they were referred to *books*, not *pictures*, for improvement.

"Hervey, speaking of the stars, says, 'On a careless inspection, you perceive no accuracy or uniformity in the position of the heavenly bodies; they appear like an illustrious chaos, a promiscuous heap of shining globes, neither ranked in order nor moving by line; but what *seems confusion* is all regularity; what shows like *negligence* is really the result of the most masterly contrivance. Ostade's pictures call this passage to my mind, so accurately does it describe the principles on which he constructs his work."

10. COLOR.

Opie says, "Color, the peculiar object of the most delightful of our senses, is (in the poet's language) the dye of love, a hint of something celestial. The ruby, the rose, the diamond, the youthful blush, the orient morning, and the variegated splendor of the setting sun, consist of, or owe their charms principally to, color. To the sight it is the index of gaiety, richness, warmth, and animation; and should the experienced artist, by *design* alone, attempt to represent the tender freshness of spring, the fervid vivacity of summer, or the mellow abundance of autumn, what must be his success? Coloring is the sunshine of the art, which clothes poverty with smiles, and renders the prospect of barrenness itself agreeable, while it brightens the interest and doubles the charms of beauty.

"It will, therefore, be useful to the artist to study the associations of color with our ideas of character. White, the symbol of innocence, and the tender tints of spring, analogous to the opening of human life, become the proper decoration and accompaniment of childhood and youth; greater strength and vivacity of color suit riper age. And thus advancing through every gradation and depth, till we come to black, 'staid wisdom's hue,' every actor that enters on his scene; the young, the old, the male, the female, the slave, the hero, the magistrate, the prince, the philosopher; in short, all stages of humanity, from the infant 'mewling in the nurse's arms,' to the decrepitude of second childhood, will derive from the freshness, brilliancy, harmony, force, gravity, or sombreness of his tints its characteristic color and shade of difference, both in regard to complexion and dress, the essence of the accident.

"Color not only pleases by its thousand delicate hues and harmonious gradations, but serves in nature, and must be employed in art, to characterize and distinguish the various qualities and textures of different bodies and surfaces, as the tenderness and warmth of flesh, the hardness of stone, the polish of metals, the richness of velvet, and the transparency of glass, in all their varied positions of light, shade, or reflected light, and of proximity to, or distance from, the eye. Nor is its operation merely physical and confined to body. Every passion and affection of the mind has its appropriate tint and coloring, which, properly adapted, lends a powerful aid in the just discrimination and forcible expression of them; it heightens joy, warms love, inflames anger, deepens sadness, and adds coldness to the cheek of death itself.

"Like M. Angelo in design, Titian in coloring may be regarded as the father of modern art. He first discovered and unfolded all its charms; saw the true end of imitation; showed what to aim at, when to labor, and where to stop; and united breadth and softness to the proper degree of finishing. He first dared all its depths; contrasted all its oppositions; and taught color to glow and palpitate with all the warmth and tenderness of real life."

Beechey says, "A poetic imagination, expression, character, or even correctness of drawing, are rarely united with that power of coloring which would set off these excellencies to the best advantage; and in this, perhaps, no school ever excelled the Dutch."

Reynolds says, "The striking brilliancy of Rubens's colors, and their lively opposition to each other; the flowing freedom of his outline; and the animated pencil, with which every object is touched, all contribute to keep alive the attention of the spectator. Rubens was, perhaps, the greatest master in the mechanical part of the art, the best workman with his tools that ever wielded a pencil. This portion of the art, though it does not hold rank with the powers of invention, or of giving character and expression, has in it nevertheless what may be called genius."

Opie says, "The artist in colors should invoke the aid of background, chiaroscuro, and picturesque effects, while he aims at action, meaning, and elevated, life-like, truthful expression."

Fuseli says, "To color, when its bland purity tinges the face of innocence and sprouting life, or its magic charm traces in imperceptible lines the forms of beauty; when its warm and ensanguined vigor stamps the vivid principle that animates full-grown youth and the powerful frame of manhood; or, in paler gradations, marks animal life; when its varieties give truth with character to individual imitation; or its more comprehensive tone pervades the scenes of sublimity and expression, and dictates the medium in which they ought to move, in order to strike our eye in harmony;—to color, the florid attendant of form, the master of the passions, the herald of energy and character, what eye, not tinged by disease or deserted by nature, refuses homage? The principles of color, as varied, are also as immutable as those of nature

"To no colorist before or after Titian did nature unveil herself with that dignified familiarity in which she appeared to him. Omitting here all notice of his other transcendent excellencies, his color only, considered as a whole or in subordination, is our object. Manifold as the subdivisions of character are,—angelic, devout, authoritative, violent, brutal, vigorous, helpless, delicate,—and various as the tints of the passions that sway them, appear,—elevated, warmed, inflamed, depressed, appalled, aghast,—they are all united by the general tone that diffuses itself from the interior repose of the sanctuary, smoothens the whirlwind, that fluctuates on the foreground, and gives an air of temperance to the whole."

Reynolds says, "Coloring is true when it is naturally adapted to the eye from brightness, from softness, from resemblance, because they agree with their great prototype, nature, and therefore are true,—as true as mathematical demonstration, but known to be true to those only who study these things."

Burnet says, "Color, though holding the station of middle tint, is, nevertheless, more capable of giving the true representation of natural objects, than the most scientific arrangements of chiaroscuro; and by the judicious management of it, a picture is rendered pleasing and attractive.

"It appears that strong color requires rich, deep shadow to support it and render it a portion of the light. The warm, rich browns of Titian, Rembrandt, and Correggio authorize us in this conduct.

"Grandeur of effect is produced by two different ways, which seem entirely opposed to each other. One is, by reducing the colors to little more than chiaroscuro, which was often the practice of the Bolognian school; and the other, by making the colors very distinct and forcible, such as we see in those of Rome and Florence; but still the presiding principle of both these manners is simplicity

11. SYMMETRY.

Ruskin says, "Symmetry is the *opposition* of *equal* quantities to each other; while proportion is the *connection* of *unequal* quantities with each other.

"In all perfectly beautiful objects there is found the opposition of one part to another, and a reciprocal balance obtained. In animals the balance is commonly between opposite sides, but in vegetables the opposition is less distinct, as in the boughs on adverse sides of trees and the leaves and sprays on each side of the boughs."

Symonds says, "The pleasure derived from similarity enters largely into the beauty of symmetry. This side is like that,—this curve corresponds to that,—and it is like with a difference, the difference being in place or material. It is similarity which constitutes the pleasure of witnessing the successful production of likeness.

"Mere likeness, without difference, becomes distasteful sameness or dull uniformity; just as mere variety, without likeness, would be intolerable.

"The symmetrical beauty of the human face and head is mainly dependent on the bony structures. The beauty of expression, or the beauty belonging to variety, results from the action of the muscles in the play of the features."

12. LIGHT AND SHADOW.

Quintilian says, "Zeuxis, among the Greeks, discovered the principle of light and shadow." According to Haydon, "The most powerful examples of this principle, will be found in the Dutch, Flemish, Spanish, Venetian, and English schools.

"Light and shadow are one thing,—light and dark another. Rembrandt is the great master of light and shadow. Here the lights are the effect of real lights, and the shadows of real shadows, produced by the direction of the lights upon the objects. The Venetians are the model for light and dark—*i. e.*, the production of the effect of shadows by real dark colors, and lights by light colors, though both are in the same light,—indeed in one mass of light without any shadow at all. This is a magnificent artifice. The lights and darks of a picture are regulated just like color. The subject should regulate and be subservient always to the nature, character, expression, and object of the composition."

Reynolds says, "Raphael never acquired that nicety of taste in colors, that breadth of light and shadow, that art and management of uniting light to light and shadow to shadow, so as to make the object rise out of the ground with the plenitude of effect so much admired in the works of Correggio.

"Leonardo da Vinci's conduct and management of light and shadow consisted in opposing a light ground to the shadowed side of the figure, and a dark ground to the light side.

"Some of our most eminent artists have, by a precisely opposite procedure, produced superior splendor and effect. That is, they joined light to light and shadow to shadow.

"The favorite mode of giving objects relief and great effect; of representing a figure, as if we could walk around it; affords to many the highest species of gratification."

Opie says, "By light and shadow all objects and parts of objects are made to project or recede, to strike or retire, to court, or to shun the attention of the spectator, agreeably to truth and propriety. What, as a drawing, was flat, tame, and monotonous, by the aid of this principle, chiaroscuro, bursts forth at once into roundness and reality; entire figures are detached from their ground, seem surrounded by air, and spring forward to meet the eye with all the energy of life.

"Thus the painting of a Venus, by an ancient artist, was said to start from the canvas, as if she wished to be pursued. It gives depth, and marks the various distances of objects, one behind another; and if drawing be the giver of *form*, light and shadow must be allowed to be the creator of body and space.

"In addition to this, if properly managed, it contributes infinitely to expression and sentiment; it lulls by breadth and gentle gradation, strikes by contrast, and rouses by abrupt transition. All that is grave, impressive, awful, mysterious, sublime, or dreadful in nature, is closely connected with it. All poetic scenery, real or imaginary, of 'forests and enchantments drear,' where more is meant, than is expressed; all the effects of solemn twilight and visionary obscurity that fling half an image on the aching sight; all the terrors of storm, and horrors of conflagration, are indebted to it for representation on canvas. Antonio Allegri, who was at the head of the Lombard school, was commonly styled, from the place of his birth, Correggio.

"Of this extraordinary man, who, in the words of Milton,

> "Untwisted all the strings, that tie
> The hidden soul of harmony;"

we are told by some, was born and bred and lived in poverty and wretchedness, and died at the age of forty, from the fatigue of carrying home a sack of half-pence or copper money, paid him for one of his grandest works. He died of a fever at Correggio. According to the best authorities, however, he does not appear to have ever been in poor circumstances, and the above account is probably a mere fable.

"Ovid, speaking of Cyllanus, the fairest of the Centaurs, celebrates him as vying in perfection with the most admirable statues:—

"A pleasing vigor his fair face expressed;—
His neck, his hands, his shoulders, and his breast
Did next in gracefulness and beauty stand
To breathing figures of the sculptor's hand."

Fuseli says, "The term chiaroscuro, adopted from the Italian, in its primary and simplest sense, means the division of a single object into light and shade; and in its widest compass comprises their distribution over the whole composition. Whether the first derives its splendor from being exposed to a direct light, or is produced by colors in themselves opaque, its exclusive power is to give substance to form, and place to figure, and to create space.

"Fra Fillippo Lippi was, perhaps, the greatest master of light and shade anterior to Lionardo da Vinci; but he was not so great a master of chiaroscuro as to dispute the validity of Lionardo's title to being the first who completely developed its powers.

"The first ideas of chiaroscuro, as of expression, character, form, and color, originated in Tuscany, with Masaccio, Lionardo da Vinci, Michael Angelo, and Bartolomeo della Porta.

"The Roman school, like an oriental sun, rose not announced by dawn, and setting, left no twilight. Raffaelle established his school on the drama. Its scenery, expression, forms, history, lyrics, portrait, became, under his hand, the organs of passion and character.

"A certain national, though original, character marks

the brightest epoch of the Venetian school. However deviating from each other, Titian, Tintoretto, Jacopo da Ponte, and Paolo Veronese, acknowledge but one element of imitation, nature itself."

13. EXPRESSION.

Fuseli says, "Expression is the vivid image of the passion that affects the mind; its language and the portrait of its situation. It animates the features, attitudes, and gestures which invention has selected and composition arranged. Its principles, like theirs, are simplicity, propriety, and energy. It is important to distinguish the materials, and the spirit of expression. To give this, we must be masters of the forms and of the hues that embody it. Without truth of line, no true expression is possible; and the passions, whose inward energy stamped form on feature, equally reside, fluctuate, flash, or lower on it in color, and give it force by light and shade. To make a face speak clearly, and with propriety, it must not only be well constructed, but have its own exclusive character. Though the element of the passions be the same in all, they neither speak in all with equal energy, nor are circumscribed by equal limits. Though joy be joy, and anger be anger, the joy of the sanguine is not that of the phlegmatic, nor the anger of the melancholy, that of the fiery character."

Beechey says, "English artists, up to Reynolds's time, had made portrait a mechanical operation. They painted the body without reference to the soul of the sitter. They had to learn how nature might be elevated, and how to combine refined taste and poetic feeling (expression) with the executive portions of the art."

Reynolds says, "If I had never seen any of the works of Correggio, I should never, perhaps, have remarked in nature the expression which I find in one of his pieces; or if I had remarked it, I might have thought it too difficult or perhaps impossible to be executed.

"Of mere *likeness* in portraiture Reynolds thought very little, and used to say that he could instruct any *boy* whom chance might throw in his way to paint a likeness in a portrait in half a year's time; but to give an impressive and just expression and character to a picture, or to paint like Velasquez, was another thing. What (he said) *we* are all attempting with great labor to do, he does at once.

"Du Piles recommends to us, portrait-painters, to add grace and dignity to the characters of those whose pictures we draw. In this he is undoubtedly right. Persons of high character and dignity should be drawn or taken in such an attitude that the portraits must seem to speak to us (*express*) themselves,—to express their true character, and their most elevated condition and intelligent state of mind.

By Raffaelle's happy correspondence between the expression of the countenance and the disposition of the parts, his figures appear to *think* from head to foot. Men of superior talents alone are capable of thus using and adapting other men's minds to their own purposes."

Opie remarks, "The genius of Raffaelle to invention united expression, grace, and propriety, such as in an equal degree never before or since fell to the lot of one man. However great and various his powers, his peculiar strength—that wherein he has never been rivalled and can never be surpassed—was *expression*. To this all his efforts tended; for this he invented, drew, and composed, and exhausted nature in the choice of his subjects to display it. Every effect of mind on matter; every affection of the soul as exhibited in the countenance, from the gentlest emotion to the utmost fury and whirlwind of contending passions; from the demoniac frenzy of the possessed boy in the Transfiguration to the melting rapture of the Virgin Mother contemplating her Divine offspring; may be found so faithfully and energetically represented on his canvas that we not only see but feel, and are, by irresistible sympathy, made participants of his well-imaged joys and sorrows. By this he attracts every eye, warms every heart and sways it to the mood of what he likes or loathes. This is what has made him, if not the greatest, certainly the most interesting and the most universally admired of all modern painters, and rendered his name in the general mouth, synonymous with perfection.

"The history of no man's life affords a more encouraging and instructive example than that of Raffaelle. The path by which he ascended to eminence is open and the steps visible to all. He studied all the artists of his own and preceding times; he penetrated all their mysteries, mastered all their principles, and grafted all their separate excellencies on his own stock. His genius, like fire, embraced and gathered strength from every object with which it came in contact, and at last burst forth into a flame to warm, enlighten, and astonish mankind."

Cousin says, "Expression is addressed to the soul, as form is addressed to the senses. Form is the obstacle to expression, and at the same time is its imperative, necessary, only means. Art succeeds, by care, patience, and genius, in converting an *obstacle* into a *means*.

"Expression is essentially *ideal*,—what it tries to make felt is *not* what the eye can see and the hand touch,—evidently it is something invisible and impalpable."

Haydon remarks, "Lawrence once took a portrait of Curran, whose features were mean and harsh. In the first sittings, he saw so little of the *true man* that he almost laid down his palette in despair of making anything more than a common or vulgar work. But Curran, in discoursing on art, on poetry, on Ireland, became transfigured to the painter's eye. 'I never *saw* you till now" (said the artist),—'you have sat to me in a mask,—do give me a sitting of Curran, the orator!' "

He wrote of Byron, as follows: "Lavater's system never asserted its truth more forcibly than in Byron's countenance, in which you see all the character; its keen and rapid genius, its pale intelligence, its profligacy and its bitterness; its original symmetry distorted by the passions; his laugh of mingled merriment and scorn; the forehead clear and open, the brow boldly prominent, the eyes brightly dissimilar, the nose finely cut, and the nostril acutely formed; the mouth well made, but wide and contemptuous even in his smile, falling singularly at the corners, and its vindictive and disdainful expression heightened by the massive firmness of the chin which springs at once from the centre of the full under lip; the hair dark and curling, but irregular in its growth; and the general effect is heightened by a thin, spare form, and, as you may have heard, by a deformity of limb."

Allan Cunningham says of a portrait of M. Angelo, by Lawrence, "With such skill did he seize the manly features of the swarthy Italian, and manage the crimson velvet, the damask, the gold, and the marble, which he lavished on the picture, that thousands are reported to have crowded to see it."

A person in Rome says, "It may be cited, as the most poetical, enthusiastic delineation of acute genius, without flattery, that has ever been executed. Its animation is beyond all praise. I heard Canova cry out when it was mentioned."

"Lawrence" (says Haydon) "has been called the *second* Reynolds,—not from being an imitator of the style of that great master, but from possessing very largely the same singular power of *expressing* sentiment and feeling, and of giving beauty and often dignity to his productions. He was capable of great exertion, having once painted 37 hours without ceasing!"

Of Gilbert Stuart, whose *forte* in portrait-painting was expression, Dr. Waterhouse says, "In conversational powers Stuart was inferior to no man among us. He made it a point to keep his sitters talking, each in their own way, free and easy. This called up all his resources of judgment. To military men he spoke of battles by sea and land,—with the statesman on Hume's and Gibbon's history; with the lawyer on jurisprudence or remarkable criminal trials,—with the merchant in *his* way, and with the man of leisure in his,—with the ladies in all ways. With the farmer he could descant on every point relating to agriculture; upon cattle, upon butter and cheese-making, &c., &c. In sum, he could be, literally, 'all things to all men.'

"Stuart" (says his biographer) "read men's characters as easily as the newspapers. Earl Mulgrave employed him to paint his brother, Gen. Phipps, who was going to India. On seeing the picture, the nobleman was much disturbed, exclaiming, 'This picture looks strange, sir,—how is it? I see—I think I see insanity in that face!'

"'It may be so,' (replied Stuart), 'but I painted your brother as I saw him.'

"The first news of the general was, that insanity, never previously suspected, had driven him into suicide!"

16

Washington Allston says, "Stuart was, in the widest sense, a philosopher in his art. He animated his canvas, not with the appearances of mere *general* life, but with that *peculiar distinctive* life which separates the individual from his kind. He seemed to dive into men's thoughts, for these were made to rise and speak on the surface."

"Henry Inman's frank and winning address," (says his biographer) "united to rare conversational powers, always gave him an advantage with sitters, which he used with happiest effect. He seldom failed to beguile them, by his talk, of the consciousness that they were sitting for a portrait, when he would seize upon the most natural and characteristic expression of countenance, from which he had thus banished the formality and constraint, which so few, in such a position, can lay aside by any effort of their own.

"Inman excelled in getting a good expression for his sitters, however ugly or stupid the latter might be. '*This*' (Lawrence said) 'the painter might and should get,—else the fault was in himself.' Inman rarely failed of obtaining a likeness, and yet his portraits almost always looked better than the originals."

"John Trumbull" (says his biographer) "was commissioned to paint a portrait of Washington, for the City of Charleston, S. C. For the period, T. selected the evening before the battle of Princeton. T. says, 'I told Washington my object; he entered warmly into it; and as the work advanced, we talked of the scene, its dangers, its almost desperation. He *looked* the scene; and I happily transferred to the canvas the lofty expression of his animated countenance, the high resolve to conquer or to perish. The result was, in my opinion, eminently successful, and Washington was satisfied.'"

Sir Charles Bell says, "Expression is to passion what

language is to thought. It is also curious that expression appears to precede the intellectual operations.

"The expression of emotion may be introduced even into the highest works of art; but it requires great taste to portray it without offensive exaggeration.

"That posture of the body is most expressive when it seems arrested in some familiar action.

"The expression of laughter is pure in the highest degree, indicating unalloyed pleasure, and will relax, by sympathy, even the stubborn features of a stranger.

"In the animated human countenance, we see the eyes full, clear, piercing, full of fire,—appearances indicating feeling, thought, mind.

"Model the lips for the expression of eloquence and of the softer passions, and the mouth becomes beautiful.

"Expression is of more consequence than shape,—it will light up features otherwise heavy; it will make us forget all save the qualities of the mind.

"On a lady's face we like at least to see the loveliness that lurks in expression. M. Angelo, in addition to all his other endowments, was a master of expression.

"Every artist should study the peculiarities of the faces of his sitters, for thus he learns to observe nature; to behold, in their minute varieties, forms which would otherwise pass unnoticed; to catch expressions so evanescent, that they must escape him, unless he is ever on the alert to call, by the excitement of conversation, into the sitter's face the highest intellectual expression of which it is capable.

"The angles of the mouth are full of expression. The lips, being the most mobile of all the features, are the most direct index of the feelings.

"There is expression in the grasp and shake of the hand in saluting,—in some, this act being chilling and depressing, while in others it is warm, heart-kindling, soul-gladdening."

Sir Charles Bell says, "If it be allowable to give examples, I would say that, in the countenance of Mrs. Siddons, or of John Kemble, was presented the highest character of beauty belonging to the true English face. In that family the upper lip and nostrils are very expressive; the class of muscles which operate on the nostrils was especially powerful; and both these great tragedians had a remarkable capacity for the expression of the nobler passions. In their cast of features there was never seen that blood-thirsty look which Cooke could throw into his face.

"It is also said that we are taught by experience alone to distinguish the signs of the passions in man; that in infancy we learn that smiles are expressive of kindness, because accompanied by endearments, and that frowns are the reverse, because they are sometimes followed by blows.

"We have already remarked that expressions peculiarly human chiefly affect the angle of the mouth and the inner extremity of the eyebrow; and to these points we must principally attend in all our observations concerning the expression of passion. They are the most movable parts of the face; in them the muscles concentre; and upon the changes they undergo, expression is acknowledged chiefly to depend. By elevating or depressing the angles of the mouth and inner extremities of the brow, we can readily convey the expression of grief or laughter.

"When the angles of the mouth are depressed, as in grief, the eyebrows are not elevated at the outer angles, as in laughter.

"When a smile plays around the mouth, or the

cheek is raised, as in laughter, the brows are not ruffled, as in grief."

Haydon says, "Of Raffaelle's *expression* the basis is common sense, and Titian's color is equally founded on common sense.

"Aristides and Timanthes were as fine in expression as Raffaelle. Aristides painted a beautiful mother dying of the plague, and with her last effort pushing the dear, smiling baby from her infected nipple; Timanthes, the sacrifice of Iphigenia at Aulis; and with the greatest skill concealed the father's face to excite greater sensibility to his agonies.

"Susceptibility to the expression of the passions, or the beauty of color, can never be *taught*, even though your instructor were an angel from heaven. You can teach to draw and compose pretty fairly; but to invent and to color, if by nature you are deficient in imagination and eye, no instruction on earth can give you.

"In the expression of dignity in portrait no heads exceed Reynolds's, though Titian's and Vandyke's are more delicate in execution. He was a great man, but certainly a superficial thinker; and yet, considering his incessant practice in individual resemblance, it is extraordinary that he wrote as he did.

"There were never two men so totally opposite in art as Reynolds and Lawrence, and great instruction may certainly be attained by a comparison.

"Lawrence got his expression and likeness by an intense perception of the individual parts and keen discernment of the best look of the sitter, and I believe no one ever surpassed him in catching the best expression of the face,—Reynolds got the same by a masculine comprehension of the masses. Reynolds's men had all the air of rank without being dandies,—Lawrence's were all dandies without being men of rank.

"Such were the gentleness, the sweetness, the chastity, the beauty, and bewitching modesty of Reynolds's women, that you would have feared even to approach them,—while you feel quite sure you might compliment Lawrence's women without much fear of offending.

"Lawrence's great power was seeing, transferring, and identifying the happiest expression of the sitter; and no man can testify to his power better than myself. I had under my own eye several of the nobility he had painted. For the first half hour I saw no resemblance. At last some lucky remark lighted up their features, and in these few moments I witnessed Lawrence's choice."

Cousin says, "The great law which governs all others is expression. Every work of art, which does not express an idea, signifies nothing. In addressing to one or another sense, it must penetrate to the mind, to the soul, and bear thither a sentiment or thought capable of touching or elevating it. From this fundamental rule all others are derived."

Haydon says, "Stothard could not tell a story by expression; yet there was an angelic sweetness in everything he did. He seemed to have dreamed of an angel's face in early life, and to have passed the remainder of his days in trying to combine in every figure he touched something of its sweetness."

14. PORTRAIT.

Howard says, "The coarsest portrait of a valued friend may give us more real pleasure than the finest picture of a stranger by Vandyke himself. Our personal affections and ties will always bid defiance to any rivalry from art; but works of fiction do not pretend to vie with realities; their aim is to give an agreeable stimulus to our imaginations or affections by reproducing to our notice whatever is permanently grand, beautiful, emphatic, or expressive in our observations and conceptions of nature wherever found."

Haydon says, "Do you suppose I undervalue portrait,—that delightful art which brings down to us the beautiful and intellectual, the hero and the sage of past ages, and carries onward the resemblance of those equally celebrated now for the admiration of ages that approach? How often have I studied Vandyke's and Reynolds's portraits with delight, enthusiasm, and profit!"

Opie says, "It has been my aim, in my little work, to treat chiefly of portrait. Not that characteristic portrait by which Silanion, in the face of Apollodorus, personified habitual indignation,—Apelles, in Alexander, superhuman ambition,—Raffaelle, in Julius II., pontifical fierceness,—Titian, in Paul III., testy age with priestly subtlety,—and in Cæsar Borgia and Machiavelli, the wily features of conspiracy and treason. Not that portrait by which Rubens contrasted the physiognomy of philosophic and classic acuteness with that of genius, in the conversation-piece of Grotius, Mauritius, Lipsius, and himself. Not the nice and delicate discriminations of Vandyke; nor that power which, in our day, substantiated humor in Sterne, comedy in Garrick, and mental and corporeal strife (to use his own words) in Samuel Johnson. On that broad basis portrait takes its exalted place between history and the drama.

"The portrait I mean is that common one as widely spread as confined in its principle,—mere human resemblance. The artist's aim and the sitter's wish are mostly confined to external likeness.

"Since liberty and commerce have more levelled social ranks, and more equally diffused opulence, private importance has increased, and family connections and attachments have been more numerously forced. Hence portrait-painting, which formerly was the exclusive property of princes, or a tribute to beauty, prowess, genius, talent, and distinguished character, is now become a kind of family calendar, engrossed by the mutual charities of parents, children, brothers, nephews, cousins, and relatives of all degrees."

Haydon says, "There is something in the thoroughbred, regularly drilled portrait-painter, which no imaginative painter ever got, or ever will get.

"It is curious that portrait-painters, when they paint high art, are always too individual for even a likeness; and when the historical painter paints a portrait, he is more individual than the portrait-painter. The portrait-painter selects the best of what he sees, but still keeps the likeness. The historic painter selects the best of what he sees, to realize what he imagines. The painter of high art makes a portrait of what he *imagines,* by the help of his model, without retaining an atom of likeness; the portrait-painter of what he sees. Thus, when a portrait-painter comes to high art, he cannot help making a portrait of his model; and when the historical painter comes to portrait, he cannot idealize without losing likeness.

"Though Fuseli had more of imagination and conception than Reynolds; though West put things together quicker than either; though Flaxman and Stothard did what Reynolds could not do; and Hogarth invented a style never before thought of in the world; yet Reynolds is undeniably the greatest artist of the British school, and the first artist in Europe since Rembrandt and

Velasquez. It is impossible for any one to look at a portrait by him, without instruction, benefit, and delight."

Says Northcote, "It is in painting, as in life,—what is greatest is not always best. I should grieve to see Reynolds transfer to heroes and goddesses, to empty splendor and airy fiction, that art which is now employed in diffusing friendship, in renewing tenderness, in quickening the affections of the absent, and continuing the presence of the dead.

"As every man is always present to himself, he has, therefore, little need of his own resemblance; nor can he desire it but for the sake of those he loves, and by whom he hopes to be remembered. This use of the art is a natural and reasonable consequence of affection; and though, like other human actions, it is often complicated with pride, yet even such pride is more laudable than that by which palaces are covered with pictures which, however excellent, neither imply nor excite the virtue of the owner."

Reynolds says, "When a portrait is painted in the historic style, as it is neither an exact, minute representation of an individual, nor completely ideal, every circumstance ought to correspond to this mixture. Small excellencies should be *viewed,* not *studied,*—they ought to be viewed, because nothing should escape a painter's observation."

Haydon says, "The proportion and shape of the bones are visible in the head, joints, hands, feet, and shoulders; the bones are moved by the muscles, influenced by the will, excited by an idea or an intention of the brain,—*how,* the profoundest anatomists are not wiser than we are.

"The interesting muscles of the face and head are the hidden causes of the expression of the passions by feature."

15. SCULPTURE.

Agesander says, "Sculpture is an art of much more simplicity and uniformity than painting. It cannot, with propriety and the best effect, be applied to many subjects. The objects of its pursuit may be comprised in two words, form and character; and these qualities are presented to us in but one manner or style. Imitation is the *means,* and not the *end,* of art. It is employed by the sculptor as the language whereby his ideas are presented to the mind of the spectator.

"Thus from the character and posture of the figure, Apollo, he is supposed to have just discharged his arrow at the great serpent, Python; and by the head retreating a little towards the right shoulder, he appears attentive to its effect. What we would remark is the difference of this attention from that of the Discobolus, who is occupied with a kindred purpose, watching the effect of his discus, or quoit. The graceful, negligent, though animated air of the one, and the vulgar eagerness of the other, furnish a singular instance of the judgment of the ancient sculptors in their nice discrimination of character. They are both equally true to nature, and are alike admirable. We may remark, that grace, character, and expression, though words of different import, and so understood, when applied to paintings, are used indiscriminately, when we speak of sculpture. These qualities are exhibited in sculpture rather by form and attitude, than by the features solely, and therefore can be expressed in but a very general manner.

"Though the Laocoön and his two sons have more expression in the countenance, than perhaps any other antique statue, yet it is only the general expression of pain; and this passion is still more forcibly expressed, by the writhing and contortions of the body, than by the features."

Barry says, "Socrates was himself a sculptor by education. A Mercury and a draped marble group of the Graces by him are noticed by Pausanias, as standing in the Propylæa, leading to the Acropolis at Athens."

Agesander, the sculptor, says, "The figure of Laocoön is a class. It characterizes every beauty of virility verging on age. The prince, the priest, the father are visible; but absorbed in the man, they serve only to dignify the victim of one great expression."

Haydon says, "At my first entrance among the Elgin Marbles the first thing I saw was the wrist of the right hand and arm of one of the Fates leaning on her thigh, which, mutilated as it was, proved that the great sculptor had kept the shape of the radius of the ulna, as always seen in fine nature male and female.

"I felt at once, before turning my eyes, that *there* were the nature and ideal beauty joined, which I had gone about the art, longing for and never finding. I saw at once I was among productions, such as I had never before witnessed in the art; and that the great author merited the enthusiasm of antiquity, of Socrates and Plato, of Aristotle, Juvenal and Cicero, of Valerius Maximus, Plutarch and Martial.

"If such were my convictions on seeing this dilapidated but immortal wrist, what think you they were on turning round to the Theseus, the horse's head, and the fighting Metope, the Frieze, the Jupiter's breast?

"I saw that union of nature and ideal perfected in high art, and before this period pronounced impossible. I bowed to the immortal spirit that still hovered near them.

"M. Angelo was a tremendous genius and a grand

moral being, with a vast power of intellect. His effect on the art was vital; but he did not allow, like the Greeks, the unalterable principles of life to keep in check his anatomical knowledge of the human figure. He often overstepped the modesty of truth, and gave a swaggering air; every figure of his looks as if he was insulted, and was preparing to return a blow; if they sleep, they seem as if they would kick. His art is a perpetual effort; his figures always seem irritated and in a passion.

"In poetry of sentiment the Medici Tombs would, perhaps, have competed with Phidias; for M. Angelo, being a painter as well as Phidias, combined in his sculpture a knowledge of *effect*. But in the naked figures, both at the Tombs and in the Sistine Chapel, he must yield to Phidias.

"But why is Phidias superior to M. Angelo in the naked? Because his most abstract and heroic figures were based on common sense."

Washington Allston says, "Of M. Angelo I know not how to speak in adequate terms of reverence. With all his faults, even Raffaelle bows before him. As I stood beneath his colossal prophets and sibyls,—still more colossal in spirit,—I felt as if in the presence of messengers from the other world, with the destiny of man in their breath,—even in repose terrible!"

Vasari gives a long list of painters and sculptors who formed their taste and learned their art by studying his works. Among these he names M. Angelo, L. da Vinci, Pietro Perugino, Raffaelle, Bartolomeo, Andrea del Sarto, Il Rosso, and Pierino del Vaga.

Ruskin says, "The chisel of Mino da Fiesole leaves many a hard edge, and despises down and dimple; but it seems to cut light and carve breath, the marble burns beneath it, and becomes transparent with very spirit."

CHAPTER XXV.

MISCELLANEOUS REMARKS FROM VARIOUS AUTHORS.

Sexes, how distinguished: Barry, Opie, Fuseli, Apelles—Analysis of Da Vinci's Last Supper: Howard, Ruskin, Lawrence, Burke, Cuvier, Dryden, Mrs. Siddons, Reynolds.

BARRY says, "There is a general character distinguishable in the sexes as contrasted with each other. The whole and every part of the male form, taken generally, indicates an aptness and propensity to action, vigorous exertion, and power.

"In the female form the appearance is very different. It gives the idea of something rather passive than active, and seems created not so much for the purposes of laborious utility, as for the exercise of all the softer, milder qualities."

Opie remarks, "Lionardo da Vinci was considered, in his time, one of the first luminaries of modern art, and one of the most extraordinary of men. If it be true that 'one science only will one genius fit,' what shall we say of the man who, master of all mental and all bodily perfections, excelled equally in painting, sculpture, poetry, architecture, chemistry, anatomy, mathematics, and philosophy; who renders credible all that has been related of the 'admirable Crichton,' who attempted everything and succeeded in every attempt; who, sailing round the world of art, touched at every port and brought home something of value from each?

This was Lionardo's glory. His genius gave the death-blow to flatness and insipidity by the invention of that deep tone of color, strength of shadow, and bold relievo which, afterwards carried to perfection, enchant us in the dreams of Correggio, and electrify us in the mysterious visions of Rembrandt."

Fuseli says, "The name of Apelles, in Pliny, is the synonym of unrivalled and unattainable excellence. He knew better what he could do, what ought to be done, at what point he should arrive, and what lay beyond his reach, than any other artist. Grace of conception and refinement of taste were his elements, and went hand in hand with grace of execution and taste in finish. The acuteness and fidelity of eye and obedience of hand, possessed by him, form precision; precision, proportion; proportion, beauty; that is, the little more or less, imperceptible to vulgar eyes, which constitutes grace, and establishes the superiority of one artist to another.

"Such were the principles on which Apelles formed his Venus, or rather the personification of female grace; the wonder of art and the despair of artists; whose outline baffled every attempt at emendation, while imitation shrank from the purity, the force, the brilliancy, the evanascent gradations of her tints."

Howard says, "Those works which, for ages, have maintained their reputation as chefs d'oeuvres, must be held to have supplied a large amount of real instruction in art; and the artist, in the beginning of his career, will act far more wisely in adopting the most approved rules, than in attempting to form them directly from nature; for, unless he avails himself of the science of his predecessors, he can have slight chance of advancing far in his art.

"A sketch-book should be the artist's inseparable

companion, in which he may note down, on the spot, every interesting group, figure, action, fall of drapery, or other characteristic circumstance which may interest his fancy, in his daily haunts. This practice will increase his facility in drawing, and gradually supply him with stores of incomparable value. This was the habit of Da Vinci and M. Angelo, of Flaxman and Stothard; and it has, doubless, led to some of their most exquisite inventions and compositions. The beautiful groups of the Sistine Chapel; the attitudes of the prophets and sibyls in the same place; and many of the figures in the 'Last Judgment,' are probably taken immediately from nature.

"No man has hitherto been master of all the parts of painting in an equal degree of perfection. M. Angelo excelled in composition and drawing, but not in color. Raffaelle was distinguished for expression and grace; but had neither the greatness of style of his rival, nor the sweetness and unction of Correggio; while Titian, a perfect colorist, was deficient in form."

"THE LAST SUPPER" OF LIONARDO DA VINCI.

Howard remarks, "In this picture the subject required that the apostles should be placed six on each side, with the Saviour in the midst. At each extremity of the table are three figures (more separated than those next to them) which are combined in two close and varied groups. One of these is more connected than the other with the principal figure, which gives due predominance to the central mass, and prevents the composition from appearing too positively divided into triads. The heads are at unequal distances, and form in themselves an agreeable waving line. There is an ingenious modulation in the arms and in the conduct of all the hands;

every figure presents a different quantity; and the principal line being horizontal, the forms above it are contrived to pass from one end to the other, in a sort of undulating chain. It would be difficult to point out a more perfect specimen of intricate grouping, than that of Peter, Judas, and John; Peter, stretching over Judas, with the impetuosity belonging to his character, addresses the affectionate John, who (his hands clasped in grief) inclines toward him; Judas leans back to support himself, and assumes the firmness and surprise of innocence.

"This, with another group, as energetic, and almost as fine, on the other side, is happily opposed to the calm resignation of the Saviour, producing great richness and effect in the centre, and a fine alternation of action and repose throughout. Nothing is neglected in this profound work, which, from the variety of its excellencies, may be esteemed a school in itself."

A brief pointing out of the persons of the piece by name may be of service to the reader. We quote from Gio Gherardo De Rossi.

1. In St. John, nearest to Jesus, sweetness and purity are expressed, as in the downcast eyes, &c.

2. Judas, the traitor, between John and Peter, leans his right arm on the table, with the purse in his hand, and turns eagerly to Jesus, as one who would hide his treason under affected frankness.

3. Peter looks full of ardor and more agitated than the rest; he touches John's shoulder, while speaking in his ear.

4. Andrew, Peter's brother, has before him a dish of fish, probably symbolizing his vocation; his hands are raised and outspread, and his face manifests a bewildered surprise.

5. James the Greater, who sits next, seems amazed, and is touching Peter's arm, as if to address him.

6. Philip, at the end of the table, on the right, wears the Roman dress. His face expresses doubt,—perhaps as to whether he had rightly understood Christ's remark, —and a question as to who was the traitor.

On Christ's left we see, first,

7. Thomas, who also seems astonished, and manifests a sort of half-doubt as to whether this supposed treason is a fact.

8. Jude, or Thaddeus, the next, expresses much affliction, and, in his excitement and agitation, his fore-finger is raised as if in enforcement of some suggestion.

9. Simon appears painfully excited, and as if anxious to clear himself of suspicion; while, by opening his vest with both hands, he might be supposed to symbolize the exhibition of a heart free from the guilt in question.

10. Matthew, formerly a publican, and thus versed in the world's ways, appears to be questioning his neighbors about the matter under consideration.

11. Bartholomew has a look of sincerity, and appears to be talking with James the Less in a mood of indignation at the treachery revealed.

12. James the Less wears an expression of habitual goodness, and would seem to repeat and confirm the words of the Master.

The Master himself, seated at the centre of the table, has his eyes cast down as if shunning to meet those of the betrayer. Purity, holiness, and grief are depicted on the face, which the painter, however, after putting forth his utmost efforts, still pronounced imperfect.

Fuseli says of the picture, "Sublimely calm, the Saviour's face is an abyss of thought, and broods over the immense revolution in the economy of mankind, which presses inwardly on his absorbed eye; while every face and every limb around him, roused by his mysterious word, fluctuate in restless curiosity and sympathetic pangs.

"Neither during the splendid period immediately subsequent to Lionardo, nor in the interval between that time and ours, has a face been produced of the Redeemer, which I will not say *equalled*, but even *approached* the sublimity of Lionardo's conception, and in quiet and simple features of humanity embodied Divine, or, what is the same, infinite and incomprehensible powers.

"The moment is that, in which the Saviour says to his disciples, 'One of you will betray me!' On every one of the innocent men, the word acts like lightning; he who is farther distant, distrusting his own ears, applies to his neighbor; others, according to their variety of character, betray raised emotions. One faints; one is fixed in astonishment; this wildly rises; the simple candor of another tells, that *he* cannot be suspected. Judas, meanwhile, assumes a look of intrepidity; but, though he counterfeits innocence, he leaves no doubt of his being the traitor.

"Da Vinci said, he wandered about for a year, perplexed how to produce a face representing so black a soul as that of Judas. At last, in a street haunted by villains he met with a man, whose face, with some alterations and additions, answered his purpose."

Ruskin says, "That virtue of originality, which men so strain after, is not newness,—it is only *genuineness*.

"Lawrence had a true enthusiasm for his art, and would not hastily dismiss anything for which he was to be paid, as a picture. He detained his sitters often for three hours at a time; had generally eight or nine of these sittings; and all the while studied their looks anxiously, and seemed to do nothing without care and consideration."

He greatly admired Reynolds, and, amid all the wonders of art, which he saw in a visit to Italy, his love of Reynolds's works seemed to increase daily; and though still considering M. Angelo as the head of all that was sublime, he looked upon Raffaelle, Correggio, Titian, and Reynolds as the gods in art, at whose shrines he should hereafter bend. Of Turner, too, though an opponent to him in the Academy, he spoke in terms of no ordinary praise. He declared that Reynolds excelled all other masters save Rembrandt, the most complete imitator of the effect of nature that art had ever produced.

"An artist should have fine pictures in all parts of his house to catch his eye and entrap him into reflection as he passes by. By such artifices he keeps his attention ever on the alert."

Edmund Burke says, "The painter, who wishes to make his pictures what fine pictures ought to be, nature elevated and improved, must first gain a perfect knowledge of nature as she is. Before he makes men as they ought to be, he must know how to make them as they are; he must acquire an accurate knowledge of all the parts of the body and countenance. To know anatomy will be of little use, unless physiology and physiognomy are joined to it."

Says Haydon, "Show me a hero, a poet, a painter, a musician, a tyrant, a murderer, a thief,—all, remember, illustrious in their respective departments, and in which their phrenological development does not prove the truth of phrenology, and I yield.

"The great proportion of mankind can be modified by education and circumstance; but there are some so constituted, inefficiently or powerfully, that no circumstance or training, in the latter instance, will ever turn them aside from realizing their burning impressions, or, in the former, elevate them to produce anything.

"The man was wrong who found fault with nature for not placing a *window* before the heart, in order to make visible human thoughts and intentions. There is, in truth, provision made in the countenance and outward bearing for such discoveries.

"Cuvier reduces the varieties of our species to three,—the Caucasian, or white; the Mongolian, or yellow; and the Negro, or black. The Caucasian, to which *we* belong, is known by the beauty of the oval-formed head, varying in complexion, and color of the hair. From this variety the most civilized nations have originated—ourselves for instance.

"In every head, painted by M. Angelo, Raffaelle, Titian, Correggio, Rubens, or Vandyke, you behold a knowledge and mastery of the skull.

"On beholding the Elgin Marbles, I foresaw at once a mighty revolution in the art of the world for ever. I saw that union of Nature and Ideal perfected in high art, and before this period pronounced impossible. I thanked God, with all my heart and my whole being, that I was ready to comprehend them from dissection. I bowed to the Immortal Spirit, that still hovered near them. I instantly predicted their vast effect on the art of the world, and was smiled at for my boyish enthusiasm!

"Fame cannot spread widely or endure long, which is not rooted in nature and matured by art.

"Dryden said there was no royal road to knowledge; and we may say, there is no railroad to perfection in art.

"In using nature for poetic invention, Reynolds, Vandyke, and even Titian and Rubens fail. Reynolds, especially, could elevate what he saw, if he kept the elements of what he had before him. The instant he left his model, he was abroad.

"Mrs. Siddons, as the Tragic Muse, is more poetical than his own inventive Tragic Muse in Garrick, between her and Comedy. Mrs. S. was an *elevated* portrait, while the other was his own invention, and the two completely illustrate the principle laid down. Reynolds was a great artist in the second rank; but with a different education and in a different period, he would have been a great artist of the first rank: but his genius for high art was not intense enough to make him a great artist in spite of time and education.

"As the painter has but one moment; first, his subject must be one of palpable interest, big with the past and pregnant with the future,—next, his actions must be doing, his passions expressing, his lights and shadows fleeting; something must be past, something must be coming, and he chooses the point of interest, the point between.

"Reynolds's broad, masculine touch; his glorious, gemmy surface; his rich tones; his graceful turn of the head, will ever be a source of instruction to the great artist, let him practise in what style he may."

PORTRAIT.

Burnet says, "Alexander would never sit for his portrait to any one but Apelles, who knew how to ennoble the likeness; while Cromwell desired Lely to represent all his warts and excrescences. A very little practice will soon convince an artist that most of his sitters will be actuated by the feelings of Alexander, rather than by those of Cromwell.

"Lawrence used to say, that even in the majestic head

of Mrs. Siddons there were parts and forms which did not appear to belong to Mrs. Siddons, and should, therefore, be omitted in her portrait. To every head where character as well as resemblance is required, the same remark will apply.

"In regard to actual resemblance, there are those whom nothing will satisfy but a real, striking, startling likeness,—a something which a child might not only know, but mistake for the reality. Those who demand *such* proof from art, may find it in the merest daub, in the harshest caricature, but will look for it, in vain, in the finest pictures.

"To Titian, the father of portrait painting, we must look for most of those qualities which ennoble and dignify the subject,—simple and unaffected air of the figure, grandeur in the contour, and the greatest breadth, alike in the light and shade, and the color.

"In the portraits of Titian we find every portion of the countenance laid out with reference to its grandeur and its greatest breadth and dignity. For example, the pupil merges in the outer line of the iris, thus giving its greatest bulk, while the upper and lower eyelids are extended, by shadows, to the eyebrow; the darks of which are carried out by a union and dependence with the adjoining hair; thus making the extreme boundary of every feature its definition.

"By the study of the antique, in the first instance, we acquire a more perfect knowledge of form, indicative of beauty and correct discrimination of character. The want of this previous study is perceptible in the early German and Flemish schools; and the adoption of it has stamped a grandeur and dignity on the works of the great masters of the Italian schools.

"Giving a work the exact look of *nature,* unless combined with the scientific arrangements of refined art, may create wonder in the ignorant, but seldom gives satisfaction to persons of refined taste. It is mentioned of a portrait by Titian, of Charles V., that on its being placed on the terrace, in the sun, the passers-by took off their bonnets, thinking it the emperor himself."

But I must, however unwillingly, bring these extracts to a close. I cannot but think that I shall have the reader's approbation for having occupied so many pages of this volume in such a way. For, if I mistake not, the heliographer and the artist, in whatever department, and the general reader not less, will find entertainment and direct instruction and matter for useful reflection in these utterances of many of the ablest and most accomplished minds in both the past and the present time. If such be the result, I shall not regret the time and labor expended in bringing them into such order as I have been enabled to give them.

NOTE.— *What High Art is.*—"High art," says a modern critic, "if there be any such thing, must be that use of the arts which has the effect of elevating and refining the morals. Thus, in painting, while the delineation of the subject, the harmony of all its features, and the combination and blending of the colors, must be so perfectly true to nature as to satisfy the highest and most intelligent perception of excellence, the subject itself, or its treatment, must be suggestive of ideas tending to elevate the moral sentiments; without which, no picture, however admirable the execution, can be called a work of high art. Historical pictures, therefore, unless recording some event in which great principles were involved, are not necessarily high art, although it is common so to consider them.

"Music, which specially appeals to the feelings, proves the correctness of this theory, the devotional being universally acknowledged as the highest order. Still, it is very questionable whether the use of such a term is justifiable, under any circumstances, because there are many pictures that would suggest various ideas to different people; so that what would excite in one man merely sensual desire, in another might call into activity the highest and purest sentiments of which the human mind is capable."

CHAPTER XXVI.

ON COLORING PHOTOGRAPHS.

Introduction—Necessity for color to an artistic photograph—Influence of white and black on colors—Blonde and brunette complexions—Water colors—Coloring in oil, some knowledge of drawing requisite—Concluding remarks.

As the subjects treated in the foregoing chapters have been so discussed, as to indicate to the student, the amateur, and the general reader, the principles lying at the basis of a good portrait, and giving it value both as a *likeness* and a work of art,—the truth of which principles is confirmed by the opinions of the ablest and most eminent artists of former times;—so I here introduce a chapter upon finishing and coloring the Photograph in several of the most approved styles in vogue. These styles, if carried skilfully into effect, will impart to a portrait a permanence, and a charm, which ever satisfies and delights, without tiring.

Here the practical Photographer and the professional Artist work together—the Camera and the Pencil are companions.

THE PRINCIPLES OF HARMONIOUS COLORING.

As I have repeatedly shown in the present volume, a heliograph which, chemically and mechanically, may be pronounced perfect, may, when considered as a work of art, be exceedingly imperfect. I need scarcely add, that judgment and taste enough may be shown in its production, in the arrangement of position, and the distribution of lights and shadows, to entitle it to the name of *picture*, while, regarded as a *portrait*, it may still be very defective. The effect of color may, in many instances, be absolutely essential to anything like a faithful reproduction of the original.

To obtain good results in coloring, it is not requisite merely to possess the manipulative aptitude to imitate, with somewhat of success, the color of the object copied. One of the first requirements in the education of the painter, is a knowledge of the value of his colors; of their relations and harmonies; and of their results in juxtaposition and combination. As in music an exhaustless world of beauty and delight is produced by the various combinations and sequences of seven different sounds, so in painting a source of beauty, scarcely more circumscribed, results from the combination and arrangement of three primary colors; and in painting, as in music, the beauty consists not in any single color, any more than it does in any one note, but in the relation it is made to bear to others.

True it is, that, in this respect, the field of the portrait painter is perhaps more contracted than that of the painter of works of imagination and fancy, or even than that of the landscape painter; while the province of the colorist of heliographic pictures is more limited still. Nevertheless, without some acquaintance with the principles of harmonic coloring, he can hardly hope even to approximate to the best results. And while in portraiture the painter is required to reproduce, in many respects, as nearly as possible, the colors inherent in the object represented, still in the selection of colors for draperies, backgrounds, &c., greater freedom is allowable; and he may employ such analogies or contrasts of color, as, while producing a harmonic total, give value and effect to the colors of the complexion. To aid the colorist in this particular, I will here present a very brief summary of the leading principles belonging to this subject, limiting myself to the bare statement of them, with as little comment as possible.

The source of all color is light, and a beam of white light is divisible into three separate rays,—blue, yellow, and red. These constitute the three (so named) primary colors, and by their various combinations every possible hue may be obtained. White light, when decomposed by passing through a prism, yields what is entitled the *solar spectrum*, which consists of the seven colors seen in the rainbow, arranged in the following order:—violet, indigo, blue, green, yellow, orange, and red; and hence it was formerly thought, that each of these was an elementary color. Subsequent observation, however, has shown, that all, save blue, yellow, and red, are produced by these overlapping or impinging upon each other.

These colors, in their several combinations, are named *hues*. These hues, when weakened by commingling with white, are called *tints*, and when deepened by admixture with black, are entitled *shades* or *shadows*. The varied gradations of tints and shades of a single color, constitute a *scale*.

The presence, in felicitous proportions, of the three primary colors, or their combinations, in a picture produces *harmony*.

Any two primary colors mingled in certain proportions, produce a *secondary* color which is *complementary* to the remaining primary color. For instance, the mixture of blue and yellow produces green, which is complemental to red.

The mixture of yellow and red produces orange, which is complemental to blue.

The mingling of red and blue produces purple, which is complementary to yellow, as may be seen by trying the experiment indicated by the following diagram.

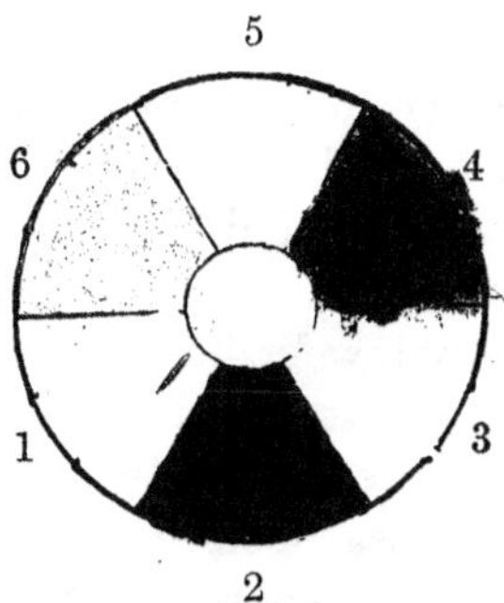

Divide a circle into six equal parts, numbered 1, 2, 3, 4, 5, 6, as in the annexed diagram. Let the spaces 1, 2, 3, be colored blue; 3, 4, 5, yellow; and 5, 6, 1, red.

It will appear, that the space 1 is now colored *purple*, by the combination of red and blue, and that it is located opposite to its complementary, yellow, the remaining primary.

The space 3 is colored *green* by the combination of blue and yellow, and is opposite to its compl mental, red, the remaining primary.

The space 5 is colored *orange*, by the commixture of yellow and red, and is opposite to *red*, its complementary.

These combinations may be carried, with like results, to an extent virtually unlimited. For example, the combination of any two *secondary* colors produces a *tertiary*, which is complemental to the remaining *secondary*.

Thus, the mixture of orange and green produces *citrine*, which is the complemental of *purple;* purple and green produce *olive*, which is complementary to *orange;* purple and orange produce *russet*, which is complemental to *green*, and so on.

This description of the relations of colors is not a mere

arbitrary one, nor is it the result of fancy or taste; but it is based on absolute inherent principles. These relations exist, as a physical necessity of our organs of sight, as may be demonstrated by a few simple experiments.

If, for example, a red wafer be laid on a sheet of white paper, and the eye be steadily fixed upon it for a short time, and then transferred to another part of the paper, a similar spot will appear before the eye, but of *green,* the color complementary to *red.* This spot, named an *ocular spectrum,* will remain visible for a few *minutes,* till it is gradually removed by the white light reflected from the paper.

If the same experiment be tried with a *blue* wafer, the color of the spectrum, thus produced, will be *orange;* if with a yellow wafer, a *purple* spectrum is the result, and so on with the others.

This principle is applicable to every combination and variety of tint. Thus, if a *red* inclines somewhat to *yellow,* as in *scarlet,* then the complemental, *green,* will incline a little to *blue,* and become a *bluish green.*

If, contrariwise, the red inclines a little to *blue,* as in crimson, the complementary will incline somewhat towards *yellow,* and become a *yellowish* green.

These combinations may be multiplied by gradations, so minute and delicate, that to enumerate them is impossible.

The *quality* of their relations, however, may be illustrated by the appended diagram, wherein the *complemental* of each color will be noted in the space directly opposite to it; each pair exhibiting a harmonic balance of the three primary colors.

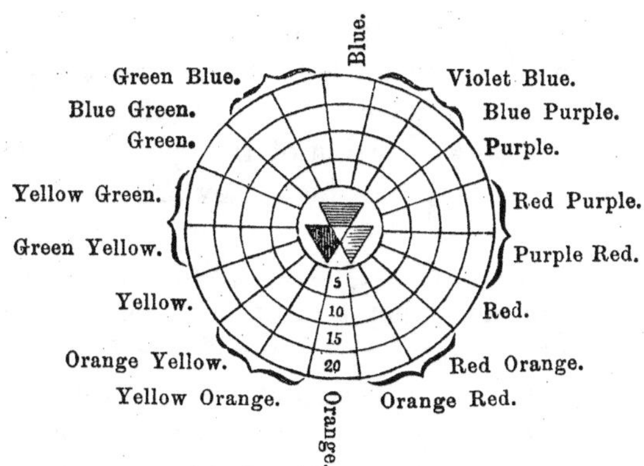

Each pair of colors, comprising a *primary* with its complemental *secondary*, exhibit also, sundry special contrasts peculiar to themselves.

For instance, blue is, at once, the *coldest* color and the most *retiring*, while *orange*, its complemental, is the *warmest* color and the *most advancing*. Every combination of colors, as it approaches towards *orange* or blue, is, in its effect, warm or cold, and, in a picture, wears the appearance of approaching the eye or receding from it.

Yellow is the brightest of colors, and is most nearly allied to light; while *purple*, its complemental, is the darkest of colors.

We may here state that *white and black*, which *contrast* most perfectly as *Light and Darkness*, are not considered as colors: *white*, which most nearly resembles *light*, being regarded as representing a combination of all colors, and *black*, like *darkness*, the absence alike of *color and light*.

Red is the most positive and exciting of all colors; while *green*, its complemental, is the least stimulative and most soothing of all colors.

It may be noted that, while each combination of two

primary colors produces a new and perfect *hue*, each subsequent combination tends to create *neutrality.* The neutral *tints*, however, which are thus produced, partake in a greater or less proportion of the special characteristics of the primaries, to which they are most closely allied.

Complemental colors in juxtaposition, mutually contribute to enrich each other, and produce what is entitled the harmony of *contrasts.* For instance, *purple and yellow*, of like purity and intenseness, become each the brighter from contact with each other,—the yellow becoming intensified by the additional yellow rays reflected from the *purple*, and the purple having its richness enhanced by the purple rays yielded by the yellow. From the same cause neutral tints, put in juxtaposition with *full hues*, appear to be tinged with the complemental colors of such hues. *Gray*, for example, placed in juxtaposition with *red*, takes on the appearance of greenish gray, *green* being the complementary of red.

Colors not complemental to each other, are reciprocally injured by contact.

For instance, blue and purple put in juxtaposition are both injured; the *blue* growing greenish from the yellow rays emitted by the purple taking a russet tinge from the *orange* rays reflected from the *blue.*

From this fact, it appears that *neutral* tints put in contact with *full hues*, should, in order to yield the best results, incline to the complemental of such hues.

For example, *olive* placed in juxtaposition with *yellow*, should, to produce the finest effects, incline to *purple* rather than to *green*, purple being complementary to yellow.

Over and above the results produced by contrast of *hue*, that flowing from contrast of *intensity* should be considered. If two tints, of like color, but of different degrees of depth or intensity, are placed side by side, the deep tint will appear still deeper, while the light tint will appear still lighter, the difference in intenseness appearing greatest at the points of contact.

Contrasting colors, also, of various degrees of intensity, are doubly modified by contact; in *brilliancy* of hue, as before described, and likewise in *intenseness*, the deepest color appearing still deeper, and the least intense appearing still more diluted.

Hence, all colors gain depth by contact with white, as the white takes the complemental tint of the color near it. Contrariwise, black tends to weaken the colors in its immediate vicinity.

The influence of the several hues on black is varied in a similar way, its depth being materially modified by contact with colors having luminous complementaries. For instance, black, in juxtaposition with purple, loses depth from being tinged with the yellow rays emitted by the purple; in contact with blue or green, it grows rusty from the orange or red rays reflected by these colors.

On the other hand, black is intensified by contrast with orange, yellow, or red.

The juxtaposition of gray, which is a commixture of white and black, imparts brilliancy to all pure colors.

Besides the harmony resultant from judicious contrasts, there is the harmony of *analogy*, produced by the combination of the several gradations of a single color in its own scale, or of the hues and broken tints in the order wherein they occur in the solar spectrum. A measureless sum of pleasing effects may be obtained by the judicious arrangement of analogous tints in harmonic relations. Being, however, less striking, much nicer perceptions, and more skilful management, are required to produce felicitous effects.

It has been already remarked, that the laws regulating harmonious coloring are not suggested by fancy, but are based on absolute inherent relations. A very little observation of nature will furnish pleasing illustrations of both species of harmony. A striking instance of the harmony of analogy may be witnessed in the beautifully graduated and blended colors of the rainbow; and, moreover, in almost every landscape, where the blue of the far distance blends with the cool greens and grays of the middle distance; and these merge into the warmer greens, yellows, and browns of the foreground; while, if the sun be setting in the landscape, every object is beautified by the play of golden lights and purple shadows. With specimens of the harmony of *contrast,* nature teems in every garden, meadow, and moor: as witness the damask rose, with its yellowish green leaf; the scarlet holly berry, and its deep green foliage; and the well-nigh unvaried mingling of yellow gorse and purple heather.

In applying these principles to the coloring of protraits, it were well to remember, that M. Chevreul,* whose investigations of this subject entitle him to the highest rank, as an authority, while discussing the harmony of colors, as belonging to the human complexion, considers the *blonde,* or fair complexion, as always allied, more or less, to an *orange* tint throughout; remarking that, as the color of *light hair* is essentially the result of a commingling of red, yellow, and brown, we must esteem it as a very pale orange brown.

---

* To the student, who would make himself thoroughly familiar with the subject, may be recommended M. Chevreul's work, on "The Simultaneous Contrasts of Colors;" as also Mr. Redgrave's excellent little "Manual of Color."

We may, further, refer him to our chapter entitled, "The Harmony of Colors, pp. 67–83."

By this we are to understand merely that orange is the *full* hue, to which *blonde* complexions approach most nearly. In what is termed decidedly *red* hair, the orange, certainly, is sufficiently *pronounced,* as also, though, to be sure, in a less degree, in auburn and chestnut hair, the approach to orange growing less decided, as the yellow or brown tint predominates.

He adds, "the color of the skin, though of a lower tone, is akin to that of the hair, except in the red parts; and, moreover, *blue* eyes are, really, the sole portion of the *fair* type, which exhibits a *contrast* of color with the *ensemble;* for the red parts produce, with the residue of the skin, merely a harmony of *analogy* of hue, or, at most, a *contrast* of *hues* and not of *colors;* and the portions of the skin nearest to the hair, the eyebrows, and the eyelashes, present a harmony of *analogy,* either of *scale* or of *hue.*"

In the *fair* type, then, the harmonies of *analogy* manifestly prevail over the harmonies of contrast.

When *hazel* eyes exist in the *fair* type (as is often the case), in combination with *chestnut* hair, the analogic harmony is perfect. In the several complexions usually classified under the title Brunette, wherein black or dark hair predominates, there is a prevalence of the harmony of contrast.

"In fact" (remarks Chevreul), "the hair, eyes, and eyebrows contrast, in color and tone, not alone with the white of the skin, but also with the red portions, which, in this type, are actually redder, or less rosy, than in the blonde type. Nor should we forget, that a *decided* red, combined with black, communicates to the latter the aspect of an exceedingly deep color, either blue or green."

A proper understanding of the principles here indicated, will enable the colorist to secure fidelity to nature, in the particulars absolutely inherent in his *model,* while he so arranges the draperies, background, &c., as to impart value to the complexion, and produce a harmonious and perfect picture.

The putting into verse of maxims, of any species, is so valuable an aidance to the memory, that it has been styled the "Shorthand of Thought;" and it will be scarce needful to allude to the trite quotation from Fletcher of Saltoun, wherein he declares, without qualification, that a "Nation's verse exerts a higher and more potent influence than its laws," in order to justify the annexing to the present chapter of the following lines, from the facile pen of Henry Hopley White, Esq., of England, aptly embodying, as they do, the principles to which this chapter is devoted. It is entitled:

"THE RELATIONS AND HARMONIES OF COLOR."

Blue—Yellow—Red—pure simple colors all,
(By mixture *not* obtained) we *primaries* call;
From these, in various combinations blent,
All other colors trace their *one descent.*

Each mixed with each,—their powers, combined, diffuse
New colors, which are *secondary* hues;
Yellow, with red makes orange; with blue, green;
In blue, commixed with red, is *purple* seen.
Each of these hues in harmony we find,
When with its complementary combined;
Orange, with blue and green, with red agrees,
While purple tints, near yellows, always please.

The secondaries tertiaries produce,
And citrine, olive, russet, bring to use,
Thus green and orange, blent, produce citrine,
While olive springs from purple, mixed with green;
Orange and purple, mingled, russet prove,
And wrought upon by the law, named above,

The complemental *secondary* hue
Harmonious with each tertiary we view.

Thus citrine, olive, russet, harmonize
With purple, orange, green, their true allies;
These hues, by white diluted, *tints* are made,
While by black deepened into darkest shade.
Pure or combined, the primaries, all three,
To please the visual orbs, must present be;
If the support be lacking even of *one*,
In that proportion, harmony is gone:
Should red be unsustained by a due share
Of blue and yellow *pure;* combined they are
In green; which, secondary, thus we see,
The harmonizing medium of the three.

Yellow, for light, contrasts dark purple's hue,
Its complemental, made of red and blue,
Red most exciting is,—let nature tell
How grateful and how soothing green's soft spell.

So blue *retires*, beyond all colors *cold*,
While orange *warm, advancing*, you behold;
The mingling of two primaries makes a hue
As perfect and decided as 'tis new:
But all the mixtures, which the three befall,
Tend to destroy or neutralize them all,—
Nay mix them, three parts yellow, five of red,
And eight of blue, the colors all are fled;
When primaries are not *pure*, you're sure to see
Their complementals *change* in due degree.

If red (with yellow) to a scarlet tend,
Some blue its complemental green will blend;
So, if your red be crimson (blue with red),
Your green with yellow would be varied;
If yellow tends to orange, then you find
Purple (its complement) to blue inclined;
But, if to blue it leans, then mark the change,
Nearer to red you see the purple range.
If blue partakes of red, the orange then
To yellow tends;—if yellowish, you ken,
The secondary orange glows with red.
Reader, farewell! my lesson now is said.

H. H. W

WATER COLORS.

The colors, required for coloring photographs, are the same as are employed for miniature painting, with such difference in their combinations, as the tone of the photograph renders necessary. The following list comprises all that are essential; and if used perfectly pure, they will not injure the picture.

Antwerp Blue, Chinese White, Bistre, Chrome Yellow, 1, 2, 3, Black Lead, Cobalt Blue, Blue Black, Cologne Earth, Bright Roman Ochre, Constant White, British Ink, Crimson Lake, Bronze, Dragon's Blood, Brown Madder, Emerald Green, Brown Pink, French Blue, Burnt Carmine, Gallstone, Burnt Sienna, Gamboge, Burnt Umber, Green Bice, Cadmium Yellow, Green Oxide of Chromium, Carmine, Chalons Brown, Hooker's Green, 1, 2, Chinese Vermilion, Indian Lake, Indian Red, Prussian Blue, Indian Yellow, Prussian Green, Indigo, Purple, Intense Blue, Purple Brown, Intense Brown, Purple Lake, Italian Pink, Purple Madder, Ivory Black, Raw Sienna, King's Yellow, Raw Umber, Lamp Black, Red Chalk, Lemon Yellow, Red Orpiment, Light Red, Rose Madder, Madder Carmine, Roman Ochre, Malachite Green, Sap Green, Mars Brown, Scarlet Lake, Mars Orange, Sepia, Mars Red, Sepia Page's, Mars Yellow, Sepia Warm, Naples Yellow, Smalt, Neutral Tint, Terra-Verte, Olive Green, Ultramarine, Orange Ochre, Ultramarine Ashes, (Olive Vermilion, 2), Vandyke Brown, Venetian Red, Payne's Gray (for Scarlet), Verditer, Permanent Crimson, Vermilion, Pink Madder, Yellow Lake, Yellow Ochre.

Carmine.—This is a brilliant red, inclining to crimson,

very clear in its pale washes, and in its full touches intense. As it is somewhat fugitive in its nature, it should, in flesh tints, be used with caution.

Burnt Carmine is a rich, deep crimson, very useful in the full touches of drapery.

Rose Madder.—A most valuable color for flesh,—its pale washes being delicate, clear, transparent, and very permanent.

Pink Madder.—Similar to the last named, but somewhat deeper in tint.

Crimson Lake.—Somewhat akin to carmine, but less brilliant; chiefly useful in draperies.

Venetian Red.—A beautiful color for flesh; works well and is permanent. Its pale washes are very clear, and slightly modified with Indian Yellow, it constitutes, in the hands of the miniature painter, a valuable general tint for most complexions, though for photographs it is often too deep.

Light Red.—Is analogous in general character, but more inclining to orange.

Indian Red.—A powerful red, of a purplish hue. It works well and is durable, but is useful only when in combinations, as a shadow for flesh.

Vermilion.—A very brilliant red, not generally suitable for flesh tints, as it is heavy and does not work well. With a little lake, it is useful for the lower lips of children.

Orange Vermilion, No. 2.—Works more favorably than the last preceding, and, as suggested by its name, it inclines somewhat to yellow. (This color, which is one of Newman's, is the nearest approach to a pure scarlet, that is permanent.)

Roman Ochre.—Useful for dark flesh, as also for dra

peries. It is used, moreover, in combination with sepia, for light hair.

Yellow Ochre.—Used in combination for light hair, and also in landscape backgrounds.

Indian Yellow.—A brilliant and intense yellow, which works well. From its purity of tint, it is a most useful yellow for mixing in flesh tints. For many photographs, however, it is too intense.

Cadmium Yellow.—A very brilliant and durable color for draperies, as also useful in producing orange tints.

Gamboge.—A fine, rich yellow, useful in forming green combinations. It, moreover, washes well, but is not suitable for flesh.

Lemon Yellow.—A beautiful light, vivid, and permanent yellow, useful in draperies for high lights.

Yellow Lake.—A bright, transparent yellow, though somewhat fugitive.

Italian Pink.—A yellow very like the last mentioned, but deeper and richer.

Naples Yellow.—A fine light yellow, which, when mingled with pink madder, is valuable as a general wash for flesh, and alone, where a body color is needed for the high light. Like most mineral colors, it is damaged by impure air, and, therefore, the picture should ever be carefully protected from this.

Raw Sienna.—A brownish yellow, which is permanent, and works favorably, and is specially useful in backgrounds.

Burnt Sienna.—A fine, transparent brown, of an orange tint, valuable in dark, warm complexions, as likewise in backgrounds.

Brown Madder.—A rich russet brown, which works well and is permanent; which is useful for the darkest touches in flesh, and for lowering red draperies. When united with blue, it makes a delicate gray, useful in flesh shadows.

Burnt Umber.—A good brown, useful for hair, draperies, and backgrounds.

Sepia.—A cool, translucent brown, useful equally in its full touches or pale washes, and valuable for hair, whether in combination or alone. With lake, or lake and indigo, it yields a fine transparent black for the shadows of draperies, of either silken or woollen fabric.

Sepia, Warm.—Similar to the substance just named, in its every property, though of warmer tint.

Vandyke Brown.—A fine warm brown, useful, from its great transparency, in glazing numerous other tints, which it both warms and deepens. Care in its use is requisite, since it is liable to "*work up,*" when a large amount of it is employed.

Neutral Tint.—A valuable gray, which may be modified for almost any shadow, by the addition of other tints.

Purple Madder.—A deep warm purple, of great richness and intensity, which works well and is permanent, and is, moreover, useful for very deep, warm shadows.

French Blue or French Ultramarine.—A fine blue very closely resembling the tint of genuine ultramarine, while working to better results.

Cobalt.—A bright, durable blue, which enters largely into the shadow colors of flesh.

Prussian Blue.—A deep blue, useful in draperies, and with the addition of carmine constituting all varieties of purple and violet. It should not be used in flesh, as it is liable to turn green.

Indigo.—A good dark blue, useful in combination for producing a variety of greens for backgrounds.

Ivory Black.—A rich translucent black, in its washes inclining somewhat to brown.

Chinese White.—A valuable, permanent white, of great body and working well; useful for the light of eyes, lace, &c., and also for giving body in draperies.

BRUSHES, ETC.

The operant's pencils should be moderate-sized sables. When charged with water, they should terminate in a good point, with no uneven hairs, and should spring well on being pressed with the finger.

For large washes, a few good camel's-hair pencils should be provided. For *hatching*, a sable, of which the point has been worn off, will serve sufficiently well.

Small pencils should be discarded, as tending to produce a feeble, wiry effect, which is extremely undesirable.

Good pencils are essential, alike to comfort in operating, and to the production of excellence in results.

THE PHOTOGRAPH; TO CHOOSE AND PREPARE IT.

To obtain fine results in coloring, it is requisite that the photograph approach, in some degree at least, to excellence. It is important, that the distribution of light and shade, in the picture, be effective and natural; that, throughout, it be properly focussed and sharp; and, that it be a clear, well-defined, and bright photograph.

A direct vertical light for producing the portrait should be avoided, since the effect of light and shadow, so obtained, is generally unnatural,—the intense light at the crown of the head often imparting, even to dark, glossy hair, an aspect of grayness, while the shadows under the eyes, nose, and chin, appear unpleasantly heavy.

A portion of skylight joining a side-light, and both facing the north, will furnish the best picture. The sitter should be placed somewhat back from beneath the skylight, while the head quarters a little from the side-light. The whole figure will then be well illumined; the deepest shadow on the face of a three quarters' view (which, as being usually the best, we are speaking of here), will be on the retiring cheek, while the partial profile will be well lighted and clearly defined on the shadowed cheek.

The position of the head in relation to the body is a matter of taste. When both are placed in one and the same direction, the effect is most simple; while the turning of the body in one direction, and of the head in another, imparts to the figure greater animation. Care, however, should be taken, not to give too much movement to the figure, or to put it in a strained unnatural posture. See chapter on sitting, pp. 105–112.

The background should be of a tint somewhat about midway between the highest lights and the deepest shadows of the picture, in order to give to all parts due relief, and produce the best effects in coloring. If the sitter be placed a few feet from the screen, serving as a background, the figure will possess greater relief.

Sufficient space for background should be secured both above and around the figure; since nothing looks clumsier, than a picture with scarce any background, as though the sitter were cramped for space. The position of the figure on the background, is the sole means of indicating the size and proportions of the model. A figure placed high on the plate, suggests a tall person, while a figure low down in the picture, intimates a short one. A background, instead of being crowded with useless objects, should be devoted to a few simple items, that neither agitate the feelings nor draw off the attention, which *ought* to be fixed upon the principal figure or object.

For water colors, the tone of the picture is of considerable importance. A warm neutral tint or gray is the best tone for coloring. Heavy shadows of purple, brown, or of an inky tone, are very undesirable, from the lack of harmony between these tones and the natural shadows of flesh.

TO MOUNT THE PICTURE FOR COLORING.

The first step in preparing the photograph, is to mount it on a card-board. For this purpose a solution of gelatine, or of clean fresh glue, should be used. Paste or gum water should be avoided, as these are prone to generate acid, which would injure the picture.

The gelatine or glue should be brushed over the back of the photograph, which should then be laid on the board. A sheet of clean paper should now be placed on the surface, and then pressed gently yet firmly down, and finally the picture should be put under a weight. The items of its subsequent preparation depend somewhat on the process of its production. As the various photographic papers, through the diverse processes they are subjected to by operants, present almost numberless varieties of surface, no *universal* mode of procedure can be prescribed for preparing a surface to receive water colors.

To apply water colors to paper with facility and effect, it should have a surface whereon the colors wash easily, sinking in sufficiently to allow other colors to be worked over them without washing up. To secure such surface, the photograph will invariably require some preparation.

In a matter so important and so greatly affecting success, not less than comfort, in working, we would urgently recommend "Newman's preparation;" which, applied to the picture, gives a fine surface, whereon the colors wash easily, and enables the operant to produce the most brilliant results.

This preparation should be applied with a camel's hair brush, and spread evenly over the whole surface of the picture, which then should be dried. For the most part one application will suffice, and this may be ascertained by trying a corner with a little color.

If it wash on easily, without sinking too far into the surface, it is ready for coloring. If, contrariwise, it is much absorbed, it will, especially if the operant be a tyro, require another application. Before beginning to color, the surface may advantageously be washed with clean water and a brush, and then dried.

Some albuminized paper requires no preparing, though it is, mostly, improved by one application. If the colors work greasily on albuminized paper, a little prepared ox-gall may be united with them.

Besides its use for preparing the surface to receive the color favorably, this "preparation" is invaluable, as a medium for adding to the water colors in vogue. In any preparation for this purpose, it mixes readily with water in whatever proportion, and has the important property of becoming insoluble when dry, so that a wash of color, wherewith it has been combined, is not liable to work up in applying another wash over it. The colorist is thus enabled to obtain a depth and transparency resembling those of oil colors, and wholly unattainable by mingling the colors themselves on the palette.

In employing it, only a small portion of color should be mixed at one time,—not more, indeed, than is requisite for immediate use; since, when the color mixed therewith has once dried on the palette, it is unfit for subsequent use. The palette and pencils should, moreover, be washed before the color hardens, or its removal will be troublesome.

The "preparation," so often alluded to, may frequently be used profitably both upon salted and albuminized paper, to which dry colors should be applied, in case they do not "bite" or sufficiently adhere.

METHOD OF COLORING.

Though the coloring of photographs differs, in some items, essentially from that of miniature paintings, yet, as both the management and manipulation of the colors are similar, the amateur should, at the outset, know somewhat of the principles on which water color painting is based.

The operant, wholly unacquainted with these, will be surprised to learn that, by mixing his colors to the tint desired, and then simply washing them on to his impression, he will obtain but a meagre and unsatisfactory result. There is scarce any part of a human face so flat, as to be correctly represented by a simple wash. It is so full of inequalities, that the gradations of light and shade are, virtually, numberless; and these gradations between the high lights and deepest shadows, are named "pearly tints," "demitints," or grays. In using these, and indeed all gradations of color, upon the local flesh tint, in order to obtain transparency and depth, it is requisite to employ "hatching," or "stippling."

Hatching consists in working on the color in short strokes, following, as closely as possible, the form of the features:—for instance, the strokes nearly horizontal on the forehead, while circular about the eyes, mouth, and general contour. These strokes are then crossed with similar ones, avoiding, however, the forming of direct right angles. This should be done with a firm touch, making every little stroke as even as may be.

Stippling is a process somewhat similar, save that fine dots, with the point of the brush, are employed in place of lines.

The effect, in either case, is to impart depth and transparency, while also retaining greater purity of tint, than could be produced by any washing of mingled colors.

The amateur would profit at the outset, by procuring a few skilfully composed and painted miniatures, whereof he should next obtain photographic copies. These let him color, copying minutely the several tints of the originals. Thus he will learn what are the various colors used in producing, in the original, the desired effect, and what are the modifications of these made necessary by the tone of his photograph.

As a general rule, warm, gray-toned photographs are best for coloring; that for fair persons, especially for ladies and children, a light impression, free from abrupt, heavy shadows, but perfect in half-tone and definition, is best; while for dark persons, especially for strongly marked men's heads, a more vigorous impression may be advantageously employed.

Let the learner endeavor to effect his object by one bold touch, rather than by several hesitating attempts. Nor let him forget, that, in water colors, the first tints should be conserved, pure, and brilliant, as they may easily be lowered, subsequently, to any tone required; but, if once rendered dull or muddy-looking, nothing can restore their purity.

We subjoin a few maxims, applicable alike to every mode of coloring, whether in oil, water, or dry colors.

The substance of them has been already presented, but the colorist may find it useful to have them stored in his memory, in this epigrammatic form.

I.—Flesh, while receding from the eye, appears to grow colder in tone.

II.—The edges of all cast shadows are gray.

III.—The high lights of flesh should be of a yellowish white.

IV.—As light is color, every gradation to shadow is a gradation from color, and, therefore, the color in shadows should never be too bright.

V.—Local colors are found neither in lights nor shadows.

VI.—Warm colors (or those approaching to orange) advance; while cold colors (or those approximating to blue) retire.

VII.—Contrasts yield brilliancy of effect, yet they should never be violent or inharmonious.

VIII.—Colors should be laid on with the least possible rubbing with the brush, to preserve them fresh and bright.

IX.—Harshness should be avoided, and every line should be softened; for in nature there exist no real outlines, though the boundary of vision is distinctly marked.

X.—Let all cast shadows be kept of a single tone, and always warm (save at the edges), varying, of course, with the local tint.

XI.—Let reflected lights be kept warm, unless the object they are projected from be visible, then they partake of its especial color.

XII.—Where the outline of a figure is ungraceful, it may judiciously be hidden, to some extent, in the shadow of the background.

XIII.—Massing together lights and shadows, will secure breadth of grandeur and effect. A background will greatly aid in this respect.

XIV.—Every portion of the background should appear to recede from the figure, which should never seem to be cut in or inlaid.

XV.—Breadth of light and shade should be properly preserved, or the most careful manipulation and elaborate finish will be tame and ineffective.

A perpetual reference to the duplicate photograph, will enable the operant to preserve the likeness of his picture; while continual attention to these maxims will enable him to impart to it some value as a work of art.

TO PAINT THE HEAD.

The photograph being prepared, ascertain whether it be in a condition to receive the color by trying one corner. If the color be too much absorbed, another sizing will be desirable; but while a slight absorption of the color renders more care necessary, it has the advantage of enabling the artist to gain depth and transparency, by working over his previous painting without disturbing the color.

The picture should be placed on a small desk, the light falling upon it from the left hand. A piece of clean paper should be kept over the lower part, whereon to rest the hand while painting the head; as, otherwise, it will get greased with the hand and with difficulty receive the color. A duplicate copy, clearly and strongly defined, should be ever near for reference.

Naples yellow, with a little madder pink, will be best for a general wash, the slight opacity having a good effect in softening the harshness of the shadows, too common in many photographs.

Commence by giving the retiring shadows of the forehead, eyes, and mouth, a wash of gray, composed of Naples yellow and cobalt, the green or blue tint predominating, as the complexion is dark or fair. Next give a general wash of Naples yellow with a little pink madder. While this is drying the hair may be colored; the tone of the picture materially modifying the choice of tints to be employed.

The eyebrows and eyelashes may now be touched, and the pupil put in with sepia, while the iris is put in with sepia and cobalt, if the eye be gray or blue, or with burnt sienna if the eye be dark. The lips should now be colored with vermilion and pink madder, the upper lip being kept in shadow. The lips of children require more vermilion, and of aged persons more pink madder.

The shadows around the mouth and nostrils may now be touched with brown madder and pink madder. Finally, heighten the general flesh tint by *hatching*, using the color thin and flowing, while following the form of the face.

If high finish be not desired, the head might now be finished by enhancing the color on the cheek with vermilion and pink madder.

These photographs are called "tinted" paintings. More elaborated, however, will often be required. In such case, proceed to wash in the general tint of the background, and commence the draperies by giving them the general wash; next heighten the color of the cheek with vermilion and pink madder.

Hatch over the shadows of the forehead with a bluish gray, and with a light tint of the same *hatch* over the receding cheek, the temples, and about the chin.

Put in the blue shadows beneath and at the corners of the mouth, and then *stipple* the socket of the eye with a cool green. The reflected lights may next be warmed by *stippling* with the flesh tint; finish the lips by *stippling* with vermilion and pink madder, making a little Chinese white for the high light, if needful. Touch the edge of the upper eyelid with Indian red, and soften the shaded side of the iris with shadow color. The sclerotic or white of the eye, in many persons will require slightly touching with cobalt, and the corner next the nose with pink madder.

The hair may now be finished, keeping it in mass to avoid the effect of wiry hairs. Work on the edges of the hair and flesh with gray, to avoid the appearance of the hair being cut into the face.

The chief work on the head will now be to give it finish and softness, by *stippling* in the grays and pearly tints, and to impart spirit and character by putting in the deepest "touches" about the eye with sepia and pink madder, mixed with a little dilute gum arabic, and about the mouth and nose with sepia and gum-water. The light in the pupil of the eye must be carefully put in with Chinese white.

The neck, bosom, hands, and arms, having been washed with the local tint, may now be completed. The tips of the knuckles, fingers, and elbows, may be *hatched* with pink madder, and the divisions of the fingers touched with the same.

In finishing the draperies and background (the next process), the choice of colors must be determined by the complexion of the model.

Lastly, go again over the face and give it the finishing touches. The high lights in the photograph should be strictly preserved throughout. If it be a copy of a daguerreotype, &c., the high lights may require to be *imagined* and strengthened. A little gum-water, used in

19

the deepest shadows of the hair, eyes, &c., gives transparency, if required, and the picture is completed. But avoid using gum-water *too freely*, especially in the draperies.

COLOR OF HAIR.

The various colors of hair are so numerous, and the tones of photographs so varied, as to make it impossible to give any special combinations of color for painting hair. We may, however, present some general hints.

In such heavy photographs as require it, some body color may be used. Chinese white or Naples yellow added to the color, for lights, will answer.

Flaxen Hair.—The lights may be made with Roman ochre, and the shadows are often greenish.

Auburn and Chestnut Hair.—The lights should be neutral, inclining to purple; the local color burnt umber, and the shadows glazed with lake.

Bright Red Hair.—Hair of this color should usually be somewhat subdued. Roman ochre may be used for the lights; for the local color Venetian red, and sepia, or burnt Sienna. Shadow with sepia and lake.

Dark Brown Hair.—Lights, purple; local color, sepia; shadows, warm.

Raven Black Hair.—Lights, neutral; local color, indigo, lake, and gamboge, in requisite proportions.

Gray Hair.—Cobalt and sepia, properly modified with neutral tint and umber.

DRAPERIES.

We have before remarked that, in portrait painting, certain colors, inherent in the model, *must* be rendered accurately, by being colored with the utmost fidelity, while the management of others is very much under the operant's control, and by their judicious arrangement, he gives to the essential colors their utmost value, while preserving the harmony and keeping of his picture. Under this head, comes the management of draperies. We here refer the operant to the previous statement of the principles on which is based the harmony of color.

Blue is somewhat troublesome for the artist, as such a mass of cold color makes it requisite to introduce something warm to conserve the harmony of the picture. In painting, use cobalt for the lights, and French blue and lake for the shadows.

Yellow.—All positive colors, in any mass, should be avoided, or used with subdued brilliancy.

Red.—Whether vermilion, carmine, or lake be used, sepia and lake, in modified combinations, will make a good shadow color.

For uniforms, a most brilliant scarlet is produced by first washing with cadmium yellow, and when this is dry, using vermilion over it, and shadow with carmine and sepia.

Purples, greens, orange, and all compound tints, are produced by the mixture of some of the primaries. Practice must enable the operant to select the most appropriate for the moment.

White.—Chinese white is the most useful and durable. The middle tints may be made of cobalt and Indian red, and the shadows of sepia.

Black.—Sepia, indigo, and lake; or gamboge with the latter two make a good transparent black for silks, &c.

Gold Ornaments.—May be touched with Roman ochre, the lights with Chinese white and chrome or Naples yellow, and the shadows with burnt umber.

Cloth Fabrics.—These, unlike silks, are often painted

in opaque colors; and then it is best to partially cover the photograph with the local color, and paint the lights and shadows upon it.

The deep shadows of all draperies are improved by adding a little gum-water, which, however, should be used sparingly.

BACKGROUNDS.

These should be devoted to repose, and should never be so painted, as to distract attention from the principal figure. The fewer objects here introduced, the better.

When white spots occur in the background, they should be touched with a somewhat deeper tint of the local color, which is commonly lampblack or sepia.

VIGNETTE PHOTOGRAPH.

This is a pleasing style of photograph, not requiring the same degree of finish as others, but looks very well when *tinted* as before described.

GELATINIZING POSITIVES.

As especially applicable to stereoscopic photographs, and partially, to paper positives generally, it may be well to describe a mode of coating pictures with gelatine, successfully practised in France, and excelling all other varnishes in its results.

To 20 grs. of the purest gelatine (Italian gelatine is the best, and isinglass will not answer), add 1 oz. of cold water, and put it near a fire till dissolved, and then strain it through muslin. Take a proper-sized piece of well-polished plate-glass, free from imperfections, and after cleaning it thoroughly and drying, sponge it over with prepared ox-gall. Before the gall is dry, cover the plate with a hot solution of gelatine, and put it away to set where it will be free from dust.

When the gelatine is sufficiently set, lay the picture gently upon it, face downwards, pressing it and taking care to avoid air-bubbles; then leave it some hours to harden thoroughly. When the gelatine is perfectly dry, a penknife, run round the edge of the picture, will readily separate it from the glass, and present a highly polished surface, exhibiting the smallest detail with the greatest delicacy and beauty.

MEZZOTINT PHOTOGRAPHS.

Touching up paper prints in light and shade, chiefly requires care and some knowledge of drawing. The colors to be used must somewhat depend on the tone of the photograph. Indian ink plain or tinted is generally pleasing.

GENERAL REMARKS.

In concluding these remarks on painting in water colors, we repeat, that they are merely suggestive, and will require continual modifying to suit the complexions to be imitated, and the tone of the photograph to be colored. A right method of coloring is the main consideration.

PHOTOGRAPHIC COLORS.—POWDER.

Dry colors are used for coloring positives on glass, silver plate, or albuminized paper. They are employed in the state of an impalpable powder, and are so prepared, as to adhere to the surface of the picture by the simplest manipulation.

Newman's colors, after a large and varied experience,

we pronounce incomparably better than any other we are acquainted with. They are also the cheapest, as well as the best in vogue.

VARNISH.

A varnish for glass positives, to give the operant the greatest facilities, and present, when completed, the most artistic effect, should *not* (as has been thought by many, both manufacturers and photographers) exhibit a hard, glassy surface, from which the colors must blow like dust; but a surface which, while free from *tackiness*, should present a tooth to the color. On such a surface the dry colors will adhere like crayons. A varnish, of such properties, has lately been introduced by Mr Newman, and sold by American stock dealers.

METHOD OF COLORING.

The method of coloring is nearly the same, whether on daguerreotypes, glass positives, or positives on paper. The first of these are colored exactly like glass positives, and not usually being varnished, when once colored throughout, they are finished.

Our own method of dealing with the glass positive is to color first on the collodion surface. Commence on the forehead, using flesh No. 1.

Having, with No. 1 flesh, colored the lights of the forehead, next, with No. 2 flesh, fair or dark, begin on the lights of the cheeks, softening into the shadows, and joining the high lights already colored. Speaking generally, fleshes, reds, greens, and yellows, may be advantageously employed; while browns, purples, light blue, and some other colors are best till after varnishing.

The first coloring finished, carefully blow away every

particle of color, which has not adhered to the surface, as it will else run with the varnish. Let the varnish be now flooded on, as collodion is, with like care to insure an even coating, and drained off at one corner. The former objection to dry colors, their tendency to *fade*, is here obviated by the varnish combining with the color on the plate, and making a coating like that of oil paint.

In the second and last coloring, the high lights should be touched with No. 1 flesh, the local tint with No. 2 flesh, and the cheeks heightened with Nos. 1 or 2 complexion.

In the backgrounds almost every color may be used, though various combinations of the grays, greens, browns, and purples are most useful.

Positives on glass, produced by the "Alabastrine process," may effect finer results with dry colors, than can be obtained on any other species of glass picture. The picture is varnished before beginning to color; we then proceed as in the second coloring above, using tints similar to those prescribed for water colors.

Positives on albumenized paper or on salted paper, sized with its appropriate preparations, may be colored in the same way, though, as a rule, the latter should be colored in oil and water colors.

ENLARGED PICTURES; COLORING IN CRAYONS.

Since the introduction of the Solar Camera, life-size and other enlarged photographs have begun to excite popular attention. These pictures, from causes both inherent and incidental, require, more than any other photographs, some aid from the artist's touch.

The nearer the picture approaches the life-size, the

more palpably is felt the need of the hues of life, and thus the colorist's aid becomes imperative.

To meet either the want of color or of finish, nothing, perhaps, is more suitable, than the employment of colored crayons, or black and white chalk. We shall, therefore, give a few suggestions as to the mode of using these.

PREPARATION OF THE PHOTOGRAPH.

Enlarged portraits, by the solar camera, are commonly, in this country, produced by the process of development-printing, and therefore are on plain paper, without an albumen surface. Any kind of paper, with a surface somewhat rough, which will present a tooth to the chalk, will answer.

Should the surface, when tried, fail to "bite" sufficiently, rub it with pumice or sepia powder, till a proper surface is obtained. A surface, in imitation of the pumice paper prepared for pastel painting, is produced by applying to the paper a warm solution of isinglass, and then dusting, through a sieve, pumice or cuttle fish powder, till an even surface is obtained, which, on drying, presents an excellent tooth. This treatment is suitable only for pictures, which are to be finished in colored pastels. In most cases, drawing paper, especially after the size is removed by a final wash in hot water, will serve every purpose.

FINISHING IN MEZZOTINT.

Prints, developed on plain paper, have generally a somewhat unfinished effect, which may, however, by a few skilful touches, be wholly removed. The crayon tint to be used will depend on the tone of the picture, and will consist of black, grays, browns, purples, and white; the last to be sparingly used in putting in such high lights as those in the eyes, &c.

COLORING IN PASTELS.

To color in pastels requires considerable skill and knowledge of drawing; but, if well done, no coloring is more effective or suitable for finishing life-size photographs.

It is best beginning with the face, and the tints here used will be like those described in the instructions for water and oil colors. The face being first colored, and the color blended, great brilliancy may be secured by *hatching* over the features with tints of the same scale, but in a higher key. Great care only will keep the picture from being cold and chalky on the one hand, or raw and red on the other. The works of M. Louis Gratia supply the finest possible models for the imitation of the student.

The best mode of preserving the picture is to place a glass at the back as well as the front of the canvas, as this will fully protect the colors from injury.

COLORING IN OIL.

The photographer, who would color his productions *artistically*, should possess a knowledge of drawing. Some colorists have given the palm to water colors, for the inadequate reason, that the use of oil requires an artist's experience and skill. If, however, the water color advocates rightly judge that the use of oil demands greater ability and skill, their argument must assuredly recommend oil colors, as, in their use, they guarantee the talent and competency of the colorist. To the writer (long experienced in the use of both oil and water colors), it seems that, *in either art,* the persons possessing the highest degree of artistic merit will best succeed; and that it is no less easy to do a *little* in the one than in the other.

To prepare the photograph, mount it free from dust, coat it carefully with "Newman's preparation," (of which two applications will sometimes be requisite,) and let it be rolled by some hot presser.

The operant will require nut oil and poppy oil, varnishes, brushes, palette, rest stick and palette knife, together with the following colors, which should be gotten ready prepared, viz., white, Naples yellow, yellow ochre, raw sienna, burnt sienna, light red, extract of vermilion, vermilion, pink madder, crimson lake, &c., &c. Procure also a megilp tube, and some sugar of lead; the one as vehicle, the other to aid colors that are bad driers.

The student, who mixes observantly the tints above named, will at once perceive their uses in the various stages of his work; and his practice will suggest all the modifications which his model may demand.

PAINTING THE PHOTOGRAPH.

Employ sufficient megilp with your colors to make them thin and transparent; but let the lights be opaque and well coated with color.

Consider carefully the gradations of tint by which the hair and flesh are softened into each other, and note the shadows cast by raised or over-falling locks, &c.

Use gray and shadow tints to blend the hair and the flesh.

Black coats are first glazed with a warm, transparent black, into which paint the lights with different tints of black and white, strengthening the shadows with vandyke brown and a little lake and bitumen.

All draperies may be treated as recommended in the case of a black coat.

COLORS FOR HAIR.

Light Hair may be made with vandyke brown and ochre, with raw umber for the shadows; the same for the local tint, and the same, mixed with Naples yellow, for the lights; the grays are identical with those used for the flesh.

Dark Hair.—Use a little black with some vandyke brown and lake; for black hair use a larger proportion of warm black. Bitumen is useful in this part of the work, as also is brown madder, mingled with French blue. In painting hair, preserve carefully the grays or half-tones.

SECOND PAINTING.

When the first painting is perfectly dry, soften the work by passing over it a brush charged with poppy oil, and rub in the oil, with a piece of soft leather. Glaze the entire face with a proper tint; repaint the shadows with transparent colors; strengthen and brighten the lights; improve the blues, greens, and grays of the flesh, and soften the lines; repaint the background, and blend its tint with a clean, soft brush; strengthen the folds of draperies; employ glazing tints wherever practicable; and preserve the colors warm, clear, and bright.

THIRD PAINTING.

The second painting having dried, complete the picture with transparent touches and markings, to strengthen the shadows, force the lights, and secure a masterly and artistic style of finish. When this is thoroughly dry, the picture is ready for varnishing.

Those, who cannot draw, should use their colors well-thinned with megilp, to preserve their transparency. And they, who can draw, should not, conceitedly, neglect that care to preserve the life-like truthfulness of the picture, without which it is impossible to succeed in photographic coloring.

PORTRAITURE.

The class of photographic portraits, chiefly in favor at the present day, and known as *Cartes de Visite*, or album portraits, make larger requisitions on the operant's knowledge of art, with its principles in regard to composition and arrangement, than any other phase of photography has hitherto done.

It should, at the outset, be remembered, that the mere delineation of an object, or the mere production of a likeness, does not constitute a picture. To constitute a good portrait, and, at the same time, to produce a pleasing picture, the original should be represented under such circumstances of position, arrangement, light and shade, and accessories, as shall suggest character, while also conducing to pictorial effect.

One of the first considerations, in connection with portraiture, and especially where the full-length figure is shown, will be as to *position*. This has much to do with the expression of character, as well as pictorial effect.

The figure should rarely, if ever, be in the middle of a picture, or equidistant from each side; nothing is more destructive of pictorial effect, than such a position. Generally, more space should be in front of the figure than behind. If the figure be placed equidistant from the top and bottom of the picture, it is still more destructive of pictorial effect and suggestive verity, than if equidistant from the sides. The distance from the top and bottom is the chief means of suggesting the height of the figures. The higher the head is towards the top of the picture, the taller will the figure appear; and the wider the space overhead, the shorter will be the appearance of the model.

Not less important than position, is a *purpose* in such position. It is not meant by this, that the sitter should always be engaged in some occupation, but care should be taken to avoid the appearance of total vacancy, or of the self-consciousness of having a portrait taken.

As regards composition, the greater the *simplicity* the better will be the result.

It is, moreover, desirable that the heaviest part of the picture, alike in form and color, should be at the base.

Contrast, in both lines and tones, is an important element in pictorial effect. These, however, should never be harsh or violent, as these properties destroy one of the most important requisites in a picture, *breadth.*

An essential element, in securing a harmonious contrast of tones, is the judicious lighting of the model. A direct front light should be avoided, as destructive of all *relief.* Let the light fall on the model at an angle of about 45°; direct vertical light should be avoided, while side light may be used freely.

In grouping for portraiture, small portraits admit the exercise of considerable discretion, and make the task less difficult than in larger photographic groups; fewer accessories being requisite for the purposes of composition.

CONCLUDING REMARKS.

The general principles of coloring have sometimes been reiterated in the directions for different kinds of coloring. Where reiteration has been avoided, it should be remembered, that the instructions for one style of coloring will often be found to comprise hints applying equally to all styles. Bearing this in mind, it will appear, it is thought, that nothing essential, which could aid the amateur in gaining a practical acquaintance with the subject, has been omitted in this chapter.

PICTURE FRAMES.

Oil pictures require gilt frames, unless the pictures have in them much yellow, in which case the contrast "kills" the painting. Ebony, or oak, or black walnut must never be used, if there is much brown in the picture.

Gilt frames are too bright for the ordinary run of water colors, unless a strip of white, more or less wide, intervenes between the painting and the frame. Water colors, however, sometimes look well in a narrow gilt frame, provided such frame be little more than a plain fillet, and the prevailing tone of the drawing be dark, with much brown. Lithographs and engravings require the same treatment as water colors.

The simple rule, then, is that the frame should "bring up" the picture, and not "kill" it by its higher brilliancy. A wall of paint or paper in olive-gray or pale-gray is the best possible, as its mass in some degree neutralizes the gilt frame, and thus tends to set off the pictures.

In very large pictures a gilt frame is almost a necessity. It is only in cases of smaller cabinet pictures that the gold is too bright. The best method of showing a picture is one, that is impracticable in ordinary rooms and galleries. For it should be surrounded by neutral hangings, and be illumined by its own peculiar light, and not by that, in which the spectator stands, and be viewed through an opening, as in a diorama. Then the work of the painter's pencil becomes almost as animated as is Nature's self.

NOTE.—It is found, singular as it may appear, that the gilding on a broad frame draws the eye away from the picture *less*, when completely covered with small ornamentation, than when it is plain. The flat surface *glares* more, than a surface subdivided and broken up, though the latter may be the richer.

CHAPTER XXVII.

PORTRAITS—SEVERAL VARIOUS MODES OF PRODUCING OR FINISHING PERMANENT SOLAR IMPRESSIONS.

The Ivorytype, a picture printed through a negative on artificial ivory, introduced in England, by Mayall of London; also a photograph, colored and sealed upon plate-glass, called the "Ivorytype," introduced in the United States by Wenderoth, 1855.

The Alabastrine, a positive upon glass, colored on the back of the film, and finished with a solution invented by Wharton Simpson, called his redeveloper. For sale by E. & T. H. Anthony, New York.

The Diaphanotype, a good photograph, cemented to glass and painted on the back in oil colors.

The Hallotype and its variations, are pictures, made on a similar principle with the above, finished in either water or oil colors, or both, on back and front. The two last named are said to be mere applications of Grecian or Oriental painting to photography.

The Melainotype, a positive collodion picture made upon japanned iron plates.

The Sphereotype, simply a collodion positive on glass, with certain peculiarities in the method of making and mounting the picture.

The Crayon, or Spherical Vignette Daguerreotype, a picture representing the head and bust, made spherical by pressing it over a convex glass paper-weight, or other oval surface, and cased with a convex glass over the impression.

The Hillotype.—Having learned, that I, as well as others, was misled in regard to the mode in which these pictures were made, I feel that the explanation, given below, is due to the public.

IVORYTYPES—OR, PHOTOGRAPHS ON ARTIFICIAL IVORY.

THIS is an invention of the distinguished heliographer, J. E. Mayall, of Regent Street, London. These pictures are declared, by English writers on sun-painting, to combine the merits of the daguerreotype and the photograph, exhibiting the delicacies of outline and the beautiful middle tints of the former, devoid of the unpleasant *glare* which so intercepts its effects, and the accuracy and distinctness of the latter without its attendant deficiencies.

They are taken upon a species of artificial ivory, possessing all the excellencies of the real substance without its defects. This imitation is a compound of barytes and vegetable albumen, which, kneaded together and rolled into sheets, is permitted to dry, and is then submitted to a polishing process, whereby a surface of the smoothest texture and purest ivory color is obtained, constituting an admirable recipient for the image, as a basis for the artist's operations.

Plates of this material are manufactured expressly for photographs, to be colored in imitation of miniatures upon ivory, and may be procured at Risler Heilman's Photographic Depot, Paris, France.

The process of printing must be performed wholly by *timing*, as it cannot be inspected while going forward. Two or three trials will determine the amount of time required. A good, vigorous negative is best for printing on artificial ivory. (See chapter on printing on ivory, wood, linen, silk, &c. Second part.)

I have elsewhere remarked, that connoisseurs and writers on art have been accustomed to pronounce heliography a mere *mechanical* operation; as incapable of attaining a higher rank than that of being a faithful copyist—a literal transcriber. Since the appearance of this invention, we perceive the tone of the critics to be changing. The following is a single brief exemplification of this change: "*Photography,*" says an able writer, "*has never trod so closely on the footsteps of the painter's art, as in the pictures on Mr. Mayall's new patent material.*"

Another writer says: "It is not a little curious that the salt, by which the sensitiveness of this artificial ivory to the photographic image is produced, is one, the very existence of which is denied by many English chemists.'

THE AMERICAN IVORYTYPE.

This picture was recently invented and introduced by Wenderoth. It is a colored photograph, finished so as to resemble a miniature or portrait on ivory.

The mode of making it:—Select a vigorous, clearly defined impression, with margin enough to allow for mounting upon the painter's stretcher or painting-board. Dampen the print with a sponge dipped in clear water; then paste its edges upon the stretcher, and, with a clean paper over its face, rub the print down smoothly. When dry, it will be tight and firm for the artist to operate upon.

Or mount it upon a sheet of glass, with its edges ground to hold the paste.

The photograph is now colored upon the face, as a miniature, with permanent colors; but colors much stronger than are commonly employed on surface-painting, as the manner of mounting the completed pictures upon plate-glass has the effect to lower the tone of the colors used.

As transparent colors are reduced, or lose considerably in tone by the mode of mounting, they should be painted-in much more strongly than for surface-painting; while the body-colors should be kept down or reduced in tone, since they are heightened, or made more brilliant and vigorous by the manner of mounting.

The colored print is now mounted on a perfectly clean sheet of plate-glass, face downward, as follows: melt bleached, pure white wax, and while hot, pour it upon the glass plate, which is also made and kept hot on a steel or iron plate, or a soapstone slab, under which one or two spirit lamps are continuously burning. While the wax is quite liquid, take the print by the ends, spring it in the middle, and lower it gently into the heated wax, carefully pressing from the middle outward both parts of it down into the wax, and then with a strait-edged paper-folder, of ivory, or bone, or some similar article suited to the purpose, press and work out all the air-bubbles and superfluous wax. This operation must, of course, be executed while the plate is quite warm.

The paper-folder should be carefully rubbed from one extremity of the print to the other without lifting it therefrom, or suspending the process, as a mark would thus be left on the picture, which will be thoroughly saturated with wax, and which, if properly handled, will be transparent, smooth, and beautiful.

Some artists use a compound of one part gum dem mar to eight parts wax; or Canada balsam and wax; or gum elmer and wax; same proportion of one to eight parts of wax. Others use a larger proportion of the gum-varnishes.

Finally the picture is finished, by placing upon its back and firmly sealing to the glass a clean sheet of white paper or card-board; with a card-board border or mat between the picture and the paper, and with small lumps of hard wax stuck upon the dark or opaque parts of the picture, so arranged as to keep them about $\frac{1}{16}$th or $\frac{1}{20}$th of an inch asunder. This distance must be determined by the effect or appearance produced, and regulated by the judgment of the artist, when the picture is ready for the frame. Sometimes a duplicate *tinted* print of the face is placed behind, to give more color or vigor.

To produce this picture in its perfection requires the highest degree of artistic skill.

THE ALABASTRINE PROCESS.

By Wharton Simpson,
Editor of the Photographic News.

Pictures, by this process, are taken upon a surface of

polished glass. The shadows are of purple velvet, put behind the glass and showing through it. The lights are produced by calomel, a purely white chloride of mercury, an excellent material for the purpose, when spread upon such a background.

The picture is colored as a miniature; not, however, with colors applied to the *front,* as in other processes, but to the *back* of the film, so as to show through, without hiding any of the beautiful details of the photograph.

Frederic Scott Archer, who first applied collodion to photography, discovered the means of whitening collodion positives with bichloride of mercury. This deposit, however, is too opaque, and has a ghastly appearance. This defect has been remedied by the alabastrine solution discovered by Mr. Wharton Simpson. This solution modifies the action of the bichloride, and causes it to form a thinner precipitate, of an alabastrine or pearly whiteness. Mr. Simpson has also discovered a varnish that does not discolor the whites of the picture; and still further, a penetrating varnish, by means of which the colors, put upon the back of the film, are made to show through without hiding any of the details. As a consequence of these improvements, this process is pronounced, by not a few good judges, the best, for portraiture, now existing. For smoothness of surface, delicacy of detail, and artistic beauty of effect, there is nothing comparable with it.

Nor is the manipulation at all difficult, since you have only to take a good collodion positive, fix and wash it, then place it upon a levelling stand, and pour over it a little of the solution in question. In about one hour the re-development is complete, and the dull lights of the positive are changed into the whiteness of pearl.

The alabastrine solution may be procured of the stock

dealers generally. It requires no special directions for its application, as it may be left indefinitely on the picture without injuring it.

This process, however, has its difficulties, which have hitherto prevented its general use. They do not pertain to the process itself, but to the preservation of the beautiful shadings in the high lights. These, apparently, are injured by a too dense precipitate of calomel, which makes the picture look flat in the lights, and, when over-exposed, also fogged in the shadows.

To remedy these defects, the positive should be somewhat under-exposed, whereby the shadows are kept black and vigorous, while the re-developing solution whitens the faint details, and renders visible what before could scarce be discerned.

Next, the effects of light and shade on the sitter, should be carefully studied. The model must look round and not flat; the contrasts between light and shade must be not too strong; and the shadows must be relieved by the reflex lights produced by white screens. The process does not seem suitable for out-door views, or subjects exhibiting strong contrasts of light and shade, or improperly illumined by cross-lights, or a generally diffused glare.

In coloring an alabastrine portrait only four colors are used, viz.: white, black, vermilion, and light-red. The shadows are first painted with mixed black and vermilion, which make a warm, transparent color.

Then the edges of the shadows are painted with a mixture of black and white (the lead color of house-painters), blended partially into the shadows.

Next the local flesh-color is laid on all over the lights. This is made by mixing white and light-red, and is blended into the gray edges of the shadows.

Some vermilion is then applied to the cheeks, lips, &c., and some gray to other parts, and this constitutes the first painting of a face.

The principle to be observed is, that the shadows are not a cold, dirty black, but a warm red in their deepest parts, where reflex lights enliven them, while their edges only are gray; the edge of a shadow being the part of the model, where the light strikes the rounded surface at a tangent.

There is nothing to compare with a well-colored alabastrine portrait. The beauty of a small portrait consists in the delicacy and perfection of its details. A miniature on paper is far too coarse, and will not bear close inspection. Its eyes are indistinct and fishy, while in a direct positive on glass, as in a daguerreotype, you can trace numerous exquisite gradations of shade within the iris. Paper, even when albumenized, will not bear close examining or magnifying with a lens.

For portraiture, then, the alabastrine process is well worthy the careful attention and the diligent study of the photographer.

THE DIAPHANOTYPE.

This picture is a variation of the principle described under the head of Hallotype, and originated with E. C. Hawkins, of Cincinnati, Ohio. It is made as follows:

A good plain positive paper photograph, after being well fixed by the hyposulphite, is thoroughly washed to secure permanence. It is first worked up in ink, and the completed picture is the finer in proportion to the amount of work and retouching devoted to it by a skilful operant.

For large pictures, heavy plate-glass, of a quarter-inch thickness, is pronounced the best; it gives the picture an *enamelled* appearance, and is not easily broken or effaced. Cleanse the plate carefully, and with a brush go over the entire surface, while in a horizontal position, with a mixture of four parts fir balsam and one part dem mar varnish thoroughly incorporated. Meanwhile, let the photograph to be "put down" float on a pan of clear water, face upward. When the picture is soft and pliant, lift it carefully to avoid wetting the upper surface, and lay it on a sheet of bibulous paper to absorb the superfluous moisture.

The picture being now placed face uppermost, the balsam surface of the glass is firmly pressed down upon it. After lying there about five minutes, so that the balsam may permeate the picture and expel the moisture, a little linseed or nut oil is poured upon the plate, and the excess of balsam is removed by rubbing with the finger.

It is also a good method to rest the plate on one edge or corner, with the glass surface uppermost, and, with the index-finger slightly bent, to press against the picture in the centre, and draw the finger towards you. Thus you may remove all the superfluous balsam as well as the air-bubbles. Keep turning the glass from corner to corner till every blister is removed. Lay it flat, and continue rubbing with the finger-tip, till a smooth, level surface is secured. Finally pour oil upon it, and let it remain there till you are ready to paint it.

The painting-easel differs from the ordinary one in not growing narrow towards the top, but in making the two supports parallel, and also in having two back legs instead of one. See engraving.

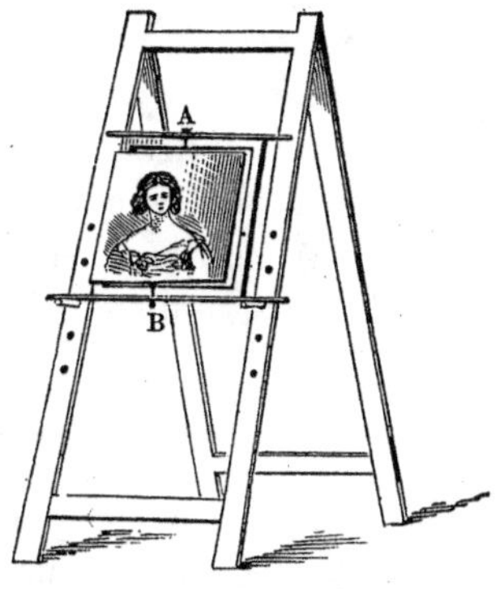

The frame in the centre has a pin A, on which it swings; allowing you, while painting the photograph, which is attached to the posterior surface, to swing it round and examine the front surface, and thus ascertain what is done, and what remains to be done towards completing the picture. B indicates a dark cloth, designed to shut off the light during the process of painting.

The surface of the photograph, whereon you paint, must be perfectly free from balsam, and clean generally. After the glass with the adhering picture has been fastened in the frame, it must be cleansed with a rag dipped in turpentine, then wiped dry; and, finally, a few drops of oil rubbed over the surface, just enough to oil it properly, and no more.

In painting commence with the eyes; next go to the high lights of the forehead, nose, &c.; then proceed to the lower lights, and so on down to the shadows of the flesh. Put the tints firmly in their places and blend them, then paint the hair, and lastly the drapery and background.

The colors requisite are white, Naples yellow, brilliant yellow, chrome yellow, raw sienna, yellow ochre, Roman ochre, scarlet lake, vermilion, Venetian and cobalt blue, permanent blue, Prussian blue, burnt Roman ochre, burnt sienna, Vandyke brown, and ivory black.

A good diaphanotype (as its surface is in oil) can be painted only with a good body of color. Thin painting gives but thin, flat, dead pictures, devoid of all good effects.

The peculiarities, belonging to the manipulation of this picture, make it very difficult to finish by any save well trained, skilful artists of genius. The number, therefore, is small of those, who succeed in producing creditable pictures. When well executed, they are exquisitely beautiful, and promise to be durable.

THE HALLOTYPE.

This is a species of picture, patented by J. Bishop Hall of New York, January 20th, 1857. Its principle consists in *combining* two or more pictures, which are fac-similes or duplicate impressions on semi-translucent material, so as to form one picture. The principle may be applied to engravings, lithographs, &c., as well as to photographs. If applied to the last named, let two copies be taken on photographic paper in the ordinary way. Make the paper of both partially transparent with oil. Cement each to a separate glass with copal or other varnish, which should first be applied to the glass, and partially dried to the state, called "tacky." In putting the picture on the glass, press carefully out all air-bubbles between the paper and the glass. Each being then dried, or nearly so, scrape all excrescences thoroughly from the back. Then put on the pictures one or more coats of copal, or other proper varnish. These being dried, join the two glass plates, so that the pictures shall *coincide,* then cement and exclude from air.

Such is the simplest form of this picture. Different effects are produced by attaching to the glass the *front* picture *only,* and placing the second some way behind, so as to correspond to the other. So, by *cutting out* certain parts of the back picture, and thus permitting more light to reach the front one, fine effects are obtained. Other effects, again, are procured by other variations. These pictures wear somewhat of the appearance of wax figures.

Mr. Hall's *originality* in this invention has been questioned—whether justly or not, we leave the reader to decide—merely placing before him certain authenticated historical facts.

The system of putting color on the *back* of the image has been practised in Germany ever since 1824; was patented there in 1827, and applied to engravings and lithographs.

M. Minotto, a few years since, applied the same principle to photography. His application was in three different modes:—

1. The paper, bearing the image to be colored, is held up to the light, so that the operant can pencil on the back the outlines of the various tints; then put the colors, either oil or water colors, on the different portions of the back of the paper.

2. Begin by varnishing the paper, then dry, and finally color on the back. Here the colors being seen at once, may be corrected at pleasure, and the crayon-sketching is needless. Of course colors must be used, which will *take-* on varnish.

3. Trace the outlines of the picture on a separate paper, and apply the colors thereon. Then affix this paper to the one bearing the image, the outlines of the two being made to coincide, and, the two being pressed together, the colors shine through.

The advantages, possessed by this over the other two, are: 1st. We preserve uncolored (though varnished) the original image produced by the light.

2d. The colors may be easily corrected by painting over the primal tints.

3d. We may give the same image several different

aspects, by executing a number of various-colored duplicates, and thus change the tints of the dress, hair, &c.

4th. We may *cut out* the paper bearing the colors, and apply it upon several backgrounds, to find which suits best.

These operations are all simple, yet require care. The paper should be even-textured, and neither too thick nor too thin, as either excess produces different defects; and the colors should be very vivid, their force being diminished by the veil of the photographic paper, and the varnish should be colorless.

"The chromatint," the right to practise which was sold a few years ago for $25, as a new invention, was a bare-faced *filch* from Minotto. Whether the "hallotype" was, or was not, borrowed from the same source, our readers must determine for themselves.

Furthermore, Wenderoth affirms unqualifiedly, that all three of these differently-named processes are nothing other than applications of Grecian or Oriental painting to photography.

VARIATIONS OF THE PRINCIPLES OF THE HALLOTYPE.

One of these is to seal the photographic proof to a smooth fine card-board, cut of the same size as the glass, with the face up, and colored with water colors.

Then make a duplicate proof transparent with sweet oil; take the excess of oil off by placing it between sheets of blotting paper; then tint the eyes, cheeks, &c., slightly with transparent oil colors.

Next take the proof mounted on card-board, and color it on the face with dry colors (using stumps) or oil, or water colors; then put the two together, making the lines to match, and seal with gum arabic dissolved in water, a little "ropy."

Another successful mode (if executed by a skilful artist) is to color the proof slightly and carefully with water colors, before it is made transparent with oil; then seal the two together with gum dem mar. This is the most satisfactory picture, though gum arabic is best, if it can be used without making air-bubbles.

THE COPYING OF ENGRAVINGS AND DRAWINGS BY SIMPLE CONTACT AND WITHOUT THE USE OF THE CAMERA.

This process, which presents no difficulty, is very convenient in numerous cases: *e. g.* when an engraving or drawing is to be transcribed in the same proportions as the original. It may be compared to the process called by engravers *counter-drawing,* and in this respect may be extremely useful to them; since, without injuring the original, they can transfer, with readiness, a drawing or engraving, &c., to a metallic plate as often as they may wish.

To obtain this result, procure a silvered plate, of the same size as the engraving to be copied. This plate is iodized and brominized in the usual manner as for a daguerreotype. When it has received the sensitive coating, apply to it in the dark the engraving, in such a manner that its surface may be in contact with the iodized and brominized surface of the plate. Then place over the engraving a smooth plate of glass, of suitable dimensions, designed to assure the perfect contact of the engraving and plate, without, however, intercepting the luminous action to which the whole is to be submitted. These arrangements being made, raise with both hands, at the same time, the engraving, plate, and glass, which press gently together; then expose them to diffused light from five to fifteen seconds, according to its intensity. In the sun, from two to five seconds would suffice. Then carry the whole into the dark; cautiously remove the glass and engraving; submit the plate to the mercurial vapors; and, if the operation has been carefully performed, the impression will speedily appear. After it has been carefully developed, it may be washed and fixed by the ordinary methods of treating photographs.

THE HILLOTYPE.

The pictures thus styled, and exhibited to the Patent Office Committee, chosen by the United States Senate, in 1853, were probably made on the same principle mentioned above, with some variations—*colored prints* being used, and the impression made on daguerreotype plates afterwards varnished or lackered, and finished over strong heat. No portraits from life were exhibited, and the few, cautiously shown to private persons, were probably common daguerreotypes, carefully colored by hand, and secured by amber-varnish or some other translucent substance. The one which fell into my hands, after the publication of Mr. Hill's book, was examined by me under a strong magnifier, and proved to be only an ordinary colored daguerreotype—the dry colored powder being undeniably and distinctly visible on the face and hair. Such was, probably, the substance of the *trick,* which created so much excitement throughout our country, and injured the heliographic artists to the amount of many thousands of dollars. It seems to have been started merely to get money, and, backed up by the respectable title of Reverend, it had a very considerable run.

CRAYON OR VIGNETTE DAGUERREOTYPE.

A picture of this kind, where the head and bust, or the head *alone* is taken upon a light ground, may be greatly improved, and enhanced in beauty, by giving it a spherical surface.

This may be effected in several different ways. Take the vignette picture upon the one-sixth size, or medium plate, or even smaller, with light ground. When gilded, place the picture or plate, face up, upon a glass paper-weight, not over two inches in diameter, smooth and convex or oval.

Then with a tin ring, large enough to touch the plate on all sides, without injuring the picture, press gently down upon the plate, so as to give it a form regularly and completely spherical. Finally mount, or set in a case under an American miniature spherical glass, and the effect will be exceedingly beautiful.

THE SPHEREOTYPE.

This picture was patented in 1856, by Bisbee, a heliographic artist of Columbus, Ohio.

It is simply a positive collodion picture, taken upon glass, by placing a mat before the plate, with an opening of the same size as that with which it is to be mounted, or placed in the case. Through this opening *alone* does the light pass and act upon that portion of the sensitive coating of the plate, which is thus reached in the camera.

Afterwards develop, wash, fix, and finish in the ordinary mode. Mount, or set in the case, with a matt behind or beneath the picture, as well as over or before it. By this means a *spherical* appearance is imparted to the picture, and hence it takes its name. When skilfully finished in dry colors, this style of spherical positive picture is pleasing.

THE ECTOGRAPH.

{ Patented by WILLIAM CAMPBELL,
Jersey City, N. J.

The name ectograph was adopted, as giving some intimation of the manner in which the picture was finished; *i. e.* "from behind."

The picture is made as follows:—

Take such a negative as is customary for the solar camera; *i. e. full in detail, but not dense,* and *wholly without fault.* No pains should be spared in this first step, as every after-step will faithfully reproduce whatever failing there may be.

Place the negative in the copying camera, and turn it towards a clear, though not too strong, north light—the sky being, if possible, made to serve as the background; as every object that intercepts the light, however distant, will palpably affect the resulting photograph. When the sky cannot subserve this purpose, then any purely white object, sufficiently large to cover the negative when at a distance, will answer.

The negative being in position, the finest French plate glass should be used for the positive. The details of this process may be found in any work on photography.

Supposing a perfect positive to have been obtained, the subsequent process described below is very simple.

The picture may be varnished, or not, at the operant's choice. The application of a clear, good varnish may possibly be of some utility, though Mr. Campbell says he has tried both methods, without detecting any difference between their results. The positive must now be coated on the collodion side with a thin layer of white wax, and, being held to the light, must be colored either with oil or water colors. If water colors are employed, the wax must be prepared to take the color kindly, by slightly rubbing it over with a little ox-gall or soap and water. A very little will suffice.

If the operant be unused to coloring, he may first varnish the wax and then color. If he does not succeed to his liking, he can rub or wash the color off and commence anew. Whereas, without so varnishing, and if the color be laid *immediately* upon the wax, it cannot be removed easily, if indeed at all.

If elaborate work be desired, the lines and shades of the photograph will indicate *where* to put the colors, and taste will prescribe how to arrange them. Dispatch, however, is sometimes of moment, in which case the whole drapery of the figure may, with a full brush, be covered in ten minutes with one color, producing an effect as beautiful as could be desired.

Be it noted, that the materials used in this process must be of the best quality, and all the appliances and manipulations marked by perfect cleanliness.

Thus the glass should be the finest plate; the wax should be sun-bleached (as no other will answer); and the colors should be brilliant in hue and not liable to fade. With such appliances and care there need be no apprehension of failure. For formula, see Volume Second.

The PORCELAIN PICTURE.—This was invented by J. Wallace Black, of Boston, Massachusetts. It is made upon a species of porcelain glass, manufactured expressly for Mr. B., to apply to this object solely. It resembles both the alabastrine picture and the ectograph in being a positive, copied on glass from a negative.

It is a rich and beautiful picture, even without coloring, and has all the fine details of the daguerreotype, without its reflection. It is susceptible of being so colored as strongly to resemble a miniature on ivory, but surpasses this in truthfulness. It is believed to be durable.

For formula, see Volume Second.

CHAPTER XXVIII.

Microscope at first undervalued—Pope—Addison—Ehrenberg's discovery thereby, 1839—Infusoria at Berlin—Luneburg—Virginia, U. S.—Tripoli powder, Infusoria—Microscopic vegetables abundant as animals—Ocean mud and pond scum, organic life, viz., desmidiæ and diatomaceæ—Divine ends subserved by infusoria—Calcareous earth eaten in South America—Guinea, Finland, China, &c., composed of organic remains—Islands formed by animalcules—Ocean phosphorescence by same—Red Sea thus colored—Lewenhoeck—Codfish milt—17,000 divisions of butterfly's eye—In one pound cochineal 70,000 insects—Divine purpose in animalcular creation—Serve as scavengers—Prevent diminution of earth's existing matter—Services of microscope to commerce—Jurisprudence, sciences, arts, &c.—Life-saving application of microscope in France, &c.—Connection of microscope with heliography.

THE CAMERA AND THE MICROSCOPE—OR MICRO-PHOTOGRAPHY.

THE important aid rendered by the microscope to the heliographic art, makes some account of this instrument, and of the various discoveries achieved by its means, not irrelevant to the present work. Of these discoveries I shall first and chiefly speak, reserving my description of the instrument and of the nature of its connection with our art to the second part of this treatise.

The microscope, strangely enough, met with little favor on its first introduction. For reasons peculiar (it would seem) to that day, a slur had been cast upon entomology and kindred pursuits, as dealing with *minute* and of consequence (according to the vulgar estimate) *useless,* if not despicable objects. Not unnaturally, this reproach was reflected upon the microscopists and their instrument, since the entomologist employed it habitually in the pursuits thus contemned. It is, certainly, a strange spectacle to see Pope and Addison devoting the talents, then wielding so potent and wide an influence, to heaping ridicule upon a class of philosophers, to whom we owe the revelation of a veritable universe, not less curious or replete with wonders, than the universe disclosed to us by the telescope. Nor is it less strange, that a British peeress should have been declared a *lunatic* on account of her enthusiastic devotion to entomologic studies; and that an attempt to invalidate her last will and testament should have been made on this pretext solely.

To enhance to the utmost the absurdity of this vulgar prejudice, it so chanced that, at this very date, all *minutest* products of *human* skill were more inordinately prized and more passionately sought after, than ever before or since.

But it is time I commence what must, perforce, be both a brief and a desultory account of the discoveries effected through the microscope. I shall ask the reader's attention first, to the composition of our globe's crust.

In 1839 Professor Ehrenberg published the remarkable fact of his discovery, by this instrument, of a stratum of soil, in the Prussian city of Berlin, composed almost wholly of living infusoria. It lies about fifteen feet beneath the surface, and is from twenty to sixty feet thick. Of the mass of minute siliceous infusoria, constituting most of this stratum, a considerable portion is still living and reproducing. Oxygen for sustaining life can reach these animals only in the water, which percolates this infusorial mass, as well as the superincumbent soil; and yet life is actively existent throughout this enormous population. Situated beneath the pavement trodden by the city's inhabitants, a few separate cubic feet of this stratum swarm with a population, outnumbering, a billionfold, the human crowd above.

At about the same date, in the vicinity of Hanoverian Lüneburg, and one foot and a half below the surface, was found a bed, twenty feet thick, of light siliceous earth, consisting entirely of the shells of defunct infusoria, so minute as to be invisible to the naked eye, and identical with infusoria still living in neighboring ponds.

In Virginia, also, are extensive beds of siliceous marl, composed mainly of infusorial shells. Their forms are discerned, by the microscope, to be of exquisite beauty, as well as of incalculable variety; and the least stain left by the evaporation of a drop of slightly muddy water, is perceived to be teeming with these beautiful and tiny forms. Richmond and Petersburg, of that state, are built upon strata, several yards thick, of infusorial bodies.

The metal-polishing powder, called tripoli, procured chiefly in Bohemian Bilin (and the state of Maine, in U.S.), and forming series of beds fourteen feet thick, is composed wholly of the siliceous shields of infusoria in very complete preservation, though the interior organism is comparatively gone, from (supposed) exposure to a high temperature. The shop of a single Berlin druggist is reported to contain above a ton-weight of this substance yearly; and yet the supplying beds seem hardly diminished. How minute these creatures are, *individually*, may perhaps be approximately conceived from the statement, that *one cubic inch* of this powder, weighing 220 grs., contains forty thousand millions of single organisms!

Minute, however, as some of these creatures are, they are yet quite complicated in structure, having a mouth, several stomachs, and sundry mobile processes named *cilia* (eyelashes), a millionfold more delicate than the eyelash of a human infant! Some possess exquisitely carved shields, of pure translucent flint, distinct and unvarying for the same species, and, therefore, supplying a means of classification. Of the smallest of them, ten million million individuals would be required to fill the space of a cubic inch; and yet each has every organ needful for life, enjoyment, and reproduction, with all conditions corresponding to its nature and wants!

But discoveries still more interesting and important than these were made by Ehrenberg, in the same year (1839), while prosecuting special researches into the form of the harbor of Wismer, in the Baltic Sea. He ascertained, that from one-twentieth to one-fourth of the mud there deposited, consisted either of living infusoria, or of the empty shells of dead ones. It being found, that upwards of 200,000 lbs. of mud are deposited here weekly, it follows that, during the last century, the deposition must have amounted to 3,240,000 hundred weight, one-tenth of which consisted of infusorial animalcula!

At Pillau, M. Hagen found, that half the total volume of mud often consists of infusoria. He estimates, that from 7200 to 14,000 cubic metres of pure infusorial organisms are here annually deposited in the form of mud. By consequence, a century would accumulate from 720,000 to 1,140,000 cubic metres of tripoli stone or infusorial rock.

Ehrenberg discovered, moreover, that the Nile mud, immemoriably famed for its fertilizing properties, contained these infusoria in such prodigiouss abundance, that every particle, of half a pin-head's size, contained at least *one*, and frequently *several* of them!

Yet universal as is the prevalence of microscopic animal life, hardly less abundant are various forms of vegetable life, too minute for discrimination by the naked eye. The green scum of the wayside stagnant pool and the mud of the ocean, are alike found to be teeming with organized vegetable existence.

The plants discovered in these two states are divided into two families: the desmidæ, inhabiting *fresh* water *solely*, and the diatomaceæ, *salt* water principally. Though *styled* plants, however, they bear little or no similitude to other vegetable beings. They are circular, triangular, and even parallelogramic in shape; and, possessing the singular property of assimilating to their organisms the silex existing in solution in the waters they inhabit, their bodies are indestructible. By consequence, these bodies form incessantly enlarging beds at the bottom of the ocean, as well as of lakes and ponds. This process having been going on from the dawn of time, we now find extensive rocky strata, chains of hills, beds of marl, and soils of every description, whether superficial, or raised from far depths, composed, in a greater or less degree, of these plantal reliques; while some large tracts of country are literally built up with the same.

According to Dr. Hooker, the waters and even the ice of the whole Antarctic Ocean, between the parallels of 60° and 80° South, so abound in these plants, that the sea wears everywhere a pale ochrous shade. The same plants are probably dispersed uniformly over the whole ocean, though from their minuteness imperceptible, save when massed abundantly together, as in the icy sea. On this vegetation, the animal occupants of these waters depend largely for sustenance, while their defunct organisms form deposits, which are to ultimate in islands and continents.

But these Diatomaceæ also perform long journeys on the wings of the wind. Darwin, having collected an impalpable dust, which fell on the ship Beagle, when sailing to the west of the Cape de Verd Isles, found it, on microscopic inspection, to consist of the skeletons of diatomaceæ, ejected probably from some volcano then active. These siliceous skeletons, being indestructible by fire, constitute, jointly with infusoria, portions of the ashes and pumice vomited from the eruptive crater.

Besides supplying food to classes of animals, these plants prepare the soil for the production of higher vegetable organisms, through the minute division of the siliceous particles laid up in their tissues, whereby these particles are rendered fitter for assimilation by such organisms. Nor is there reason for doubting, that the diatomaceæ, like other vegetables, decompose carbonic acid and liberate oxygen, thus performing a due share of that life-sustaining function of the plantal world.

It is well known that chalk beds constitute a quite considerable portion of the globe's crust. This chalk is composed almost entirely of shells and corals, the reliques of animalcular life. So minute are these shells and corals *individually*. that one million of them are embraced by a *cubic inch* of chalk! These shells consist mainly of foraminifera, which swarm in unimaginable numbers in our seas, and are incessantly augmenting the existent sub-oceanic deposits. The miliola species of the foraminifera so abound in the valley of the Seine, that Paris and the towns of the neighboring territory are, almost exclusively, built of them; nor is the south of France hardly less prolific of the same.

On the banks of the Orinoco, the Meta, and the Magdalena, in South America; in Guinea and the island of Java; in Finland, in Swedish Lapland, in China, and elsewhere, the natives make more or less use of various species of calcareous earth for food; and in periods of extraordinary scarcity, subsist principally thereupon.

The microscope has disclosed, that all these varieties of earth consist mainly of the remains of organized beings.

In January, 1687, a great mass of black paper-like substances fell during a storm in Courland, and the learned in vain endeavored to detect its nature. Some of it, however, having been preserved in the Berlin Museum, was finally examined through the microscope, and found to be a matted mass of minute organisms, comprising some thirty species of infusoria, together with a few confervæ. Thus the instrument, once so contemned, revealed, in one instant, a truth, which had baffled the most earnest inquiry for one hundred and fifty years!

So in 1736, an overflow of the Silesian river Oder cast a paper-like substance on shore, which, a century later, was discovered by the same microscopic scrutinist (Ehrenberg), to consist of nineteen several species of infusoria, with a filamental tissue of confervæ.

From these facts we learn, that animalcular life enacts a vast and important part in forming the solid crust of our globe. Indeed, as regards this end, the agency, exerted by the whole immense residue of the animal kingdom, is quite inconsiderable, compared with that of these tiny creatures.

We have noticed, moreover, the existence of animalcules in the seas, with the various purposes they fulfil therein; one of which is the formation of new islands and continents. In what inconceivable numbers they occupy the sea, may be illustrated by an estimate of Scoresby. Thus, portions of the Arctic Ocean, frequently covering an area of twenty or thirty square miles, are made turbid by the multitude of animalcules therein contained. He estimates that 80,000 persons working without cessation from the date of man's creation to the current hour, could count only the animalcula comprised within the compass of two miles of this turbid water! What, then, must be the sum, representing the total of organic existences in the Polar Seas, where *one-fourth* of the Greenland Sea, for ten degrees of latitude, consists of water *completely surcharged* with animalcules?

As Humboldt remarks, it is still a moot point, whether life is more abundant on the land or in the ocean. That natural phenomenon, the phosphorescence of the sea, which is witnessed in all latitudes, and is beautiful in all, but is, in the tropics, beautiful beyond expression, is now ascribed to the light-emitting powers of innumerable minute animalcules sporting on the waves. This light is considered electro-magnetic, and is evolved from the animal concerned by its voluntary vital act. With these light-emitting living organisms are mingled, in phosphorescent waters, vast quantities of organic matter, the reliques of *dead* animalcules, which shine by the chemical decomposition, set up in all decaying organic substance.

Besides the diatomaceæ, before spoken of, other classes of minute vegetation abound, in certain seas, in numbers beggaring all calculation. Thus, the Red Sea derives its title from the presence therein of a species of extremely minute algæ of red color. The same plant was found by Darwin in other seas.

But the land and the waters do not *exclusively* teem with microscopic animal and vegetable life. The atmosphere also is, at all times, copiously charged with it. By evaporation, by sudden gusts of wind, and kindred means, these creatures are uplifted into the air, and after having been borne by its currents whole degrees, it may be, of latitude or longitude, are dropped upon the land or into the water, there to recommence their ordinary vital functions. The yellow meteoric sand or mist, often falling upon the Atlantic, and sometimes carried even to Central Europe, was discovered, through the microscope, to consist of siliceous shelled animalcula.

But, besides these *already developed* animals and vegetables, the atmosphere contains multitudinous *germs* of life, such as eggs of insects and seeds of plants, which by means of hairy or feathery crowns, are carried forward on vast aerial journeys. So, too, the vivifying pollen of the blossoms is borne by winds, by birds, and by winged insects, often across lands and seas, to the plant which it is needed to fructify.

Perhaps no physical phenomenon is more wonderful, than the seeming omnipresence of fungus-germs in the air. A morsel of ripe fruit, a little water spilled on a bread-crumb, a drop of stale ink, or a neglected bottle of medicine may, either of them, furnish evidence of this fact. Very shortly the decomposing mass is enveloped by a velvety covering, which speedily acquires a luxuriant growth. Beneath the observer's eye, myriads of delicate forms lengthen, swell, burst, and scatter their invisible germs into the surrounding air. Fries declares, that in a single individual of the fungi, he has reckoned above 10,000,000 seeds—adding, that, being so numerous and so light, it is difficult to imagine a place from which they can be excluded. They have been found living within the lungs of a living man; they are in the waters, since a fungus envelopes the fish of our ornamental ponds; and they penetrate the bowels of the earth, for a luminous fungus lights the coal mines of Dresden. Guano from Ichaboe Island contains more beautiful dratoms, than any other known substance, of course having been swallowed by the birds.

The phenomenon of colored snow, commonly red though occasionally green, is familiar to scientific men.

It is now ascertained, that this phenomenon is due to the presence therein of both vegetable and animal life.

Before proceeding to inquire what offices in the grand system of creation are subserved by the varied forms of microscopic existence, we insert a description of a few additional discoveries effected through this instrument.

Thus, Lewenhoeck, the microscopic observer, calculates that a thousand millions of animalcula, which are discovered in common water, are not altogether so large as a grain of sand. In the milt of a single codfish there are more animals than exist upon the whole earth; for a sand-grain is bigger than 4,000,000 of them. The white matter, that adheres to the teeth, also abounds in animalcules of various shapes, to which vinegar is fatal; and it is known that vinegar contains animalculæ in the form of eels. A mite was anciently thought the limit of littleness; but now we are not surprised at being told of animals twenty-seven million times smaller than a mite. Monsisa de l' Isle has computed the celerity of a little creature, scarce visible from its smallness, which he found to run three inches in half a second. If now you suppose its feet to be the fifteenth part of a line, it must take five hundred steps in the space of three inches; *i. e.* it must shift its legs five hundred times per second, or in the ordinary pulsation of an artery.

The proboscis of a butterfly, which winds round in a spiral form, like the spring of a watch, serves for both mouth and tongue, by entering the hollows of flowers and extracting their juices. The seeds of strawberries rise out of the pulp of the fruit, and appear themselves like strawberries, when viewed with the microscope. The farina of the sunflower seems composed of flat, circular, minute bodies, sharp-pointed round the edges; the middle of them appears transparent, and somewhat resembles the flower it springs from, The powder of the tulip is shaped exactly like the seeds of cucumbers and melons. The farina of the poppy looks like pearl-barley. That of the lily is very like that of the tulip. The hairs of the head are tubular fibres. The sting of the bee is a horny sheath, which includes two bearded darts; and that of the wasp has eight beards on the sides of each dart, somewhat like the beards of fish-hooks. The eyes of gnats are pearled, or composed of many rows of small semicircular protuberances, ranged with the utmost exactness. The wandering or hunting spider, who spins no web, has two tufts of feathers attached to its paws, of exquisite beauty and coloring. Its feet have a comb on each, which enable it to move on and fashion its web. A grain of sand will cover two hundred scales of the human skin, and also cover twenty thousand of the pores from which issues the perspiration. Justly has a philosopher (Mr. Baker) observed: "To the Deity, an atom is a world, and a world is but as an atom."

The following facts are mentioned, to show how man's mechanical ingenuity has been favored by means of the microscope:

In a certain museum was exhibited a golden chain, of 300 links, all being but an inch in length, fastened to and dragged along by a flea. And Mr. Baker narrates his having seen, and examined with a microscope, a chaise having four wheels, with all the usual apparatus pertaining thereto, together with a man seated in the chaise, all framed of ivory and drawn forward by a flea, without any seeming difficulty. The weight of the whole establishment, flea inclusive, was barely a single grain. The same gentleman, at the same place and time, also weighed a brass chain made by the same artificer, containing 200 links, with a hook at one end and a padlock and key at the other, all about two inches long, and found it to weigh less than one-third of a grain. He speaks also of having seen a quadrille table, with a drawer in it, an eating table, a side-board table, a looking-glass, twelve chairs with skeleton backs, two dozen plates, six dishes, a dozen knives and as many forks, twelve spoons, two salts, a frame and castors, together with a gentleman, lady, and footman—all contained in a cherry-stone, and not filling much more than half of that! In our day may be purchased cherry-stones highly polished, with ivory screws, each containing one hundred and twenty perfect silver spoons! And it is reported, that a certain Oswald Merlinger fabricated a cup of a pepper-corn, which held twelve hundred other little cups, turned in ivory, each of them gilt on the edges, and standing upon a foot, and that so far from being crowded or wanting room, the pepper-corn would have held four hundred more! So, one pennyworth of crude iron can, by art, be manufactured into watch-springs, so as to produce a thousand pounds sterling!

Lewenhoeck reckoned seventeen thousand divisions in the cornea (anterior coat) of the eye of a butterfly—each of which, he thought, possessed a crystalline lens. Spiders are similarly supplied.

By microscopic examination, it has been discovered, that spiders have four paps for spinning their threads—each pap having about one thousand holes—and the fine web itself is the union of four thousand separate threads. No spider spins more than four webs—and if the fourth be destroyed, it seizes on the webs of others.

Every pound of cochineal contains seventy thousand insects boiled to death—and from six hundred thousand pounds to seven hundred thousand pounds are taken annually to Europe for dyeing scarlet and crimson colors.

It will, of course, be understood, that the microscope is concerned alike in the discoveries and the manufactures alluded to above.

The question, *for what end* have the multitudinous forms of animal and vegetable life first revealed to us by the microscope, *been created,* is not yet fully settled by the savans. That one of their offices is that of *scavengers,* is however obvious enough. Feeding, as both kinds do, on decaying animal and vegetable particles, they aid in conserving the salubrity of our air, by removing one principal cause of its taint.

A second and still more important function of theirs, would seem to be the arresting the *diminution* of the *existing amount* of *organized* matter on our globe. For when such matter has reached that stage of *decay,* immediately preceding its decomposition into the elemental gases; or (in other phrase) its passage from the organic to the inorganic world; these swarming myriads of nature's invisible police intercept the escaping organized atoms, and retrovert them into the *ascending* stream of animal life. Having first converted the dead particles into their own living substance, they become themselves the food of numerous other animals; and thus, by ascensive gradations, the identical atoms, which were on the eve of escaping from the realm of organic matter, come eventually to be a part of the highest organic beings, man himself inclusive. These animalcules may well be compared to the minute capillaries in the animal body—receiving organized matter in its state of utmost attenuation, and on the point of escaping from the system, and turning it back, by a new route, towards the central and highest portion of that system.

Monads, the smallest of creatures *known,* are said to swim by myriads in a *drop of water.* It has been computed, that, within this compass, five hundred million could be comprised! The monad is never found longer than the twelve-thousandth part of an inch.

In a cubic inch of a certain kind of mould, consisting wholly of animalcula, Ehrenberg estimated, that over forty-one millions of distinct beings existed!

The services, moreover, transcend all estimate, which the microscope is capable of rendering alike to commerce, to jurisprudence, to science, and to the arts, useful and ornamental, of life.

Thus, Professor Owen, by a microscopic inspection of a *fragment* of fossil-tooth, demonstrated the existence, immemorial ages since, of an animal belonging to the genus of the modern sloths; but of a bulk so enormous, as to be able to uproot and push down the largest trees of the Tropic forest—an act which this animal was accustomed to perform, for the sake of feeding, as do contemporary sloths, on their leaves and tender shoots. In fact, neither the hammer nor the blow-pipe is so essential to the geologist, as the microscope. Through the latter, he has already made many valuable discoveries in his superb science; and by these discoveries has already been constrained to *re-classify*, to a not inconsiderable extent, the fossilized animal tribes. At the same time, it is manifest, that he has but just *entered* upon a vast field of kindred discoveries.

Hardly, if at all, less important is the microscope to *chemical* science. A European professor of medical jurisprudence, some years ago, discovered an infallible test for detecting the presence of arsenic. It is briefly this: Take the contents of the alimentary canal of a person supposed to be arsenically poisoned, and apply them to small strips of copper ribbon, prepared in a certain prescribed mode. Dry these strips and put them in a clean glass tube, to the bottom of which the flame of a spirit-lamp is applied. If arsenic be present, it soon crystallizes in a brilliant zone round the upper end of the tube. It is known, that arsenious acid forms beautiful crystals of an octohedral figure. To remove, then, all shade of doubt whether this zone be arsenic, or not, apply the microscope. If it *be* such, the octohedral figures will instantly appear. How momentous this discovery is to the interests of justice, is plain at a glance.

Another illustration of the worth of this instrument in legal concerns, is furnished by an incident that occurred in France twenty years ago. A murder had been perpetrated—the body was found, covered with blood—and the murderer was entirely unknown. A certain person, however, being suspected, his domicil was searched, though nothing suspicious was discovered, except a hatchet, whereon were some stains and a few hairs. On inspecting the hatchet with a microscope, the hairs were found to be those of an *animal,* and the man was cleared. Very probably the preservation of life was, in this case, due to this once contemned instrument.

Some years ago it was found by microscopic investigation, that the Paris milkmen were accustomed to defraud their patrons by first removing the cream of the milk, and then restoring the richness of its appearance, by adding thereto the *brains of calves* or *sheep.* With an instrument of a power of from three hundred to five hundred diameters, fragments of *cerebral* substance were distinctly perceived beside the milk globules.

The microscope, moreover, is employed in selecting wet-nurses, as it reveals great diversities in the quality of the milk of different women.

The merchant, too, is beginning to find this instrument of great utility in his business. It enables him to detect the *adulterations* of commodities, from teas, sugars, and drugs, down to guano itself; while by examining the textures of manufactured fabrics, he can determine whether or not they are made of the material alleged.

The foregoing statements will suffice to show the vast importance of the instrument which discloses to us such a world of wonders; for the singular beings, thus brought before us, bear no resemblance to those which are visible to the unaided eye; and their modes of progression, existence, and increase are, in most respects, entirely dissimular.

But life, with its rich endowments, is theirs; and, though millions can be contained within the bulk of a mustard-seed, yet each individual of this vast assemblage is, in its organization, as perfect as an elephant which, in its size relatively to this sentient atom, is as a universe in comparison with ourselves. The living creatures of the microscopic world are, probably, far more numerous than those which are perceivable by the naked eye. And, from the splendid discoveries already made, we may reasonably infer that, if our vision could become indefinitely more piercing, and progressively advance from the minutely visible, through the successive realms of the invisible, exploring onward towards the inmost shrine of nature, new scenes of beauty would be incessantly unfolded, and new fields of divine display would continually reveal that God was still present in His creative energy, and that we saw but the "hidings" of His power and wisdom.

The microscope, in connection with heliography, has become indispensable. By a simple contrivance, the minutest infusoria and vegetable monads can be photographed and enlarged to almost any extent, and the outlines of their beautiful and delicate germs perfectly preserved. The minute spots and striæ on the navicula; the structure of many of the confervæ; cross-sections of many of the polysphoniæ, and other marine algæ, have been represented by the aid of the microscope and the camera more perfectly than it could be done with human hands.

The reader is referred to Vol. 2d, for a brief description of the mode of making these pictures; and if amateurs and professionists will but direct their attention to the study of the microscope, they will, in a short time, be able to master this beautiful branch of photography.

CHAPTER XXIX.

HISTORY OF THE HELIOGRAPHIC ART IN THE UNITED STATES.

Camera obscura—Professor Draper's early researches—Used bromine and sensitive paper—Made the first sun-portrait—Professor Morse's early experiments and their success—A. S. Wolcott and J. Johnson—their discoveries and performances—Dr. Bird—Joseph Saxton, first daguerreotype in Philadelphia—Drs. Goddard and Parker—Professors J. Frazer and W. R. Johnson—Messrs. Mason and Cornelius—Professors Grant and Davis—Drs. J. E. Parker and Wildman—Mr. Reed—Mr. Langenheim, his services to heliography—First brought talbotype and stereoscope to United States—Van Loan, Anthony, Edwards, N. G. Burgess, Charles Williamson, Fizeau, Cady, Gurney, Brady, Quail, Haas, and Lawrence, of New York—Southwerth & Hawes, Whipple & Co., and French, of Boston—Thompson, Schriver, Mayall, M. A. Root, of Philadelphia—Mr. Root bought Mr. Mayall's stand, 140 Chestnut St., 1846—Beckers—Faris, of Cincinnati, Ohio—Hesler, of Illinois—Fitzgibbons, of Missouri—Crystal Palace, New York—Shives—Howard—Sun-painters in United States—Decline of daguerreotype—McClees & Germon, crystallotype—Collodion process, 1852—Drs. Charles Cresson and Langdell—Cutting—Rehn's Photolithography, &c.

IT will not be irrelevant to the following history, if I preface it with a brief extract from an English work of a century or more old.

"We may well imagine," says its author, "that could a young painter but view a picture by the hand of nature herself, and study it at his leisure, he would profit by it more than by the finest performances from the hand of man.

"Now nature is constantly forming such pictures in our eyes; the solar rays, coming from exterior objects, entering the pupil and being refracted by the crystalline lens, stamp on the retina at the bottom of the eye the object, to which the pupil is directed. The soul, receiving instant intelligence of this image, *sees* the object it represents.

"A method was discovered of imitating this natural process, entitled the camera optica or obscura, which may be named 'an artificial eye,' and this is too familiar to the reader to need describing here. We may imagine how the pictures thus formed must have charmed the earliest beholders. Our author rises into enthusiasm in their description."

He remarks, that "the best of the modern Italian painters have been greatly aided by the instrument, as, probably, many tramontane artists as well."

He says, he "was present when an able artist first saw a camera. He was enraptured with it, and his delight increased the longer he examined it, and he confessed, that these pictures were incomparable."

"Another of equal eminence," he says, "declared, that an academy, with the camera and a few casts of the finest Greek busts, would alone suffice to revive the pictorial art."

Our author, therefore, counsels the young painter to study these divine pictures his life long, as he can never give them too much attention.

What would have been the ecstasies of his artist-friends and his own, could they, like ourselves, have seen these impressions permanently fixed, and even heightened in beauty by the brilliancies of color in the hand of genius?

Our author, however, spoke wisely in advising the painter to study assiduously and long even the unstable images projected by the instrument. Very likely such study may have helped the great masters in creating their pictured immortalities. Very likely, too, the same study may have been one among the causes, that impelled our eminent savant, Professor J. W. Draper, M. D., to go so deeply and largely into those studies to which heliography is related, and which, among numerous discoveries, led him so far, that he was able to make the first human photographic portrait the world ever saw. How much the art and its affiliated sciences are indebted to him will presently appear.

Desiring to give an authentic history of the introduction of heliography into this country, as well as of its subsequent progress therein, I addressed letters to Professors John W. Draper and S. F. B. Morse, the latter of whom brought home from Europe the first accounts on the subject, which were published in the New York Observer, requesting of them to detail, for my use, their earliest experiences in the art.

Prof. Draper, in his reply, referred me to his statement in relation to the matter contained in a communication to the New York Mechanics' Institute, of which the following are extracts:

"Nearly ten years before any one in America had turned attention to the subject, I had been occupied with the chemical effects of light, and had published in the Journal of the Franklin Institute and elsewhere a good deal in relation to it.

"For years before either Daguerre or Talbot had published anything on the subject, I had habitually used 'sensitive paper' for investigations of this kind. It was thus (as you will find by inspecting the above-named journal for 1837), that I had examined the impressions of the solar spectrum; proved the interference of chemical rays (*i. e.* their destroying of each other's effect); investigated the action of moonlight, and of flames, either common or colored, red or green; and also the effects of yellow and blue solutions and other absorbing media; the decomposition of carbonic acid by light, &c. In these experiments I used the preparations of bromine, recently so much spoken of. The *then* difficulty was in *fixing* the impressions. I had long known what Wedgwood and Davy had done in copying objects; had amused myself with repeating some of their experiments; and had even tried, though unsuccessfully, the use of hyposulphite of soda, having learned its properties in relation to the chloride of silver from Herschel's experiments, but abandoned it because I found it removed the blacks no less than the whites. This want of success was probably owing to my having used too strong a solution, and kept the paper in it too long.

"When Talbot's experiments appeared in the spring of 1839, they interested me greatly, as I had been at work so many years on the action of light. I repeated what he published with variations. I tried to shorten the long time required for getting the picture of a house or tree, by using lenses of large aperture and short focus, and from this germ portraiture finally arose. This was prior to the publication of anything by Daguerre.

"It was during my repetitions of Talbot's experiments, that I recognised the practical value of the experiments I had made in 1835 and published in 1837, respecting the chemical focus of a non-achromatic lens, and saw that the camera must be shortened in order to obtain a sharp picture.

"My first knowledge of the particulars of Daguerre's process was from their publication in the London Literary Gazette, which contained Arago's Report of the meeting of the Academy of Sciences, on August 19th, and this I saw at the time of its arrival in New York. I do not remember the date, but it strikes me it was in September. I at once bought some of the common silver-plated copper, and directly after tried Daguerre's process. I believe I was, at that moment, the only person in America, who had any practical skill in experiments with light; but then I had had ten years' experience in such matters. Those, who know the failures and disappointments, incident to photographic experiments, can fully appreciate the worth of such a schooling in a delicate operation like Daguerre's. I succeeded, without other difficulty than the imperfection of the silver-plating, in copying brick buildings, a church, and other objects seen from my laboratory windows.

"I now returned to the attempts at portraiture, and upon the principles I had ascertained *before* Daguerre's publication, I resorted to a lens of five inches diameter and seven inches focus, which I still have. I dusted the sitter's face with flour and pushed the back of the camera to the violet focus. At this period I did not well understand the manner of illuminating an object, and making the trial in a room succeeded in getting an impression. But, observing that the dark spots of the dress impressed themselves, I perceived it was needless to whiten the face, and found on trial, that the forehead, cheeks, and chin, whereon the light fell most favorably, would come out first.* By augmenting the illumination and prolonging the time, I could get the entire countenance. At this time the problem of portraiture might be regarded as virtually solved.

"About this time I became acquainted with Professor Morse, and we subsequently had a building on the top of the New York University, in which we took many portraits, at first with a four-inch lens, and then with

* This was the first portrait taken from life.

an achromatic lens and plates, both French, which we imported.

"In March, 1840, I wrote to the editors of the London and Edinburgh Philosophical Magazine, stating my success in solving the problem of photographic portraiture; and in the following September I published a detail of the whole process. Meanwhile I had forwarded specimens to Europe, and had received letters of acknowledgment.

"From the foregoing statements, it will be seen that my connection with portraiture dates back to the summer preceding the publication of Daguerre's process; that I had secured various *partial* successes; but that within a day or two after the daguerreotype was made known here by the above gazette, I had accomplished the object.

"Photographic portraiture implies the use of a lens of large aperture and short focus, together with a knowledge of the correction for the chemical focus, and perhaps the use of bromine. All these things I knew before Daguerre was named on this side the Atlantic. How any doubt can now be entertained as to who took the first sun-portrait, passes my comprehension.

Yours, truly,
J. W. DRAPER.

Messrs. Stetson, Cohen, Seely,
Committee of Mechanics' Club."

The remark in the closing sentence of the above interesting letter is confirmed by the following extract from an article, by Sir David Brewster, in the Edinburgh Review for January 1843:—

"Dr. Draper," we believe "was the first who, under the brilliant summer sun of New York, took daguerreotype portraits. This branch of photography seems not to have been regarded as a possible application of Daguerre's process, and no notice is taken of it in the reports to the French legislative bodies. We have been told, that, at that period, Daguerre had taken no portraits, and when we consider, that twenty or twenty-five minutes were then deemed necessary to get a daguerreotype landscape, we do not wonder that portraiture was unthought of in this connection."

Besides those mentioned in his letter, Professor Draper has published numerous other memoirs, having more or less connection with the heliographic art: *e. g.*, on the analogy of the chemical rays and radiant heat; on spectral appearances and latent light; on the tithonometer, an instrument for measuring the chemical or actinic power of the sunbeam; on a new imponderable; on the negative rays of the sun; on the phosphorescence of bodies, &c. These are a portion of a series of papers which, collected, would make a considerable volume. Many were published in London, and have been translated into the languages of Germany, France, and Italy, and published in those countries. Many, too, may be found in the Franklin Institute Journal from 1834 to 1839. Besides all these, he has written a treatise on physiology, illustrated by himself, by means of micro-photography. He was chosen first president of the New York Photographical Society, and has been annually re-elected until now. He continues to investigate every new phase of the art, and is one of the best practitioners among our scientific amateurs. His son, Dr. Henry Draper, has constructed the largest reflecting telescope ever made in the United States; and, with it, has taken perfect photographs of the moon, over two feet in diameter. He has favored me with many facts on Lunar Photography, Actinism, &c., and has kindly aided me with his counsels and suggestions in the preparation of this work, which I take this occasion to thankfully acknowledge. Within the present year he has published an octavo entitled: "The History of the Intellectual Development of Europe;" a work pronounced by many his chef d' œuvre, and, like his other writings, not only doing great credit to himself, but reflecting high honor on the American name. Our limits forbid our speaking more fully of his multitudinous performances.

I mentioned, that I wrote to Professor Morse, as well as to Professor Draper. My letter to the former contained the following queries, viz.:

1st. When did you commence your (photographic) experiments? I was told by an Englishman (name lost), that your first successful effort was an impression of your coat hanging upon the wall. Is this the fact?

2d. How long was the time required to obtain this impression?

3d. Of what kind were the instruments employed by you?

4th. Who first followed you in your experiments?

5th. Who began the taking of portraits?

6th. Who made the first portrait in New York city?

The professor's very obliging reply was as follows:

POUGHKEEPSIE, Feb. 10th, 1855.

My dear Sir:—

Yours of January 30th I found on my table, on my return to New York, after an absence of some days. I have been and am still much occupied, but will give you as satisfactory answers as I can, to your questions.

To question 1st, I answer, that I was in Paris when Daguerre's discovery was announced in the winter of

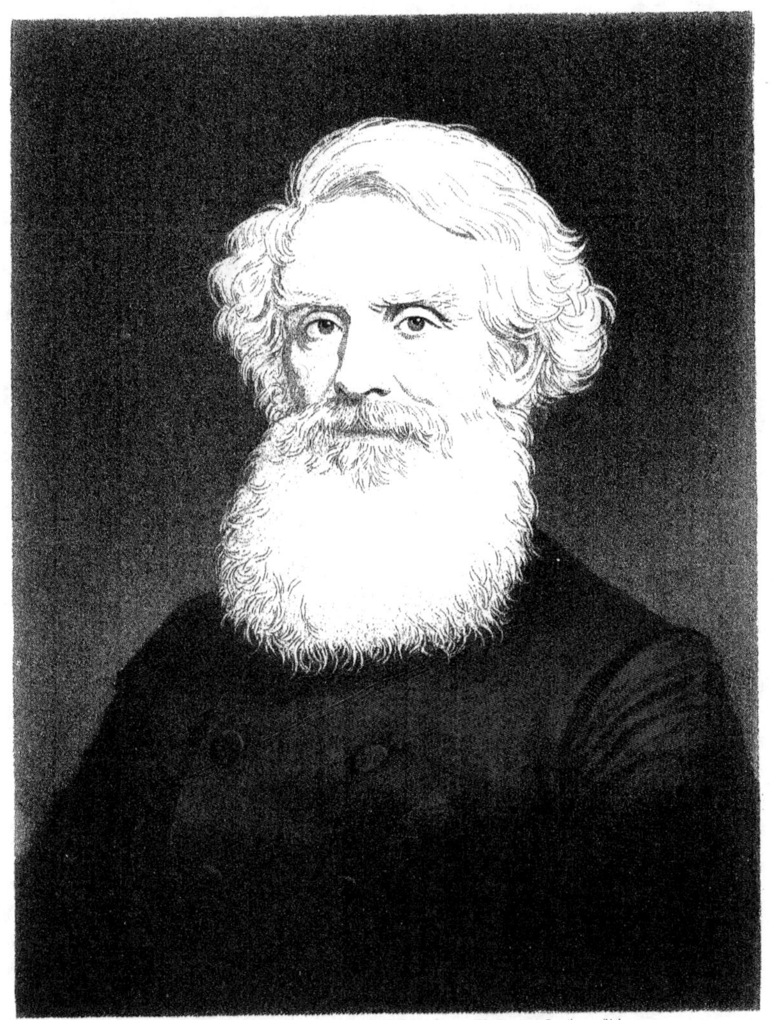

Engraved by John Sartain, Phil.a after a Photograph from life.

I am truly Yours,
Sam.l F. B. Morse

1838-9. Early in the spring of 1839, I had the gratification of being invited by Daguerre to see his results in private. He had not then shown them, except to the Royal Family, to Arago, and to a few others. His *process* was then secret, awaiting the action of the Government, respecting the pension to be granted him in case he would publish his process. My letter, announcing the discovery and my examination of the results, was written to my brothers, the editors of the New York Observer, about the first week in March 1839, and was published by them, I think, in April following. This was the first knowledge of the discovery obtained by the American people. In July or August of the same year, I think, Daguerre received his pension, and the process was published. Some copies of the work were immediately sent to this country, one of which I received the latter part of August or September; and immediately I had made for me the apparatus from the description in the book. This, I find, answers questions *first* and *third.*

To question 2d, I reply, that as soon as the apparatus was made, I commenced experimenting with it. The greatest obstacle I had to encounter was in the quality of the plates. I obtained the common plated copper in coils at the hardware shops, which of course was very thinly coated with silver, and that impure. Still I was enabled to verify the truth of Daguerre's revelations. The first experiment, crowned with any success, was a view of the Unitarian Church, from the window on the staircase, from the third story of the New York City University. This, of course, was before the building of the New York Hotel. It was in September, 1839. The time, if I recollect, in which the plate was exposed to the action of light in the camera, was about fifteen minutes. The instruments, chemicals, &c., were strictly in accordance with the directions in Daguerre's first book.

To question 4th, I answer, that there were *several persons* who immediately began experimenting. An English gentleman, whose name at present escapes me, but who is (I believe) now living in Mexico, obtained a copy of Daguerre's book, about the same time with myself. He commenced experimenting also.

But an American, named Wolcott, was very successful with a modification of Daguerre's apparatus—substitututing a metallic reflector for the lens. Previous, however, to Wolcott's experiments, my colleague and friend, Professor John W. Draper, of New York City University, was very successful in his investigations; and with him I was, for a time, engaged in attempting portraits.

As to taking portraits, in answer to your 5th question, I would say, that in my intercourse with Daguerre, I specially conversed with him in regard to the practicability of taking portraits of *living persons*. I well remember that he expressed himself somewhat sceptical as to its practicability, only in consequence of the *time* necessary for the person to remain immovable.

The time for taking an out-door view was from fifteen to twenty minutes; and this he considered too long a time for any one to remain sufficiently still for a successful result. No sooner, however, had I mastered the process of Daguerre, than I began to experiment with a view to accomplish this desirable result. I have now the fruits of these experiments, taken in September or the beginning of October, 1839. They are full-length portraits of my daughter, single, and also in group with some of her young friends. They were taken out of doors, on the roof of a building, in the full sun-light, and with the eyes closed. The time was from ten to twenty minutes. The following is a transcript of the daguerreotype alluded to.

(Fig. 6.)

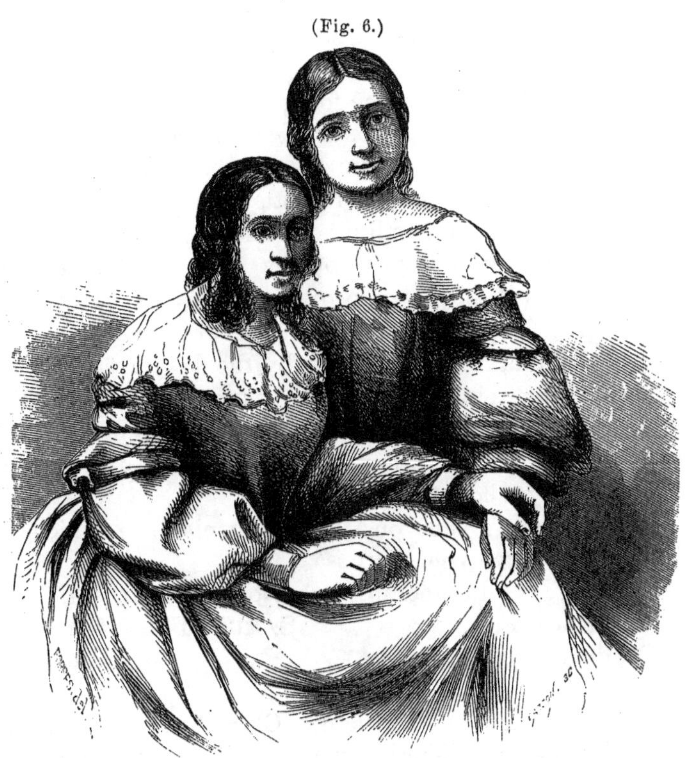

As the eyes in the daguerreotype, from which the above engraving is copied, were tolerably well defined, we presume, that, at the taking, they were open a part of the time, and a part of the time closed. Therefore, we represent them as open.

About the same time, Professor Draper was successful i ı taking portraits; though whether he or myself took the *first* portrait, I cannot say. Soon after, we commenced together taking portraits; causing a glass building to be constructed for that purpose on the roof of the

University. As our experiments had put us to considerable expense, we made a charge to those who sat to us, to defray this expense.

To the 6th question, the foregoing is, to some extent, an answer. But Professor Draper's other duties calling him away from the experiments, except as to their bearing on some philosophical investigations, which he pursued with great ingenuity and success, *I* was left to pursue the *artistic* results of the process, as more in accordance with my own profession. My expenses had been great, and for some time (five or six months), I pursued the taking of portraits by the daguerreotype, as a means of reimbursing these expenses. After this object had been attained, I abandoned the practice to give my exclusive attention to the telegraph, which required my whole time.

I have thus given you a hasty reminiscence, which, I hope, may serve your purpose.

Respectfully, your obedient servant,

M. A. Root, Esq., Samuel F. B. Morse.
Philadelphia.

At a session of the Mechanics' Club, April 14th, 1858, Mr. John Johnson detailed the early attempts at daguerreotype portraiture, illustrated by the apparatus employed in 1839, by specimens of pictures, and by original documents of that period. He was of the firm of Wolcott (Alexander S.) & Johnson (John), who commenced working the daguerreotype process soon after its publication in this country, October 6th, 1839. About this time, they obtained two pretty successful impressions, one positive and the other negative, a fact which perplexed them not a little. Their first portrait was made on the 6th or 7th of October.

Early in February, 1840, Johnson, Senior, visited England, and arranged with Rev. Richard Baird to patent and work in that country an apparatus got up by Mr. Wolcott. The latter, after examining the camera described by Daguerre, thought that an image could be obtained in less time, than by that, by employing a reflector of wide aperture and short focus. Therefore a reflector, designed for taking portraits from life, was determined on, having eight inches diameter, and twelve inches focal distance for parallel rays. While engaged upon this, Mr. Henry Fitz, who had, in former times, been associated with Mr. Wolcott, and was well versed in optics, returning from abroad, offered Mr. Wolcott his valuable aid. This was gladly accepted; the reflector was properly polished, and experiments in daguerreotypy were tried with tolerable success. It was this apparatus for which English patents were obtained by Johnson, Sr., and Rev. Mr. Baird, and enrolled June 14th, 1840, it having been previously exhibited in London, March 23d, 1840.

Mr. Johnson, Sr., paid Daguerre £150 for the use of his process, as Claudet subsequently paid him £200 for the privilege of using three cameras. Still later, Rev. Mr. Baird purchased the whole of Daguerre's right in England.

On May 8th, 1840, Mr. Wolcott procured an American patent for his reflecting apparatus.

Mr. John Johnson seems to be of opinion, that Mr. Wolcott and himself were the first who took portraits in New York by Daguerre's process. The first after them (he says) was a Mr. Prosch, who was followed by numerous others, most of whom employed Wolcott's reflector. Till the beginning of 1840 (he continues), no means of abbreviating the time of sitting for a portrait was in use, or had even been attempted, save Wolcott's instrument above mentioned. Early in this year, Wolcott tried bromine for this purpose, but unsuccessfully. Mr. Johnson intimates, that he and Wolcott were the first users of this chemical in New York. He moreover states, that he and his establishment were the earliest to employ chloride of iodine to secure short sittings. He further declares that, in 1842, he discovered a combination of chemicals (now known in London, as "Wolcott's mixture"), which was very sensitive to the action of light.

Our limits allow us no further present space for Mr. Johnson's reminiscences. If the *seeming* clash between some of his statements and those of Professors Draper and Morse, be pronounced by our readers a *real* one, it is beyond our power to harmonize them, and we must leave to each individual to settle his own views.

I now proceed to detail summarily the progress, in the United States, of the art thus introduced.

In 1839, and on the very day of the publication of Daguerre's discovery in the Philadelphia daily papers, Dr. Bird, then chemical professor in one of our medical schools, was asked, at a gathering of several scientific men, what he thought of this new mode of copying objects with the sunbeam?

The Doctor, in a lengthened reply, pronounced the whole report a fabrication—a new edition of the famed "moon-hoax"—such a performance being, in his view, an intrinsic improbability.

Much to his credit, however, he soon after gave the subject a thorough investigation, and examining, with the requisite appliances, every new phase assumed by the art, he mastered each successive discovery and improvement as fast as they appeared, so that, at his decease in 1854, he was probably the ablest writer on sun-painting in the United States.

Joseph Saxton, a cultured man of genius (who was not present on the above occasion), had, on the day in question, carefully examined the same subject, and had concluded that Daguerre's announcement was literal truth. He forthwith proceeded to experiment in the art, according to the following method.

He constructed a camera by fixing an ordinary sunglass in one end of a cigar-box; while a seidlitz powder box, with an aperture in its top somewhat smaller than the plate to be used, and containing a few flakes of dry iodine, served as a coating box. His mercury-bath was made by excavating a hole through a dogwood-block, and attaching thereto a piece of sheet iron so bent, as to hold a little quicksilver. And finally, for a plate, he burnished a piece of silver one and quarter by two inches in size.

With these primitive implements he produced, that day, the first heliograph ever made in Philadelphia, a transcript of which, in size and appearance, can be seen on next page. The original was recently presented to me for this illustration by a member of the Philadelphia Historical Society, George M. Justice, to whom it belonged. The picture represents the old Arsenal and the cupola of the old Philadelphia High School, taken from a window of the United States Mint, in which Mr. S. was an official.

I have in my possession another view taken by him, soon after, from the same window, and representing certain buildings west of Broad street. It was presented to me by Mr. Saxton himself.

These heliographs naturally created no small excitement among the curious in such matters; and from this date many of our Philadelphia savans began cultivating the art.

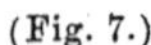

(Fig. 7.)

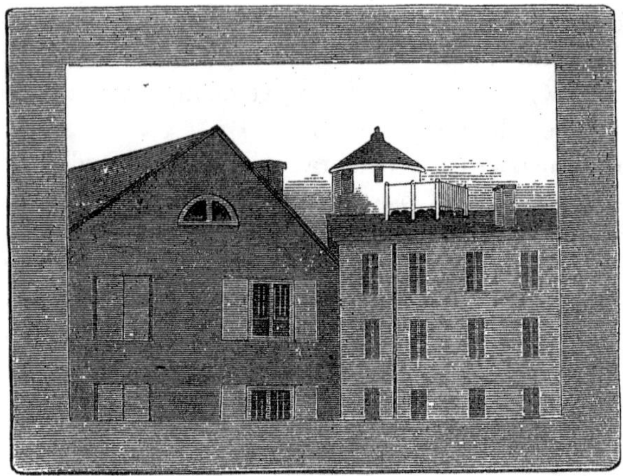

Among these were Robert Cornelius, Drs. Paul Beck Goddard, Parker, Bird, and Kennedy, Professors John Frazer, and Walter R. Johnson, William G. Mason, engraver, Dr. Wildman, and many others. Some of these have kept pace with the progress of the art, through all its phases, while contributing largely thereto.

In the United States, Dr. Goddard (at the time engaged with Dr. Hare, Professor of Chemistry in the Pennsylvania University) merits special mention for his services to the new art. His claim to the introduction of bromine, as a sure and valuable accelerator, is sustained by the record of it in the Journal of the American Philosophical Society for 1840.

In English heliographic works, John Goddard, a London optician, has erroneously received the credit of having earliest suggested this use of bromine.

In Daguerre's process, dry iodine had, hitherto, been exclusively employed for acceleration. This substance,

(Fig. 8.)

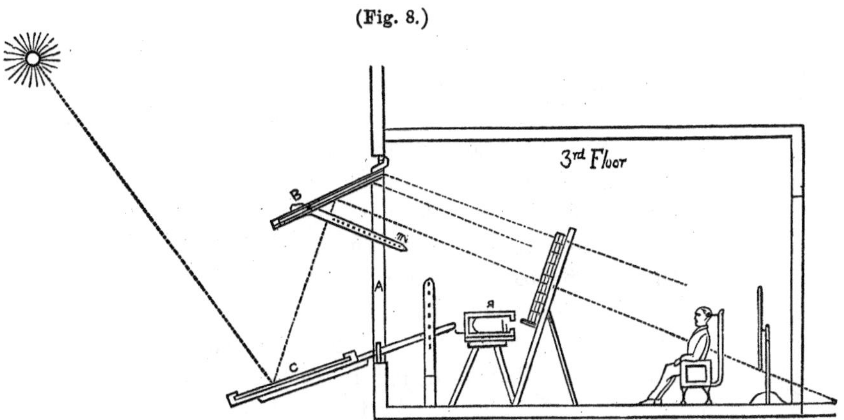

however, is slow-acting even for views; while for portraiture, its use, by itself solely, is impracticable.

In 1839, Professor Grant, of "Calcium Light" notoriety, and Mr. Davis, of Boston, Massachusetts, made daguerreotypes, on the third day after the discovery was published in Boston.

The first Philadelphian who produced portraits, was Robert Cornelius. Importing his lenses, he himself manufactured the cameras, plates, and mats, he employed. For coating the plates, he used dry iodine exclusively; and by several large reflectors, set at different angles, both within doors and without, he was enabled, in strong sunshine, to concentrate upon his sitter light enough to obtain through a side-window facing south, an impression within from one to five minutes. (See Fig. 8.) Mr. Cornelius obtained much of his knowledge of the proper mode of proceeding, *e. g.* the arrangement of lights and shadows, the use of reflectors, &c., from a visit to the rooms of Wolcott & Johnson, corner of Chambers Street and Broadway, New York. These gentlemen were taking portraits at the date of this visit, which (Mr. Johnson thinks) was early in April, 1840, and theirs were the first rooms open for portraiture in the United States. Meanwhile Dr. Goddard, privately experimenting for the discovery of an accelerator, had, with bromine, gotten views, and even portraits, in the open air instantaneously.

Subsequent to this discovery of his, Mr. Cornelius, with bromide of iodine, procured fair impressions, even without reflectors, in from ten to sixty seconds—and this too within doors.

It was auspicious for the new art, that it won the interest of the distinguished dental surgeon, of Philadelphia, Dr. J. E. Parker. At this early date he surpassed all others in producing out-door views of street-scenes, buildings, &c. He and Mr. Reed, an ingenious silver-plate manufacturer, effected numerous improvements in the apparatus used. Their bromine-box, alike peculiar and admirable in construction, was charged with pure bromine, and is yet in the Doctor's possession in good working order. Dr. P. is also among our ablest microscopists, and takes a deep interest in micro-photography and the progress of the art generally.

Mr. Mason having, as a professed engraver, been previously skilled in metal-polishing, very naturally excelled in preparing plates. For cleansing, he used clean, fine cotton-wool together with well washed rotten-stone. And for polishing he employed rouge on a small hand-buff, made of a wooden block, about two and a half by three inches in dimensions, covered either with common, or cotton flannel in five or six thicknesses, over which was drawn fine buckskin; and on this buff the rouge was thrown by striking thereon the muslin bag containing the same. The buff was rubbed circularly over the plate, which was held fast by sealing wax upon a block matching the plate in size.

In 1839 Mr. M. produced, by the light of a small gas-burner, a perfect copy of a certain engraving. This was, probably, the first picture ever taken by artificial light. It is still perfect, and remains in his possession. The exposure was one hour. He also made a daguerreotype on steel at this date, which he presented to the writer. Mr. Mason's pictures exhibited a pure and exquisitely finished surface. And indeed some of the heliographs produced at that early period (1839 and 1840, or twenty-four years ago) by him, as also by Messrs. Goddard, Cornelius, and Parker, are rarely transcended even now, despite the improvements made in the art and its appliances.

Among these early amateurs was Dr. Wildman, a gentleman of considerable mechanical genius, a most able practising dentist, and skilful manufacturer of artificial teeth. At that date, and without receiving any aid or suggestions from the experiments of others, he produced several views, which, for beauty of delineation and tone, for fidelity of detail, and for artistic effect, have never been surpassed even to this day. They are still perfect, and promise to endure for ages.

The earliest experiments were performed, either with single lenses, or with plano-convex lenses variously combined. These were succeeded by the achromatic object-glasses of Voigtlander & Sons, of Vienna, after Professor Petzval's calculation. The latter were introduced into the United States by Langenheim, Voigtlander's brother-in law. He took up the art where Cornelius left it, and for several years was the leading photographer, not only in Philadelphia, but probably in the world. And the fact should be commemorated, that he has done as much as, if not more than, any other to advance this art, and render it worthy the notice of the most intelligent and cultured classes in the community. In just recognition of his liberality, skill, and artistic enthusiasm, six or seven valuable gold medals were conferred upon him by European sovereigns, on their receiving from him a large panorama of Niagara Falls.

In 1848, he introduced, at great expense, the talbotype into the United States, by which he printed from paper negatives.

In 1850 he also introduced the stereoscope here, and by his efforts the American Stereoscopic Company was established. After this had been effected by many years' hard labor, and the public had learned to appreciate and demand these interesting pictures of scenes and objects both familiar and distant, the London Stereoscopic Company was encouraged to send hither an artist to take views, as also to establish an agency in New York. By this agency, with the furtherance of the booksellers in our large cities, the stereoscope has been circulated throughout the land, and thousands of families are drawing alike entertainment and instruction from this beautiful variety of the solar sketch.

Professors Draper and Morse, Dr. Chilton, and Messrs. Wolcott, Johnson, Fitz, &c., of New York, appear to have commenced experimenting with the daguerreotype, about simultaneously with our Philadelphia savans. They continued practising the art as amateurs, improving, the while, its instruments and manipulative methods until its practicability and utility were both demonstrated.

Mr. Johnson, of New York, claims that Wolcott & Johnson were the first to make photographic portraiture a profession for pay in that city. He says, that all the time they could so use was devoted to this object, and to preparing apparatus, plates, &c., long before the close of 1839, and subsequently still more vigorously, while they were preparing rooms for the purpose.

In the Journal of the Franklin Institute, for October, 1839, Professor J. F. Frazer, of Philadelphia, published a translation (made by himself from the French) of a full and detailed description of the new sun-painting process discovered by Daguerre. Following the directions therein given, he succeeded in producing a daguerreotype picture. His further prosecution of the study of the art was prevented by the pressing duties of his professorship, and the specimen he then produced has unfortunately got lost. For the amount of practical interest, however, then taken by him in heliography, we are happy to give him this mention among its earliest devotees.

At a visit made by Niepce, the after-associate of Daguerre, to England, in 1827, he exhibited to his friends, and left with them, several specimens of sun-limnings, produced by himself, nearly as perfect as those of Daguerre, made public in 1839.

Mr. Bauer, one of these friends, says he received from Niepce copies of engravings, fixed permanently by the action of light; copies of scenes from nature; also metallic plates thus engraved, and engravings copied therefrom. Mr. Bauer's belief was, that no engraving tools were employed upon these, but that the drawings were fixed by the action of light, and the plates subsequently engraved by a chemical process discovered by Niepce.

As early as 1829, Niepce and Daguerre formed an agreement to prosecute the new art together.

At the inauguration of the opening of a railroad to Courtrai, Belgium, in 1839, a daguerreotype picture was taken of the locomotive-engine, the wagon, train, and cortege, &c., exactly at the moment when the inauguration address was commenced. The time required for taking the impression was seven minutes.

It was reported that the Russian Czar offered Daguerre 500,000 francs ($100,000) for his secret, which was refused. Daguerre got from his own government only a 6000 franc pension per annum, which was only the 6 per cent. interest of 100,000 francs; *i. e.* $1200 per year.

As we have before stated in another place, the first who took portraits in Philadelphia was Robert Cornelius—followed by Thompson, Retzer, and John Plumb, for whom Truman Shew acted as agent. The earliest daguerreotype portrait from life, taken in Philadelphia, was probably one of Dr. Kennedy, the principal of the Polytechnic Institute, by the late Professor Walter R. Johnson in 1839.

The first portrait of this kind, made and *sold* in Philadelphia, was one of our long and well-known optician, John McAllister (founder of the house, now entitled McAllister Brothers), by Robert Cornelius, now the head of the firm of Cornelius, Baker & Co., our enterprising chandelier manufacturers.

Fizeau's discovery of the process for securing the impression on the plate by a coating of gold, which was introduced into Paris, in 1842, was soon after brought to the United States.

Laborde, Professor of Sciences in Corbigny, Navarre, was the first to recommend coating the plate a second time, or returning it from over the bromine back again to over the iodine, for a short time, before exposing it in the camera. This great improvement, which completely changed the *cold blue* linen collars, shirt-bosoms, &c., to a pure *natural white*, was introduced into Philadelphia by Samuel Van Loan, and into the country at large by John Johnson, of New York, early in 1844.

The earliest implements used by our heliographic operants were rude indeed, and their failures, of course, numerous. Vigilance, however, and persistent energy would achieve an occasional success. Such a specimen would be circulated among friends, as a something marvellous; although, as compared with some of the best present productions of the art, it may have been a flat, indistinct, leaden-looking thing, which a breath might almost blow away. For the now familiar process of securing the impress by gilding was then unknown.

After the successful experiments of Messrs. Draper & Morse, in New York, and of Cornelius, in Philadelphia, together with the improvements made by them and others in the heliographic apparatus and manipulative methods, and the great advance consequent thereon in the mode of obtaining portraits from life, quite a number of persons directed their attention to the art from the hope of making it a source of profit. They secured the services of individuals possessing activity and mechanical skill, who contributed to the progress of the art and its rapid introduction to public notice. Thus the chief towns of the Union became, ere long, familiar with the productions of the solar pencil.

Among the most prominent of those who earliest entered this field, were the elder Van Loan, Anthony, Edwards, &c., in New York; Southworth in Boston; and Thompson in Philadelphia. Thompson was, in 1855, the leading American heliographer in Paris.

J. Gurney commenced practising the art in 1841, and has closely applied himself thereto ever since (twenty-two years) in all its phases. He has uniformly striven to make it a reputable vocation, by producing the finest possible specimens in the various styles of the art.

Mr. A. Morand commenced practice in 1841, and has continued it with the feeling of a true artist down to the present date. He succeeded the elder Van Loan, corner of Chambers Street and Broadway, New York. In 1842, he introduced the daguerreotype into Brazil, South America. He waited upon the emperor, Don Pedro II., and took daguerreotypes for him, his family, and many of his friends. He took one instantaneous portrait of his majesty, as he alighted from his carriage in front of his palace. He also took the portrait of the wife of the French Prince De Joinville, and was present at her marriage to the prince. He commenced practising the art, in Brooklyn, New York, in 1860, and has often been favored with the valuable advice of the most eminent artists, such as Page, Huntingdon, Elliott, and Inman.

Few only of those, who commenced practising the art, as a calling, in 1841, have followed it through all its changes and improvements, so as to stand, to-day, in the front rank of its practitioners. Among these I am happy to name J. Gurney and A. Morand, of New York, and Samuel Broadbent, late of the firm of Broadbent & Co., Philadelphia. Mr. B. commenced as a pupil with Professor Morse, and for several years practised in the South. He came to Philadelphia in 1851.

Thomas Faris, a native of Ohio, commenced practice in 1841, and introduced the art into that state. He has still in his possession daguerreotype portraits, in good preservation, which were made by him twenty-two years ago. He introduced also the use of bromine into Ohio, and was, for many years, the leading daguerreotypist in Cincinnati, of that state.

To these should be added the intelligent and enterprising John Plumb, who early established galleries in most of the large cities of the United States; placing them under the supervision of his employés, in whose charge they flourished for the first four years. With so many "irons in the fire," however, he necessarily neglected some of them. The consequence was, that he became sadly reduced through the heedlessness and wastefulness, if not the absolute dishonesty of his agents. So that, from being possessed of a competence, the year 1847 found him literally penniless. Most of his fine establishments passed into the hands of those in whom he had confidently trusted.

In 1844–7, the leading practitioners of the art were Southworth & Hawes, Litch & Whipple, French & Hale, Chase & Ives, in Boston; and in New York, Anthony, Edwards & Clark, the proprietors of the National Gallery, J. Gurney, Edward White, and M. B. Brady.

Messrs. Anthony Brothers (Edward and Henry T.), originally civil engineers, were prompted, on the appearance of the new art, to make themselves practically acquainted with it. E. Anthony accompanied to the Aroostook territory in Maine, the commissioners appointed to run the boundary line between the United States and the British Dominions. He then took, for our Government, photographic views of the "Highlands," involved in that controversy between the two governments, which Lord Ashburton and Mr. Webster were appointed to settle. These views are preserved in the national archives, and, so far as we know, this was the first recourse ever had, by any government, to the services of the sun-painting art.

They also took from life in 1839, or early in 1840, the portrait of a laborer, standing on the sunny side of a house at Tarrytown, with the lens of a telescope.

The firm of Anthony, Edwards & Clarke took daguerreotype portraits of the members of Congress, in 1843 and 1844; and in 1845 published the large and fine picture entitled "Clay's Farewell to the Senate." The portraits in this picture were striking for life-like artistic effect. This was the first notable engraving taken from daguerreotypes, extant at that date (1846), when this firm stood at the head of the art in New York.

Edward Anthony, the head of both the above-named firms, has, from the outset, manifested a deep interest in the art, and has been zealous and liberal in promoting all the measures adopted and the efforts made for its advancement. In 1854, he offered two magnificent and valuable prizes, to be awarded to the two artists who should produce the three best and the three second best specimens of the daguerreotype. This offer, of course, was made, as a stimulus to those engaged in the art.

The first prize, a massive silver pitcher, highly ornamented, was awarded to J. Gurney; and the second, two beautiful silver goblets, to Samuel Root. The competitors were quite numerous, and there was no great difference in the manipulative or artistic excellence of the effects produced. A favorable subject, as a model, or some lucky circumstance, probably determined the award, as there was no very decided difference in the specimens presented, all being highly creditable to the makers. The condition, attached by Mr. Anthony to his offer of these prizes, was that each competitor should furnish him a full description of the process whereby he operated—to be published for the general benefit. This was done, and the processes of each were published.

Henry T. Anthony, a member of the Photographic Club, and a brother of Edward, was (we believe) the first who took instantaneous views by the collodion process;

the first not only in the United States, but (so far as we know) in the world.

The following paragraph is extracted from an exceedingly complimentary letter, written by Thomas Sutton, Esq., of England, editor of the "Photographic Notes," to Mr. H. T. Anthony, in reply to a letter by the latter, accompanied by some of his instantaneous photographs, and asking Mr. S. how these compared with similar results obtained in Europe.

"In reply to Mr. Anthony's query about us European photographers, we can only say we *know of no pictures, save two or three of Wilson's best,* which could *be put in comparison with those he has sent;* and we old stick-in-the-mud fellows must take care, or the Yankees will go ahead of us."

In copartnership with a brother, he is, at present, one of the largest stock-dealers in the United States, manufacturing and keeping ever on sale, the best qualities of all the materials and implements employed in the profession.

Next after them in New York, followed Gurney, Brady, Haas, and Lawrence. In 1845–6, F. Langenheim, in Philadelphia, was generally acknowledged to be the first scientific and practical daguerreotypist in this country, and probably in the world. He has skilfully applied the new art to the manufacture of magic lantern slides, of an exquisite quality. His micro-photographs are far superior to any we have seen made by others on either side the Atlantic. Following him were Van Loan, Mayall, Plumb, and Simons.

Mayall became sole proprietor of the since widely known establishment at 140 Chestnut Street, in 1845. On June 20th, 1846, he disposed of it to M. A. Root, and returned to London, where he now has a flourishing establishment, in which all branches of sun-limning are successfully practised.

Through Mr. Shadbolt, the able editor of the London Journal, I have learned that Mr. M. has been honored with the patronage of England's Royal Family. This, I trust, will compensate him for his many years of zealous devotion to his favorite art, with his indefatigable efforts to place it high on the list of honorable professions.

In 1842, John A. Whipple, of Boston, Massachusetts, manufactured the chlorides of iodine and gold, and hyposulphite of soda for daguerreotype amateurs. The firm of Litch, Whipple & Cannon was formed in 1846, and dissolved in 1848.

In 1849, Whipple, by help of the Cambridge Observatory telescope, supervised by Dr. Bond, daguerreotyped a group of double stars; and a few months later, by the same help, he took excellent daguerreotypes of the moon. These were the first pictures of the kind ever obtained by the new art.

In 1860, he took stereoscopic views of the moon on collodionized plates, and as two views of the same object, taken at slightly different points, are required to represent such object *stereoscopically*, Mr. Whipple took his first view of the moon in February 5th, and the second in April 6th. The moon having changed her position and aspect during the interval, the two pictures, when properly mounted and seen through the stereoscope, were represented as one moon, alike interesting and wonderful to behold. These are perfect marvels for their *rotundity* of effect, the moon standing out as round as a billiard ball. The definition is both clear and beautiful. The time of exposure was from four to five seconds each.

Whipple introduced the use of steam-power in polishing plates, as also in other branches of his business, thereby saving much time and labor. He still prosecutes daguerreotypy, in connection with all other branches of sun-painting. He has tested the art in all its phases, and has, probably, labored as diligently and done as much to make it popular and useful, as any man in the United States. He has generally been first in introducing improvements. His largest lenses, which are also the largest in the country, were constructed by Alvin Clarke, of Boston.

He was among the first in the United States to enlarge daguerreotypes up to life-size, by his own arrangement of lenses. Having a condenser fixed in the roof, the light is thrown down through a small set of lenses upon the paper, which is fixed upon a platform so arranged with weights and pullies, as to be elevated or lowered, as required to regulate the size of the impression. He made at once with a camera the largest street-view ever taken. The negative was 5 ft. × 3,—and the finished proof, when trimmed and mounted, was 4 ft. 6 in. × 2 ft. 6 in.

Whipple's galleries, which occupy the upper part of three buildings, cost over $25,000, and are admirably appointed; every appliance is convenient, and of the most approved construction. He employs nearly forty persons, mostly females. His work, of all styles, stands deservedly high, and is appreciated by the intelligent and opulent, and his business is large and profitable.

My personal interest in the art commenced with its earliest appearance in Philadelphia in 1839, and for the next few years, I devoted to its study and practice the whole time and attention not absorbed by my ordinary vocation. In 1844, I commenced practice in Mobile, Alabama, having bought out John A. Bennett, a young practitioner there. From Mobile I went to New Orleans, where, for some time, I paid attention to the art. In the same year I opened a gallery in St. Louis, under the name of Root & Miller, and another in Philadelphia, under that of Root & Collins.

Since June 20th, 1846, when I commenced giving my undivided time and labor to sun-limning, in Philadelphia, I have strictly maintained my original prices, or else have advanced upon them; and have constantly striven to make the profession as widely popular and as lucrative as possible. To this end I have expended nearly $20,000 in advertising, &c., in order to draw public attention to the excellencies of the art, and to the value of first-class specimens of the same, as subserving a multitude of most important ends.

My extra-liberal use of "printer's ink," coupled with my reputed success in producing good pictures, not only augmented largely my own business, but induced hundreds beside to adopt the same vocation. So that, at the close of the first sixteen years from its introduction, nearly every village of note in the United States had at least one heliographer, who made it his head-quarters, while most of our large towns had from two to a dozen.

In 1849 I opened a gallery at the corner of Franklin Street and Broadway, New York, under the supervision of my brother Samuel. In 1856, this was sold to Mr. Faris, and my brother commenced practice in Dubuque, Iowa.

In 1852 I opened a gallery in Washington, D. C., under the care of a former pupil of mine, John Clark, who, at this date (1863), has a flourishing establishment in New orleans.

In 1856 I was severely injured by a railroad collision, and was confined to my house, crippled and helpless, for nearly four years. Within this period most of the first part of this volume was prepared and put on paper.

The total number practising the art, in 1860, throughout the United States, was believed to exceed ten thousand. It was, however, undeniable that a great proportion of this number were not qualified to achieve even a high *mechanical* success therein, being ignorant alike of its theory and practice.

Of this large number of operants, we regret the necessity of saying, that the proportion is inconsiderable who appear to us to be artists in judgment, feeling, and executive genius, or in the discipline obtained from scholastic training or self-teaching. Nor is the sum very considerable of first-class proficients, even in the chemical or mechanical departments. This remark applies, with slight if any difference, to all the main sections of the United States.

Within the interval from 1851 to the present date (1855), practitioners have grown so numerous and the resulting competition so sharp, that prices have gradually sunk from a moderate amount to the bare cost of the often indifferent materials employed. So that heliographs, not unfrequently, were sold for one shilling apiece.

Now that this state of things is attended with evils of no slight moment, will (I suppose) be freely conceded. Among these is the disrepute thus cast upon the art and its professors, as are also the hindrances thereby put in the way of its development, and its progress towards that eminent status and that multiform utility, which both, under genial auspices, are capable of attaining.

Let us not, however, forget that this condition of affairs has its own compensations, and that even cheap photographs are not without some benefits to the community. Their cheapness brings them within reach of all, however little cultured and however depressed in the social scale. It is rare to find any one of these, which has not in it *something* to fix and reward the attention; and multitudes of the humbler classes are not, by education, qualified to appreciate the highest products of art, so as to give them instant preference to the lowest.

Very many, therefore, may draw both pleasure and mental profit from pictures, which the able connoisseur would fling contemptuously aside.

Let us not, then, despise what is capable of delighting and advantaging any considerable number of our fellow-beings. To borrow the language of a friend, who believes that "God hath made of *one blood* all nations upon earth,"

"The desire for specimens of art may be as strong with the poor in their cabins, as with the rich in their palaces; and the poor widow, as she pays her twenty-five cents (which, probably, are her whole savings, through many weeks, from her scanty pittance), for a likeness of her cherished one (perhaps her only son bound for the field of war), who is about leaving her, it may be to return no more, will feel a glow of gratitude to the art that has enabled her to have always within view a 'counterfeit presentment' of one so fondly loved. She will, moreover, be quite as happy in this her possession, and possibly as respectable, as the opulent ladies and gentlemen, who ride in their carriages, for their costly portraits to the studios of the highliest famed celebrities of the art."

If thus the indifferent sun-painting may be a *solace* in a multitude of cases, of which the above is an example, and a positive delight in as many others, so it may also serve as a partial means of culture to the whole community of the lowly poor, by training, to some extent, within them a taste for the beautiful in nature and in art, as also the capacity to judge between various degrees of merit; thus tending to elevate and to bring them nearer, in intellectual condition, to those more favored of fortune.

In 1848, John Quail invented, and employed for several subsequent years, in his daguerreotype gallery in Philadelphia, a multiplying camera, with a very convenient plate-holder, having both horizontal and perpendicular movements, whereby several impressions could be taken at one sitting. This camera still exists. He also used a "greasy buff, magnetized" with spermaceti oil, and took pictures of children, almost instantaneously, and usually without the "head-rest."

Mr. Cady, of New York, in 1851, took instantaneous views of steamboats while leaving the wharf, with the wheels in rapid motion. The waves, the spray, and objects generally, were defined as beautifully as though standing still at the taking.

Alexander Beckers, in 1851, made instantaneous views in Broadway, New York, wherein all moving objects were clearly and beautifully delineated on a silvered plate. He also invented and, for many years, used a movable plate-shield, which comprised lateral and perpendicular movements, that brought the image into the middle of the plate and through the centre of the lens.

In the Crystal Palace exhibition, at New York city, in 1853, our leading daguerreotypists placed there on show the finest collection, probably, of daguerreotypes, ever brought before the public, either in this or any other quarter of the world.

The daguerreotype business was at its zenith in 1853, since when it has been declining. And I venture the prediction, that this decline will go on till large numbers, especially in our principal cities, have abandoned it. By this means, I think, it will ultimately fall into the hands of comparatively a few—such, moreover, as are qualified for it alike by native genius and by education, and who will so practise all its several branches, as to secure the approval of the most accomplished connoisseurs. It will *then* attract the regards of artists more than it has heretofore done, and will essentially aid them in their own special departments, and, at the same time, will be patronized by amateurs and by the more opulent classes of the community. In such circumstances, sun-pictures will be far more likely than now to be appreciated, and to receive the awards due to their absolute merits.

In 1855, Hesler, of Chicago, Illinois, excelled most others in his daguerreotype views. He had a genuine love of his art, and worked it with veritable artistic feeling. His subjects were usually well chosen, and the mechanical and chemical manipulations displayed evidence of a genius, of which the profession should be proud. He did much to elevate his art both in excellence and in public estimation.

Fitzgibbons, of St. Louis, Missouri, also exhibited great energy and skill in his street-views, his pictures of steamboats, his portraits of Indians, &c. These, taken in 1852–3, were wonderful for delineations, depth, tone, and beauty.

But to proceed with our history.—In Paris, where Daguerre's discovery was first made public, it lies at present in partial abeyance, if it be not well-nigh forgotten; while photography, by the albumen and collodion processes, has been carried to a high degree of excellence. The march of improvement is, at this moment, not less steady and rapid than at any prior date, and men of science and accomplishments, all over Europe, may be found taking solar portraits and views, both as professionists and amateurs.

Talbot's process (patented in 1840) was purchased by William & F. Langenheim, and by them introduced, at great expense, into the United States, in 1849. Unhappily for the purchasers, this process proved impracticable, and was soon superseded by the albumen process, first practised (as already stated) by Niepce St. Victor, in Paris, whereby pictures were impressed on glass, and entitled "Hyalotypes." In 1850 this process was patented by Langenheim, and at the "World's Fair" in the Crystal Palace, in London, he received a medal for the superior excellence of his specimens.

John A. Whipple and William B. Jones, of Boston, also obtained, in 1845, a patent for a certain variety of the albumen process, styled by them the "Crystallotype." In the hands of Whipple, one of the most original geniuses in the profession, and more especially (perhaps) of J. Wallace Black, who was noted for his extraordinary energy and skill, this picture was greatly improved and to some extent brought to the knowledge of the Boston public. Strictly considered, we believe this process is simply that of Niepce, whose description of it was translated for Whipple, and for this he procured a patent from the United States Government.

In New York, several daguerreotypists in 1853 essayed the introduction there of this process for portraiture, but they did not succeed. It is suited only for views, and for transcribing pictures, where prolonged exposures can be had.

McClees & Germon introduced Whipple's crystallotype into Philadelphia, and, after much trouble and heavy expense, succeeded in producing some very fine pictures, as also in copying good daguerreotypes so well, that but slight labor was requisite for an artist to make of them very pleasing and creditable productions. McClees copied and transferred to boxwood blocks, ready for the engraver, an admirable *fac simile* of the Japan treaty, which was faithfully cut upon wood, stereotyped or electrotyped, and printed in the Japanese language. This may be seen in Perry's account of the United States treaty with Japan, published in 1853.

Mr. Schreiber who, in 1850, succeeded Langenheim in Philadelphia, has practised the albumen process with fair success. He has excelled, especially, in copying *poor* daguerreotypes.

The collodion process, discovered, in 1850, by Le Gray, of Paris, and Frederick Scott Archer, of London, was, in 1851, introduced to the English public, together with its formulas.

In January and February of 1852, Dr. Charles Cresson, of Philadelphia, was by myself supplied with cotton for making collodion, and instruments for experimentation. Early in February he obtained encouraging results, and in March he produced views and portraits, at brief exposures, in a series of experiments with iodine, bromine, and sundry other substances, suggested by the late John Price Wetherill, Esq.

In 1853, Dr. Giles Langdell, now of Philadelphia, procured, while residing in Boston, a published account of Archer's process, and, after several experiments, succeeded in making very good collodion portraits on paper. My impression is, that he was the first to operate successfully with this process in the United States.

After considerable improvements, this process was first introduced, in 1854, into various daguerrean establishments, in the Eastern and Western States, by Cutting & Rehn. In June of this year, Cutting procured patents for the process, though Langdell had already worked it from the printed formulas.

The process has since been introduced, as a legitimate business, into the leading establishments of our country. The positive branch of it; *i. e.* a solar impression upon one glass-plate, which is covered by a second hermetically sealed thereto, is entitled the "Ambrotype," (or the "imperishable picture"), a name devised in my gallery.

Isaac Rehn, formerly a successful daguerreotypist, in company with Cutting, of Boston, perfected and introduced through the United States the "Ambrotype," or the positive on glass. Since then, he has investigated and mastered, on its appearance, every new phase of the heliographic art. Portraiture in all its branches—from the small and exquisite stereoscopic picture, up to the life-size by the solar camera enlargement—has been executed, with remarkable excellence and beauty, by his artistic genius and skilful manipulation.

Not content with limiting his attention to this branch alone, he turned his investigations to other branches also; *e. g* photo-lithography and micro-photography. His productions, in these two departments, so useful and important for numerous purposes, have proved him to be a perfect and successful master of both. Government gave him large orders for patent office delineations. So, too, the scientific members of the Philadelphia Academy of Natural Sciences have expressed themselves surprised and delighted with his exactly and beautifully executed representations of microscopic objects, enlarged thousands of times, and photo-lithographed clearly in all their minutest details.

A distinguished scientific gentleman and heliographic amateur, in a recent letter to me, writes of Mr. R. as follows:—"Mr. Rehn knows more about photo-lithography than any other man in the world! I judge from the beautiful specimens of his work, some of which you sent me. *I saw nothing in Europe like them!*" We congratulate our friend R. on calling forth a judgment so eulogistic from so capable a judge and art-critic.

This species of picture (the Ambrotype) had, at the very outset, an extraordinary popularity, which, however, for reasons stated otherwhere, has palpably and generally declined; so that, at present, comparatively few are made. Positives taken upon enamelled or japanned iron plates, instead of glass, are, at this date (1863), quite popular.

The principal use now made of the collodion process, is in taking and printing positives on paper from a negative taken upon glass. From *one* such negative an indefinite number of paper positives can be made. And, all things considered, these pictures must, probably, be pronounced the finest of sun-limnings as yet produced. Some, however, would doubtless insist upon at least one exception—the daguerreotype.

Charles Williamson who, in 1849, had been for a while in my employ, opened a photographic establishment in Brooklyn, New York, in 1851. He introduced the "Cameotype," which was simply a small vignette daguerreotype, making a pretty picture, tastefully got up and cased. He kept pace with the improvements in the art, always introducing these, as suggested by scientific amateurs at home and abroad, employing first-class artists, and, for the most part, supplying his customers with artistic and satisfactory portraits. He employs, at present, about forty persons, and has one of the best appointed, most beautiful and popular establishments in our country.

C. C. Harrison, so widely known as a manufacturer of camera lenses and tubes, for heliographic use, was, in 1846, a daguerreotype manipulator. He prosecuted this business for several years, making, the while, lenses both for his own use and for sale. The value of his lenses eventually became so extensively known, and the demand for them so great, that he was constrained to give his undivided attention to this manufacture, in which he has, at present, constantly employed over thirty workmen. Up to May 15th, 1863, he had constructed eight thousand eight hundred and seventeen of the lenses in general use, and three hundred and seven of his new globe lenses, so highly prized for landscape-photography, copying, &c. (See chapter on Optics. Part Second.)

M. B. Brady commenced the daguerreotype practice in 1843. He received, in 1844, the first medal ever awarded by the American Institute for the best specimens exhibited, and, in subsequent years, received several others. The first medal was awarded to him at the London Crystal Palace, in 1851.

He has always been energetic and untiring in his efforts to improve and elevate the art—employing, at high prices, the best artists to finish portraits in India ink, water, and oil colors for his patrons. He took the photographs of the members of the United States Senate and House of Representatives, and combined them in a single group, just before the rebellion broke out. He has also photographed "war scenes," or "incidents of the war," having eighteen or twenty assistants employed on the work for months.

The most remarkable productions of his establishment for artistic effect, and that *expression*, which imparts to a picture an air of intelligence and thought, were a series of photographic representations of Mr. Forrest in his various dramatic characters, finished in India ink. In these pictures the several characters were admirably expressed, and told each its own individual story. For the series Mr. F. paid $1000.

The work was, in all its departments, executed in the finest style of the art, and was, in the highest degree, creditable to Mr. Brady.

Sundry other species of pictures, chiefly variations of the collodion process, have been invented in this country, receiving their names either from their inventors, or from some circumstance associated with them. I shall here do little more than enumerate them.

1st. The Hillotype is so styled from Rev. L. L. Hill, of the interior of New York, who attempted thereby to produce pictures, colored as in nature. As his endeavor succeeded but partially, if at all, and as there appears to have been deception in the matter, I shall meddle with it no further.

2d. The Hallotype was invented by J. Bishop Hall, of New York city, and patented in January 1857. Its principle consists in a certain mode of *combining* two or more pictures, which are fac simile or duplicate impressions, so as to constitute one picture. There are numerous varieties in the application of this principle, and some items of the process have been practised in Europe for over thirty years.

3d. The Diaphanotype is a method of applying the principle of the hallotype, originating with E. E. Hawkins, of Cincinnati, Ohio. The picture has an enamelled appearance, and being cemented to plate-glass, and colored on the back in oil colors, it is believed to be durable.

4th. The Melainotype is simply a collodion positive, made upon an iron instead of a glass plate, the invention of Professor H. L. Smith, of Kenyon College, Gambier, Ohio. The Ferrotype plate, so named, manufactured by V. M. Griswold, of Ohio, has a similar appearance.

5th. The Sphereotype was patented in 1856, by Bisbee, of Columbus, Ohio. It is nothing else than a positive, impressed on glass in a certain peculiar way, and is named from its spherical appearance, when finished and encased.

6th. The Atrephograph is an invention of James M. Letts, of Dundee, New York. The name in English, is "not reversed," and denotes its character. It is simply a collodion positive taken upon glass, which is coated, first with India rubber dissolved in chloroform, and then with collodion. After the impression has been fixed and washed, it is flowed over with thin transparent varnish or with water, and, while damp or "tacky," it is rolled off upon black paper, upon thin cards, or japanned leather having a fine polish.

In a daguerreotype the reversal, above mentioned, does occur—the right and left sides changing places. (Mr. Johnson, of New York, remarks, however, that "it does not occur, when the picture is produced by the reflecting camera," constructed by his former partner, A. S. Wolcott.)

7th. The "Imperial Photograph" is a picture taken, in the usual way, on a plate 20 by 17 or 17 by 14 inches,—or on a small plate and magnified to that size by the solar camera or other means,—and then completed by the artist. It was introduced to the public by M. B. Brady, of New York city.

In 1854, after the introduction of the albumen process into some of the leading establishments of our principal cities; and before the collodion process had attracted much notice, or had been successfully worked by any of our American practitioners; Messrs. Gurney, Fredericks & Pennebeart, very greatly to their credit, introduced into New York from Paris several accomplished practical artists, who had had much previous experience in coloring photographs, with both oil and water colors. This proceeding served to corroborate a statement of mine, repeatedly made in the heliographic journals, viz.: that this art belongs to the category of both the fine and the useful arts; that it merits the attention and is certain, eventually, to secure the skill and endeavor of able artists, who are versed in working in Indian ink, crayon, pastel, and oil and water colors.

In 1854, soon after artists were employed to finish photographs in colors, &c., occasion called for pictures of this kind, enlarged to a size not producible by ordinary camera lenses; and Woodward's solar camera, now so widely known, was invented and patented. This instrument, and others designed for the same purpose, are described elsewhere in this work. (See Part Second.)

In 1858, Mr. Shives invented and patented another enlarging instrument, whereby direct light and a condensing lens are employed, in lieu of Woodward's reflector. This is capable of enlarging pictures to any size required. (See chapter on enlarging cameras. Part Second.)

A solar or enlarging camera was also patented by Mr. Howard, of Reading, Pennsylvania. It is manufactured and kept on sale by George Dabbs & Co. (See Chapter, Second Volume, on enlarging cameras.)

Portraitists generally are now constrained to concede the capabilities of the *collodion process* in skilled and competent hands, and are glad to avail themselves of its great advantages. Thus a superior photograph, taken by an operant of genius and feeling under favorable auspices, may be variously finished; *e. g.* in Indian ink or colors, upon diverse materials; and be by him improved and idealized, without losing in the least the verity of the picture. Indeed it may be affirmed, that *only* by heliographic aid can likenesses, *perfectly* truthful, be obtained of the "human face divine."

So well is this fact apprehended at this date (1860), that not a few of our leading heliographers have introduced, while others are, from time to time, introducing into their establishments, thoroughly educated and skilled artists to finish, in colors or Indian ink, photographs for those who, on perceiving the exact truthfulness of these representations, appreciate and pay liberally for such portraits of relatives and friends.

In fine, all indications promise that the era is rapidly drawing nigh, when sun-painting shall be recognised as one of the fine arts; nor this alone, but as one among the most useful of all the useful arts. That such are its capabilities and its possibilities is a doctrine which, as the reader will find, is earnestly advocated in this work from the first to the last of its pages.

Messrs. Case & Getchell, successors to Measury & Silsby, of Boston, have also a large and popular establishment in that city. Their cartes de visite and larger photographs are, for beauty and artistic effect, surpassed by few, if by any. They closely resemble the productions of the celebrated Disderi, of Paris, which are the finest I have seen of their class, and are veritable gems of art.

Among the most remarkable productions of the solar camera that I have met with (and these are numerous), none are superior to certain full, life-size portraits produced by Mr. Burnham, of Boston. They are taken on "cartoon" paper, seven feet by five feet, and are purer, softer, and more beautiful in their lights and gradations, while their shadows are bolder and more forcible than those of the finest crayon drawing.

Mr. Miller, of Boston, an artistic heliographer, and equally able and well skilled in all branches of the profession, took several exceedingly interesting stereoscopic and larger-sized views, in the crater of a volcano, at one mile's depth, on Fayal, an island of the Portuguese Azores. The smoke and the steam rising from a gushing spring (hot enough to boil eggs in three minutes), to nearly the summit of the crater, and flowing gracefully over to one side, was so exquisitely reproduced by him, as to constrain every admirer of art to bless the "light-sketching pencil," when wielded by artistic genius.

Mr. Miller also devised an admirable solar or enlarging camera, of simple construction, which is widely used in the Eastern States, and vended at moderate rates by John Sawyer & Co., Boston.

The first successful heliographic views, taken from the balloon, of which we have any account, were by J. Wallace Black, formerly of the firm of Whipple & Black, Boston. In consequence of the incessant swaying, twisting, and rolling movements of the balloon, as well as its rapid flight, the operations were extremely difficult.

The instrument used was an 8–4 Voigtlander lens and camera, of open or full aperture, affixed to a side of the balloon-basket. It had a stop, or a sliding pasteboard for excluding light, having in its middle a hole as wide as the tube, and, in length, twice its diameter. One end of this slide closed the camera tube till ready for exposure.

Being arranged with India rubber springs set by a trigger, these, when all was ready, were snapped, and the slide changed ends; admitting the light through the lens, as the aperture in the slide passed, and making the impression *instantaneously*.

Some of the views are very fine, and the results of the

experiment are highly creditable to Mr. Black, as an able, energetic sun-limning artist, whether stayed by the solid globe or cleaving the unstable air. After his former partner, Whipple, had represented the moon and stars above, he soared aloft and pictured the earth he left below.

Mr. Black's success for the last five years in all branches of his profession, is probably without a parallel in the United States at this date (1863). He has one of the most extensive and best-planned establishments, now existing, for every department of the art. He gives constant employment to over sixty persons, male and female.

The excellent specimens here produced, coupled with his energy and courteous deportment, have placed him where he now stands,—in the front rank of the profession.

The card picture has given a new impulse to the heliographic art.

The French were its inaugurators, and gave it the name of Carte de Visite. Messrs. C. D. Fredericks & Co., Broadway, New York, with their characteristic enterprise and energy, introduced the making of portraits and views, of this class, into the United States.

In 1860, J. E. Mayall, of London, was honored with a commission to visit Buckingham Palace, and take card-portraits of the Queen, Prince Albert, and the rest of the royal family. The sale of these small pictures, at a moderate rate, gave the British people the pleasure of possessing life-like representations of their universally loved queen and her interesting family. Imitating this high example, distinguished persons, of every rank and pursuit, availed themselves of the photographer's services, and left with him a negative impression of themselves, from which thousands could be printed. Thus their friends and acquaintances, and the curious alike in Great Britain and in foreign lands, could easily procure portraits of the country's notabilities, whose names so often appeared in books and the public journals of the day. The natural result was, that the sun-painting art received an impulse which has carried it to a height before unparalleled.

The Messrs. Appleton, of New York, were (we believe) the first booksellers in the United States, who introduced stereoscopic pictures to the public. The influence, given them by their eminent standing and large resources, in this branch of traffic, enabled them to popularize this new species of photograph, and to put hundreds of thousands, ere long, in circulation throughout the land.

More recently, they have commenced manufacturing the cartes de visite, consisting of portraits of celebrities and of citizens generally, and have made an arrangement with A. A. Turner, who employs over forty persons, in producing such pictures as are likely to be in demand, to be put on sale at their counter.

It is auspicious, both for the art and its practitioners, that a house so eminent and influential as the Appletons, have become so connected with this new variety of the art.

To show, by a few statistics, how high is the elevation which the art has now attained, we introduce the few lines below. They prove that, as at the outset a few hundreds of dollars would start a daguerreotypist in practice, now as many thousands are required to set up a photographer.

The first who had the foresight and courage to risk seven or eight thousand dollars, in fitting a ground-floor reception room, and pay $4000 per annum for rent alone, for the single purpose of prosecuting our art, was Rufus Anson, of Broadway, New York. His bold venture was justified by the speedy increase of his business fourfold.

Charles D. Fredericks & Co., of New York, took a house at $9500 rent, and expended eight or ten thousand dollars in fitting it with a ground-floor, office, and reception room, and furnishing the establishment throughout with appliances for carrying on all branches of the business to the best advantage. The spirited enterprise was a rich pecuniary triumph.

In Philadelphia, O. H. Willard, Rehn, Hurn, Cooper, Gutekunst, Hipple, Turner, Morgan, and some others, have also ground-floor reception and sky-light rooms, elegantly and expensively fitted up.

Although the advance of the heliographic art has, within the last five years, been rapid almost beyond calculation, yet, strange to say, comparatively few of the profession appear to have kept a complete set of books, comprising a full and accurate account of their business transactions.

Mr. A. Bogardus is one of these few. Commencing the daguerreotype practice in New York city, in 1846; in 1862 he refitted the old Root Gallery, 363 Broadway, and made his spacious and convenient rooms pleasantly attractive to his numerous visitants and friends.

Order the most complete is visible throughout. Mr. Montgomery, his book-keeper, has devised and introduced a perfect system of accounts and check books, specially adapted to the photographic business, whereby all confusion in the management of affairs is prevented. No losses, moreover, are now sustained, but much on the contrary is saved.

In the first year after opening in Broadway, the business amounted to over $33,000, and between twenty five and thirty persons, male and female, are employed therein.

The Messrs. Lewis, father and sons, of New York city, have, during the last twenty years, been widely known throughout the United States, as inventors and manufacturers of the finest qualities of almost every species of instrument used in the daguerreotype, as well as the heliographic business in general. The profession are deeply indebted to them for their valuable improvements, which have essentially aided in the prosecution and advancement of the art in all its numerous branches.

R. A. Lewis, manufacturer of Lewis & Holt's celebrated collodion, Chatham street, has, after twenty years' experience, and persistent energetic effort, created a business that requires from thirty to forty employés, male and female, to take and fill orders. The amount of materials used, and the number of card-portraits, and of plain and finished pictures of the several styles, taken by this establishment, are absolutely amazing.

1. *Blue Glass*,—for sky-lights, first suggested to M. B. Brady, by H. H. Snelling, in May, 1849.

2. *Instantaneous Daguerreotypes*,—first practically made by H. H. Snelling, in September, 1849, at which date he invented an electric camera-box for that purpose.

3. *Condensing Mercury bath top*,—to prevent the escape of mercurial fumes into the room, invented by H. H. Snelling in 1851. Never adopted.

4. *Pantograph, for enlarging Photographs*,—invented by H. H. Snelling, in July, 1853. First used in 1855, by C. D. Fredericks.

5. *Colors*,—to be employed in printing bank notes, to prevent photographic counterfeiting, first suggested by H. H. Snelling, in 1854.

6. *Resinized Paper process*,—discovered by H. H. Snel-

ling in 1856, and first put in practice in December of that year.

7. *Printing in Colors by Carbon process*,—first attempted and executed by H. H. Snelling, in July, 1858, one year before any other attempt.

It may not be generally known, that Daguerre had so strong an objection to having his portrait taken, that he never (it is believed) sat to but one photographer; and this was our countryman, Charles R. Meade, of the firm of Meade Brothers, in New York. Mr. Meade being in France, in 1848, visited Daguerre's Chateau, at Brie-sur-Marne, for the purpose of taking his portrait,—not being aware of Daguerre's objection to being thus represented. Mr. Meade's request was politely but firmly negatived, as had been the request of many others,—among them two artists from the United States. Eventually, however, through the urgent persuasion of his wife and niece, Daguerre was induced to sit, and five or six daguerreotypes of him were taken by Mr. Meade, from which numerous copies were afterwards produced in the various modes of representation. The artist also took a daguerreotype of Daguerre's Chateau at this time. In 1853, his brother, H. N. Meade, took one of Daguerre's monument, in the cemetery of Brie, and worked in the laboratory where Daguerre made all his experiments. He also visited M. Niepce St. Victor, and saw him make daguerreotypes *in the natural colors* by the camera solely. These, however, could not be rendered permanent.

In 1841, Charles Fontayne began daguerreotyping in Baltimore, Maryland. In 1846, he removed to Cincinnati, Ohio. In this year he discovered the property of the camera to throw a magnified image on a screen. In 1853, he made some collodion pictures. In 1854, he produced life-size photographs—the first ever made in the United States, *he* says; and his statement is backed by H. H. Snelling. In 1855, he made two full-length portraits, of five and a half by seven feet size. In 1858, he invented a machine for rapid photographic printing, designed for illustrating books, which, with the most sensitive paper, and by development, produces four prints per second, or fourteen thousand four hundred per hour. By enlarging the condensing lens to twenty inches, fifty thousand per hour might easily be produced. Mr. Fontayne says, he made several large pictures with the condenser some years before this was patented by Mr. Woodward. He is now printing with his machine, large quantities of pictures on albumen paper, as well as vignette portraits.

In May, 1854, Mr. Holmes, Broadway, New York, invented the double camera for taking two pictures at once, and got it patented by the United States Government. This invention comprises both a mode of producing two pictures at once, and a double box, whereon the tubes or lenses are fastened, and worked upon an angle or a parallel to the object, as required for stereoscopes, &c.

In August, 1862, he made improvement in backgrounds, with ornamental floor-ground combined in perspective upon the back-ground—giving depth and finish, in illustrating interior or exterior scenes.

Our history of the art in this country has occupied so much space, that a few paragraphs more must close it. We would gladly speak at some length of many other American photographers, whom we cannot even *mention* for lack of room.

The few names, added below to the list already given, are of men, with most of whom we have been personally acquainted; men who, commencing with the daguerreotype, and struggling manfully with the numerous difficulties attending the introduction of a new art, have kept pace with all its improvements, and mastered all the new phases and forms it has assumed, and have done very much towards raising it to that position of popularity and lucrativeness which it at present holds. The young aspirants to excellence and distinction in this now highly reputable, extensively useful, and profitable profession, may study with advantage the history of these pioneers; finding a healthful stimulus to their career, in the tireless energy, the unwearied patience, and the indomitable perseverance, which that history discloses.

Among this class are Gabriel Harrison and Douglas, of Brooklyn, New York; Griswold, of Columbus, Ohio; Ryder and North, of Cleveland, Ohio; Perkins, Pollock, and Whitehurst, of Baltimore, Maryland; Page, of Washington, D. C.; George S. Cooke, Charleston, South Carolina; Porter, Cincinnati, Ohio; Webster & Brother, Louisville, Kentucky; Long and Brown, St. Louis, Missouri; Samuel Fassett, Chicago, Illinois; S. Root, Dubuque, Iowa; H. S. Brown, Milwaukie, Wisconsin; Douglas Hovey, Rochester; Arthur Cobden, Troy; Henry Glosser, New York; D. C. Collins, New Haven, Connecticut; and John Keenan and Reimer, Philadelphia.

This enumeration has been extended far enough for the purposes of a mere historic record. A few facts and comments will complete what we have to say here.

Landscape Photography, executed by artists possessing the genius of a Cole, a Durand, a Hart, a Church, a Webber, a Sontag, a Hamilton, or a Russell Smith, has hitherto received but little attention in the United States. Government, however, has employed some in various public works, while others, under private patronage or as amateurs, have produced battle scenes and views of different military operations, as well as of landscapes noted for sublimity or beauty. In Europe, highly accomplished art-amateurs have produced, and are still constantly producing exquisite views and "choice bits" of scenery, architecture, &c., which are highly prized and promptly secured, wherever put on sale.

Colonel Nicholas Pike, formerly our minister for several years to Portugal, practised as an amateur, while abroad, all the various processes, whereby landscapes have been taken in Europe. He moreover became personally acquainted with many who had made discoveries and improvements in this branch of photography; with scientific amateurs, editors of journals, authors, &c., engaged therein, and was (we believe) the first to introduce the dry process into the United States.

Since his return, Colonel Pike has practised, as an amateur, all the varieties of the art which have successively appeared; and he now understands the whole art, both theoretically and practically, quite as well as, if not better than, any other amateur in our country. As the corresponding secretary of the New York Photographical Society, he was by his position, as well as by his rare photographic knowledge and skill, enabled to render me (as he has actually done) most valuable aid in collecting facts and preparing the second, or practical part of this work. His love for science and art in general, and his special devotion to the heliographic branch of the same, have appeared to make of this a pleasing task; and while I can congratulate my readers on their thus enjoying the results of the Colonel's labors, I am happy in having this opportunity to present my grateful acknowledgments for his kind services in my behalf.

PHOTOGRAPHIC JOURNALS.

The first journal of this class, which was established in the United States, for promoting the interests of the photographic profession, and the improvement of the art, was started, in 1850, by S. D. Humphrey, in New York city, and is now widely known, as "Humphrey's Journal of Photography, and the allied arts and sciences."

This was soon followed by the "Photographic and Fine Art Journal," edited by H. H. Snelling.

These journals labored long, assiduously, and faithfully for the advance of the art. Unfortunately for the proprietors, there seems to have been too little intelligence in the Photographic Fraternity, to give to both these publications a liberal and living support.

Mr. Snelling's energetic and generous efforts not being appreciated and sustained by those, who were so greatly benefited by the vast amount of various information, which he carefully gleaned from every available source, domestic and foreign, and laid monthly before them; his journal was finally suspended, and his subscription-list was transferred in 1860 to the "American Journal of Photography," conducted by Charles A. Seely, A. M.

From this date the collodion process began to attract general attention, and to engage the efforts of all who were interested in sun-painting; and under these circumstances, the art has progressed with marvellous celerity. By the fostering care of more intelligent professionists and amateurs, scientific institutions, and government patronage, it has been placed on a solid foundation, invested with artistic dignity, and made a vocation that promises large and constantly enlarging pecuniary returns.

Treatises on the art have been published in the United

States, by Snelling, Hill, Humphrey, Seely, Gage, Cole, Simons, Hewett, Bisbee, Waldack, Burgess and others; while probably over one thousand have appeared in Europe.

The last two of the above named have passed through several editions; Burgess having recently issued his tenth. His work is a neat, well-arranged little handbook, of much practical value to the student and the amateur of the art.

Mr. N. G. Burgess was in Paris, early in 1840,—the period when Daguerre, through his recent discovery, was "the observed of all observers,"—and naturally made some investigations of the art, as then known (and practised). His business there brought about an acquaintance with one of the artisans, who had taken part in constructing Daguerre's first sun-painting apparatus. From him and another person he took his earliest daguerreotype lessons, and sketched some of the public edifices of Paris. Owing to his imperfect appliances, his pictures (he says) were very unsatisfactory. Hearing that Professors Draper and Morse had produced portraits from life, he proposed to the artisan, above mentioned, to attempt his (Burgess') portrait. The result, however, of eight or ten minutes' exposure to the solar ray was so wretched, that the experiment was abandoned, under the conviction that portraits could never be thus taken.

Mr. Burgess saw Daguerre, and says his manner was reserved and distant. He appeared very nervous and restless—symptoms ascribed to his being affected with dyspepsia.

The following are extracts from the speech of Professor S. F. B. Morse, at the annual supper of the National Academy of Design, April 24th, 1840:—

"Gentlemen:—I have been requested to give my opinion of the probable effects to be produced, by the discovery of Daguerre, on the Arts of Design. It is known to most of you, that, for many months, I have been engaged in experiments with the daguerreotype, more particularly for the purpose of forming an intelligent judgment on this point.

"The daguerreotype is undoubtedly destined to produce a great *revolution* in art, and we, as artists, should be aware of it and rightly understand its influence. This influence, both on ourselves and the public generally, will, I think, be in the highest degree *favorable* to the character of art.

"Its influence on the artist must be great. By a simple and easily portable apparatus, he can now furnish his studio with *fac-simile* sketches of nature, landscapes, buildings, groups of figures, &c., scenes selected in accordance with his own peculiarities of taste; but not, as heretofore, subjected to his imperfect, sketchy translations into crayon or Indian ink drawings, and occupying days, and even weeks, in their execution; but painted by Nature's self with a minuteness of detail, which the pencil of light in her hands alone can trace, and with a rapidity, too, which will enable him to enrich his collection with a superabundance of *materials* and not *copies*;—*they cannot be called copies of nature, but portions of nature herself.*

"Must not such a collection modify, of necessity, the artist's productions? Think how perspective, and, as a consequence, proportion also, are illustrated by these results. How the problems of optics are, for the first time, confirmed and sealed by nature's own stamp! See, also, what lessons of light and shade are brought under the closest scrutiny of the artist!

"To the architect it offers the means of collecting the finest remains of ancient, as well as the finest productions of modern architecture, with their proportions and details of ornament, executed in a space of time, and with an exactness, which it is impossible to compress in the ordinary modes of an architect's study.

"I have but a moment to speak of the effect of the daguerreotype on the *public taste.* Can these lessons of *nature's art* (if I may be allowed the seeming paradox), read every day by thousands charmed with their beauty, fail of producing a juster estimate of the artist's studies and labors, with a better and sounder criticism of his works? Will not the artist, who has been educated in Nature's school of truth, now stand forth pre-eminent, while he, who has sought his models of style among fleeting fashions and corrupted tastes, will be left to merited neglect?

"I should feel, gentlemen, that I had been greatly deficient, if I did not add a few words attesting my admiration for the genius of the great discoverer of this photogenic process. I have for months been occupied with experiments, repeating those of Daguerre, and modifying both the apparatus and the process, by my own experience and the suggestions of scientific friends, and, as the result of all, I must say that, at every step of my progress, my admiration for his genius and perseverance has increased. I could not but constantly reflect, if, with the details fully revealed, of a process, whereby a *sure result* could be obtained, so much to discourage be encountered, what must have been *his* discouragement, who, when one experiment after another failed, had only darkness, uncertainty, and doubt for his comforters! And yet he triumphed over all, and in the lists of fame the name of Daguerre will deservedly stand by the side of Columbus and Galileo, and Papin and Fulton.

"Gentlemen, in closing, I offer you the following sentiment:—Honor to Daguerre, who has first introduced Nature to us, in the character of *Painter.*"

CHAPTER XXX.

HISTORY OF THE HELIOGRAPHIC ART IN EUROPE.

Rapidity of the progress of the art and its numerous applications—Camera obscura discovered two hundred years ago—Crystallizing of various salts by light, discovered in eighteenth century—Investigations of these subjects in that century by several savans—Wedgewood and Davy first tried to fix images by light in 1800–3—Unsuccessful—Hyposulphite soda discovered by Herschel, 1819—Niepce, Daguerre, and Talbot first fixed images in Europe—Anecdote of Daguerre's wife and Dr. Dumas—Variations of the calotype by different operants—Waxed-paper process—Glass plates for pictures suggested by Herschel—Albumen, gelatine, &c., used for coating such—Collodion now preferred to all other coatings—Variations and improvements made by several practical photographers and amateurs.

AMONG the most extraordinary phenomena of modern days may be counted the rapidity with which the sun-painting art has been developed, and the great variety of applications, both useful and ornamental, which have already been made of it. But twenty-four years have elapsed since Daguerre made known his process to the world, and submitted to public inspection pictures, which in comparison with those now produced, would be called quite inferior, and even poor: and yet within this brief interval, heliography has become one of the most valuable and generally prized of existing arts. The beautiful toy, entitled the Camera Obscura, and the observation of the effects of the sunbeam on certain chemically prepared surfaces, were the two main agencies to which the discovery of our art was due.

The camera obscura, one of these, was discovered about two centuries ago, by Giovanni Baptiste Porta, a Neapolitan physician.

It seems strange, that the ancient philosophers should not have observed and applied to some use the chemical properties of light, which are, in many ways, so obvious, even to casual inspection. If they did so, no record of their proceedings has hitherto reached us.

There is a tradition existing, that the Oriental jugglers possessed for ages a secret process, whereby they could rapidly transcribe a person's profile by the agency of light. Whatever the fact may once have been, this class of individuals are not known to possess any such knowledge now.

The alchymists of the middle ages, in their search for the philosopher's stone and the elixir vitæ, chanced upon a peculiar combination of silver with chlorine, an element with which they were unacquainted, and which they named *horn-silver*, from the resemblance borne to horn by the white precipitate obtained through fusion. As early as the 16th century they noticed, that this silver was blackened by light; but, as they failed to get gold, as they expected, from this substance, they merely recorded the blackening, without investigating the phenomenon further. The 18th century brought a more thorough examination of this curious fact, and about the same period, the effect of light in the crystallizing of various salts was first observed. In 1722, Petit published his investigations of this latter subject, while Chaptal published his in 1788, and Diezé his in 1789.

Scheele studied closely the phenomenon of the blackening of chloride of silver by light; more especially the influence of the several prismatic rays in producing this effect; and published the results of his studies in 1777. He discovered, among other things, that the violet ray wrought this change much sooner than any of the other colors.

In 1790, Sennebier found, that fifteen minutes' exposure to the violet ray imparted to chloride of silver the same blackness which it required twenty minutes' action of the red ray to produce.

In 1801, Ritter discovered, that the chemical action of light extends *beyond* the colored rays of the spectrum, there manifesting itself through invisible rays.

In a recent publication of Lord Brougham, he states, that in 1796 he had published in the "Philosophical Transactions" a paper on light and color, containing remarks on the effects of exposing a plate of ivory, moistened with nitrate of silver, to the sun's rays passing through a narrow aperture into a dark room. The secretary of the society, for reasons of his own, *omitted* these remarks, and thus, it *may* be, *delayed* the discovery of heliography for nearly half a century.

Scheele's researches, mentioned above, seem to have had a powerful influence upon the scientific world, for he was followed, in the same or similar tracks of inquiry, by numbers of the leading savans in all parts of Europe. Among these may be mentioned Berard, Seebeck, Berthollet, Wunsch, Sir William Herschel, Sir Henry Englefield, Dr. Wollaston, Count Rumford, Morichini, Configliachi, Berzelius, and that admirable specimen of womanhood, Mrs. Somerville. Sir Humphrey Davy also made some curious discoveries, which, with those made by the others above named, constituted a mass of materials, which brought the world to the verge of the great discovery we are recording.

But the following experiment, detailed in sundry old books, is so definite in its forward-pointings, as to cause wonder that more was not made of it: "Dissolve chalk in aqua fortis to the consistence of milk, and add thereto a strong solution of silver. Keep this liquid in a well-stopped glass decanter; then cutting out from a paper the letters you would have appear, paste it on the decanter, and lay the latter in the sun's rays, so that the rays may pass through the spaces cut out of the paper and fall on the surface of the liquid. Then will that part of the glass through which the rays pass, be turned black, while that beneath the paper remains white. Special care, however, must be taken that the bottle be not moved during the operation."

It is not very unlikely that the experiments next mentioned were suggested by this.

The earliest known attempts at *fixing* images by the chemical influence of light, were those of Davy, and of Wedgwood, the great improver of English porcelain manufacture. In the "Journal of the Royal Institution," of 1803, appeared a paper by the latter, with appended comments by the former, entitled "An account of a method of copying paintings upon glass, and of making profiles by the agency of light upon nitrate of silver."

White paper, or white leather, saturated with a solution of *nitrate* of silver (instead of the chloride) was selected as the impressible surface. They made numerous experiments, with greater or less degrees of success in getting the images of objects. Neither, however, was able to produce a surface sufficiently sensitive to receive proper impressions from the subdued light of the camera. Davy used to better purpose the solar microscope for obtaining images of small objects. He states, moreover, that he found the chloride *more* sensitive than the nitrate of silver.

Having no agents to *fix* the images and to prevent the coloring of the white parts by exposure to light, these gentlemen relinquished their experiments. Iodine was not discovered till 1811, and hyposulphite of soda was discovered by Sir John Herschel only in 1819; and without these indispensables to the art, heliography could not advance further than Wedgwood and Davy had carried it.

In 1814 Joseph Nicéphore Niepce, a retired business man, residing at Chalons, on the Saone, directed his attention to the chemical effects of light, with the object of "fixing" the images of the camera. Having found that the sunbeam would alter the solubility of various resinous substances, he spread a thin layer of asphaltum on a glass or metal plate, and placed this in the camera. Five or six hours after he found on the plate a latent image, which became visible by the application of a solvent to the surface of the plate.

Thirteen years later (in 1827) Niepce experimented with the art at Kent, in England. Some of the pictures there made are still left. They somewhat resemble the daguerreotypes, though far inferior to them.

Louis Jacques Maude Daguerre, resided about nine miles from Paris, at the town of Brie upon the Marne; was a painter by profession; a member of the French Academy of Fine Arts and other similar institutions; stood high as a scientific man; and was, moreover, much esteemed for his goodness and geniality of character. In 1824 he began experimenting, to fix the images of the camera by various chemical agencies, employing, like Wedgwood, both the chloride and nitrate of silver spread upon paper. In 1826 he became acquainted with Niepce, and from that time forward the two pursued their researches and experiments jointly. In 1829 a copartnery contract was executed between them for mutually investigating the subject. Niepce had, in 1826, already solved the problem that had baffled Wedgwood and Davy, and made his copies of objects insensible to the rays of the sun. He called his discovery "Heliography," or Sun-sketching, a more accurate title than "Photography," or Light-sketching, since the pictures are *not* produced by the light-rays, but by the actinic rays of the solar orb.

The reader, I think, will be interested in the following anecdote in relation to Daguerre, related by the distinguished French chemist, Dumas. A lady, says he, came up to him at the close of a lecture in 1825, and said: "Monsieur Dumas, as a scientific man, I have a question, of vital importance to myself, to ask you. I am the wife of Daguerre, the painter. For some time he has let the idea seize him, that he can *fix* the image of the camera. Do *you* think it possible? He is always at the thought; he can't sleep at night for it. I am afraid he is out of his mind. Do *you*, as a man of science, think it can ever be done, or is he mad?" "In the present state of knowledge," said Dumas, "it cannot be done; but I cannot say it will always remain impossible, nor set the man down as mad who seeks to do it."

If *such* was Daguerre's mood fourteen years before he had brought his process to a fitness for publication, we may form some conception of what his discovery must have cost him. At any rate, he exhibited the true temper of one of the few whom genius predestines to immortality.

In 1829 Daguerre and Niepce, for the first time, employed for blackening the heliographic plate, iodine, which was discovered in 1811, by M. Courtois, of Paris, in the kelp or ashes of sea-weeds.

Niepce died in 1833, and his son Isidore succeeded him, as copartner of Daguerre in heliographic researches and experiments.

In January 1839, Daguerre announced his great invention, which has since, by common consent, borne his name. In the following July, the Chamber of Deputies voted to Daguerre an annual pension of 6000 francs (subsequently increased to 10,000), and one of 4000 francs to Isidore Niepce, on condition that they should publish to the world a full description of the processes by which their pictures were produced, and also make known all the improvements which might, from time to time, be made therein. Reversions of one-half these several sums were, by the same law, secured to the widows of Daguerre and Niepce.

At the time the copartnership was formed between Daguerre and the elder Niepce, it appears, that both made their experiments chiefly on plates of copper or silver, coated with different kinds of varnishes and essential oils, without the use either of iodine or mercury. Finally, however, after a long course of observations and experiments, Daguerre exposed an iodized plate in the camera, and then over boiling mercury in an iron crucible. At first there was no favorable result; but, on repeating the experiment, he found, after the exposure of the plate to the mercury, a dim shadow on the outer edge of it, and the thought occurred, that *here* the heat had been less intense. Whereupon he reduced the temperature, and obtained a picture. Daguerre remarks, that the image is finer on copper plated with silver than on silver. If such be the fact, does it not intimate that electricity plays a considerable part in the operation? (See chapters on Galvanizing and Actinism.)

Daguerre employed only iodine in coating the plate. Since that date, as we shall see further along, great improvements have been made by using *accelerating* substances, and thus rendering the plate far more sensitive to the action of light. Among these accelerators are bromine, chloride of iodine, and finally, a compound of the three, of which I shall speak with some detail hereafter.

On January 31st, 1839, Henry Fox Talbot communicated to the Royal Society his photographical discoveries, and, on the 21st of February following, he published a description of his methods of preparing the paper used in his processes. He did this by dipping the paper into a solution of common salt, and then applying to the surface a solution of chloride or nitrate of silver—mostly the latter. After getting the image in the camera, he fixed it by again immersing the paper in a *strong* solution of common salt. He was able to make paper so sensitive, as to obtain the picture of an object, under full sunshine, in half a second. The paper here referred to, was that used by him for taking copies of objects by means of the solar telescope.

Whether Talbot's attention was first turned to heliographic researches by Niepce's communication to the Royal Society in 1827, or whether he had commenced his investigations before this, I know not. It is understood, however, that he conducted his experiments independently, and without even being acquainted with the Frenchman.

On March 14th, 1839, Sir John Herschel made a communication to the Royal Society, recommending the use of hyposulphite of soda as a fixing agent. On February 20th, 1840, he sent to the Society a paper on the "chemical effects of light in the solar spectrum," wherein he recommends using this solution hot in the case of iodide of silver, as this salt is less readily dissolved by the cold solution of the hyposulphite, than is chloride of silver.

In 1840, Rev. J. B. R · de used, with good effect, the hyposulphite solution to fix, and the infusion of galls to accelerate, the formation of the picture. At the same time the former is known to have been habitually employed by Daguerre, Robert Hunt, and others, in addition to Herschel.

In the last paper named, Herschel also recommended the employment of iodide of potassium, to convert the nitrate of silver on the paper into iodide of silver, and gave, moreover, the peculiar properties of the iodized paper.

In July 1841, Robert Hunt read, before the British Association at Plymouth, a paper "On the influence of the yellow ferrocyanide of potassium upon iodide of silver, and on the high sensitiveness of the same, as a photographic preparation," giving also instructions how to prepare the iodized paper.

Iodized paper was used likewise by Ryan, Lassaigne, and others; and it seems pretty certain that this paper, as prepared according to the instructions given by Herschel, Hunt, and others, was an article of commerce, before the patent for the Calotype of Talbot had been obtained.

I have already stated, that in 1839, Talbot published to the world his photographic discoveries, together with his methods of producing his pictures. From this period he continued his studies and experiments until 1842, when he published and procured a patent for a process, which was a considerable improvement upon his original one, and was called by him the "Calotype," from the two Greek words, καλος τυπος, "beautiful sketch." In this country, however, I believe his pictures are oftenest entitled Talbotypes, on the same principle that Daguerre's are called Daguerreotypes. Talbot subsequently obtained a second patent for his calotype process, in which he had introduced still further (supposed) improvements. To what extent the calotype is now in vogue across the water,

I know not. I believe, however, that albumen, collodion, and some other pictures have, to a great degree, taken its place.

It will fall next in the order of this historic summary to give some account of several variations of heliography on paper, which closely followed, and may be supposed to have been suggested by Talbot's discovery. I have space merely to name these, with their discoverers, leaving to the reader to seek their description elsewhere.

1. The Chrysotype. This process was communicated to the Royal Society, June 1842, by Sir John Herschel.

2. The Cyanotype was also a discovery of Herschel. He describes several varieties of this process, which it were hardly worth the while to introduce here.

3. The Chromotype was, substantially, a discovery of the French savans, Pontin and Becquerel. Under this specific name, however, it appears to have been first announced to the British Association, in 1843, by Robert Hunt.

4. The Catalissotype was communicated in 1854 to the British Association by Dr. Thos. Woods, of Dublin.

5. The Amphitype is another of Herschel's discoveries. Its name "double sketch," is derived from the fact that two pictures are produced by the same action of light, with different subsequent manipulations.

6. The Anthotype seems to have been a joint production of Herschel, Chevreuil, and Robert Hunt. Its nature is defined by its etymology "flower sketch," the juices of various flowers, bruised and treated with small portions of alcohol, being used for washing the paper, instead of mineral solutions. See Prof. Draper "On the Growth of Plants," 1860.

7. The Gaudinotype takes its name from its French discoverer, Gaudin.

8. The Energiotype was a discovery of Robert Hunt,

and made public through the Athenæum. I suppose it was thus named from the sensitiveness of its impressible surface, and the consequent *energy* with which the sunbeam acts upon it.

9. Thermography means, etymologically, heat-sketching. The process, a very curious one, was discovered by Moser, of Koningsberg, in Prussian Poland.

The above variations of the talbotype are not known to be much used, or ever to have been, by professional heliographers. They have, however, subserved a good purpose by enlarging our knowledge of the materials, the agencies, and the methods of operation pertaining to the general art. (See Prof. Draper's Tithinotype).

10. The waxed-paper process has been and still is much more in vogue than either of the above. Its invention is generally ascribed to Le Gray; though some hold, that its first announcement to the public was due to Fabre. A peculiarity of this process is, that the first step is to saturate the paper with pure white wax. A great advantage of paper thus prepared is, that it may be used some time after excitement, and that even the hottest weather does not impair its capacity for use. For this reason it is very serviceable to excursionists and travellers. This process has been very successfully practised by several eminent photographers, among whom Mr. Fenton has been one of the most successful.

11. Albumen process. Sir John Herschel is said to have first suggested glass plates for heliographic uses. M. Niepce de St. Victor, nephew of Niepce, the associate of Daguerre, published, in 1848, a mode, devised by himself, for applying albumen to such plates. Blanquart Everard followed; and albumen, gelatine, serum, and other substances were successively recommended for application to glass. Albumen, however, employed according

to Le Gray's directions, is found to answer better than any other of these. The methods of Mayall and Negretti are also good.

12. Collodion process. Collodion, at present, is put by general consent at the head of all heliographic agents. It is prepared from gun-cotton. Gun-cotton, according to an English authority, was discovered by Schönbein, a German professor in the Swiss University of Berne, in 1841. He made it by dissolving cotton in a mixture of nitric and sulphuric acids. The German's claim has been somewhat contested, but the matter is unimportant. Collodion—a name taken from the Greek κὸλλαι, "to adhere"—is made by dissolving gun-cotton in ether mixed with alcohol. The best authorities make Dr. Josiah Curtis, of Boston, Mass., the discoverer of it, early in 1846. The first use of it was its application to wounds, in place of the ordinary bandages. An attempt was made, in Philadelphia, 1848, to use collodion for heliographic purposes, by Frederick Langenheim, at the suggestion of Dr. Chas. S. Rand, of the same city. The attempt failed; and Frederic Scott Archer, of England, is generally accredited as having first used it successfully. He published his process in 1851. Collodion soon came into general use, and numerous variations, greater or less, from his method became common, to which we shall briefly refer.

The applications of collodion may be ranged under two principal heads.

1st. The Ambrotype, a positive picture made upon a collodion-covered plate of glass, upon which is laid a second plate, hermetically fixed thereon by some adhesive substance, so that neither air nor water can reach the impression. Hence the title, derived from the Greek *Ambrotos*, immortal, imperishable.

2. A negative picture is impressed upon a plate, and

from this are printed indefinite numbers of positives upon prepared paper. The latter species of picture is at present in most general vogue.

In the waxed-paper process, we saw, that by means of the wax, papers, *already excited,* might be kept for some time before being placed in the camera, and yet answer an equally good purpose as if used immediately after excitation. This property in prepared heliographic surfaces would obviously be a great convenience for travellers and excursionists, who might desire to take views under circumstances that made it difficult or impossible to sensitise these surfaces at the moment.

As it were equally desirable to impart the same property to collodion surfaces, several attempts have been made to this end. Three of these, which have been successful, I will briefly mention here:—

1st. Messrs. Spiller & Crookes effected this purpose by nitrate of magnesia—a collodion plate, sensitised as usual, being dipped in a bath, of which that substance forms one of the ingredients.

2d. Shadbolt's Honey process, in which a syrup, made with pure honey and distilled water in equal parts, takes the place of the nitrate of magnesia in the above process.

3d. H. Pollock's Glycerined Collodion process, wherein glycerine, an ingredient of several neutral fats and oils, subserves the purpose of nitrate of magnesia and of honey in the two processes above named.

4th. Dr. Taupenot's Collodio-Albumen process, which consists in first coating a plate with collodion and exciting it, and then putting upon this a coating of albumen and exciting it, after which the plate is ready for the camera. This twofold coating serves the two purposes of keeping the plates sensitive for a considerable time and of increasing the rapidity of their action. This is thought by some to transcend all other processes in the quality of its results.

5th. Gutta Percha, as a sensitised medium; as a substitute for glass, &c. It is not settled whether the discovery of the heliographic capabilities of this substance is due to Mr. Archer or Rev. J. B. Reade.

It is used in three ways:—1st. You coat a glass plate with gutta percha; upon this you put a collodion coating and produce a picture in the ordinary way; and the gutta percha basis being then detached from the glass, you have a substitute for the latter, which is as tough as leather, while flexible and portable. 2d. You may iodize a sheet of gutta percha, and take pictures upon it without using collodion at all. 3d. You can employ a mixture of gutta percha and collodion in the same way. 4th. You prepare a glass plate with collodion, and conduct the process in the usual mode. The picture being completed, you pour over it the gutta percha solution. The latter being cold, the united films are separated from the glass in a single sheet.

The ivorytype is an invention of Mr. Mayall, of Regent Street, London. These pictures are taken upon an artificial ivory, a compound of barytes and vegetable albumen. A plate, made of this substance, is treated substantially as you treat the paper in producing the talbotype, and the result, especially if touched up with a skilful pencil, is a picture exhibiting all the delicate beauties of the finest miniature painting upon ivory.

The dry collodion process is commonly regarded as the invention of Fothergill, but has been varied more or less by Muller, Neville, Norris, Mayall, Powell, Col. Pike, and many others, so that we shall not attempt to decide whose process is the best. Probably some may prefer one, and some another. What is common to most, is to coat the plate first thinly with albumen, which being dried slowly, a coating of collodion is then put on, and the plate is treated in the same manner as in the wet process. Muller varies the process of the others, by first collodionizing and sensitising the plate, and then pouriug on a mixture of two liquids—the first composed of white of egg, creosote, and distilled water, and the second of honey, animal charcoal, and water. The advantage of the ury collodion process is, that the plates may be used long after being first prepared.

In concluding this chapter on the history of the heliographic art, it is thought that it may prove of some interest to append the following table, compiled with much care for the British Association, by Robert Hunt, and printed by that body in their Reports for 1850. It is believed that the dates of discovery are accurately given, the date of publication being, of course, in all cases, taken where there was the slightest doubt.

Silver.		
Nitrate of	Ritter	1801
—— (photographically employed)	Wedgwood and Davy	1802
—— with organic matter	J. F. Herschel	1839
—— with salts of lead	J. F. Herschel	1839
Chloride of	C. W. Scheele	1777
—— (photographically employed)	{ Wedgwood	1802
	{ Talbot	1839
—— darkened, and hydriodic salts	Fyfe, Lassaigne	1839
Iodide of (photographically used)	{ Herschel	1840
	{ Ryan	1840
—— with ferrocyanate of potash	Hunt	1841
—— with gallic acid (Calotype)	Talbot	1841
—— with protosulphate of iron (Ferrotype)	Hunt	1844
—— with iodide of iron (Catalysotype)	Woods	1844
Bromide of	Bayard	1840
Fluoride of	Channing	1842
Fluorotype	Hunt	1844
Oxide of	Davy	1803

Silver.		
Oxide of with ammonia	Uncertain	
Phosphate of	Fyfe	1839
Tartrate—Urate—Oxalate—Borate, &c.	Herschel	1840
Benzoates of	Hunt	1844
Formiates of	Do.	1844
Fulminates of	Do.	1842
Silver Plate.		
With vapor of iodine (Daguerreotype)	Daguerre	1839
With vapor of bromine	Goddard	1840
With chlorine and iodine	Claudet	1840
With vapor of sulphur	Niepce	1820
With vapor of phosphorus	Niepce	1820
Gold.		
Chloride of	Rumford Herschel	1798 1840
Ethereal solution of	Rumford	1798
Ethereal solution of, with percyanide of potassium	Hunt	1844
Ethereal solution of, with protocyanide of potassium	Do.	1844
Chromate of	Do.	1844
Plate of gold and iodine vapor	Goddard	1842
Platinum.		
Chloride of	Herschel	1840
Chloride of, in ether	Herschel	1840
Chloride of, with lime	Herschel	1832
Iodide of	Herschel	1840
Bromide of	Hunt	1844
Percyanate of	Do.	1844
Mercury.		
Protoxide of	Uncertain.	
Peroxide of	Guibourt.	
Carbonate of	Hunt	1844
Chromate of	Do.	1843
Deutiodide of	Do.	1843
Nitrate of	Herschel	1840
Protonitrate of	Herschel	1840
Chloride of	Boullay	1803
Bichloride of	Vogel	1806

Iron.		
Protosulphate of.		
Persulphate of.		
Ammonio-citrate of.		
Tartrate of.		
Attention was first called to the very peculiar changes produced in the iron salts, by	Sir John Herschel	1845
Cyanic compounds of (Prussian blue)	Scheele	1786
	Desmortiers	1801
Ferrocyanates of	Fischer	1795
Iodide of	Hunt	1844
Oxalate of	Do.	1844
Chromate of	Do.	1844
Several of the above combined with mercury	Herschel	1843
Copper.		
Chromate of (Chromatype)	Hunt	1843
—— dissolved in ammonia	Do.	1844
Sulphate of	Do.	1844
Carbonate of	Do.	1844
Iodide of	Do.	1844
Copper-plate iodized	Talbot	1841
Manganese.		
Permanganate of potash	Frommherz	1824
Deutoxide and cyanate of potassium	Hunt	1844
Muriate of	Do.	1844
Lead.		
Oxide of (the puce-colored)	Davy	1802
Red lead and cyanide of potassium	Hunt	1844
Acetate of lead	Do.	1844
Nickel.		
Nitrate of	Do.	1844
—— with ferroprussiates		
Iodide of		
Tin.		
Purple of cassius	Uncertain.	
Cobalt	Hunt	1844
Arsenic sulphuret of	Sage	1803

Substance	Observer	Year
Arsenical salts of ANTIMONY, BISMUTH, CADMIUM, RHODIUM	Hunt	1844
CHROMIUM.		
Bichromate of potash	Mungo Ponton	1838
—— with iodide of starch	E. Becquerel	1840
Metallic chromates (Chromatype)	Hunt	1843
CHLORINE AND HYDROGEN	Gay-Lussac & Thénard	1809
Chlorine (tithonized)	Draper	1842
—— and ether	Cahours	1810
GLASS, manganese, reddened	Faraday	1823
CYANOGEN, solution of	Pelouse and Richardson	1838
METHYLE.	Cahours	1846
Crystallization of salts influenced by light	Petit	1722
	Chaptal	1788
	Dizé	1789
Phosphorus	Schulze	1727
	Ritter	1801
—— in nitrogen	Beckman	1800
Phosphorus and ammonia	Vogel	1806
Nitric acid decomposed by light	Scheele	1786
Fat matter	Vogel	1806
Development of pores in plants	Labillardière	1801
Vitality of germs	Michellotti	1803
RESINOUS BODIES (*Heliography*)	Niepce	1814
Asphaltum	Niepce	1814
Resin of oil of lavender	Niepce and Daguerre	1830
Guaiacum	Wollaston	1803
Bitumen all decomposed	Daguerre	1839
All residua of essential oils	Daguerre	1839
Flowers, colors of, expressed, and spread upon paper	Herschel	1842
Yellow wax bleached	Senebier	1791
Phosphorescent influences of solar rays	Licetas	1646
	Kircher	1646
	Canton	1768
	Biot	1840
	E. Becquerel	1839
Vegetation in stagnant water	Morren	1841
Influence of light on electrical phenomena	E. Becquerel	1839

CHAPTER XXXI.

THE HELIOGRAPHIC ART—ITS PRESENT STATE AND APPLIANCES, AND ITS FUTURE POSSIBILITIES.

The three great modern discoveries: 1st. Steam—2d. Magnetic Telegraph—3d. Heliography—All tend to produce an improved human condition—Heliography, its direct effects: 1st. A substitute for travel—2d. Strengthens and perpetuates ties of kindred and friendship—3d. Makes familiar to us the great and good of all ages and countries—4th. Serves as an efficient means of general culture—5th. Is an important help to the knowledge and practice of chemistry, geology, medical and surgical science, architecture, engineering, military operations, astronomy, &c.—Journals, photographic and other, now advocate the claims of photography to be a fine art—Sir David Brewster and Claudet favor this view—Why should not the painter and photographer work together; one with the camera, and the other with the pencil?—Quotations from various eminent modern writers, specifying the benefits flowing from art in general, and the photographic art in particular.

THE tradition of a millennium, to occur at some stage of the Christian History, has, for nearly nineteen centuries, been floating through Christendom. What, at the outset, were the material form and literal sense of that tradition, is too generally known to need explanation here.

I presume, most of my readers are also aware that, during the last century, a *spiritual* construction has been put upon the term millennium, whereby it is held to signify a rapid and vast improvement in the universal condition of our race—its exaltation to a plane of intelligence, virtue, and happiness, unparalleled before. And, what is somewhat singular, these recent constructionists have agreed in placing the dawn of this new era at or near the present time. Thus, Swedenborg represents it as the "New Jerusalem descending from heaven to earth;" the event to become *distinctly manifest* (if I rightly remember) between the years 1850 and 1880; Fourier, as a series of harmonic phalanxes covering the entire globe, the process commencing at about the same date; and Father Miller, under an aspect too absurd for any but a disturbed brain to accredit.

But whether this tradition be groundless and worthless or the reverse, it is undeniable that our age, for the celerity and extent of the multiform improvements going on in man's condition, stands alone in the authentic history or even the traditions of the globe. These improvements are manifestly due to various scientific and practical discoveries, of which the most important are:

1st. Steam in its several applications to land and water locomotion, and to numerous purposes beside.

2d. The magnetic telegraph.

3d. Heliography in its multitudinous forms.

These three discoveries, in addition to all their other beneficent results, alike serve to bring the individuals of our race, however widely dissevered by material distances, into more or less close proximity and communion with each other. And if, as experience has often proved, the poet says truly, that

> "Mountains interposed make enemies of nations;"

experience also teaches, that the first and most essential step towards the mutual regard and unity both of individuals and communities is, that they should know each other alike in their dispositions and sentiments, and in their exterior modes of life. For the promotion of this end, the discoveries in question have a value beyond calculation.

My present purpose, however, is to indicate briefly what heliography has done, is doing, and promises to do for the world's future; and,

1st. Travelling, whether in foreign lands or our own, is regarded as one of the most efficient means of self-culture within our knowledge. Comparatively few, however, are able to leave home and business and bear the heavy expenses thus required.

But photography enables us to enjoy the pleasure and the advantages of travel without even crossing our own thresholds. Sun-pictures in abundance may be had at so cheap a rate, as to bring them within reach of all save the literally penniless. And in these we behold vivid and life-like presentments of all the objects which would most strongly attract the actual traveller's notice in distant countries or our own. All forms and diversities of natural sublimity and beauty—the architecture, the paintings, and the sculptures, wherewith Genius, during the lapse of centuries, has embellished the earliest civilized of modern lands, while eternizing its own memory; the stupendous or magnificent ruins, which still survive to show what the most advanced of ancient peoples could achieve; the localities wherein events have occurred, either of war or of peace, which have changed the destinies of nations; and the inhabitants of various regions of the globe, with their personal aspects, their usages, secular and religious, and their modes of life, whether private or public, domestic or social,—all these, and a myriad objects besides, may be inspected in their minutest particulars by the day-laborer, surrounded by his family at his own fireside. And he thus may often get a completer and truer impression of them, than if standing on the very sites they occupy.

2d. Photography serves to draw closer, to strengthen and to perpetuate the ties of kindred, of friendship, and of general respect and regard. The exigencies of life, in most cases, necessitate the dispersion of relatives, born and reared under the same roof, towards various points of the compass, and often to remote distances, and by this means the primal household affection almost inevitably becomes impaired, and is frequently transformed into comparative indifference, if not absolute coldness. How great are the loss and injury thus inflicted on those concerned, it were impossible to measure. For in the love of kindred is found one of the most potent preservatives of a life of purity, virtue, and honor, as also one of the most active stimulants to a laudable and manly social ambition. A nation is virtuous and united according as the households composing it are well ordered and bound together by mutual regard.

And the photographs of parents, brothers, and sisters, now within the universal reach, constitute the most effectual means of keeping freshly alive the memories of the dear absentees, long associated with us round the same fireside, and of those young days, when the world before us, under the golden rays of imagination and hope, seemed to us one vast realm of brightness and beauty and gladness. What, better than such memories, can preserve the freshness of feeling and tenderness of conscience proper to our opening existence?

3d. Photography brings within the general and daily inspection, the portraits of the patriots and heroes, the saints and sages, and the eminent in every sphere of life, and of all ages and countries. And the sight of such representations awakens the desire of learning the history of their originals, with their magnificent achievements and noble endurances. If, according to the trite adage, "evil communications corrupt good manners," good communications must work reverse effects. To breathe habitually an atmosphere of high principles and thoughts and sentiments, is to be moulded into the same image and practical character, even as the respiring of a pure and bracing air is to secure physical health and soundness and vigor. But,

4th. Photography serves as a most efficient means of general culture. In the numerous pictures which the art has sown broadcast through all civilized communities, those of all ages and conditions daily behold objects, that appeal to and awaken to activity the inborn sense of beauty and grace; that provoke to comparison between the good and the bad, and between the bad and the worse; and that gradually thus form, in even the lowliest, somewhat of an artistic judgment. But such judgment, first reared upon, and by means of, *artificial* representations, naturally finds a sphere for its exercise in the limitless domain of beauty opened to it in the material universe; in the varieties of imitative beauty created by man, and in man himself. How elevating and great is the influence of such a mental action on the character, both intellectual and moral, we have indicated elsewhere.

But the judgment, educated to the sense of the beautiful, cannot restrict itself to this single department of nature and life. It measurably extends to all other spheres as well, and thus a process of general culture is originated and carried forward, by means so simple as sun-stricken impressions on plate, or paper, or glass, numbers of which are daily gazed on by the newsboy, and even the child-beggar, at photographic doors in almost every street.

A multiplicity of other and miscellaneous uses is subserved by the photograph, a few of which I will now briefly mention. The Rev. Mr. Statham, to whom I am indebted for several facts in this chapter, remarks, that photography may, among other things, be called the "handmaid of the sciences." For example, it has

1st. Rendered important aid to chemistry. The mere fact of its being based on this science has, of necessity, multiplied students of the same to the number of the thousands interested in photography, either as professionists or amateurs. Moreover, by causing a large increase in the number of existing chemicals to be employed in the art, it has brought to light not a few entirely new combinations of matter—enough indeed to constitute a laboratory of its own. It also serves to train in the young chemist, several qualities of great utility in chemical experimentation, *e. g.* patience, manipulative cleanliness, self-reliance, and an adventurous spirit of research—all of which are essential to success in photographic operations, and which he acquires in their performance. After all, however, the uses of photography to chemistry are, comparatively, but beginning to be known.

2d. Geologic inquiry is essentially furthered by our art. A distinguished English writer aply entitles the professors of this grand science the "*Anatomists of Nature.*" The bulk of its students are forbidden, by the nature of the case, to read, in the *original*, that "testimony of the rocks," wherewith nature has registered earth's long past history, but must needs rely on such *copies* of the same, as its few privileged readers can supply. And when we consider how slow and toilsome is the task of reproducing, by hand, geologic specimens and views, and how unavoidably inexact and inadequate such representations must be, how indescribably great must appear our obligations to that art which, within a few seconds, or it may be instantaneously, grants us a *fac simile* of the scenes and objects desired, so absolutely perfect, that even under the microscopic lens, the original has scarce an iota of advantage over the transcript! But,

3d. Medical and surgical science is greatly advantaged by sun-painting. Exact copies of the aspects of morbid anatomy in general; of disease in every varying shape, and of the appearances of each several malady, at its different stages, must be of incalculable service alike to practising physicians and to medical students. Both derive therefrom the same benefit (or nearly such), as they would from inspecting the patient *in person;* and one immeasurably greater than he could from reading verbal descriptions, even the minutest, of what, after all, it is impossible fully to describe. For the photographic presentment, unlike the verbal, may be microscopically examined. To the leading European hospitals are already attached skilled draughtsmen and modellers in wax, to copy from the living patient, or the dissected corpse, any appearance throwing light on the origin or progress of the malady, which may aid in after practice. Of how much greater value would be an accomplished sun-painter in this office! Medical consultations, too, can easily and profitably be held with distant physicians, through photographic representations sent them, and this without their stirring from home or the vicinity of their own patients.

4th. The progress of architectural improvement is secured by our art. The professionist and student, of scantiest means, may possess, for models and for helpers in artistic discipline, exactest transcripts of the noblest edifices and other architectural constructions in present occupancy, in every known region on earth, and of the reliques of the finest ancient achievements in this art, which have immortalized the localities that hold the dust of long-buried nations, and which have to a considerable extent survived the assaults of over four thousand years.

For example, the pyramids, the catacombs, and the labyrinths of Egypt; the rock-temples of India, Nubia, and Petra; the weird and wondrous Babylonian remains; the matchless ruins which Greek genius left, as its memorials in both the Grecian and Italian peninsulas,—all these are at their service in pictures so exact, as virtually to answer every purpose of their originals, when viewed on the sites they occupy.

The same remarks apply to photographic transcripts of natural scenery, in the shapes of mountain and glen and expanded plain, and of river and lake and ocean, which travellers, seeking the gratification of curiosity in all quarters of the globe, have agreed to place at the highest point of material grandeur and sublimity, or loveliness; and of the localities in different lands, which have been glorified in the world's memory, by the momentous and critical events, whether of war or peace, that occurred therein, alike in the early twilight of human tradition, or within the scope of authentic history.

It is an opinion of the writer to whom we are so greatly obliged in this chapter, that a contemplation of the fine sketches, recently brought by our art within the universal inspection, has wrought the considerable improvement manifest in our contemporary architecture—an improvement visible alike in our public and private constructions.

One very important advantage conferred by the sun-picture, is that an eminent architect can supervise, at the same time, from a half dozen to one hundred works, of whatever class, during their progress from commencement to completion, without the necessity of being at the localities they occupy. This is effected simply by help of skilfully executed sketches of them, in whole or in part, at successive stages of their advancement.

Thus Colonel Bowman, the accomplished head of West Point Military Academy, is reported to have at one time superintended and directed, as he had primarily laid out, the plans of one hundred of the United States public works by the aid of these pictures, which subserved the same end as the inspection of their originals would have done.

5th. It has become a custom of manufacturers to advertise machinery, mortuary monuments, and a multitude of articles beside, by forwarding to all sections of the country and (I believe) to foreign lands, sun-stamped copies of the same, alike in their wholes and in their several parts. While the manufacturers and the persons, at what distance soever living, who are likely to need their wares, are thus essentially convenienced, the public are instructed where to apply for *any* articles which such manufacturers, from the nature of their vocations, are probably able to furnish. It is obvious at a moment's thought, that, by this means, all parties concerned may save a vast amount of time, trouble, and expense.

6th. Civil engineering, mining works, and all military operations may profit largely from photography. The reader may see *why* and *how*, without our specifying particulars. In the construction of the Grand Trunk Railway of Canada, it is said the chief engineers of Great Britain were able to supervise the work, virtually *in person*, without leaving their homes.

In war the camera is variously useful in taking views of fortifications, or other places, to be attacked, and in exhibiting the effects of cannon-fire upon breaches; in giving correct representations of the difficulties of any route to be traversed by troops; or in getting from a balloon a view of the enemy's forces, and of the mode in which they are stationed, whereby their probable movements can be conjectured.

It was recently stated, in a Richmond rebel journal, that General Gilmore, the present commander-in-chief of the United States troops before Charleston, experimented in cannon-firing at a target for three years or more, photographing each time the spot struck by the ball; and that it was through this practice he became, what that journal pronounces, the first military engineer now living. Whether this account be true or false, I know not, as, according to the adage, "a liar cannot be credited when he speaks the truth." In the nature of the case, however, it *might* be true, and it serves to verify the proposition we are now discussing. The general's recent feat of throwing a shell, charged with Greek fire, *five miles* into the pestilent city where the rebellion was conceived and came into life, and where the first decisive insurrectionary crime was perpetrated, is a further corroboration of what we have suggested, and is an ample fulfilment of what the hero had promised to perform.

Would it not, then, be a most useful arrangement to have a skilful photographic teacher attached to every military school, as also to every institution where engineering, surveying, architecture, and all other applications of the sciences to the arts are studied? For ourselves we have no doubt of this. Nor of this alone. For we would have the same official introduced into every college and higher academy throughout the land.

7th. Public order seems likely to be, in some measure, secured by the custom lately adopted, of taking photographic likenesses of all criminals sentenced, after trial, to some term of incarceration. Such persons, on the expiration of their allotted periods, will find it not easy to renew their criminal careers, while their faces and general aspects are familiar to so many, especially to the keen-sighted detective police. There would seem to be at least a *possibility,* if not a *likelihood,* that old infractors of law may be absolutely *driven* out of the "broad road leading to destruction," into the "strait and narrow way," wherein alone is found *safety,* as well as *freedom,* by the almost inevitable certainty that, in the former, he must speedily be re-arrested and doomed to a more protracted imprisonment.

10th. It is familiarly known that the sun and the moon have already been transcribed, by means of the camera, with literal exactitude. In the further large improvements certain to be made in our present photographic materials and processes, who shall measure the additions which may thus be furnished to our existing knowledge of the magnificent science of astronomy, by the camera in the handling of a skilled and enthusiastic photographic genius?

And here the reader will not merely excuse but thank me for introducing the following admirable extract from an unpublished lecture of Professor John S. Hart, on "The Progress of the Age":—

"What would an ancient Greek have thought to see a puny mortal, more daring than Prometheus, making even the thunderbolts of Jupiter his toy? And what would even Franklin have thought to see the subtlest, fleetest, and most powerful of nature's agents, not only stripped of its terrors, but made the submissive thrall, the obedient slave of man; doing his behests, running his errands, now gilding a child's toy, and now carrying a message to Congress, and exhausting in its flight even the language of metaphor, 'as swift as lightning,' it being no longer a comparison, now that lightning itself has become the agent of communication. But if Jupiter would have been astonished at the wonders of the telegraph, what would the sun-god have said to the not inferior wonders of the heliographic art? Apollo, indeed, knew himself of old to be the patron of painting; but did he ever dream that he would himself become the limner of half the human race? That those imponderable rays of his should, at man's pleasure, be gathered into a brush of light, of inimitable truth and delicacy, wherewith to trace, with microscopic exactness, the lineaments of the human face?"

They who have glanced even cursorily over this volume,—which, by the by, was commenced and carried a considerable way onward ten years ago,—may perhaps remember that, from the very outset to the close, we have advocated and in all modes striven to establish the claim of photography to a rank among the so-named Fine Arts. For a long time we stood on this ground alone, or nearly so.

By slow degrees, however, the heliographic and some other journals, on both sides the water, began to exhibit evidence that this opinion was gaining currency, till at present it would seem to be, substantially, the prevailing faith. For men, holding the most eminent positions in science and literature, have, in publications of the highest repute, expressed this view in the strongest and most unqualified phraseology they could command.

Thus, in the North British Review, of February, 1862, Sir David Brewster, the scientific luminary of Scotland, has a long essay on the heliographic art, wherein, among other kindred passages, may be seen the following:—

"Nearly fifteen years have elapsed since we directed the attention of our readers to the new art of photography, its brief history, wondrous progress, &c. Since that time, its advance has been rapid beyond the most sanguine anticipations of its patrons. New materials and processes, and numberless applications to almost every department of knowledge have illustrated its history, and *raised it* (perhaps before its time) *to the high position of one of the Fine Arts.* One step only is required to achieve so lofty a place. The sun-painter has yet to arrest the colors of nature and fix them upon his tablet; nor have we any doubt, that photography with color is a *possible* result of scientific research.

"Among the numerous applications of photography, its application to the arts of design has been so successful, that it has been regarded by its most ardent cultivators as *one of the Fine Arts.*

"That it is entirely a mechanical art (*though it is such with many of its practitioners*), we cannot admit. That it is entitled to precisely the same rank as painting and sculpture, we will not maintain; but we think it will be fully entitled to rank *above engraving,* when its processes have become more sensitive, and its instruments and methods of working more perfect.

"The want of *absolute truth* manifest in the finest portraits, is thought to be compensated by an ideal beauty, which, if not perpetuating the sitter's *happiest expression,* at least suppresses the *main defects* in his features. Youth is given to age; to the pallid cheek color; brightness to the ordinary eye; and new and fashionable drapery to complete the picture.

"The heliographer has none of these advantages in his favor. His work may, and often does *disfigure,* but it never *flatters* the human countenance. If, however, an *instantaneous* process is employed, and a minute portrait is taken with a small lens, or with a large one at a remote distance, and is subsequently enlarged to life-size, we shall have *absolute truth* in the portrait. And who would not prefer an *absolutely true portrait* of Demosthenes or Cicero, of Paul or Luther, of Milton or of Newton, to the finest representations of them which time may have spared?"

Thus far the Scottish savant. The reader will perceive, that he goes nearly the whole length of corroborating our views of the rank of heliography. And there can be little doubt that, when so short a distance remains between the goal and his present position, he will not long delay in traversing that distance.

I will now introduce a few paragraphs, of kindred purport, from Claudet, a distinguished practical heliographer, of London.

"Should photography fail of progressing beyond its present stage, it is even now a most valuable auxiliary to the artist as an agent, in whose hands its application requires discrimination and taste.

"Photography is an art in which only *genius* and *talent can attain a high position.* There is neither pleasure nor merit in doing what costs neither trouble nor talent. In the immense number of photographs exhibited during the five last years, how *very few* were there of *really fine pictures!*

"Photography would increase the taste for art-productions, and reciprocally art-productions would increase a taste for photography.

"Photography is the imitator of nature,—the drawing is perfect and the perspective correct. Photography is to the fine arts what logarithms are to mathematics; by it work is more easily and rapidly accomplished. To the artist it is a *vocabulary,* which guides him, as the hand-book of nature.

"Why has photography been invented? Simply for

this. Scientific men long since tried to learn the action of light on certain chemical agents, merely as a philosophic inquiry. Such inquiries, however, proving that light caused *changes* in such substances, a desire was awakened in artists, that the images of nature represented in the camera obscura should be fixed.

"Wedgwood was one of the earliest to enter this field, but, though he obtained photographic pictures, he could not so fix them as to protect them against the further action of light. Hence, they had to be kept in the dark, and could be viewed only by a feeble light.

"M. Niepce having learned that certain bituminous substances were rendered insoluble by light, based on this discovery a process then well known, though too slow to admit of its general application. At this stage, Daguerre and Talbot brought forward their experiments, without concert or a knowledge of each other, or of their common experiments. Both had found substances sensitive to light, but not sufficiently so to bring out a picture by ordinary exposure to its action."

They argued thus:—"If the light of the camera has not been intense enough to produce an intense impression, the sensitive surface must yet have received a light, capable of being completed by other chemical re-agents. Both ultimately succeeded in developing a latent picture; one by the fumes of mercury, and the other by a gallic acid solution.

"As photography has been invented, because needed by the fine arts, was it not absurd to suppose these arts could be injured by it? A photographer of taste, judgment, and feeling, though not a painter, might yet be competent to *pose* a model, so as to give the greatest grace to a picture,—while a painter could not fail to find among the productions of such many excellent models for study, as photographers daily pose numerous subjects, while the painter arranges only what he can paint." So writes Claudet.

And here we must express our wonder, that one so acute as Claudet, after going so far, did not advance one step further, and suggest what we have long believed would occur in the not distant future: *i. e.* a union of the pencil and the camera in the production of portraits. The one only point, wherein the sun-painting falls below (or is liable to fall below) the pencil-painting is, that he who operates with the camera, being restricted to a single sitting, of a few seconds' duration, may fail to catch, in those seconds, the sitter's best and most *individualizing* expression; while the wielder of the pencil, who may have sittings *ad libitum,* may behold his subject in all various moods, and among these may detect and transfer to his canvas the very expression desired.

Now it is by lights and shadows added to colors, that expression is represented; and frequently a few minutes only are required for the painter to put into the picture this absolute essential to a veritable portrait. The most protracted and laborious portion of his task, is what precedes even the attempt to secure the expression; *i. e.* the taking of the contour and ensemble of the head, the face, the form, the drapery, &c. And yet by no genius nor skill can be produced with the pencil, so exact a transcript of the original in these particulars, as can the artist-genius with the camera.

Why, then, should not the painter be also a practical photographer, and with the camera perform in a few seconds all this preliminary work, which, with the pencil, would cost him days, and must, after all, be inferior to the work produced by the sunbeam? And these preparative operations being executed, and this in a manner absolutely perfect, let him then, with the pencil dipped in colors, perform what remains towards completing the representation of the expression, which he has awaited the proper moment to discern and to catch? Or why at least should not the painter and photographer work together—one with the camera and the other with the pencil; both possessing kindred artistic genius?

So obvious seems to us all this, that we cannot account for the neglect to adopt, long since, the method here proposed. Possibly one reason may be, the obstinate and absurd prejudice prevailing against heliography, as (in vulgar parlance) a mere mechanical process, coupled also with the flocking into the profession of numbers totally unfit for its requirements both in organization and education.

But such a prejudice cannot much longer exist, while so many of the leading scientific men of the day are boldly and emphatically vindicating for sun-painting a rank among the Fine Arts. And we believe, and long have believed, that the time is not far off, when the union of the camera with the pencil will be formally consummated to the exaltation of both, alike in fact and in general repute.

How near Sir David Brewster came towards suggesting this very movement, will appear from a paragraph, which we take from the essay of his before quoted, and which is as follows:—

"Is it not possible to make the *absolute truth* in photographic portraiture, when attained, as *pleasing* also as we could desire?

"When Chantrey, in conversation with Sir Walter Scott, saw and transferred to his marble that happy expression, which characterizes the baronet's bust, might not the *same expression* have been still more accurately taken by a camera concealed behind the sculptor?

"Why, then, should not the painter's studio be so constructed, that the portrait of a lady or gentleman may be taken, unknown to them, by the camera, while they, in conversation with the artist, or with their friends, have unconsciously assumed their best posture and happiest expression?"

It will here be seen, that Sir David accepts the *substance* of our suggestion, while, in *form,* he so far differs from us in dividing the work between *two* persons, while we would unite its two portions in a single operant. Time alone, we think, and not a long time either, will be required to bring him on to the same platform *we* at present occupy.

It will not be irrelevant to the general strain of this chapter, if, in closing, I cite a few passages from some of our most eminent modern writers, as having both an *intrinsic* and an *illustrative* value.

It is remarked by Opie, the painter, that "the progress of the arts and sciences is the *exact criterion* of cultivation among nations;" and Sir Joshua Reynolds says, "That a relish for the excellencies of refined art, is attained only by cultivation of taste, or improvement of mind, or whatever relates to it."

The following paragraphs are from an excellent English writer:—

"Art affects national prosperity, intellectual culture, and material and social happiness; art shows us man, as he can by no other means be made known; gives us nobler loves and nobler cares, and furnishes objects by the contemplation of which we are taught and exalted—and every department of art, whether practised by the painter or sculptor, the engraver, architect, and engineer must, from its association with photography, gain rather than lose.

"The first useful application of painting was, probably, as an intelligent mode of conveying information. Indeed in Ancient Egypt the same hieroglyphic, and in Ancient Greece the same word, signified writing and painting.

"Religion gave birth to the arts. It was to ornament temples and sacred precincts, that sculpture and painting were first introduced; and in the most ancient monuments of India and Egypt, as in those of the Middle Ages, architecture, sculpture, and painting are the material expressions of *religious* thoughts.

"Among all nations of remotest antiquity colors had the same significance. This conformity indicates a common origin, which extends to the earliest state of humanity, and develops its highest energies in the religion of Persia, in which the *dualism* of light and darkness, personified in Ormuzd and Ahriman, presents, in effect, the two types of colors, which become symbolic of the two principles of benevolence and malevolence, as recognised under every form of religion.

"The symbolic language of colors, intimately connected with religion, passed into India, China, Egypt, Rome, and Greece, and reappeared in the Middle Ages. These indications of color have an important significance in the Scriptures; in mythology, heraldry, architecture, &c., explaining much of the origin and analogy of languages and customs. They tend to elucidate the apparent obscurity of the Sabean or Mithriac worship (*i. e.* the adoration of the heavenly bodies); of Egyptian and Chinese hieroglyphics; of the Orphic and Eleusinian mysteries; and of ancient and modern art; symbols reaching down even to our own days, and connecting (like the color of the North American Indians) the past and the present, the old world and the new, and the Indian with the progenitor of mankind, Adam signifying, literally, 'Red Earth,' or the Red Man.

"The covenant between God and man recorded in Genesis,—the visible token, that God, all-merciful, had accepted Noah's offering, was ratified by colors; and the rainbow, the symbol of safety for all aftertimes from a second general deluge, and typified in mythology by Iris, the messenger of the gods and of good tidings, has become symbolic of regeneration, which is the covenant of God with man.

"The name 'Shem,' (which signifies 'splendor,') was given to the progenitor of the Asiatic or Red Races, every one of which (according to Ruskin) possesses, by *simple instinct*, a supremacy over color, which no race beside has even approached, and possesses it despite the overthrow of their dominion, the extinction of their virtue, and the defilement of their religion,—while to Japhet (a name denoting 'extension') were assigned the treasures of the sullen rock, and stubborn ore, and gnarled forest, whereby they were to achieve their destiny, as they spread, to a greater or less extent, over the vast lands and still vaster waters which together constitute our globe. Meanwhile Nature matured, in the sand, the brilliant gem, and, in the shell, the precious pearl, which were the heritage of him, whose name was 'splendor.'"

Ruskin, the most eminent, perhaps, of contemporary art-critics, remarks: "No law within my knowledge, is more severely without exception, than *this* of the connection of pure color with profound and noble thought. The fact is, that of all God's gifts to the sight of man, color is the holiest, the most divine, the most solemn."

To such as may have looked carefully over the foregoing citations and comments, I would put this question:

"Can it be, that an art, which by the most cursory examination is shown to have an infinity of uses, many among them of the highest and noblest quality and of inestimable moment, which renders to most, if not all of the sciences addressing the eye, as also to multitudes of the practical arts, both the useful and the ornamental, such efficient aids as raise them to a height otherwise wholly unattainable,—can such an art be a baldly mechanical one, capable of being rightly applied by one devoid alike of genius and education; an art, which must be shut out from the pale of the fine arts, although furnishing to each of those arts appliances and means, that promise to make of them pursuits more elevated and offer more various utility, than hitherto they have even begun to be?"

To subserve all the ends we have specified,—ends, of which numbers have already been accomplished by many both of professionists and of amateurs,—it must be in the hands of genius, and of none beside. With us it is an axiom, that an art, which requires genius, and cannot otherwise fulfil its proper ends, must needs be ranked among the Fine Arts. In that rank, therefore, we place heliography.

CHAPTER XXXII.

HELIOGRAPHY—ITS ARTISTIC CHARACTER AND RELATIONS.

Wrong opinions of heliography almost universal—Now changing for the better—Heliographer must study as largely as the painter—Artistic studies needed by him—Bodies, how existing in nature?—Elements of a picture, what?—Photography and painting, in what alike?—Former derives nothing from color; latter very much—Differences between the two, what?—Expression constitutes the portrait—Examples of same—Dress, its influence—Color and position important—Size of portrait, how determined?—Descriptive and historic sketches—Difficulty of getting best expression—Distribution of light important—Great difficulties in getting photographic groups—Conditions requisite.

As we have repeatedly hinted before, the public at large, and the professors of the fine arts, and (what is still stranger and more to be regretted) the scientific amateurs of heliography, have habitually looked upon this art, rather as a mere chemical and mechanical process, than as belonging to the category of painting and sculpture, governed by the same laws as these, and capable of producing kindred effects.

But, everywhere in this volume, the reader will find very different views advanced. Again and again have we claimed for sun-painting the character and title of a fine art, and this claim we have advocated with our utmost ability. And we have done so, not alone on these pages, but in many successive contributions to our photographic journals for the last seven or eight years, during which this work has been in hand.

As the months and years have rolled on, we have been

gladdened to find, now in some scientific or artistic publication, and now in some address to a photographic society, an occasional paragraph, wherein the capabilities of our art were measurably recognised, and its artistic quality and claims in some degree conceded.

Not indeed that *full justice* was awarded to it, or its true character and possibilities were even proximately comprehended. Nor, in any heliographic hand-book, or treatise for the general information, have we met with more than some brief and inadequate allusion to this point, with the single exception (quite recent in its date) of a text-book, comprised in one hundred pages, by M. Disderi, an eminent French photographer. Here we find a far higher rank assigned to photography, than we have seen accorded to it otherwhere.

We are, however, by no means satisfied even with *his* views of our art. In our opinion he underprizes its possible reaches of performance, and places it much below its merits. Still he presents many valuable hints, which, as indicating considerable progress in the true direction, seem to us worthy of examination. As confirming, moreover, by his high authority, many of the views advanced in this work, in the maintenance of which, at its commencement, we stood almost if not entirely alone we have found an additional reason for introducing here some extracts from his treatise. Our limits, however, will restrict us to what follows, in which I have often adopted the thoughts, rather than the words of the writer, and which is accompanied with criticisms and comments of my own.

At first view, the photographic reproduction of nature would seem to require nothing more than a knowledge of certain chemical materials and optical instruments, and of one simple method of applying the same. But experience teaches that this knowledge, how complete soever, will not of itself insure a perfect transcript of the reality; since we find it necessary to vary our mode of operating, according to the nature and surroundings of the object to be represented.

Thus, one way of proceeding will probably produce vigorous effects; another is requisite when "softness" is desired, or when the objects are uniformly and properly illumined; and it is always essential to combine the distances according to the power of the instrument, so as to secure in the image the same proportions that exist in the model.

Thus, to appreciate the effects of the light and distance, and all the circumstances modifying the scene, requires a knowledge quite other than that of the appropriate chemicals. It demands of the operant to note carefully the effect produced, and to study the causes producing it; *e. g.* the distribution of the lights and shades; the relative intensity of the different colored masses; the perspective of the flat surfaces; and lastly, the proportions of the various objects.

Therefore, for the simple reproduction of nature, taken at hazard and without choice of particulars, the photographer should possess, besides an acquaintance with the laboratory, a very different order of knowledge; and he is constrained to a course of study very like that required by the artist, as a basis for his art.

The aim of photography, however, is *not* merely to reproduce nature taken at hazard. These operations should be guided by a choice, determined by the ideas or temperament of the individual. It is on this account, that the productions of different operants are marked by peculiarities, which reveal the author's personality. In fact, each individual selects his subject according to his special idea of the beautiful; in the scene to be represented, he arranges the parts, and combines the chiar' oscuro according to his taste; and even in the execution he finds multitudinous combinations for the general aspect of his work.

THE ARTISTIC STUDIES REQUIRED BY THE PHOTOGRAPHER.

These are nearly as vast as those of the painter himself. Like him, the photographer should study the laws of beauty, of producing it by composition; the forms, the disposition of the parts, the chiar' oscuro, and the execution. To *feel* that a thing is beautiful, does not suffice to constitute an artist. The individual must know *why* it is so, and whether this beauty may be expressed by the art he studies; and he must know the key to all the combinations of means, whereby the ideas and sentiments are to be expressed. The photographer can no better dispense with such knowledge than the painter. It must not, however, be forgotten, that photography and painting are two different arts, notwithstanding these striking analogies between their objects and the means of attaining them. We will attempt to present a few points of the distinction between the two.

First, then, photography, unlike painting, derives no aid from color. To painting color is a powerful resource; completely modifying the combinations that preserve its other parts. To render a parallel between the two arts possible, and make the comparison clear and distinct, photography must be compared with cameo-painting or drawing. The analogy would then be perfect, so far as the visible aspect resulting from the material employed is concerned; since photographic drawing may be obtained in all shades and on many various substances, always producing the same aspect. This consideration is important from the fact that the general color pervading the whole, being appropriate, must increase the harmony, the beauty, and the significance of the subject.

Let us endeavor to distinguish, in their "*ensemble*," the fundamental causes determining the character and import of the natural spectacle, which is the common basis of both arts.

Bodies exist in geometrical forms, and are located in different parts of the space that expands before our sight; the light illuminates them by distributing its rays over their surfaces, thereby not only rendering their forms perceptible, but also revealing two properties belonging to the essence of the bodies, and completing the total of the elements constituting the natural spectacle, viz., color and tone.

It may be remarked that different bodies present not only different colors, but also different degrees of brilliancy, *under the same light* and *in the same place*—they are more or less light or dark; they have a light which belongs to them naturally, and shows itself independently of all coloring. This distinction between the natural color of bodies and what may be termed the chiar' oscuro or tone, is of considerable moment with respect to photography, as it serves to fix, with much exactness, the limits to be observed in representing nature.

The elements of a picture are the form of objects, their color, and their natural tone, revealed by the light shining upon them. The positions of the forms among themselves; the objects with respect to the light, and with respect to us, produce infinitely varied effects, by creating numberless relations between the various elements of the visible spectacle. From all these combinations will result a general effect, which will be the character or significance of the picture. It is therefore, important that the artist should know to what extent each of the elements, first enumerated, conduces to the final result; and, especially, must he unite in his imitation the elements which, by their relations, constitute the meaning of the natural spectacle.

If the painter or the photographer is struck by the beauty of an object, he should endeavor to detect the cause, or the origin of his impressions. This may be the arrangement of colors, or perhaps some felicitous contrast. This eloquence of color *may* be so potent as to dominate all the rest; so that, were we to withdraw from the picture all the expression it receives from its colors, all that remains would produce but an indifferent expression, and, very possibly, one devoid of beauty. On this account it is, that many of the photographic proofs, taken of scenes, *apparently* very effective, are in reality so often dull and destitute of the character which had arrested our attention and determined our choice.

Let us now introduce into the comparison between photography and painting a subject, that derives more of its essential significance from color.

In regard to exact imitation of nature, the two arts are strikingly similar. The photographer indeed can express the natural spectacle, with its forms, its perspectives, its lights and shades, &c., quite as well as the painter, if not better.

But, as already remarked, imitation without choice is not the sole aim of photography, and here the difference between the two arts becomes very marked. For, while the painter, by a sort of natural impulse, chooses natural objects of the most opposite character, and groups them together, modifying them in position or detail, the photographer cannot dispense with the *presence* of the objects he would reproduce. Let us try to illustrate by examples.

Thus, if a painter wished to express the sentiment of calm and tranquillity, produced by an early morning excursion into the country, with the varied scenes spread out before his eyes, he may recall many variations of the landscape, which had previously struck him; *e. g.* the curious forms of certain trees, the peculiar effect of a piece of water, &c. He assembles these scattered fragments in a single composition, and if some apparently essential part be wanting, he seeks, in the boundless field of nature, some suitable object to supply the deficiency. Imagination, memory, and present vision, all unite in furnishing the materials of the composition, and these materials, each and all, he modifies to suit his purpose.

The photographer cannot thus proceed. He must seek the scattered elements which have originated the idea he would express, not by help of imagination, but as *assembled in reality.* He thus composes his picture by a series of systematic calculations. To sum up:—The painter, in addition to the reality, which may be present, may employ the boundless resources of imagination. Contrariwise, the photographer, in his composition, is bound to the reality; while, in the execution, he is limited to exact imitation.

Whatever be the species of picture which the photographer aims to produce, he must follow the great *law of unity; i. e.* the composition should have but one decided point of interest; and the forms, attitudes, shades, &c., should unite for the expression of this.

For instance, in a portrait, the individual represented should constitute the feature of interest; the accessories, such as draperies, background, &c., should all be mere subordinate details.

In a composition representing inanimate nature; *e. g.* a group of deer—by introducing hunters, horses, &c., you destroy the unity of interest and infringe a law of art.

OF THE PORTRAIT.

At first sight, it seems sufficient, in order to produce a good portrait, that the model should remain still, and the operant employ the shortest possible method. How is it, then, that so many portraits are not at all good likenesses; and that the friends of the model are so rarely satisfied with the result of a sitting? How is it, that the different representations of the same person are so various, that they sometimes express dissimilar, and sometimes even opposite characters? The reason for all this is, that the same person is susceptible of an infinite diversity of moods, and may, therefore, present infinitely diverse aspects. Few of these represent the true and dominant character of the model. It is the expression of this *dominant character* that constitutes the portrait, and not a *mathematically exact reproduction of the features and form.* As the first step towards obtaining a good portrait, the photographer should penetrate, by whatever means at his command, the fleshly mask, which envelopes the spiritual part of his model, and ascertain his real type and character. The second step is, by animating conversation, and all other appliances, to call into the face the *expression* of such character. Thus much being done, the solar pencil will perform the rest. To avoid repetition, we would refer the reader to the four chapters on expression, especially the first two,—Vol. First, pages 246–7. He will there find the subject of portraiture discussed in full. I would also recommend his consulting, for the same purpose, the series of chapters in Part First, commencing with the seventh and extending to the sixteenth. It is only by first ascertaining the proper expression, that the artist is enabled to select the attitude, the distance, the lights and shadows, and various accessories of the picture; and knowing these, he seeks to obtain the optical combinations required for expressing the result of his observations; *i. e.* he *composes* the portrait.

The class of impressions made upon an intelligent beholder, by observing the portrait of an individual, will go far towards proving its general truthfulness or falsity. Thus the representation of a true philosopher, who has passed his life in close study and diligent research, should awaken, even independently of resemblance and similar considerations, *calm and serious ideas;* it should possess simple attitudes; an interior light distributed in tranquil masses, with half-shades, deep background, and very sober accessories. The head, as the seat of thought, should present a brilliant and luminous aspect.

On the other hand, the portrait of a soldier, who, though young, has achieved the right to command, and has distinguished himself by unusual daring, should create quite other impressions. The life, passion, and energy which are its fitting expression, would properly accord with an open-air treatment; plenty of light, without mysterious half-tones; the body firmly poised; the gestures frank, decided, and vigorous;—such should be the representation in question.

Of course, these general styles of presentment might be modified by the artist to correspond to peculiarities in the originals. In order, moreover, to make the portrait beautiful, as well as truthful, so far as may be, he should so use his appliances, as to cast blemishes and defects of the model into shade, and to bring out good points into prominence. (See chapters above referred to in Part First.)

To get the desired proportions of the figure requires no slight acquaintance with optical effects. Thus, the figure will appear much larger, if the head is placed near the top of the frame, leaving plenty of free space at each side. It will be increased or diminished in size, as it is brought towards the right or left edge, with much space above it.

Dress, too, greatly influences the proportions,—close-fitting, light cloth garments enlarging the head, hands, and extremities; while an ample flowing dress diminishes the same.

Again, he may increase the size of a head, that appears too small, by throwing the light on the face; and lessen it, by using a tint that would throw half the face into the shade. Backgrounds produce the same effects, according as they are light or dark.

The proper size to be adopted for a photographic portrait should be determined by the importance of the subject, and especially by the mode of treatment and the disposition of the scene. The place to which it is destined should also be considered—an open position requiring much larger dimensions than a boudoir, or ordinary apartment.

So the portrait may represent the individual in full length, in half length, or in merely the bust. The first gives best the complete likeness, but involves many and great difficulties.

The head should never be represented, unaccompanied by the bust at the least.

The group-portrait is often very much abused, and has

shown the worst results of any kinds of portraits. If it be so difficult to produce a good likeness of *one* person, how much more to represent *many*, and these of different ages, sexes, and characters!

The *position* of the model is important; and in this especially the artist should clearly understand the *character* of the person he would represent. The first condition of a good attitude is, that it should be in accordance with the age, stature, habits, and manners of the individual; and secondly, that it should express the greatest beauty of which the model is susceptible.

The *pose* should, moreover, express unity of aspect and be optically correct. A *dominant* movement, therefore, must be found, which harmonizes with all the other particulars.

The great difficulty in regard to the physiognomy, is to distinguish from the multitude of *different* expressions presented by the model, the one which is most *characteristic*, or best represents his *individuality*, or most accords with the sentiment intended to be exhibited by the "*ensemble*" of the portrait, and which is, at the same time, most favorable to a good resemblance. The expression giving the person's true character is (as we have said scores of times) an absolute essential.

Among other expedients to be employed, the artist should place himself in the moral state he desires to create in the person to be represented, and thus take on himself the expression he would give to him. Unconscious imitation on the part of the model may help the artist in his task.

To obtain a good result, the artist should especially be exempt from *interruption*, and Disderi thinks he should be *alone* with his model. In the case of children he deems this condition essential, as they should be photo graphed *without being conscious of it.*

That Disderi is a first-class authority is undeniable; and that he is right, as regards *interruption*, we are not disposed to deny. But with his idea of the artist being *alone* with his model, we cannot agree. For the presence and varied conversation of *congenial friends*, at a *séance*, may be an incalculable help to the artist, in producing in the sitter's mind, the mood desired—that mood, which shining out upon the face, and thence transferred to the plate, shall stamp thereon an image which leaves nothing to be wished for. No artist exists who is so flexible and electrically swift in his mental activities, as to adapt himself to scores of successive sitters per day, to each of whom but a few minutes can be granted,—*so* adapt himself, as to produce in each the state required. Our opinion, therefore, is that the company of friends of the right kind, is one of the greatest of benefits instead of the worst of hindrances.

A skilful choice and distribution of light are important to a portrait. The general effect of the lights and shadows should be appropriate to the character. Thus, if the portrait be that of a child, the scene should be conceived in a clear and smiling light, free from deep and heavy shadows. Whereas, if the portrait be that of a man of firm character, sombre and ample masses should be alternated with luminous ones; the shadows should be powerful and the lights large and frank.

It should by no means be overlooked, that all the combinations above enumerated, as requisite conditions for obtaining a good portrait, may be absolutely nullified by a false selection of color in the dress of a model. The colors most luminous to the eye, do not always produce the most energetic effects; *e. g.* red, orange, and yellow, are almost *without* action; green acts but feebly; blue and violet are reproduced very quickly. Thus a person of very fair complexion must avoid dressing either in green, or orange, or red, as the lights would be too prominent, and the whole portrait would lack energy and detail. The artist, therefore, should be very careful in choosing his model's dress. (See page 67, Harmony, &c.)

Portrait-coloring should be confined only to artists of uncommon ability and skill. For it is not only necessary to avoid losing the *likeness*, but the colors must not be so opaque, as to cover and make invisible the shades produced by the light.

From the foregoing remarks it is evident, that the production of a good portrait, combining resemblance with beauty, is a difficult achievement; and that the photographic art can be acquired only by patient study and a long and constant observation of nature.

ANIMATED SCENES—DESCRIPTIVE AND HISTORICAL SUBJECTS.

It is most especially in the treatment of scenes wherein the personages are supposed to be in action, that the photographer must possess the clearest possible idea of the particular language and multiform resources of his art. In the impression produced by animated nature, color often makes a considerable item. Many photographers, in their quest of interesting subjects, have been attracted by those Southern lands which have inspired so many painters; but the specimens they have brought back have often failed of giving a clear or pleasing idea of the regions they wished to represent. The reason of which is, that they have been carried away by those brilliancies of color and costume, which are not within the scope of their art, to the neglect of scenes which photography might have pictured. While observing nature, the photographer must often ask himself, if the scene he admires would retain the same expression, if devoid of color?

Although strictly obliged to imitate *reality*, the photographer may, nevertheless, sometimes unite the elements of the scene he would represent. He may, in fact, *compose* the scene he wishes to reproduce, by choosing the personages; giving them costumes appropriate to the parts he would have them take, and combining the different effects of light and distance.

In a vast atelier (sitting-room) properly organized and fitted up with backgrounds, reflectors, and all requisite accessories, the intelligent and skilled photographer, aided by capable models, may therefore essay the most complicated and difficult pictures, provided the subjects do not necessitate attitudes which depict and illustrate the passions, as, for instance, in the episodes of battles by Salvator Rosa. Might he not represent *interiors* like Van Ostade, Pierre de Hooge, Chardin, Granet, &c.? Might he not attempt to exhibit the sentiment of Schaeffer, and the style of Watteau; or the meritorious compositions executed in the manner of Ducq, Terburg, Teniers, &c.? Why should he not treat historic subjects like Paul Delaroche, in his picture of the death of Henri Duc de Guise? And, by constructing an atelier sufficiently spacious, and securing a sufficient number of the most highly accomplished models, why might he not attempt those vast compositions for which Veronese was distinguished?

Certainly the photographer might *attempt* these and kindred compositions; but whether such attempts would issue in *triumphs* or *defeats,* is a question which it were impossible to answer decisively, and not easy to answer at all.

The remarks already presented concerning the portrait, show how difficult it is to produce a *single* figure, marked by that *expression* which alone constitutes it a portrait, truthfully representing the original. How would it be possible to apply the many nice expedients required for begetting that expression in *one,* to *numbers* small or great,—numbers who must, at *one and the same instant,* exhibit, in face, form, position, &c., each the character he is intended to embody and manifest?

It is evident that, by no *unaided endeavors of his own,* can he prepare the group for the moment of taking by the camera. If prepared at all, the models must almost wholly *prepare themselves.* By a sort of *self-magnetization,* they must place themselves in the several positions of the persons they mean to represent, and identify themselves completely with such persons. The enormous difficulties attending the achievement of such results, are obvious at a glance; and Disderi seems to reckon them so many and great, as to imply an absolute impossibility.

We admit fully the *difficulties* of the case, but we cannot recognise its *impossibility.* A Garrick, a Kemble, a Kean, a Mrs. Siddons, a Mrs. Jordan, a Fanny Kemble, a Forrest and a Booth, a Murdoch, a Davenport, and a Charlotte Cushman, have once lived, and before the eyes of multitudinous beholders, have been able to reproduce, to the minutest particular, the various characters they assumed to represent. Has the advance of our race ceased? Has its utmost goal been reached? Does the future enfold in its teeming bosom, no duplicate *fac-similes* of the Kemble, the Siddons, and their compeers of the days foregone? Fac-similes? Why not even *superiors* to those sons and daughters of fame,—those worthy wearers of the civic crown?

Why, then, may not the time, how far distant soever, actually become the *time instant,* wherein shall live multitudes, capable of executing tasks immeasurably harder than the one in question? For ourselves, we look forward to the era wherein the sun-painting art, improved beyond our present conceptions, shall depict groups, comprising multitudes, who, each unaided, shall represent to the most vivid life, the most brilliant characters, encompassed by the sublimest or loveliest scenes, and engaged in actions which thrill and exalt the spectators to a mimic heaven on earth! Who shall say that representations like these may not be among the most potent of earthly influences, for civilizing, refining, and elevating our kind?

Disderi admits that, even now, some inanimate scenes and some human groups may be regarded and treated as proper subjects for the camera. For example, the culture of the fields; the different trades; military and every-day life, all furnish the photographer with subjects, which periodically appear under nearly the same conditions. In regard to these the operant should proceed in the same manner as with the portrait. He should first endeavor to ascertain its true character and significance, and then cast about for the means of reproducing it to the best advantage.

On the whole, however, he speaks discouragingly of the capability of photography for representing descriptive or historical subjects, or indeed groups of any class, whether animate or inanimate. As we have already stated, however, in the many causes which, in his view, render such representation impracticable, we behold only difficulties, which time and persistent systematic endeavor may eventually overcome. For the stage men and women are carefully educated and disciplined. For the equitation and the ground and lofty tumbling of the circus; for the exhibitions of the tight and slack rope; for jugglery; for singing and dancing, and a multitude of kindred displays, individuals are prepared by a lengthened and rigorous course of training, and, as the result of such training, they are enabled to execute feats, which, to the uninitiated, seem more like miracle than prosaic every-day actualities.

Why, then, may not education and discipline, if sufficiently thorough and protracted, fit men and women for models to represent such scenes and living groups as the photographer may wish to transfer to plate or paper, be they as complicated and beset with difficulties as they may? No limit can be set to the possible development and progress whether of art or artists, and of the appliances required by them, whether inanimate or human; and what may, perhaps, be impracticable to-day, may cease to be so a generation or a century hence.

And the models required by the photographer for these large and complex representations, may serve besides to entertain and instruct the public, by composing and exhibiting "tableaux vivants." In these spectacles may be presented the sublimest and loveliest scenery of all lands, and the grandest and most beautiful monuments of human genius, skill, and labor, in both the ancient and the modern worlds, together with man himself, of every nation, tribe, and aspect on earth, and engaged in every various occupation pertaining to earthly existence. By the same flexible appliances, the most thrilling and critical scenes and actions, which are commemorated in history or imagined in romance, together with the heroes or geniuses, the sages or saints or martyrs, who have borne a part therein, may be reproduced before the contemplation of the present generation with the vividness of living reality. What incalculable means and materials of instruction, of refinement, and of elevation, not less than of recreation and amusement, are here presented! And, after serving this primary and most important end, they may serve the photographer in producing pictures of whatever is most interesting and instructive, either in the vast and multiform world of reality, or the still vaster and more various world of imagination and inventive genius.

From these slight suggestions we leave the reader to form his own conclusions, as to the importance and dignity of our art, and the magnificent purposes it is capable of subserving.

INDEX.

www.ingramcontent.com/pod-product-compliance
Lightning Source LLC
LaVergne TN
LVHW020938110826
845150LV00004B/898

* 9 7 8 1 4 2 5 5 5 2 1 5 2 *